BRITAIN SINCE 1945

By the same author

Shell Shock: Traumatic Neurosis and the British Soldiers of the First World War
The British Migrant Experience, 1700–2000: An Anthology (with B. Piątek and
    I. Curyłło-Klag)
Between Two Cultures: Poland and Britain (editor)

Britain
since 1945

Aspects of Identity

Peter Leese

First published 2006 by
PALGRAVE MACMILLAN
Houndmills, Basingstoke, Hampshire RG21 6XS and
175 Fifth Avenue, New York, N.Y. 10010
Companies and representatives throughout the world

PALGRAVE MACMILLAN is the global academic imprint of the Palgrave
Macmillan division of St. Martin's Press, LLC and of Palgrave Macmillan Ltd.
Macmillan® is a registered trademark in the United States, United Kingdom
and other countries. Palgrave is a registered trademark in the European
Union and other countries.

ISBN-13: 978-1-4039-4805-2   paperback
ISBN 10: 1-4039-4805-4   paperback
ISBN-13: 978-1-4039-4804-5   hardback
ISBN-10: 1-4039-4804-6   hardback

This book is printed on paper suitable for recycling and
made from fully managed and sustained forest sources.

A catalogue record for this book is available from the British Library.

A catalog record for this book is available from the Library of Congress.

10   9   8   7   6   5   4   3   2   1
15   14   13   12   11   10   09   08   07   06

Printed in China

Contents

Shelton State Libraries
Shelton State Community College

List of Maps, Figures and Illustrations

Maps

Figures

Illustrations

Preface

The beginnings of this study are not difficult to trace: it was in the autumn of 1992 that I travelled to Poland for the first time, one of about thirty lecturers chosen to participate in the Oxford-based Higher Education Support Programme set up by Professor Zbigniew Pełczyński. None of us knew quite what to expect, though each of us knew the name of a city we would be living in, and the name of the institution where we would be teaching. My final destination, while it was not entirely clear to me as I stepped onto the plane in London, was a teacher-training college in Kraków. There I had to unravel the intricacies of British geography, as well as 'British Life and Institutions', a subject that didn't sound too promising, not to mention that I had never heard of it before.

Initially, making presentations and leading discussions on both the subjects seemed a relatively straightforward task. Geography might include geological formation, population change or environmental issues; 'British Life and Institutions' might refer to almost anything from eating habits to political systems. Quickly, though, the artificial separation of geography from life, and of history from both of these, began to trouble me. Another set of questions emerged when in 1995 I took up a post at the Jagiellonian University, began to teach an MA Seminar on British society and culture, and started to tackle more detailed topics related to Scotland and Wales as well as Ireland. In particular, I continually encountered a mismatch between the intricacies of personal family history – the individual and collective experience of belonging and participating in a society – and the generalities that appeared to constitute 'Life and Institutions' as a subject. (Subsequently I found one account that concentrates on the family and personal experience in the context of wider national events, Mary Abbott's excellent *Family Affairs: A History of the Family in 20th-century England*.) This study developed from my own efforts to balance these intimate and institutional aspects of life in Britain, to navigate between native subjectivism and diagrammatic objectivism.

Working at a distance from Britain, exploring its past and present from a non-native point of view or, more correctly, from a bi-cultural perspective, imposes a particular set of demands: to recognize the potential validity of both native and non-native opinion, to answer the simplest question with a convincing degree of nuance and complexity. Whatever success I may have achieved in meeting these demands is mostly owed to my students, who have constantly forced me to rethink my own approach, and who have frequently come up with their own surprising observations and insights. I am grateful, too, to the Higher Education Support Project, and subsequently the Civic Education Project, for giving me my first foothold in Poland. Equally to the Jagiellonian University, for allowing me to take a year's paid leave to finish writing this account. I spent the year in Britain with family members from both England and Poland, and they deserve special thanks for their patience and support. My various anonymous readers were also by turns encouraging and challenging in their comments, and I am grateful for their assistance. Without any one of these contributions this book would never have appeared. I have only myself to blame for whatever omissions or oversights remain.

P.J.L

Acknowledgements

The author and publisher wish to thank the following for permission to use copyright material:

Mary Evans Picture Library, for the photographs of West Indian Women on p. 46, Lewis Merthyr Colliery on p. 14, and the 'New Look' dress on p. 30.

Topham Picturepoints for the photographs of the Hindu Temple on p. 155, the rave party on p. 176, the New Age travellers on p. 140, London Stock Exchange on p. 124, Cumbernauld on p. 68, David Hockney on p. 86, and the striking miners on p. 102.

Every effort has been made to trace the copyright holders but, if any have been inadvertently overlooked, the author and publisher will be pleased to make the necessary arrangements at the first opportunity.

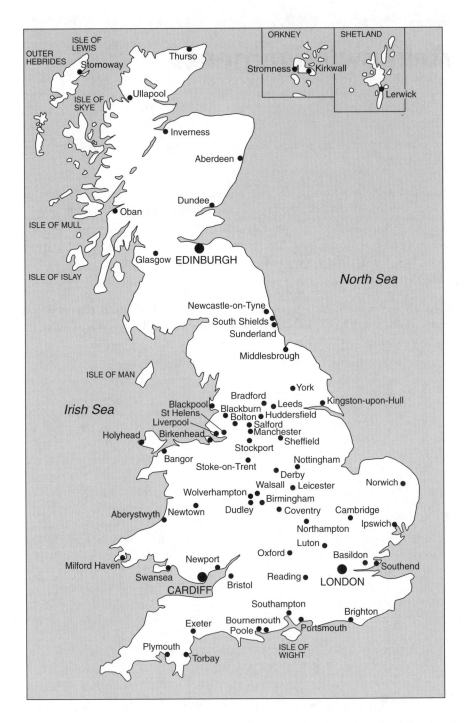

Map I Scotland, Wales and England: main towns and cities

Map 2 Northern Ireland: main urban centres and regions

Introduction: A Montage of Identities

This is not a book about foreign wars, the symbolism of flags or the local loyalties of football fans. It is an account of how identities within the United Kingdom, past and present, have been formed and maintained in particular regions and cities, among certain sub-groups within society, in some areas of the collective imagination. In the debates of recent years on the nature of 'Britishness' and its constituent parts, identity has been viewed as a function of the nation state as well as a backdrop to the various nationalist political campaigns in Wales, Scotland or Northern Ireland.[1] But underlying questions of public political debate, matters of constitution, administration and legal framework, are the cultural roots of identity that also form the nation: individual mentality, family and neighbourhood life, local landscape, patterns of work or tradition. The problem for any such account is that identity is elusive. It cannot be recorded directly in a documentary format, but it can be shown indirectly by compressing time into a symbolic sequence, by juxtaposing a series of images, by showing a run of photographic 'stills': by montage.

In this portrait, identity does not refer to a particular set of essential values, but rather to a continual historical process of individual and collective reinvention. Duration, location and a specific set of social relations shape this remaking; symbols or uncertainties are equally a part of identity formation. For the individual, it is social groups, particularly kin, who take precedence in the process; neighbourhood as well as regional circumstances also mould values and aspirations. As well as a process, identity is a function. It provides values, actions and hopes that influence life choices and which regulate the formation and performance of relationships. It is within these individual and collective connections that concepts of inclusion and exclusion, 'us' and 'them', begin to emerge. Particular, localized combinations of social and spatial circumstance will account for the many, at times conflicting, notions of community that are held by individuals and groups, as, for example, in Northern Ireland.[2]

From such instances it is clear that collective unity exists at many levels, and that the nation as a collection of all peoples in all places is only one such level. Identity resides, too, in subsections of any society, not because all members necessarily feel or think alike, but because they share a framework of experience: agreement as well as conflict may be the product of local conditions. Switching off the party political broadcast and attending to daily affairs, we also observe, reflect on, and make a common life. Peer groups, common leisure interests and work all bring people together in various combinations, bonds form, individual and collective senses of the self are reinforced, adjusted, revised. Self- and collective identities are also made as they are 'told'. This is as true for individuals when they recount anecdotes and life stories as it is for neighbourhood and for national communities as they present local folklore and 'the story of our nation'. Because they are continually adjusted to help us interpret and understand our daily existence as well as national affairs such narratives can never be finalized.

*   *   *

One beginning to the story of 'Britishness' is the notion of 'core' and 'periphery', which develops to encompass the 'four nations', and eventually produces a 'multicultural' model. Before describing how *Britain since 1945: Aspects of Identity* expands on such models of British identity to incorporate regional and local culture zones, particular social constituencies and imaginative activities, some explanation of these earlier versions may help orient readers.

The idea of core and periphery has long been a staple in discussions of 'Celtic' culture, of non-native populations, and of the arts. A variation on this theme is the long-running debate over the relative merits of province and metropolis.[3] Hence the opinion of nineteenth-century poet and cultural critic Matthew Arnold (expressed in the 1860s, but representative of similar attitudes towards Scotland and Ireland both before and afterwards) that the Welsh language, and by implication any distinctively native culture, was 'the badge of a beaten race, the property of the vanquished'.[4] In addition to this metropolitan or Anglocentric perspective, this propensity to ignore what is considered geographically or linguistically on the outskirts, there is the tendency to forge definitions that disregard supposedly 'marginal' social groups. As with Arnold's views on 'Celtic literature', these attitudes can partly be traced back to the Imperial moment, when the position and contribution of an immigrant, for example, was judged by the adoption of native traits and values. Journalist Walter Besant's 1903 comment on London's then new immigrant Polish Jews: 'In the free air of Anglo-Saxon rule they will grow; you will not know them again', expresses this attitude.[5] Another topic in the conventional national story relates to the imagination, to the preference for telling 'Britishness' by reference to 'popular' or 'high' arts (usually the latter is privileged). Historian A. J. P. Taylor thus distinguishes between 'high-grade' literature, which was 'beyond the masses', and 'low-grade' literature, which provided 'the masses' with 'their own form of cultural satisfaction'.[6]

Against such definitions an alternative, more inclusive school of 'British' or 'four nations' history has emerged since the mid-1970s. The moment is significant as it coincided with the final collapse of Britain's imperial past, and with the rise of 'peripheral' nationalist dissent: increased sectarian strife within Ulster expressed as mirror-image hatreds between loyalist and republican; in Scotland, the simultaneous new exploitation of North Sea oil and the beginning of a worldwide fuel crisis, which strengthened the devolutionist agenda in national politics; in Wales, the continuing rise of language and other cultural forms of nation-building.[7] It is from this time, too, that 'Englishness' gradually becomes problematic: a competing ethnicity rather than a set of unquestioned values.

Hugh Kearney, in one of the early reinterpretations of British history from the 'four nations' perspective, stresses the importance of the local in the many indigenous ways of living across the Isles. While the web of connections among native regional cultures is far more intricate that the following summary would indicate, Kearney's 1989 description of 'culture zones' begins to hint at how place, ways of living and community interact. In outline Kearney identifies ten local 'regions': (1) North-West Wales: the most rural part of the country, still strongly influenced by Protestant Calvinism and Methodism, home to many speakers of that old, difficult Celtic language, Welsh; (2) South Wales: more cosmopolitan and urban, centred on cities such as Cardiff, mainly English speaking; (3) South-West Scotland: the most heavily populated and urbanized part of the country, centred on the River Clyde and Glasgow; (4) the Western Islands, the Hebrides, and (5) Orkney and Shetland, which constitute subcultures in themselves; (6) Northern England: in recent times marked by industrial decline and recession, progressively more separate from (7) Southern England: which has greater prosperity, and which is increasingly dominated by (8) London: such that fifty miles in any direction (today much more) is commuter territory; (9) Protestant Northern Ireland: which gives its political allegiance to London, but is more strongly linked to Dublin and Glasgow; (10) Catholic Ireland: which willingly admits it is shaped by American culture, but reluctantly acknowledges English connections.[8] By Kearney's definition, then, the notion of a multiplicity of cultures – ways of living that coexist within the common boundaries of the political state – relates as much to the often-unacknowledged native regional distinctions of language, religion and economy as to the much more visibly distinct patterns or boundaries of settlement and custom.

Britain since 1945: Aspects of Identity uses the 'four nations' model within the confines of a recent political formation, the United Kingdom, but expands it as well by considering particular social groups and acts of creative imagination. Additionally, it explores spatial relations, the plurality of overlapping individual and communal definitions, and the numerous cultures that cut across familiar boundaries in the national-historical landscape.[9] Recent thinking on the relation between local landscape and individual experience, on how 'sense of place' is experienced and structured and on how 'social memory' informs individual and self-definition, also informs this account.

Alongside the 'four nations' school for example, *géohistoire* (associated with the French history journal *Annales*) has stressed the complexity of lived human experience among a mass population, the importance of locality not just as a framework within which particular human experience is played out, but as a *milieu* within which it is lived. Hence Fernand Braudel's investigations into the lived human experience as it is connected to local landscape or region.[10] In this view there is an intimate, intricate connection between the individual, the locality and the nation; identity is constituted within the collective experience of national events, but these are registered by each individual within the local context of his or her life, within the realm of the personal. One way to understand these interlinking levels of individual and collective apprehension is by reference to what Norman Davies has called 'multiple identities'; similarly, Eric Hobsbawm has referred to identities as 'hats' which can be worn and discarded as the occasion requires.[11] Recent sociological work on the changing nature of 'place' in the context of 1990s globalization gives some examples of the material individuals use to design and make their headware.[12] A sense of belonging may come from local accent or language use in Glasgow, Belfast or Newcastle; from traditions of work specialization; from provision of services; from patterns of leisure, including, despite the opening disclaimer, participation in and support for local sports; from youth cultures, or even pub signs; but more importantly, from the fabric of daily life that sustains and connects all of these within the local community. Additionally, regional newspapers and television create a distinct journalistic form of local knowledge, as does district folk belief, folklore, festivals and eccentric or well-known characters in the vicinity. At the same time each individual makes a personal sense of place, belonging and self through encounter and intervention within the public environment. As one study reports:

> Different buildings and different spaces and areas of [Manchester and Sheffield] help to create discrete 'mental maps' of each city for diverse publics, which then get to be institutionalized for members of each public as 'their' Manchester or 'their' Sheffield, cutting across, in the practical popular imagination, the dominant maps of the city that are mobilized by the local 'heritage industry' or members of the local growth coalition.[13]

Domestic and collective 'social memory' adds historical depth to personal and local identity, for instance in the private and shared use of photographs or stories by a family or neighbourhood. Snapshots act as an interpretative device that allows flexibility in the reinterpretation of, and in the exploration of, the connections or disjunctions between past and present. Figures 1 and 2 provide an interpretative summary of these models to describe how individual identity formation is understood in the study that follows.

The reconsideration of connections between past and present, between individual and locality, was a notable trend in late twentieth-century Britain. Urgency was added to these deliberations by the extended, destabilizing effects of decolonization and deindustrialization. Together these two processes erased various of the psychological and social certainties that had shaped many parts of the country from the nineteenth century onwards: abroad the ruthless pursuit of profit and the altruistic 'civilizing' process both lost credibility; at home the phasing out of employment opportunities and work practices cast the future into doubt. The reduction of specialized local labour markets in coal, steel or shipbuilding had dramatic effects. 'At every level in such [post-industrial] social formations, individuals are left to adapt to the void in what was their working world, their identity, their community and their social life, but in particular local contexts.'[14] Recent questions of belonging, of self- and group definition, have arisen, then, since 'place', a network of social relations, obligations and benefits, dissolves into a mere 'space', which is assessed in a global context by its capacity

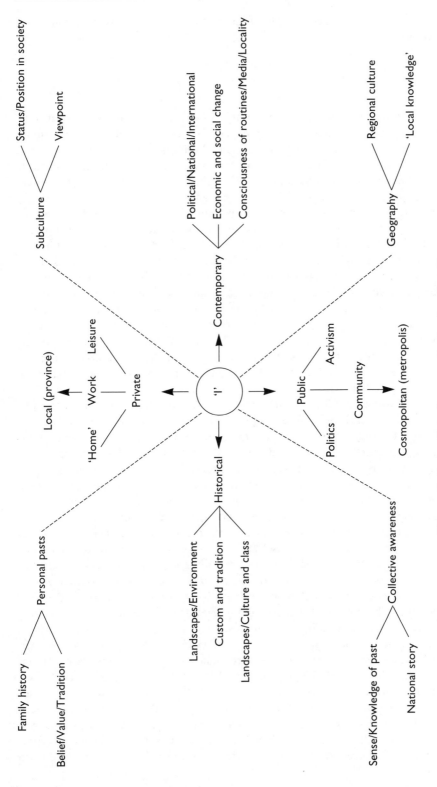

Figure 1 Formation of personal/collective identities

to yield profit. This devaluation of 'place' has knocked askew personal and collective self-image.[15]

*   *   *

It is this destabilization that has prompted, I believe, much of the recent investigation into local and national identities. Historians are well placed to contribute here, as one of the things they do best is to X-ray the past – times, places, incidents or concepts – in this case of past and present identities, to understand its inner workings. As individual and group identities constantly fluctuate, the assessment of processes of change through time is an equally relevant skill. The objective, then, is to recover past notions of individual and collective selfhood as they have changed over the past half-century or so, and as they vary among connected social groups, according to place, and in the realm of imagination and artistic endeavour. While the first purpose of this account is to argue for a revised definition of British identity, it is also intended as a guide to various aspects of postwar history, and for this reason it is designed as an 'open' text. It can be read as a whole, section by section, chapter by chapter, from 1 to 10; it can be studied by reference to any of its constituent subject strands: locality, society or the arts. It may be scanned to reveal the relationship between particular themes: local developments and the situation of women, or youth and the evolution of popular music. Or it may be read for a condensed introduction to Wales, fine arts, or the social history of cinema.

Read in its entirety *Britain since 1945: Aspects of Identity* selects subject strands and follows them through from 1945 to the present; its structure constitutes a narrative to parallel the 'intellectual montage' technique of experimental filmmakers. A group of subject strands (images) – regional, social and imaginative – is juxtaposed to create a portrait: not a photographic reproduction, but an interpretive mosaic; selected facets within the collective culture that relate to each other and that fit into the context of their times. The focal point of this study is its reading of the connection between lived experience and imaginative artefacts, the interpretation of which will allow a better understanding of self-definition, its individual and collective processes. Such a reading offers a wider than usual perspective. At the same time this vantage point enables the observation of both social and artistic formations, the consideration of what is specific to them as well as what might be held in 'common ways of living' from less familiar angles. It is important to bear in mind that the cumulative analysis, the montage as a whole, takes precedence over individual elements.

The account divides the sixty years from 1945 into four phases of regional, social and artistic development. Hence the following arrangement: Part I: 'From War, from Modernism' (1945–59); Part II: 'Pop Protest, Pop Art' (1960–79); Part III: 'Post-empire, Post-aesthetics' (1980–97); Part IV: 'Re-locating, Re-imagining' (1998–2005). With the exception of Part IV, each 'part' consists of three chapters. Chapters 1, 4 and 7, as well as the first part of Chapter 10, address the theme of 'identity in the making'. These might best be described as representations of selected localities and individuals through the period from 1945 to

2005. Each of these chapters, as well as the first part of Chapter 10, has four subsections that deal with Scotland, Northern Ireland, Wales and England, always in the same order. They draw on local history sources as well as autobiography, memoir and travel writing to describe the variety of personal and collective identities that exist within the United Kingdom (male and female, regional and national, historically inflected and present day). Again this regional aspect of the study is not meant to be all encompassing, but rather to balance out the coverage of themes – industry and the countryside, rural and urban planning, housing conditions and community life, among others – between different districts of the UK. The order of presentation in these 'regional' chapters serves as an argument for not letting 'England' stand for 'United Kingdom'; it also supports the conviction that there are revealing connections and contrasts to be found by studying two sets of historically distinct pairings: between Scotland and Northern Ireland as well as between Wales and England. The very real differences between these parts of the UK – their landscapes, customs and peoples – are not to be disguised. Nevertheless, government policy, educational and employment opportunities, countryside and city planning schemes, industrial and postindustrial development provide the common context within which life stories and collective histories are played out.

The second and third chapters in each part (2 and 3, 5 and 6, 8 and 9 as well as part 2 of Chapter 10) progress chronologically. They consist of six subsections, always in the same order: (a) women: work, social position, the family; (b) immigration and ethnicity: arrival, social position, integration and exclusion; (c) youth: fashion and consumption, 'morality' debates, employment; (d) visual arts: individuals, movements, themes; (e) popular music: sources, fashions, technology and business trends; and (f) film: genres and schools, business, actors and directors.

There are, of course, many other possible subject strands that might have been chosen for these chapters. The experience of the elderly over the last 60 years, modifications in pensions or housing policies, or in attitudes towards growing old, would have provided a different history from that which emerges through the examination of youth. But it would still be a connected history. Likewise, it is easy to imagine an account of Britain's development that explores shifting notions of masculinity and male experiences of fashion, unemployment or leisure pursuits.[16] The social groups finally included in this study represent sections of society usually not discussed thoroughly in the context of 'identity' debates. I wanted to create too a series of contrasting perspectives according to age, gender and social viewpoint. Relatively speaking, these are marginal experiences of the conventional social world which permit a variety of alternative standpoints, and which also fulfil the basic criteria of raising wider sets of issues. The focus on women gives insight into the shifting balance of gender relations as well as into the worlds of work, private and public dimensions of family life, and changes in moral values. The overview of immigrants and ethnic minorities presents Britain's self-image formed as a response to outsiders, and reveals the gradually shifting range of attitudes among new and continuing settlers as they enter mainstream society through the postcolonial era. An account of the changing responses of the young to particular social and material circumstances provides a sensitive gauge of economic values, anti-authoritarian moods and social development.

Which subject strands of imaginative expression and representation might best extend this montage of identities was another consideration. Sport might have introduced questions of local loyalty and representation between regions and internationally just as much as music. In my view, however, popular music takes precedence because in the context of this study it contrasts well with the discussion of youth; moreover, the lyrical, technological and financial changes associated with popular music are a more articulate expression of time-bound preoccupations and values. While the study of music in society might easily have been extended to 'high' culture classical works and their performance, it is visual arts that provide a contrasting model of 'elite' culture that eventually sees certain artists take on a celebrity persona and lifestyle. Painting and sculpture usher in worlds of intuition, sensual response and abstraction. The visual arts, reacting as they do to the intimacies of bodily experience and the imaginative interpretation of landscape, also present otherwise inaccessible domains of self-perception and identity formation. While film has the privilege of being both popular and elite art, both theatre and literature might have served usefully here. Film has this advantage: viewed as historical evidence of a time gone by, it combines performative art with the captured realm of past apprehension, past values and moralities, past artistic experiments and commercial certainties.

Each of the ten chapters is centred too on a major theme that is its interpretive heart. For Chapter 1, renewal and unity; Chapter 2, the establishment of welfare values; Chapter 3, the attractions and repulsions of 'America'; Chapter 4, the cultural roots of devolution; Chapter 5, the continuities of 'the sixties' within the context of postwar history; Chapter 6, images of crisis and decline; Chapter 7, the postindustrial imagination; Chapter 8, the end of consensual values and new social division; Chapter 9, prosperity and bankruptcy; Chapter 10, local and global connections. To further inform readers in their interpretation, I have added background and supporting materials: the maps that appear at the beginning of the book, the timelines at the end of each part, the appendices at the end of the book, and the final thematic Bibliography and Further Reading section. As a way of alerting readers to generational change I have included dates of birth and death in the text for many of the individuals mentioned. To understand fully this account it is important to go back to the paintings, films and songs that are discussed throughout. A visit to an art gallery, to a cinema, video or music store is recommended. An internet search can bring up all kinds of treasures – contemporary articles, reproductions of works of art – they convey with immediacy and clarity how women and men in the past have understood themselves and the world around them.

Britain since 1945: Aspects of Identity is a series of case studies: it presents particular events as well as individuals, and it demonstrates connections as well as parallels. A debate on maternal deprivation led by John Bowlby, for instance, illustrates apprehension over the role of women, youth and American culture in the postwar years. The treatment of an Afro-Caribbean during the Profumo affair of 1963 reveals the persistence of the colonial mind-set within the country as well as the gradual revision of moral attitudes. The protest and debate surrounding the 1994 Criminal Justice Act displays a clash of generational values and the continuing influence of the 1960s' counter-culture. *Yesterday's Enemy* (Val Guest,

1959), a war film made two years after the Suez crisis, views Britain's status as a world power with a newly found scepticism. The Beat, a late 1970s pop group influenced by the ska music and the fashion style of black immigrants in the early 1960s, play out the effects of the Rock Against Racism youth movement and the beginnings of multiculturalism. Jenny Saville's *Prop* (1993), a painting of a nude female torso, inscribes both the imaginative stimulus of feminism and the post-modern revival of interest in Marcel Duchamp. None of these examples denies the complexity of an individual's life experience. No person or object can be reduced to an emblem of some wider mood or trend.

Equally, no communal experience can be rendered in its totality. Political elites or nationalists tend to imagine one particular kind of collective community that may be projected and mobilized for ill or good. In the structure of this account, but also in everyday life, I see identity as a composite, a montage: a walk through a local neighbourhood dissolves into a bulletin of national and international news; a journey by car or plane wipes away the highland landscape of Inverness to reveal the metropolitan sprawl of 'London Luton'; a video installation by Gillian Wearing dissolves into a long-forgotten photographic portrait of a Second World War soldier. Filmic and historical representations have in common an incompleteness and partiality; past mentalities and forgotten mind maps are perhaps beyond recovery, but this should not preclude our efforts to bring them to light.

PART I
From War, from Modernism

Welfare's Place

I am an underdog, am I not?

On Thursday, 26 July 1945 a group of Conservative Party supporters gathered in the Kelvingrove Glasgow constituency to discuss the results of the General Election. Delayed for three weeks while the servicemen's ballot papers were collected and counted, the outcome proved unpredictable. When it did finally arrive it was incomprehensible too, at least to this particular political salon.[1] The overall swing meant no dramatic change in Glasgow as ten Labour MPs from the city had already been returned to Parliament in the election of November 1922.[2] Nevertheless, the former Secretary of State for Scotland and Tory MP for the constituency since 1924, Walter Elliot, lost his seat to Labour candidate John Lloyd Williams by 45 votes. Just as disastrous for the Kelvingrove Conservatives, Winston Churchill was unceremoniously put out of office. 'I shall write to Dave to demand how he voted,' said Mrs Blane, speculating that the servicemen were responsible. 'If he did vote Labour I shall tell him what I think of him.'[3] Expressions of sympathy and of regret for the loss of the wartime leader were difficult to suppress in the discussions of that afternoon as the collective mood lurched from bewilderment to desperate humour and resignation. When the possibility of emigration was half-heartedly raised, it was immediately quashed by general admission that Australia already had a Labour government. Finally Miss Page, who administered trust funds for aristocratic families, came around to the view that all was not lost. 'Of course I am very sorry about Mr Churchill, but I am not sure that it is not a good thing for people like me,' she said. 'Well, I am an underdog, am I not?'[4]

Miss Page's sudden conversion to the new, democratic spirit of the early post-war years gives an insight into how individual and collective loyalties gradually began to change according to time, place and shifting circumstance after 1945. While the Kelvingrove Conservatives shared with Miss Page and with many other people around the country a sense of achievement as victory and peace became a reality, they were nevertheless forced to reluctantly rethink their own sense of belonging. By scrutinizing such local perspectives, giving attention to individual voices, looking at national developments as they were lived out in Belfast, Stromness, Cardiff or Manchester, and in the rural as well as the more commonly reported metropolitan scene, the particularities of the local are gradually revealed. As the war ended observers from almost all quarters of the United Kingdom saw around them physical damage, obsolescence and the prospect of slow recovery. Road and rail networks, housing and industrial equipment were outdated, the economy struggled to supply food and clothing, technology produced rapid and

Illustration 1 Community and labour in a local landscape: South Wales mine

unexpected changes to factory and field labour. Moreover, the new welfare state, the expanded role of government, caused regret as well as rejoicing: pressing questions of how and where to live were now subject to state scrutiny and decision-making procedures that shaped millions of lives for decades to come.

In Scotland observers also saw a substantial benefit in the Labour victory. In the 1945 election 36 Labour candidates were returned alongside the new member for Kelvingrove, and collectively they sought to alleviate the severe local housing crisis by new building programmes, as well as to reduce hardship and disease rates by introducing state benefits and healthcare. In the first eighteen months or so after VJ Day, which marked Japan's capitulation and the final end of the war, unemployment increased in Scotland to five per cent. Parts of the economy were caught up in an export boom, particularly in steel, engineering and shipbuilding. Fifteen per cent of the world's tonnage was launched from Scottish shipyards in the years 1948 to 1951. The Korean War from 1950 sustained growth at the beginning of the new decade; Scottish yards produced 12 per cent of all tonnage during 1951–4; employment in the shipbuilding industry increased in the early 1950s to 27,000.[5] The economic revival passed. Only gradually, and painfully, did it become clear that this traditional mainstay industry was subject to creeping obsolescence. In the shift from war to cargo production after 1950 Scottish yards were too narrow, berths too small and technology too soon outdated. By the late 1950s, with increased antagonism in industrial relations, overseas yards were supplying ships with greater speed and efficiency: the new prosperity of the early postwar boom was to be the last success of a disappearing age. Coal and steel eventually lost their market position too as new, more efficient and cost-effective sources of fuel became available, as the European and Japanese economies recovered and became more competitive, as the first industrial nation was finally overtaken.

In the rural economy the longer-term twentieth-century trend towards mechanization and the decline of labour-intensive work now accelerated. In the islands of Orkney, a useful example precisely because of their remoteness, tractors had appeared before 1914, and immediately prior to the outbreak of the Second World War were used alongside the 5,800 working horses. After 1945, because it was now readily available for hire, the tractor came within the reach of almost every farmer.[6] By 1960 the working horse had become an unusual sight in Scottish farming. The old farm servant system was already prohibitively expensive after 1918; after 1945 changes in farming methods added to the chronic problem of rural depopulation as labour intensive techniques and specialist jobs, long a feature of rural life, now quickly disappeared. Within Orkney there was also long-term migration from the most rural districts to the towns of Kirkwall or Stromness, so that by the 1980s 40 per cent lived in a town; outward movement from Orkney was higher through the twentieth century than in any other part of England or Scotland.[7] Throughout Scotland the look of the countryside was changing too: the number of small crofts and farms fell; the large landholdings of the Forestry Commission served to rebuild timber stocks by extensive planting, which in turn led to 'the single greatest physical transformation in the Scottish countryside in the [twentieth] century'.[8]

Living in city or countryside, the people of Scotland had a shared concern for the poor condition of their housing stock, and by the early 1950s they saw improvements in accommodation and living conditions. New materials became available, new building techniques possible and government grants made both accessible. Rural and urban squalor, an absence of basic sanitation, for instance, nevertheless persisted. In 1951 only two-thirds of the Orkney population had more than two rooms to live in, 45 per cent had piped water, 23 per cent had flush toilets, 18 per cent had a fitted bath.[9] The housing shortage continued into the 1970s. In the larger cities of mainland Scotland public housing, including house building, was a high priority, yet these were not issues that could be solved simply or by any single measure. Ambitious redevelopment plans were produced in the early postwar years in an attempt to defeat overcrowding and shabby or non-existent sanitary facilities in the older housing stock, and more immediately the destruction of the war years. The *Clyde Valley Regional Plan* (1949) proposed major housing development, peripheral estates and a commitment to rebuild urban areas, including Paisley, Clydebank and Rutherglen.[10] Similarly the *Civic Survey and Plan for Edinburgh* (1949) and *Regional Plan for Central and South-East Scotland* (1948) shaped future development, this time by a policy of urban containment that favoured land-use zoning to promote agricultural and industrial growth as well as housing.[11] Central Glasgow, the densely populated heart of West Scotland, was one of many cities across the United Kingdom to demolish nineteenth- and early twentieth-century buildings and districts and thereby to disperse long-established local communities. In their wake came the new towns such as East Kilbride, established in 1947, 11 miles south-east of Glasgow, and peripheral estates such as Easterhouse. These changes meant that between 1945 and 1971 Scottish housing stock in the public sector trebled; by 1981 it accounted for one third of all homes.[12]

The prospect of education and better employment drew the young from more remote districts towards metropolitan areas; when jobs and money were scarce in the city, rural life became attractive to travellers and outside settlers. As roads and ferry services improved the most isolated corners of the Highlands became accessible to tourists, while locals could now visit metropolitan centres for themselves.[13] The interwar years were 'the bleakest time in Stromness's history', but here and in other rural districts the years after 1945 were a time of increasing self-confidence as tangible improvements including farm owner-occupation and the arrival of electricity made real the possibility of a better life.[14] The general trend was still towards the abandonment of the countryside, most of all because of lessening faith in rural ways of life. For the young, living away from the city now seemed to be isolating and inconvenient in its lack of dancehalls or cinemas; to the older generation of the 1950s it appeared that custom and community as well as local loyalties were increasingly abandoned.[15] Even greater mobility, which meant new possibilities to some, was troubling to others. 'Older people, who remembered sending twelve miles or more to fetch the doctor by horse, or chartering a steamer in an emergency, were very conscious of the advantages of telephones, cars and the air ambulance service,' as one historian put it. But 'by the 1950s they still found it strange that young people sought their social life outside the parish and could take off in cars to attend a concert or a dance at the other end of the island.'[16] While the land gradually lost its appeal as a way of life and as a viable living, transport and media communications began to invade, noticeably reducing regional distinctions. 'Many variations will be seen, for there are still great contrasts between such communities as, say Cowdenbeath and Crail, or even neighbourhoods like Inverkeithing and Aberdour', the editor of the *Third Statistical Account* for Fife reported in 1952. Yet 'there has been a standardization of dress, of speech, of manners and of the whole attitude of life.'[17]

In cities the pre- and postwar generations also had different values. Growing up in Glasgow in the 1950s, for example, Liz Heron was aware that her own outlook separated her from her parents. Mother and father had grown up in the East End of the city of Irish catholic stock. Both had left school at the age of four-teen. Their religious and national tradition expressed itself partly in anti-protes-tant sentiment, which became a rationale for personal disappointment and collective limitation. Living conditions were sparse:

> School and home were on opposite sides of the steep hill that was the main road joining the two. Trams went up and down it. We lived in a tenement block that ran its whole length, in a top-story 'room and kitchen' with no bath-room and an outside toilet shared with several other families and reached by an open staircase. At night I slept in the big kitchen on the brown leatherette bed settee, and my parents slept in the box room.[18]

Arguments with the neighbours over cleaning public areas; playing girl games and gang games on waste ground; observing the pleasure and pride in material gain: a vacuum cleaner, a boiler for the washing, were among her earliest memories. Such small pleasures contrast with the powerful constraints on her parents. The Second World War delayed her father's hope for emigration to New Zealand; he worked as a tradesman, married, became a parent, failed in business and finally put off emigration permanently. Educated in a catholic primary school, Liz Heron was confronted by two role models. One was 'Our Lady' ('Our Lady wouldn't whistle; Our Lady wouldn't go to Mass without gloves'), the other was the young women teachers, rare examples then of a catholic middle class in the West of Scotland, 'with their New Look skirts and wide-belted dresses . . .' who were all in a state of becoming engaged or about to be married, '. . . nearly all were virginal, but some on the verge of something else'.[19] Eventually, Heron found her way to a senior secondary school, and from the summer of 1958 began to lose contact with her childhood contemporaries. She now had a privilege denied to their parents: a path into higher education. The losses of the Kelvingrove Conservatives were now the gains of a younger, wider cross-section of Scottish society. Later, separation from her mother's values brought accusations of 'self-ishness and rank ingratitude'; while her father's hope was that the education he had never received might make anything possible for his daughter. Heron was left with the sense that '*by right* [we had] something more than had been intended for us'.[20]

From Molesworth Street to Rathbeg

Rights and obligations, family and community ties, nowhere ran deeper than in Northern Ireland. Describing her family background and upbringing in Cookstown in County Tyrone, for instance, Bernadette Devlin (b. 1947) notes that for 'miles around everyone is called either Devlin or Quinn, and they are all related to each other'.[21] The problem of knowing who you were talking about could be solved by using a father's as well as a son's name, hence 'John Pat Devlin, meaning John-Devlin-son-of-Pat', or by singling out an identifying trait to distinguish among the dozens of Devlin clans. All the more essential in this case as her mother's side of the family were Dan, or fair-haired Devlins, while the father's side were in earlier times Delphy or Hawker Devlins known for travelling and selling pottery. Later they became known as the Fighting Devlins 'because that's all they ever did'.[22] Born in 1947, Bernadette Devlin's subsequent career as an Irish nationalist politician, civil rights activist and MP for mid-Ulster – elected at the age of twenty-two – was testimony to the strength of such ties, and the passions they aroused. As one commentator wrote in the year of Bernadette Devlin's birth, 'it would be true to say that the Ulsterman's character, like his climate, is not a soft one. There is a hard nip about it. But it is precisely that which keeps him strong and active and enterprising, and which has made Ulster the industrial spearhead of Ireland.'[23] Three hundred years of common agricultural and peasant heritage, of shared proximity and acclimatization, thus provided a common background beyond religious and ethnic division: '. . . it would be wrong to think that the two characters [protestant and catholic] stand for two ways of life that touch only to spring apart again. For one can see them shading each other, the wet colours running together here and there. Each lend-leases itself to the other.'[24] What both Irelands shared too was predominantly a rural, peasant heritage: its people were characteristically proud, alert to the significance of the past and to the vitality of collective, group loyalties.

With the arrival of the new postwar interventionist, subsidizing government such intimate bonds were not relinquished, and Northern Ireland, like Scotland, was initially at least a net beneficiary. At the same time the political settlement enshrined in the Government of Ireland Act (1920), which set unionism at the permanent centre of regional government, and which affirmed the position of the province of Northern Ireland within the United Kingdom, was strengthened with the Ireland Act (1949), which now established the Republic of Ireland. For Northern Ireland Labour administration from the mainland now meant, for example, the introduction of the Industrial Development Acts (1949–53), allowing the expansion of business and manufacturing assisted by improved communications. Moreover, in an overwhelmingly rural region, the business of farming profited. During the war years the requirement to boost food production meant intervention and support for the agriculture sector; thereafter the Drainage and Agriculture Acts (both 1947) meant that cereals, potatoes and flax production as well as dairy stock and poultry all received continuing support.[25] The system of guarantees for prices and deficit payments in the Agriculture Act especially stimulated milk and beef production. However, farms were generally smaller and less mechanized than in mainland Britain; employment on the land fell by 27 per cent as the number of tractors doubled through the 1950s.[26] Likewise, this period saw a drift away from rural life, increasing eastward migration and urban population particularly among catholics who now came to represent 35 per cent of town dwellers.[27]

As in Glasgow, the underlying trend was towards industrial decline. The boom in the linen trade continued into the 1950s, especially while there was a worldwide shortage of textiles from the end of the war to around 1951, but in 1952 severe recession in the trade affected major centres of production and led to job losses in Belfast.[28] Ten years later some of the best known names such as the York Street Flax Spinning Company, the Brockfield Spinning Company and the Broadway Damask Company had disappeared, while the number of employees over the same period fell by 50 per cent. As in Lancashire, Belfast's nineteenth century heritage of industrial prosperity and cloth mills was no longer adequate to the changing market: low cost synthetic and natural fibre from abroad now cut demand. Likewise shipbuilding, as in Glasgow or London, continued through the 1950s: orders still came in, employees still went to work. Following an initial postwar fall in demand and related drop in employment, industry orders and employment remained until the completion of the *Canberra*, a large passenger liner, in 1963.[29] This was not enough, though, to maintain full employment or production. The period 1951–61 saw a 28 per cent drop in industrial textile production as well as a 16 per cent fall in shipbuilding repair and marine engineering works. Both of these industries were overwhelmingly based in Belfast, so that while unemployment in the city continued to hover at around five or six per cent, two-thirds of those without work were former employees in either the textile factories or the shipyards. In 1953 unemployment in the Belfast district was low compared to other parts of Northern Ireland, but reached 30,000 from an estimated 250,000 insured employees.[30]

Belfast's historical development and industrial achievement, within Ireland as a whole as well as within Northern Ireland, was unique. As the parallels with the Lancashire cotton trade or Glasgow shipbuilding indicate, its progress as an urban and industrial centre are best viewed within the context of nineteenth century mainland Britain's industrial growth. Belfast and many other parts of Ireland were connected to Merseyside and the Clyde too by cyclical and long-term patterns of migration as well as settlement.[31] Thus by 1900, Belfast's expansion had far outstripped Dublin; its high levels of inward migration and outward expansion along the Lagan Valley also resembled the development of Manchester.[32] It was in this period too that the city's pattern of population zoning was strengthened with large working-class districts in the north and west, as well as mills, factories and engineering works where textile machinery was made and repaired. The Belfast Ropeworks meanwhile, together with Workman Clark, and the Harland and Woolf shipyards, were located across the River Lagan.[33]

If medium-term political and economic misfortunes were stored up during the postwar years, there were nevertheless real benefits, not always easily won, for individuals and communities. After the Second World War, Northern Ireland was relatively underdeveloped and poor compared to mainland Britain and for this reason benefited disproportionately from the new political settlement. Overall living standards, especially among the poorest working-class communities, rose steadily through the 1950s.[34] Among the beneficiaries of the new dispensation were the Devlin family, who immediately after the war lived in a small apartment:

> Some time before my second sister, Marie, was born in 1945, my parents got their independence by renting two rooms above a milk-bar in Molesworth Street. By no standards could it be called a desirable property. It was damp. It was falling apart. And it had rats. To get to the lavatory shared by all the lodgers you had to pick your way through rotting boards on the landing, and my father spent all his spare time patching the place up. He put a gate at the top of the stairs to prevent us tumbling down into the street.[35]

This was the flat where Bernadette Devlin was born in 1947, contracted bronchial pneumonia and almost died at the age of six weeks. The prospect of another child led the family to search for a new home. When the local council provided nothing the Northern Ireland Housing Trust, set up by the Government and independent of local authorities, helped the Devlin family move onto the Rathbeg housing estate in Cookstown. 'A whole house to ourselves – to begin with my mother didn't know what to do with all the space . . . We had come up in the world. Where we lived the houses had whole floorboards and good doors and windows.'[36]

While it lasted, welfare state optimism and economic boom provided the basis for large-scale redevelopment and real improvements in everyday life. Yet as the difficulty of the Devlin's move to Rathbeg shows, gains from industrial and agricultural subsidy were offset by tension between the socialist, collectivist ethos of the Labour government and staunch unionist dominance both locally and in the Stormont Parliament. Despite better housing or the potential for wider access to education and a larger catholic middle class, socio-religious separatism and disadvantage in housing or education remained unchallengeable. Sectarian segregation persisted in housing as well as in education and health services. Thus while the need for extensive slum clearance and new housing was recognized by the Housing Act (Northern Ireland) (1945), and while the construction rate doubled annually over the next twenty years, so that by 1965 around 100,000 new dwellings had been built, allocation procedures and the setting of constituency boundaries consistently divided protestant and catholic communities.

The limits on development were also evident in large-scale planning after the war. Acute concern for the urban environment was reflected in the Government of Northern Ireland Planning Commission report, *Planning Proposals for the Belfast Area* (1945), which established the new principles of controlled suburban growth, decentralized industry, decanting populations from the inner city and protecting open spaces, especially the Antrim and Down uplands and the Lagan Valley.[37] Yet the *Second Report* of the Planning Commission in 1951 admitted these efforts were frustrated by inadequate legislative powers. Outside the urban centres, the *Report of the Board on the Ulster Countryside* (1947) together with the Northern Ireland Advisory Planning Board urged the conservation of vernacular buildings and coastal districts, as well as the establishment of national parks. Within Belfast itself the population rise peaked in 1951; outside the city's limits there was continued demographic expansion. As had been feared, the new suburban sprawl moved along both sides of the Lagan Valley, down along the Belfast Lough's north and south sides.[38]

The admixture of urban and rural cultures and mentalities within Northern Ireland was noticeable between the wars in the tendency of many to commute into Belfast, and after the war in the movement of employers beyond the boundaries of the city. Here too there were similarities with the Midlands or with the south-east of England, where congestion prevented expansion and industrial peripheral estates began to develop. The rural roots of northern Irish society remained close to the surface though:

> It may seem contradictory to call Ulster society a rural one when one third of its population is concentrated here . . . [in Belfast]. But gradually you will

notice that these city workers are happily not so far removed from their country cousins in character. Almost all Ulster townfolk have relatives who are farmers and with whom they spend many a happy summer holiday. And you will notice, too, that much of the traditional rural pattern of Ulster life has been carried into the city. For example, no town of comparable size in the British Isles has so many churches and church-going people.[39]

Thus while the benefits of the post-1945 settlement to Northern Ireland, to farming and rural life, to urban and industrial conurbation, were embraced as eagerly as any other part of the United Kingdom, the outlook and attitudes of the population, rooted within a particular historical development, a specific cultural geography, remained unaltered. The common history of catholic and protestant, but above all the political settlement of the post-First World War period, enforced a social, political and cultural deadlock. While the argument that the new consumerism and improvements in everyday life went some way to lessening strident socio-religious tensions in the postwar years may be credible, the suggestion that a liberal, affluent 1960s might have diminished conflict still further remains unproven. Even if the habit of 'buying from one's own' did momentarily falter, unionism and the Orange Order dominated the political scene; even though the IRA was reactivated in 1956, its actions were of slight consequence to the Stormont Parliament.[40]

Favourites of the people

In the mining community of Onllwyn, South Wales, where public divisions were far less visible, the Labour victory of 1945 was widely seen as a vindication. Miners were among the most fervent supporters of the Party, as elsewhere, spurred on by the keen memory of the interwar slump. Consequently Labour's election success was all the greater in Wales: 25 seats in Parliament, seven of them new; by contrast now only seven Liberal and four Conservative seats.[41] Moreover, there was every reason to expect improvement, a better life, and indeed, over the ten years following the end of the war, unemployment did steadily fall. In July 1955 it amounted to 13,400.[42] Despite too the dilapidation of the mines, of machinery and production methods, the over-dependence in the Principality on heavy industry in general and coal in particular, the promise of public ownership, a reality from 1 January 1947, was cause for celebration. A mark of recognition for the contribution of the Welsh valleys to the war effort. In June 1946 Jack Dorgan, one of the Onllwyn miners, recalled his journey to London to participate in a celebration of the Allies achievements, but also of the Labour rise to power. Describing the occasion Dorgan said:

On Saturday morning . . . at 9 am we started off for Hyde Park . . . to move to our position for the Victory Parade. The sights I have seen was [*sic*] very impressive foreign Regiments from all corners of the globe . . . we were now marching rigidly to attention and [when] the order was given we all looked to the left and the king saluted. . . . As we miners marched through the streets of London the overwhelming reception which the people gave to us was terrific, and whatever the Press say or our picture shows we were the favourites of the people.[43]

The conviction that the miners had striven for the common good, in war and now in peace, was matched by the major investment which followed nationalization. The steelworks and petrochemical plants at Port Talbot as well as the steel and later the car plants in Llanelli represented the promise of future prosperity. The war had revived the Welsh economy and the new consumer society sustained it, yet as with shipbuilding and textiles, coal and steel were not to have a long-term future. Coal-related employment had already fallen by 150,000 in the twenty years to 1947, the export market disappeared and by the late 1950s cheaper, cleaner, more effective fuels were favoured for domestic use, power production and transport. The search for alternative employment, the world of redundancy payments and compensation, came to Cwmllynfell, for example, some forty miles from Swansea, when the local community was threatened by pit closure in 1959.[44]

As in Northern Ireland, the Agriculture Act (1947) ensured stable prices and a guaranteed market for goods; payment of grants from central government began the drastic process of modernization; changed techniques, no longer labour intensive, pushed forward movement into urban ways of living, now increasingly accepted as the dominant model. Consumerism was embraced here too, and as its privileges were most readily available in cities and towns, the move away from the countryside was natural. The radicalism, religious non-conformity and community traditionalism which had shaped collective and individual beliefs and values before the First World War were gradually eroded after 1945. One example of this was electrification, which arrived in many rural Welsh districts in the 1950s. While one light per room and the use of paraffin-oil lamps continued even after electricity had arrived, and while the benefits of easier, cleaner cooking and better lighting were obvious, the arrival of electricity had unexpected consequences too. In rural north Wales, Elizabeth Williams Ellis found more leisure time did not necessarily lead to better leisure time.[45] 'It was not long before aerials sprouted on the village roof-tops. The weekly visit to the cinema lost its attraction. People did not make their own amusements. The chapel and the WI [Women's Institute] meetings were not the centre of entertainment anymore. "Americanisms" crept into our speech . . . Electricity changed our whole lives far more than we anticipated at the time.'

While Welsh society gradually altered, traditional radicalism underpinned the welfare state: Aneurin Bevan (1897–1960; Minister of Health, 1945–51) used the self-help cooperative of the South Wales coalfield as a model for the National Insurance and Industrial Injuries Acts (both 1946). Building on these rights, Wales entered into the United Kingdom's affluent community of nations in the 1950s. Better roads led to increased mobility, especially in the Cardiff region; England and America could now more easily come to Wales either in person or through television after the BBC began broadcasting there in 1953.[46] As in Northern Ireland, greater material success, because it tied regional development and investment more closely to central administration, did not alter the political settlement or lead to significant moves towards greater regional autonomy.

Despite the introduction of an advisory Council for Wales (1948), a post of Minister for Welsh Affairs (1951), a capital city (Cardiff, 1955) and finally a senior Labour politician James Griffiths (1890–1975) as first Secretary of State for Wales (1964–6), the Labour Party rather than any nationalist faction dominated through the 1950s. In 1957 the question of Welsh self-determination was nevertheless bitterly brought alive by the erasure of the Tryweryn Valley – home to a Welsh-speaking community – in Merioneth, which was evacuated and flooded to provide a water reservoir for Liverpool. The decision was taken outside Wales, it was widely attacked as against the wishes and interests of the population, and its implementation was equally condemned. A sabotage attempt followed the introduction of a similar scheme at Clywedog, Powys, this time to create a dam for Birmingham.[47]

Even the districts into which affluence barely reached took something from the new age of welfare and consumerism. In the Cardiff dockland community of Butetown, more often called, with a hint of disparagement, Tiger Bay, an intracultural, multi-ethnic port community that predated the First World War was still thriving on its uniquely mixed African, Middle Eastern and Asian heritage. In an affectionate recollection of his childhood, Neil Sinclair records a local version of what became an iconic moment in the postwar era: the televised broadcast of the coronation of Elizabeth II. Among the twenty and a half million viewers watching in 1953 were Sinclair and his fellow Tiger Bay residents. There were three televisions in the neighbourhood at the time, and in years to come the locals argued over whose set was used that day. Mrs Percy's set was in the 'front room' of her house at 11 Frances Street. 'So anybody passing by could see in and know she had one.' But it was not available for public viewing. Some claimed it was the set that belonged to Eddie Gomez. Sinclair nominates the man he called 'nice Mr Shephard', who always carried newspapers under his arm and, dedicated to his cause, provided the author with his 'first impression of a communist blackman'.[48] How fully Sinclair qualified as one of the viewers of the coronation ceremony is debatable. '. . . I rushed across the park to get in the tent to see the Queen being crowned only to find all the grown-ups crowded in front. We could barely see the telly, it was so small. All I recall was a box with a bluish light coming from it as grown-ups shoved us back.'[49] Enthusiasm and rivalry for new experiences and goods was keen in Tiger Bay as Sinclair was growing up. Mr Gatehouse topped the coup of Mrs Percy's front room television when he became the first in the area to own a car, which he polished daily.

Council housing became an object of pride too for new occupants, as it was central to the urban renewal and re-housing programme of the 1940s and 1950s under Aneurin Bevan for Labour and then Harold Macmillan (1894–1986; Prime Minister 1957–63) for the Conservatives. In Swansea it was only after 1945 that the old slum districts were finally demolished, assisted by wartime bombing. Private developers were reluctant to invest in the coalfield areas so 87 per cent of the houses built between 1945 and 1951 were council properties.[50] Home improvement grants allowed 200,000 houses to install hot water and indoor bathrooms; pre-fabricated houses remained in use for a decade or more in the 'Tin Town' districts of many British towns and cities, including Pontypridd. The shortfall in adequate dwellings was not always resolved or even successfully addressed. In Caernarfon the old town within the city walls was replaced by inadequate modern development, while Cardiff City Council planned an extensive redevelopment of the area, including the demolition of Tiger Bay. Sinclair and many of his fellow residents saw this as a pretext for the destruction of a 'disreputable' district, widely believed by outsiders to be a slum area. 'Yet the home my family lived in was no slum, nor were many of the other homes I so often frequented.' Despite bomb damage, which was relatively slight, despite the disrepair and dilapidation, the community remained close-knit and could well have thrived had it been allowed to remain. Sinclair continues:

> Loudoun Square had spectacular buildings merely requiring refurbishing – Victorian and Edwardian buildings containing moulded features where chandeliers once illuminated the rooms. Given such a complete eradication of quite salvageable structures, one tends to be faced with the conclusion that the motivation was to dispose of the melting pot community that Tiger Bay represented. Over the years many of us have come increasingly to see the 'slum clearance' as – to borrow a phrase from Olwen Blackman – 'municipal vandalism'.[51]

Such affection for local community was not exceptional. The boom in private house building reached a postwar peak in 1956 when 19,524 homes were put up; suburbanization and owner occupation increased even among the working-class section of Welsh society.[52]

The same forces of 'standardization' were at work here as observed by the *Third Statistical Account* for Fife: new homes, cars, consumer goods were not to be shunned; monotonous trading estates, or the industrial sprawl of Swansea or Llanwern, could be lived with, even at the price of community spirit and neighbourly courtesy. Church attendance, attached as it was in Wales to the powerful matrix of radical non-conformity and Welsh language, gives an indication of community-mindedness. In Northern Ireland attendance figures held strong through the 1950s and long after; in Wales participation dropped, among the largest group, the Presbyterians, from 152,000 (1955) to 137,000 (1962–3) and 133,000 (1967–8).[53] New town developments also dispersed community, creating neighbourhoods with no common past, no shared values and no grounds for a common way of living. Cwmbran New Town for instance, located approximately halfway between Newport and Pontypool, was planned from the late 1940s, built beginning in 1952 and had by 1954 over a thousand houses completed. The Cwmbran area's attractive utilities and communications system drew industrialists from the English Midlands but had little to offer its population in the early postwar years. The town's shopping and recreational facilities remained underdeveloped and inadequate and, despite encouragement by the development corporation, public life did not flourish. Just as the neighbourhood districts were being completed in the early 1970s, several hundred jobs were lost.[54]

In other districts there were traditions and older ways of life more actively sustaining present-day society. In 1948 the Miners' Eisteddfod was established at Porthcawl; in the 1950s the South Wales Miners' Gala became a meeting place for the national Labour movement. Gwyn Thomas, writer and dramatist, captured the mood of early welfare socialism, based in the 1950s on greater union power and the renewal of an authentically working-class culture suspended for most of the 1940s, in his commentary for a promotional film on the 1960 South Wales Miners' Gala:

> We enter Sophia Gardens. This would have been a place denied to us in the long age but now it is part of our inheritance, and we are prepared for a day in which gaiety and thought will compete for equal place in the long years of endurance, the long years of conflict. These men have listened, thought, planned, worked. Their hands have been hands that sustained a nation. Strong creative hands on which a community can always rely no matter how the community may have sometimes treated them. Men as strong as the steel of the pit head gear that takes them down into the earth and up into the light, men as ardent as the coal they bring us, men as enduring as the hills from which they hew the stuff that keeps us alive . . .[55]

Elegy, praise of masculine virtue, respect for the integrity and achievement of industrial workers: this is a continuing celebration of wartime victory, social equality and escape from poverty into the justice of state welfare provision.

Sheep on Hampstead Heath

A year or so after Jack Dorgan's march to Hyde Park, Christopher Logue (b.1926), ex-soldier, poet and later CND activist, was also in the capital. He saw it differently:

> London was sad. A place of war-damaged, unpainted houses, cellars filled with water, stairs and windows open to the sky, static water tanks – big, four foot deep, iron rectangles brimming with black water intended to extinguish the fires started by the Luftwaffe's incendiary bombs – weed-covered bomb sites, mean 'caffs', miles apart from one another and almost always empty. There were sheep on Hampstead Heath, bound, I suppose, for grand restaurants. Very little in the shops.[56]

Despite the elation of war's end and Allied success, in Logue's London obstructions blocked off the mental and physical horizon at every turn: obsolete equipment, tense labour relations, strikes and the threat of industrial action accompanied the effects of bomb damage. As Logue suggests too, there were very immediate difficulties to overcome – in 1946 shortages of butter, margarine and cooking fat as well as bread and flour; in January 1947 the worst winter for over fifty years. The rationing of coal for domestic and industrial use and the poor availability of building materials meant that basic needs for shelter and warmth were hard to meet. By 1953 everyday life was less unpredictable, but troubling events could still have a disproportionate effect. In January gales and high tides caused severe flooding in Essex and East Anglia with deaths near King's Lynn and at Canvey Island, Essex; in December a four-day asthma- and heart attack-inducing chemical smog enveloped the capital.[57] That six years of recession should follow the end of the war was unexpected, that the resultant frustration should express itself in tense race relations, the threat of strikes in the Port of London and the takeover of empty property by squatters should have been less surprising.[58]

Terry Hamlyn (b.1935), whose father was a long-distance lorry driver, described these tensions in his account of factory work in the mid-1950s. Recalling the time with twenty or so years' hindsight, Hamlyn remembered vividly the stigmatic division between the workers in overalls and the more formally dressed office staff, who were paid less but assumed a higher social position. One result of this was the policy of different toilet facilities for 'office' and 'shopfloor'. Industrial relations were poisoned as well by mistrust and mutual suspicion.

> When the strike was called, the shop steward was not a good orator, but the assistant shop steward was. He said, 'I won't be behind you, brothers, I'll be beside you.' We all charged out of the shop. What happened? Next day he went back to work as manager of the bakery department. He'd been paid to do it. It was the same elsewhere: they would provoke a strike because they wanted to rearrange the assembly lines . . .'[59]

During more extended stoppages the buoyant job market and the economic boom meant simply that 'a lot of people got other jobs'.[60]

Antagonistic labour relations persisted in the London docks too, 1958 was a high watermark as more goods were processed than in any single previous year.[61] Cars from Ford, Dagenham, and aircraft from Vickers, Weybridge, were a part of the vehicle construction and engineering export boom to Commonwealth markets. In the industrial centres, success in the nineteeth century had been based on fabric manufacture and its production as well as coal and coke consumption, yet exports fell from 60 to 17 per cent of national commodity trade between 1870 and 1965.[62] As the rise of vehicle manufacture indicates, metal-related industry became vital to support export sales and job markets in the post-1945 period.

Holidaymakers, a different kind of export, were also beginning to be processed in large numbers following the opening of the new, modernized Gatwick Airport in June 1958. For a moment in the 1950s the variety show coexisted with the television set: an older way of life based on industrial labour, localized entertainment and leisure, collective values sat comfortably alongside forms of consumption that were more individual- or family-oriented.[63] London's sports events helped maintain the collective mood. While attendance, especially from overseas, media coverage and funding were sparse for the 1948 Olympic Games, football, speedway and greyhound racing thrived. Soccer had the highest attendance figures for Arsenal and Chelsea games; speedway had its noisy, atmospheric, floodlit stadia and the spectacle of the crash; dog racing had gambling, restaurants, corporate entertaining and its own cigarette-smoke smogs.[64] Traditional pleasures were quickly supplemented by new leisure activities; tea-rooms and coffee-houses were replaced by American-style fast food outlets. Terry Hamlyn was among those pleased by such change:

. . . the Americans moved in on Joe Lyons. The tea-shops were a waste of time, people would sit there one hour, two hours, with just a cup of tea and a cake. In fact, people used to eat in the evenings, before going to theatre or cinema – solid traditional English things, fish and chips and puddings. That was all changed. The Corner Houses closed and opened up as Wimpey Bars. It was still run by Lyons, Empire Caterers. The London Steak Houses also opened about then; they've all gone now. It was part of the Americanization of our eating habits. It wasn't seen like that. People thought, Oh, this is more modern.[65]

Older ways of living gradually disappeared from rural and city districts; country-dwellers and urbanites began to see each other differently. The landscape and function of the countryside was gradually transformed, not only by changes in the business of farming but also by the increasing presence of outsiders as visitors and settlers. One cause of these changes resulted from the new situation in which the aristocracy found itself after 1945. Faced with declining financial resources, increasing maintenance cost and death duties and the often severe damage from use as wartime billets, some owners of stately homes preferred to demolish what was seemingly beyond restoration. Lord Bath of Longleat pioneered the trend towards paying visitors (1949); Lord Montague opened Beaulieu, establishing the first motor museum as an added attraction (1952).[66] Urban life had in any case already travelled to rural districts before the Second World War with ramblers. After 1945 trips to the countryside became more common as car ownership increased, and settlement grew too as commuting expanded in the south and east of England, and as mechanization and depopulation left farming areas run down. Essex and Surrey were early bases for workers travelling into London; commuting now increased to spread across the home counties. These non-metropolitan and rural districts were now divided into local and outsider, better and worse off, traditional and modern: a variation on the theme of 'standardization' in Fife, or perhaps of the 'generation gap' on Orkney, and a parallel to the remaking of local community as observed by Neil Sinclair in Cardiff.

Wartime property requisition had different consequences in the city. The need for sufficient housing, adequate in number, facilities and location, was recognized as a pressing requirement for postwar society as early as 1941. Then and in 1944, when Professor Patrick Abercrombie (1897–1957), architect and town planner, produced his Greater London Plan, there was discussion on how possible development schemes could best meet the requirements of adequate living conditions, leisure and transportation. The end of the war saw little immediate advance; families became increasingly impatient. In Kensington there were about 8000 houses and hostels left empty after government wartime requisition and on 7 September 1946 protesting squatters began to move in. One of the organizers, Lou Kenton, who was affiliated to the Communist Party, described the tolerant view that was taken towards the squatters' illegal campaign. Even the police, Kenton stated, 'got the Armed Services Corps to provide tea and told us to ring up if we were in difficulties'.[67] London now gained its own long-standing 'Tin Town' districts of temporary, prefabricated housing. Some of the 125,000 'rabbit hutches' constructed at this time were still in use forty years later in the East End of

London. In the same part of the capital the Lansbury Estate, named after one of the district's most famous Members of Parliament, opened on Valentine's Day 1951, replacing nineteenth-century bomb-damaged terraces with blocks of large flats, mostly no more than three storeys high. This was the government's ideal housing solution: shops, parks, and other facilities all available nearby. Yet model estates were difficult to build to such high specifications: by the end of 1951 few more than 1000 homes were available.[68] Lansbury Estates were rare; Loudoun Squares were common. Ray Gosling's sentiments on 'slum clearance' echo those of Neil Sinclair. In the St Ann's district in Nottingham, Gosling noted. 'We fought against having high-rise flats, budgie boxes in the sky, and we won. We got plasterboard hutches on the ground instead.'[69]

The Abercrombie Plan also included a recommendation that was taken up in many other parts of the United Kingdom, namely satellite towns. In the case of London eight were to be built, from 15 to 30 miles away, among them two in Essex, Basildon and Harlow. Peripheral estates also grew in size and number across the United Kingdom at this time. Beatrix Campbell made her own North of England move from city to outlying estate of a Cumbrian town as a child in the 1950s:

> We got a house with three bedrooms, a bathroom, a separate living room and dining room, a kitchen big enough for a table and chairs (saving mothers from solitary confinement), front and back garden, a coal house, inside *and* outside lavatory and wash house where people stored dolly tubs and mangles, bikes and prams. And it was brand new. Estates like ours were out on the urban edge, the new boundary between town and country. Although we were city kids, we built dens in the fields behind the estate and harvested bluebells and brambles. Allotments kept people in winter vegetables and summer salads.
>
> When we moved we had one armchair and a sewing machine. The kitchen had built-in cupboards and shelves – my first memory is of sitting with my little sister in the most commodious shoe cupboard. Happiness was an inside lavatory and built-in cupboards. Unhappiness was our cold bedrooms and condensation settling like dew. So, despite seeming to have all that space, you didn't. Our new houses were cold and uncomfortable. The rent, my dad reminds me, took a quarter of his wages.[70]

Both Wythenshawe Garden City, which was a part of the interwar urban garden city movement, and the Lansbury Estate, showed that it was possible to provide adequate, well-planned developments. More often housing was inadequate, facilities insufficient. In Manchester, as in Nottingham, the new housing initiatives tended to be piecemeal, uncoordinated efforts that lacked careful planning across the region. Even the overspill estate tower blocks were not enough to replace the decaying nineteenth-century housing stock. Ninety thousand houses were demolished between 1954 and 1976; 71,000 new flats and houses were put up by the Manchester Corporation; yet in 1959 68,000 houses were declared 'grossly unfit'.[71]

CHAPTER 2

Looking New

New relations

Reuniting across the country after a separation of months or years, readjusting to civilian society and the world after war, women and men found dealings with one another subtly changed; while the fractured bones of society could be set once again in common proximity, they would not fuse in the old way.[1] Between 1939 and 1945 women's work had extended further than ever before into activities previously reserved for men: from 1941 the wartime labour shortage meant that women were obliged to register as available for work. Subsequently they might be allocated employment in a factory, on the land or in auxiliary military service. Under these new conditions there could be freedom and challenge but also sometimes too a division of loyalty between commitment to family life and demands in the world of work. A number of women recalled war work fondly. 'No matter what happiness came after that,' one Land Army worker said of her time felling trees in the Timber Corps, 'it would never be better than those three and a half years . . . They were complete freedom, where I had never known it before'.[2] The diminished certainties of human relations, the unpredictable quality of life, made new experiences, both professional and personal, all the more vivid. The loosening of moral restraints, whether pleasurable or troubling, served to further change relations between the sexes. Many women married younger; some were distressed and endured separation only with difficulty; others took partners in the absence of husbands or boyfriends, black or white American servicemen for instance. The number of births to unmarried women doubled over the course of the war to nine per cent of all births in 1945.[3]

The transition from war to peace was inevitably difficult because it required an alteration in activity, mentality and public role for women. Because too while the deprivations and sacrifice for the cause of victory might be embraced, albeit sometimes reluctantly during hostilities, the personal incentives to achieve public goals once peace had arrived could never be as compelling. Nevertheless, three or four children now became the ideal family recommended by the *Report of the Royal Commission on Population* (1949). As encouragement the report suggested better facilities for children, including playgrounds and nursery schools; greater attention to mother's needs including babysitters and rest homes; and additional assistance through state allowances.[4] These recommendations came too late to influence thinking on government policy. In 1945, the year the Commission was established, the new Labour government was already building its legislative programme on the belief that the nation's recovery was to be furthered by the promotion of the family. Elaborating on the Beveridge Report on *Social*

Illustration 2   An ideal of womanhood? c.1950

Insurance and Allied Services (1942), which recommended a comprehensive, national system of social security, the Family Allowances Act (1945), for example, took for granted that married women would favour home over career, and that benefit entitlement should depend on the contributions of the husband.[5] Single motherhood was not condoned, benefit claims to single women were granted and the allowance paid was directly to the mother: all of these measures somehow advanced state notions of motherhood, of domestic provision as state policy. Moreover, as ex-servicemen returned home the assumptions on which Beveridge based his report were initially vindicated: setting up home and starting a family was for many now the highest priority; women's full-time employment dropped from 7.75 million in June 1943 to 6 million in June 1947.[6]

Psychological, sociological and childrearing studies as well as theories further promoted models of womanhood and mothering which chimed with the early postwar 'nation building' mood. Both Donald Winnicott's radio broadcasts on 'The Ordinary Devoted Mother and Her Baby' and John Bowlby's *Maternity and Maternal Health* (1951) encouraged the sacrosanct mother–child relationship. *Forty-Four Juvenile Thieves: Their Character and Home-Life* (1946), also by Bowlby (1907–90), provides a series of psychological case studies which was expanded into a more general theory on the link between maternal deprivation and emotional maladjustment. These are stories rich too in period detail. Case No. 34, for example, concerns 'Derrick O'C' while obliquely outlining the life of his mother. Profoundly deaf, the mother of three, Mrs O'C had become pregnant at the age of 19 while the father-to-be was living in the house as a lodger. Bowlby describes her as 'rather cut off from her family', and continues 'Although fond of her children she lacked any sort of understanding of them and was inclined to shout at them. The father was a happy, pleasant man but equally unimaginative'.[7] Her oldest son, Derrick, spent most of his first three years with a foster mother, a neighbour he referred to as 'mummy Rosy'. Aged three he returned home full-time as Mrs O'C gave up work. She described him as 'nervous, spoiled and always demanding attention, and unhappy when left by his mother', but he was also 'usually top of his class and got a scholarship to a Central School'. Derrick's character defects are attributed to his separation from 'mummy Rosy' and subsequent unsettled home life 'with a mother who never wanted him and disliked him'. Like *The Neglected Child and His Family* (1948), a report by the Women's Group on Public Welfare, *Forty-Four Juvenile Thieves* fostered the welfare notion of 'problem' families.[8]

This central intimacy between mother and child which was built into policy and legislation, promoted and popularized by specialists, was at odds with other developments. From 1945 to the peak of the baby boom in 1947, two million women left work; in the following year however, there were still 350,000 more insured women workers than in 1939.[9] Full-time and fully paid jobs returned to men, despite the *Report of the Royal Commission on Equal Pay* (1946), yet demand for labour and the availability of part-time work both increased. A nationwide campaign to recruit women workers attempted to target the older age group of 35–50 while leaving younger mothers to their domestic lives, but younger women also wanted the benefits of work. Poor living conditions, opportunities and pay as well as the continued necessity to maintain a household under the troublesome constraints of austerity were powerful incentives to work; the expectation of motherhood among employers as well as confinement to traditional occupations such as healthcare, teaching and clerical work frustrated career ambitions. No matter how limiting, work offered some financial and social rewards in consolation for the frustrations of poor fruit supplies or the lack of attractive dress material. It brought closer small pleasures: a glimpse at the panache of a Rita Hayworth, at the latest chic fashions and interiors, at the possibility of a fuller life.

The dilemmas and pressures women faced after 1945 resulted from changes, readjustments, in social situation and image; men faced comparable dilemmas. If the reassurance of women as mothers and domestic providers was encouraged to smooth men's transition back into civilian life, self-conscious responsibilities were now said to accompany male privilege. 'Different' as yet had not come close to meaning 'equal' for men and women, just as 'commensurate work' did not exist and therefore neither did 'equal pay'. The generation of fathers who returned from the war was also warned off too much family involvement. Shelter, protection and resources to allow the woman's role as child-rearer were sufficient. In describing *The Purpose of the Family* (1946), J. C. Spence recommended fathers should provide 'sustenance for her [the mother's] mind and spirit'.[10] Under the pressing conditions of the early postwar years, such provision was is short supply. The aspiration towards better lives, to fuller emotional and material conditions, was partly fulfilled by the absence of war; attempts to walk a line between independence and family responsibility were still as yet thrown out of balance by the instability of the times.

What to do, what not to do

The extraordinary social upheaval of wartime disrupted many families and communities; the vast population movements of the postwar years also confused old certainties. Moving for reasons of political conscience, physical survival or economic gain, new arrivals and settlers in the United Kingdom began to reflect critically and to debate on the conditions and attitudes they found. Observing society with fresh eyes, only gradually becoming sensitized to conventions of behaviour and decorum, arriving migrants gradually drew the native population into a debate on what it meant to be British, and on how that definition should now be changed in the light of new circumstances. This process began in the early postwar years through individual encounters.

Aged 17 when he arrived from Grenada in May 1950, Ronnie Gordon was a well-educated boy schooled in the colonial vein: the romantic poets and the mother of Parliaments, he had been taught, were his heritage. Hoping to celebrate Empire Day, compulsory to schoolchildren back home, he asked for directions:[11]

> I said to him, 'I must hurry you know because I want to attend the May Day celebrations'. He said, 'my, my you're smart. May Day celebrations? What sort of celebrations are you asking for?' I said, 'Well, it's Queen Victoria's Birthday'. He said, 'Queen Victoria is dead'. Of course I knew she was dead but in Grenada we all paraded in the market square.

That the natives did not celebrate Queen Victoria's birthday with enthusiasm and spectacle was only one of many shocks. The cooler climate was not unexpected, but it did entail additional heating and clothing costs; the lowly status of many white people was a surprise though. In Grenada whiteness meant the authority of colonial rule. Nor were the former citizens of Empire the only new arrivals to be puzzled. While the South Asian and Caribbean population combined amounted to 80,000 in 1951, many Europeans had been displaced by the war, including 160,000 Poles in Britain.[12] There were also Ukrainians, among them one man who was forced into German slave labour from 1942 to 1945 and then transferred to Britain under the Displaced Persons scheme in 1948, becoming a brickworker at Kempston, near Bedford, around 1950. 'In my country,' he said, recalling his early days, 'if you go by somebody, you have to greet them. In England, they turn away. . . . You think they don't like you. . . . Then you understand that in England they do not make such greeting. You learn to be careful, what to do, what not to do.'[13]

The arrival of the *Empire Windrush* at Tilbury Docks in Essex in June 1948 is conventionally cited as a decisive moment in the twentieth century history of the United Kingdom, bringing as it did more than 400 mostly Jamaican men in search of betterment. Symbolically it began a new age in immigrant and ethnic relations, a switch from mostly white Europeans to often non-white, non-European arrivals. Yet representatives of both groups had been present in significant numbers as a part of the war effort. During and after the 1940s, and under very different circumstances, both groups engaged in the difficult, drawn-out processes of negotiating a temporary or more permanent settlement, of finding a legitimate place. Twenty-seven thousand members of the Polish Armed Forces reformed in Britain after the fall of France. The Polish Second Corps (100,000) followed in 1941, and after the war political prisoners (21,000), members of military families (33,000) and European Volunteer Workers (14,000).[14] In Scotland Polish Army camps were set up on the east coast in 1940, a Polish Wives Association in Dundee soon afterwards and by the early 1950s between nine and ten thousand had settled.[15] Polish settlement was political as well as involuntary. The Allies' settlement at Yalta recognized the new Russian-backed communist government in Poland; the Polish Resettlement Act (1946) acknowledged the difficulty of return for Poles who contested the Russian claim to power.

While the Polish community was already well established at the end of the war, reverse colonial migration developed gradually after 1945. During the war a West Indian volunteer scheme run by the Ministry of Labour and the Colonial Office encouraged migration to Britain and many worked in munitions factories or in the British armed forces, especially the RAF. Among those on Merseyside, for instance, the end of the wartime employment scheme, which had already been extended to 1946, led to immediate unemployment and the prospect of return to the depressed economy of the West Indies, a difficult choice even for those in the north-west of England, and around Liverpool particularly, where there was above average unemployment.[16] For those who had already departed at the end of the war, arrival at Tilbury or Liverpool in 1948 was a return, but under the altogether different conditions of peace. West Indians and South Asians began to arrive in the late 1940s too, especially following the breakup of colonial India in 1947. While Jamaicans were the largest group, West Indians came from all over the Caribbean; by contrast, the sending areas from the Indian subcontinent, for example in the Punjab, were clearly defined. While a few settled in Northern

Ireland and some in Wales, especially Cardiff, the large and medium sized cities of England and Scotland were a greater draw to the new arrivals.[17]

Some of the inward migrants were warmly received. Mrs Taggart came in 1944 from Palestine, she had married a Glaswegian soldier, moved to his hometown, stayed for a brief spell in Parkhead with his parents, then settled in Thistle Street in the Gorbals. Though her Jewish neighbours could not speak Hebrew and she could not speak Yiddish, she soon settled in. 'I was about eleven years in the house, it was only a single-end, a sub-let really, but I really liked the Gorbals there, really friendly people . . . There was this man with a fruit barrow and 'cos I came from Palestine he used to give me oranges and all kinds of fruit cheap.'[18] As Mrs Taggart's experience shows, the national background of immigrants affected their reception. Generally admired for their role in the war, there was nevertheless in some circles resentment at the newly expanding Polish community. Poles did not at first fit into the social or political landscape: unions feared they would work for lower wage rates; Polish men were resented too as their attentive, gentlemanly manners made them 'too successful' with local women.[19] Marrying, setting up new businesses and establishing the Polish University College in 1947 all helped keep the delicate balance between 'nation in exile' and assimilated minority; while the TUC expressed its official hostility to Polish workers in 1946, resistance to 'colonial' migrants was much greater. The provision of housing, employment and hardship relief fostered resentments which led in turn to violence in Liverpool, Birmingham and Deptford, London, in 1948–9. Meanwhile in a letter to Clement Attlee (1883–1967; PM 1945–51), 11 Labour MPs asked for the introduction of restrictions on black immigration. The Prime Minister's public response was a qualified welcome to the new arrivals. Similarly the *Report of the Royal Commission on Population* (1949) stressed the need for able-bodied workers, if they were of 'good human stock'.[20]

Despite the relative lack of connection between Britain and its European refugees, despite differences of religion, of expectations in work, of temperament too, European political or economic exiles like the Poles were able to find a way into British society, even if they judged the native population 'easy to respect, difficult to like, and impossible to love'.[21] Familiarity with the language and customs of the mother country, by contrast, hindered colonial citizens by lending a deceptive sense of familiarity to early encounters. One Jamaican ex-serviceman, Eric Ferron (b.1925), felt that beyond initial gestures of welcome adjustment was a difficult, disillusioning experience. 'I thought of my grandfather,' Ferron wrote, 'the years he spent fighting in two wars for this country, and my father who had been in the First World War. Did they believe they were fighting for freedom, for the homeland, the Empire? My war seemed to be very different. I wasn't sure what it was about, but my battle seemed to be with the homeland and I knew some of it was inside me.'[22] Natives of Jamaica or St Kitts were now born into a new 'West Indian' community in Britain; natives of Jullundur and Hoshiarpur found themselves transformed into 'South Asians': native Britons too, under the force of new circumstances, were about to embark on a long, difficult reconsideration of how they might be identified with their own changing homeland.

Trad fans and Elephant Boys

The bemused, ambiguous response to postwar immigrants betrayed a nagging anxiety towards the future, especially among adults; schoolchildren, teens and workers in their early twenties longed for that same future to arrive.

Peter Bailey's parents had a long courtship through the 1930s while they saved for their mock Tudor terrace house in the suburbs of Coventry. His mother had lived in the cramped, working-class home of her parents until she was over 30. She became a housewife after Peter was born in 1937. His father was an electrician, a skilled worker in an aircraft factory often doing overtime on rearmament orders through the war. Reconstruction and industry helped Coventry thrive after 1945. With the easing of austerity, the Bailey family could hold tea parties with games and musical entertainment on piano and banjo.[23] Bailey began to play the piano aged 10 and the following year passed his 11-Plus exam, which under the 1944 Education Act meant that he could take up a place at the local grammar school. Once at the grammar school, Peter Bailey was encouraged to think of himself as a possible Oxbridge candidate and a 'gentleman'. Jealous of the freedoms allowed to his friends at the secondary modern school, an outlet for his restlessness presented itself:

> I liked the idea of jazz before I actually heard any. Older boys talked of it in an entranced but knowing manner; it was infinitely superior to 'commercial' popular music; it was American and exotic but had its home grown heroes; it was playable on the piano; my parents would not understand it; it was different.[24]

Ex-servicemen, school, art college and university students as well as working-class youths were among the music's fans. 'Trad' jazz especially was one of the informal outlets for self-expression and self-definition at a time when institutions seemed increasingly to shape the preoccupations and activities of the young. Despite the modernizing agenda of the new welfarism, the values and tastes that guided the older generation – parents, politicians, church leaders, social scientists – often appeared so remote that they might as well have predated the First World War.

The young were among the highest priorities of the new welfare state. As early as 1939 the intention had been to extend education by raising the school leaving age; the Butler Education Act (1944) was to be the 'educational Beveridge'. Grammar, technical and secondary modern schools would match skills and intellect; access to university would be opened up by the 11-Plus exam and by the state scholarship system; children would delay their departure longer and be better qualified for further work and education when they did leave the school system. Such meritocracy was hampered as working-class children still found it difficult to get to the most prestigious schools and universities, while lack of resources, for instance due to the 5000 schools damaged in wartime bombing raids, made the transition to peace and Butler's implementations difficult.[25] Embedded in the postwar legislation too were assumptions about what would now be 'best' for the young. The Education Act gave Local Education Authorities responsibility for youth recreation and obliged them to ensure that adequate facilities such as youth clubs were provided. The Children's Act (1948) required that Local Authorities set up departments responsible for the welfare of children, including the homeless; the Criminal Justice Act (1948) stressed 'corrective training' and 'treatment' above punishment, the skills of the psychiatric social worker over those of the criminal lawyer. The Conscription Act (1948) intended as a practical, low-cost solution to Britain's military commitments and world power pretensions also changed the lives of postwar teenagers. Its unexpected side effects included the creation of a 'conscription generation', and of what the King George's Jubilee Trust called at the time a 'high hurdle' against 'the need to plan and work for the future'.[26]

Conscription blanked out the prospect of adult life between leaving school at the age of 15 and entering the Forces at the age of 18. While Peter Bailey and his peers worked their way towards university, his secondary modern school contemporaries were, so the argument went, more likely to be engaged in juvenile crime. Fears of lawlessness youth resurfaced as birching was virtually abandoned from 1941 and as the number of juveniles found guilty of indictable offences in England and Wales rose 42 per cent between 1939 and 1945.[27] While in 1938 1 per 100 of 14–17 year olds was convicted of an indictable offence, in 1951 the number was said to have reached an alarming rate of 1 in 50.[28] Social psychologists, social workers and journalists all engaged in public debate over causes: maternal deprivation and wartime disruption, the over-attention, possibly the inattention of the Welfare State too, and the 'punch drunk' BBC radio serial 'Dick Barton, Special Agent' (1945–51) which held 15 million listeners at the peak of its popularity: all were to blame.[29]

The 'spiv' – black marketeer, working-class adolescent – with his coat-hanger shoulders, pointed shoes and wide lapels, became the archetype of the postwar delinquency boom.[30] He was accompanied by 'American' style motorcar raids and outlandishly named juvenile gangs such as the 'Elephant Boys'. While knives, chains and coshes were 'un-British' if not 'fascist', the democratic redistribution of nylons and bananas was viewed less as anti-social behaviour than a pragmatic interpretation of the 'fair shares' ethos so strongly advocated by both government and people during wartime. Such activities were on the outer edge of legal 'entrepreneurship', and there was a similar suspicion of the more general comparative affluence of the young as it began to grow.

At the same time juvenile criminals caught the popular imagination in newsprint, in cartoons and in films. Among the delinquent youths on screen were Pinkie Brown (Richard Attenborough) in *Brighton Rock* (John Boulting, 1947) and Tom Riley (Dirk Bogarde) in *The Blue Lamp* (Basil Dearden, 1950). The Victorian criminal underworld was brought to mind by *Brighton Rock*'s racetrack milieu and razor gangs; the shocking murder of a policeman in the early scenes of *The Blue Lamp* reminded audiences of a more recent event, the Southgate shooting of PC Nathan Edgar in 1946.[31] Yet its 'hard-boiled' documentary style, and its belief in community, as racegoers, bookmakers and criminals cooperate to capture the murderer, had initially caused unease at the British Board of Film Censors. 'It would be disastrous,' wrote the Assistant Censor Frank Crofts in 1949, 'to treat the dangerous subject of adolescent criminals with any glamour. On the other hand, whilst it is necessary to show the criminals as mean, cowardly sneak-thieves, there should not be any prostitution or eroticism.'[32] Perhaps to counter the effects of possible glamorization, in the final version of the film the narrator explains that broken homes and wartime demoralization produced 'restless and ill-adapted youngsters' who contributed to the rise of postwar crime: 'All the more dangerous because of their immaturity.'[33] Such alarmist comment was acceptable as popular entertainment, and perhaps contained some truth, but it expressed too a censorious streak in the new welfarism. Criminal self-interest was not in this view far removed from the gradually developing youthful consumerism; the assertive impatience of the teenager could also express itself, though, through a 'licensed form of deviance' such as jazz.[34]

The smooth and the textured

Uneasiness at the future expressed in concern for lawlessness and criminality found a positive counterpart in state sponsorship of fine and applied arts, in the promotion too of a collectively 'British' vision, yet artists themselves and the mood of early postwar society were resistant. Looking back from 1955, distinguished art critic David Sylvester (b.1924) saw a shift of style from interwar to postwar. 'Yesterday's taste for smooth surfaces was the outward sign of an aspiration to order and impersonality, today's taste for rough ones that of an aspiration for freedom and singularity.'[35] Just as the intellectual debate of BBC radio's Third Programme and musical promotion of the Aldeburgh music festival was to revive arts and letters in the new mass democracy, visual arts were enlisted too, though education and improvement were not necessarily the first objective of any artist. Herbert Read (1893–1968), poet and critic, had initially hoped for a modernist art to rebuild the postwar world, but by the early 1950s found instead a 'geometry of fear'.[36] The burgeoning cultures of the young were unofficial and ad hoc, at odds with government's institutionalized efforts to redefine cultural as well as political identity; the same division existed in the world of the fine arts, where state sponsorship sought to enrich citizenship. Some artists, and others concerned with the arts, were indeed now intent on a new democratic vision to marry popular and elite, decorative and utilitarian. Yet there was a wider, more pressing requirement: for a new visual language that could replace the 'modernisms' which now seemed stripped of credibility, complicit and powerless against Europe's fall into the chaos of world war. The often dour mood following 1945 was thus well observed in Swiss sculptor Alberto Giacometti's rejection of surrealism for a critical scrutiny of the human form, newly made vulnerable. With vulnerability came recognition of the individual: no surprise, then, that Giacometti's rough singularity won high praise among critics and artists, nor that he was championed by David Sylvester.[37]

The tension between state sponsorship and individual artistic vision was expressed in response to the Picasso and Matisse exhibition held at the Victoria and Albert Museum in December 1945 and organized by the British Council. Robert Colquhoun's (1914–62) *Woman With a Bird Cage* (1946) rejected landscape or direct figurative representation in favour of semi-cubist formality, density and narrow colour spectrum. While native, everyday subject matter might coincide with wider political themes, as in the early work of Prunella Clough

(1919–99), a glance at her subsequent career shows the collision as momentary. Journalists and scholars also noted the continuing influence of modernist art on native tradition. Robin Ironside's essay on 'Painting since 1939' (1947), for example, fretted at the erosion of landscape and figurative sensibility as it had long been practised.[38] New institutions such as the Council for Industrial Design (1944), established by the Board of Trade to educate public taste and to boost exports, or the Arts Council (1946), originally the wartime Council for the Encouragement of Music and the Arts, were by their nature averse to controversy: the moderate populist marriage of tradition and modernity were their objective. An objective only partly realized.

Discovering 'schools' or collective themes among the work of artists is at best a haphazard affair. If neo-Romanticism, figuration and abstraction were among their collective concerns, artists were unwilling to be labelled as members of some movement and style. Nevertheless, several sets of preoccupations did appear in the early postwar years, some of which were more readily adaptable to a populist, political cause. Graham Sutherland (1903–80) belonged to the neo-Romantic camp in the years before the war ended, absorbing himself in tangled landscapes of emotion and, like some of his fellow artists, spending a part of the war in rural Wales. 'To see a solitary human figure descending a road at the solemn moment of sunset is to realize the enveloping quality of the earth,' wrote Sutherland in his 'Welsh Sketch Book' (1942).[39] By the later 1940s, though, a harder-edged abstraction appeared in both landscape (*Thorn Trees*, 1945–6) and portraiture (*Somerset Maugham*, 1949), together with an express intention to parallel in landscape Picasso's transformation of the human body. In figurative art Francis Bacon (1909–92) and Lucian Freud (b.1922) were linked by the London circle of artists within which they moved, and by their unsparing scrutiny of the human figure, as in Freud's *Girl With a White Dog* (1951–2) or Bacon's *Three Studies for Figures at the Base of a Crucifixion* (*c.* 1944). The latter seemed a violent expression of the moment to viewers when exhibited in 1945 because of its grotesque anatomical fusion of humanity and bestiality. Victor Pasmore's (1908–98) career also shows the fluidity of creative development as it turned from the prewar Euston Road group, to neo-Romanticism, constructivism and in the late 1940s' 'jazz' abstraction.

The Labour government's final attempt to propagate the modern through fine and applied arts came in 1951 with the Festival of Britain. Science, technology, painting and design were all to contribute to the theme of 'innovation and tradition fused', to 'declare our belief and trust in the British way of life . . . to be a nation at unity in itself and of service to the world'.[40] Modernist surrealism and neo-Romanticism were displayed in the work of Henry Moore and Barbara Hepworth; crystalline and atomic structures were transformed into furniture and tableware designs; the futuristic 'Skylon' sculpture and Dome of Discovery represented faith in tomorrow. A preference for yesterday surfaced however in the '60 for '51' exhibition of native, contemporary art, when *Autumn Landscape* (1950) by William Gear (1915–97) was awarded one of the £500 exhibition prizes. Gear, who had spent several years just after the war in Paris, was immersed in the continental experiment that sought to divine and abstract nature as well as the living forms within it. He was the only abstract artist to win a prize.

Despite his neo-Romantic affinities, Gear's painting became the subject of a drawn out, often hostile debate. As one critical voice put it, 'I like a sky to look like a sky.'[41]

While decorative or applied arts suited the purposes of welfare culture, the fine arts could less easily be turned to promote a 'native' vision of the rebuilt nation. Through the late 1940s the experimental textures that would flourish outside state patronage were primed and prepared. Sitting in a rented cottage overlooking St Ives Bay, Cornwall, in 1947, Patrick Heron (1920–99) was a part of the artistic community that became so vital within British art, with its fusion of landscape and abstract traditions, its sense of nature observed from within. 'I may swivel my head momentarily from the open window, with its prospect of the Bay,' Heron wrote, 'and for a few seconds absorb visual realities of a very different order: the reddish outline of a near chair cutting up and across the white of a piece of the wall . . . and this momentarily perceived and registered, becomes an integral part of my apprehension of the reality that surrounds me at this particular moment.'[42] Scottish-born Eduardo Paolozzi (1924–2005), who like William Gear had lived in Paris just after the war, and whose sketchbook collage *I Was a Rich Man's Play Thing* (1947) used images from advertising, comic books and magazines, looked further afield: to America. Describing that country's imaginative draw as he returned to London in 1949 Paolozzi wrote:

> The American magazine represented a catalogue of an exotic society, bountiful and generous, where the event of selling tinned pears was transformed into multicoloured dreams, where sensuality and virility combined to form, in our view, an art form more subtle and fulfilling than the orthodox choices of either the Tate Gallery or the Royal Academy.[43]

Bopping and jiving

Paolozzi's view was iconoclastic. Critics of mass as well as elite culture tended more often to regret than revere foreign fashions. Reviewing an early postwar import, a 1947 concert by the American close harmony group The Ink Spots, John Ormond Thomas, writing in the *Picture Post*, preferred gently mockery. 'A chord on the guitar and the Ink Spots are in key. The melodic drool and drawl begin, the sentimental song is being sung and swung, hummed with hymn-sincerity. Four voices nuzzle close around the theme and crane towards the microphone. Bill Kenny takes a solo, lingering on its notes and words with genuine, heart-felt feeling for the soft-jazz, saddened notes. He kisses his vowels as if he were taking leave of them for ever . . .'[44] While there was a hint of derision at The Ink Spots' concocted commercialism, there was also wry affection in these sentiments. A reminder that American popular entertainment was not newly arrived in Britain, that it had been watched in cinemas, listened to on radios, danced to on ballroom floors through the interwar years.

Dixieland jazz, the Charleston, Cole Porter and Irving Berlin were all a part of that interwar scene. After 1939 the arrival of American troops and Forces Network Radio brought the big bands, swing, the jitterbug: to the European sense of elegance, display and occasion American music now brought a feel for excitement, movement and individuality. In hotels as well as restaurants and clubs swing-based dance music flourished: 'Tango King' Geraldo and the Cuban-style rhythms of Edmondo Ross's band led the live music scene from the mid-1930s to the mid-1950s.[45] Easily adapted as light entertainment after the war, this tradition continued most audibly in the Billy Cotton Band Show, launched in February 1949 on BBC radio and broadcast until it transferred to television in 1957. Its guests included music-hall style artists, bandleaders and star names: Arthur Askey, Alma Cogan, Bob Hope.[46]

The end of the Second World War was the end of the swing era; the market for big dance bands collapsed. In America the airwaves opened up as blues, rhythm and blues or jazz became more readily accessible. In Britain the enthusiasm for American music had been curbed by a Musicians' Union dispute that meant no American bands were allowed to perform there between 1935 and 1943. As recordings were scarce too it was the BBC who fed audiences' taste for specific styles and, as the number of records grew, a Wednesday evening slot was given over on the Light Programme to traditional jazz, in 1948 with Muggsy Spanier's Ragtime Band in residence.[47] Now there were alterations in musical style, sometimes affected by union disputes, in copyright systems, and in broadcasting to reflect the taste of specialists and mass audiences. Changing technology altered how music was recorded and heard. The hand-held microphone gave a new flexibility to vocal technique, and especially a new intimacy, that in turn smoothed the upward ascent of the first postwar pop stars, including Frank Sinatra and his British counterparts, Frankie Vaughn or Dickie Valentine. Tape for capturing and manipulating studio performances widened the creative possibilities of the recording studio. The replacement of the old-fashioned 'gramophone' with the American 'record player' coincided too with the shift to vinyl, and the micro-groove plastic disc increased dramatically the number of records that could be produced as well as the standard of sound they reproduced. The single and the long-player album now allowed mass consumption.[48]

Music on stage, screen and radio, homemade music too, was popular both before and after the arrival of mass market pop music that came with vinyl. Music hall-type stars such as Max Bygraves became widely known, allowing novelty, sentiment and stand-up humour even into the BBC. The jokey wartime style of the Entertainments National Services Association (ENSA) also kept its appeal. Alongside these were the imported American musicals of the late 1940s both on stage and screen: Rodgers and Hammerstein's *South Pacific* in the West End; Leonard Bernstein's *On the Town*, which was released on film in 1949.[49] The British swing dance bands had a prolonged afterlife following their interwar and wartime heyday. 'Tango King' Geraldo, also known as 'Britain's Glenn Miller', became director of BBC Dance Music and later on his band became the first to appear on the new medium of television. Joe Loss's strict tempo dance music was first broadcast from the Kit-Kat Club in 1933 and from various hotels through the 1930s and 1940s. Initially following the style of Glenn Miller and Woody Herman, after the war he added a female vocalist and played for the World Ballroom Championships as well as society and royal occasions.

Jazz often appealed to a younger audience. The original New Orleans style had its purists, 'mouldy figs' to their detractors, who were reluctant to allow even slight interpretation or improvization on the themes of 'King' Oliver or Bix Beiderbecke. The less respectful bands played British interpretations.[50] As it emerged after 1945, interest in American jazz, no matter how it was later interpreted or played, had its roots in the local discussion and listening groups of the war years such as the Bexleyheath and District Rhythm Club in Kent. Enthusiasts were already forming their own bands in 1943 and broadcasting on the BBC by 1945. By the time George Webb's Dixielanders signed to Decca in 1945, the audience was growing. Among that audience was Humphrey Lyttelton (b.1921), a Grenadier Guard during the war, who began attending jazz clubs in London as he awaited demobilization. Within four years he was playing clarinet with Webb's Dixielanders in a Bexleyheath pub. In 1948 Lyttelton formed his own band and held a residency at a club in Leicester Square; the arrival of the Graeme Bell Band from Australia in the same year helped show that jazz was for dancing as well as listening.[51] Lyttelton defended the music against detractors in 1949:

> Its origins are purely functional, and we are content to keep it that way. We don't believe that it should be dressed up in a starch shirt and hustled on to a concert platform. Jazz never was and never will be a highly intellectual music. But it can be a dance music which is worthier of the dancers' intelligence, and has more vitality, than the dreary products of Tin Pan Alley. We play for dancing as well as for listening: and our music can only be fully appreciated if this is borne in mind.[52]

Revivalist jazz was well established with the arrival of the London Jazz Club in 1950, and Lyttelton's own club in 1951. By then fans were further split with the bebop modernists of New York whose preference was for intricate rhythmic pattern and greater dynamic range.

What connected the supporters of these partisan styles was their opposition: to the classical and intellectual approach of the BBC Third Programme and to the broken buildings and empty cafés of the early postwar years. If commercial popular music was 'dreary', if state sponsorship consisted of debating intellectuals and the middle class populism of the Festival of Britain, a roughness and texture was added to the British scene by the spontaneous enthusiasm, the dance, the amateur groups that made up the new jazz scene. Its amateurism and its improvized quality set jazz apart, provided an outlet beyond the bounds of state or commerce, allowed participants to 'throw the map out of the window'.[53]

Flames of passion

Film far more than visual arts or popular music was *the* medium of mass entertainment in the immediate postwar years: as the confidence and range of British cinema had increased during the war a number of serious film-makers, the Boulting brothers, Humphrey Jennings and Michael Balcon, the then head of Ealing Studios, saw the possibilities of the medium as entertainment, but also as a means to promote collective values, social concerns and moral education.[54] These aspirations were matched by a critical strain within some films, and a worry among critics and censors, at the possible corrupting influences of on-screen violence and sexuality. Literary adaptations by David Lean (1908–91), *Great Expectations* (1946) or *Oliver Twist* (1948) as well as more 'realist' features, *It Always Rains on Sunday* (Robert Hamer, 1947) for instance, were affirmations, though hardly uncritical ones, of the nation's heritage, the strong, intricate patterning of its social fabric. Poverty, class and the limits of progress were addressed too in less 'respectable' films and genres, notably gangster features. The futility of crime and communal efforts to expel violence and greed were acceptable critical values; the celebration of violence and charisma, of American gangsterism, were not: *Brighton Rock* (John Boulting, 1947), with its literary antecedents, was more tolerable as a film than the screen version of *No Orchids for Miss Blandish* (St John L. Clowes, 1948), from the thriller by Charles Hadley Chase.

The advantages of the cinema as mass entertainment were its low cost; with 4,600 cinemas across the country, its ready accessibility; and, with programmes changing up to twice a week, its variety. The habit of frequent attendance was born early in the war as cinema audiences increased by 30 per cent in 1941. An examination of the exhibitions between October 1948 and September 1950 showed 69.5 per cent of films shown in Britain were made in Hollywood and 27 per cent in Britain. Musicals, musical comedy, family and domestic subjects and settings, history, drama and adventure were the best rated subjects.[55] Among the top box office stars of the period were Anna Neagle, who specialized in women in British history (Queen Victoria, Florence Nightingale, wartime secret service (SOE) operative Odette Sansom), as well as a series of light comedy musicals alongside Michael Wilding such as *Maytime in Mayfair* (1949).[56] To protect and promote the British film industry against American competition the Labour government imposed a 75 per cent tariff on all imported American films which led to a boycott by American companies and a shortage of films between the autumn of 1947 and spring 1948. Eventually the tax was withdrawn and an agreement made to ensure 30 per cent of all screenings in Britain were home productions. The industry mainly damaged itself: the Rank Organisation, nearest rival to the major Hollywood studios, suffered financially, while audiences resented the recycling of older British supporting films which they had already seen.[57]

Early postwar film-making nevertheless flowered: the artistic and production values of British film were higher than ever before; they provided too a condensed, vivid portrayal of national values in the light of the recently ended war. Rank, the most important production company, tried to compete directly with Hollywood in their creation of big budget, high prestige projects, including David Lean's adaptations of Dickens. One of the most topical, popular and skilfully crafted of the features released around the end of the war was another film directed by Lean, *Brief Encounter* (1945), which used a technique often seen around this time, the 'story frame'. A 'present' at the beginning and end of the film with a 'past' or 'fantasy' element in between, suited the difficult times because it allowed a flight from the everyday. In *Brief Encounter*, the reality or fantasy of the romance between Laura Jesson (Celia Johnson), the happily married housewife with two children, and Alec Harvey (Trevor Howard), a doctor who is about to emigrate to South Africa, is less the point than the conflicting loyalties Laura feels between the needs of her children and husband as well as the certainty of everyday domesticities, than the 'flames of romance', adventure and escape which she and Alec laugh at as they watch a film trailer during one of their cinema trips. Later on Laura sits in an empty park late at night, filled with despair and disgust at her situation, the camera looks down to show her in the shadow of a war memorial. While Laura comes close to self-destruction, she finally clings to her values of loyalty and familial affection. The weight of the everyday, the sense of ambition and desire frustrated by duty and conscience is no less intense as Laura pulls back from suicide at the last moment.[58] Rather than escape by killing herself or going to South Africa, and rather than daydream in a world of fantasy, she chooses a return to personal and communal responsibility.[59]

In 1942 the Rank Organisation set up Independent Producers to provide facilities as well as financial support for a group of small film companies, among them The Archers: Michael Powell (1905–90) and Emeric Pressburger (1902–88). Arrived as an exile from Hungary in 1938, scriptwriter Pressburger was a follower of German and Russian cinema. Together with director Powell, who shared his enthusiasm, the two produced a series of films celebrating the verve of the British people and the mystery of their island landscapes. Perhaps because there was no 'frame' to these fantasies, they were regarded as eccentric, baroque creations for their time. Yet while *A Canterbury Tale* (1944), *I Know Where I'm Going* (1945) or *Gone to Earth* (1950) are self-consciously artistic interpretations of the postwar moment, steeped in neo-Romantic sensibility, they are still able to describe the clash and reconciliation of opposing cultures and class values within contemporary society. An uneasily observed need to balance tradition and innovation, and a characteristic visual flare, are evident, for example, in *I Know Where I'm Going*. Here perseverance and renewal come from the mystery of human experience, the elemental power of water and thunder, of falcon and wolfhound; and from delicate, difficult, enriching encounter with an unknown language and landscape.

Powell and Pressburger explored unsuspected personal fulfilment outside the bounds of the conventional world; Ealing Studios by contrast often displayed ambiguous, bitter and deep feeling lightened by the comic: as if Laura Jesson had developed a less hysterical sense of humour. The character and values of the nation are well established, yet the achievement of individual growth is limited by consensual insularity.[60] In *Passport to Pimlico* (Henry Cornelius, 1949), an exploration of, in the words of one character, 'you never know you're well off until you aren't', the longing for an end to irksome rationing and shortages is brought to life revealing wish fulfilment as self-indulgence, as a threat to community if it is not properly earned. Crime and the selfish individualism of black marketeers, as the film shows, are avoidable by vigilant self-sacrifice and painful discipline. *It Always Rains on Sunday* (Robert Hamer, 1947) portrays a very different London where the loyalty of housewife Rose Sandigate (Googie Withers) is tested by the reappearance of an ex-lover, now an escaped convict. Criminal activity, the limits of legality and the connection to morality are implicit themes in many of the Ealing Studio comic and non-comic films.

Ealing productions generally took a mocking, if ultimately supportive, view of postwar consensual values, and gained box office and critical accolades to match. Critics and censors often saw gangster and crime films, with their unspoken danger of disorder and violence, as disreputable and threatening. Such was the case with *No Orchids for Miss Blandish*, a studio-made melodrama, erotic, amoral and popular with audiences, which provoked questions in the House of Commons as well as the condemnation of Dr Edith Summerskill's Married Women's Association. Leading lady Linden Travers later explained such publicity only added to the film's appeal. When asked why the film proved so controversial she replied, 'Well, the kiss lasted forty-nine seconds!'[61] Audiences could happily accommodate both the values of community and the amorality of law-breaking dissent with their own critical judgements. The conflict between collective and individual ambition continued, displayed by proto-pop artists celebrating American culture, sounded by jazz fans enveloped in the dissonant honk and squawk of bebop and felt by silver-screen housewives as they struggled with their contradictory desires.

CHAPTER 3

Soap-flake Arcadia

Honey's taste

Describing the virtues of the Hoover Electric Washing Machine in July 1950, an advertisement in the *Radio Times* explained how it might satisfy the housewife's more mundane wishes. 'Heavy tiring washing days a thing of the past,' the potential purchaser learned, 'saves hours of drudgery every week. It washes everything astonishingly quickly and *spotlessly clean*. Works in an entirely new gentle-on-the-clothes principle . . .'. In 1955, and having recently given birth to her son, Cara Buckley was delighted to receive a washing machine for her twenty-first birthday. 'They weren't automatic. You still had to stand there. They had hand wringers, though my English Electric had a power ringer – it was wonderful.'[1] While there was condescension in Nicolas Tomalin's view of the later 1950s as a 'soap-flake arcadia', while washing machines left housewives with a waterlogged mass of blankets, shirts or underwear to somehow dry and air, while standards of cleanliness rose and the effort to achieve it entailed more labour, Cara Buckley still saw her new English Electric as 'a revolution'.[2] Released from maintaining basic family needs for cleanliness and sustenance by sheer physical labour; employed, though usually part-time, on low pay, and without prospects; consuming sometimes for pleasure as well as necessity: many more women could now view the prospect, if not the achievement, of an easier, more tolerable life.

With these possibilities came new policy debates, within government agencies and among experts, on the condition of marital relationships, on the nature and provision of childcare and mental health care, and on the proper status of women's work. John Bowlby's concerned advocacy of continuous mothering gained support as well as influence with the publication of *Maternal Care and Mental Health* (1951), which in 1953 became a paperback best-seller.[3] The *Report of the Royal Commission on Marriage and Divorce* (1956) displayed a similar disquiet at the institution of marriage, again influenced by the urgent need to rebuild the nation after the war, again stressing collective above individual aspirations. The Commissioners concluded that the 'tendency to take the duties and responsibilities of marriage less seriously than formerly' and the 'increased disposition to regard divorce, not as a last resort, but as the obvious way out when things begin to go wrong' should be curbed.[4] Unease with the health of marriage as a national institution, as well as with the stability and sanctity of the family, led the Wolfenden Committee's *Report on Homosexual Practices and Prostitution* (1957) to the conclusion that personal preferences and individual moral choices could be quarantined outside the realm of public affairs. Beyond instruction for parenthood and marriage, the need for personal accomplishment was voiced by

Illustration 3 Beginnings of the new society: London, early 1950s

sociologists Alva Myrdal and Viola Klein, whose work was as rooted in the 1940s as was Bowlby's, yet whose *Women's Two Roles: Home and Work* (1956) argued that even if childrearing should take precedence in early childhood, women were vital as paid employees too. The achievement of individual and wider social objectives should therefore be seen as complementary.[5] Fifteen or so years after the end of the war, Eustace Chesser's question *Is Chastity Outmoded?* was still controversial yet, with the backing of the British Medical Association, later withdrawn in the face of bitter opposition, it was possible to argue that personal satisfaction and development now mattered as much as, if not more than, collective, traditional concerns. 'When two young (or even not young) people express their attitude to each other by fully consummating their sexual attraction, they are confirming their humanity . . . The fact that it is not only "pleasant" but a natural human expression should evoke our sympathy; first and before all else. Why then do we leap for the nearest prohibition at hand?'[6]

Prescriptions, advice and injunctions did not necessarily match the aspirations or experiences of women in the everyday world. State policy and collective interest were unlikely foundations for personal fulfilment; increasing earning power and the availability of new consumer goods now began to change women's two roles. Between 1951 and 1961 women became increasingly active in the job market: the number of female employees in part-time work rose from 12 to 26 per cent; those past the childrearing phase and in their forties also began to look for further employment.[7] Yet the ideal of personal development rather than simple financial benefit remained hard to realize when working in part-time and low skilled employment. In personal relations and family affairs the model of a spotless easy-maintenance home promoted by advertisers was no more a reality than the selfless maternal devotion advocated by childcare experts. Upbringing, social position, income and employment produced wide variants in patterns of childcare and consumption: Lancashire men whose wives worked shifts in the textile industry routinely bathed and put to bed their children; enthusiasm for Formica and pressure cookers was matched by frustration at the pettiness of everyday chores as a childrearer. Divorce kept a residue of social stigma but all the same it was increasingly common.[8]

Just as the rise of part-time work was not necessarily new, but rather better recorded outside the family economy than between the wars, so possible variants of appearance and behaviour came fresh to public attention. Girls growing up in the aftermath of war were surrounded by comic book stories of adventure as much as domestic serenity; glamorous nightclub hostess Ruth Ellis (1926–55), whose complicated love life led her to murder an unfaithful lover, was tried, convicted and executed in 1955. One expression of the new 'more adventurous' female self was Shelagh Delaney's (b. 1939) *A Taste of Honey*, which premiered in 1958 as a Theatre Workshop production at the Stratford East Theatre, London, and which, with clear-eyed affection, observed the life of a working-class teenage girl in Lancashire.[9] Jo, after a brief affair with a black sailor, becomes pregnant. Her mother, infatuated with a new boyfriend, abandons the daughter. Jo sets up home with her companion Geoff, a homosexual art student, but when Jo's mother returns it is Geoff who is abandoned. The reluctant transformation from girlhood to womanhood, the quality of love between friends, family members and lovers, the conflict that these various bonds of affection generate, all are Delaney's concerns. Reviewing the play in 1958 Kenneth Tynan argued:

There are plenty of crudities in Miss Delaney's play: there is, more importantly, the smell of living. When the theatre presents poor people as good, we call it 'sentimental'. When it presents them as wicked, we sniff and cry 'squalid'. Happily Miss Delaney does not yet know about us and our squeamishness . . . She is too busy recording the wonder of life as she lives it . . . She is nineteen years old: and a portent.[10]

Whether full participants or marginal figures, women in many parts of the United Kingdom were nevertheless often beneficiaries of the new consumerism, and yet, as *A Taste of Honey* illustrates, two roles often meant contradictory aspirations: family values and sexual allure, the housewife's weekly budget and financial independence, communal injunctions to build a new society and personal ambition for respect and recognition.

Living with Jumbles

Women or men, the newest arrivals to the United Kingdom in the 1950s, from Europe, Africa, India and the Caribbean, were among those less likely to either benefit from Britain's new affluence or to achieve their personal potential. Though they were integrated into the workplace, and contributed to the economic boom, immigrants still found social acceptance as well as economic success elusive. In March 1956 journalist and novelist Colin MacInnes (1914–76) attempted to describe West African life in Britain, to show how the natives were viewed by one group of newcomers. 'A Short Guide for Jumbles' – 'the word's a corruption of "John Bull", and is used by West Africans of Englishmen in a spirit of tolerant disdain' – listens in on an imaginary conversation between an informed and sympathetic observer of the new black immigrants, much like MacInnes himself, and an averagely uninformed, hostile questioner.[11] In reply to the question 'How does one talk to Africans and West Indians?', for instance, MacInnes lists the frequently irritating statements and questions put to new arrivals, the result of either 'cheery condescension' or 'guilt-ridden tact':

> 'You won't mind my asking, but why do you people come to this country?' (Unspoken answer: 'Why did your people come to mine and, anyway, why the hell shouldn't I?') . . . 'You'll find there's a certain amount of prejudice here, but some of us are just as worried about it as you.' ('Look after your own worries, man, and leave me to handle mine.')[12]

Like his subjects, MacInnes himself was 'half English'. Raised in another former British colony, Australia, the rare advantage of his position was that he could mediate between black and white communities at a time of widespread misunderstanding and ignorance.

MacInnes' contribution was all the more useful as the increasing numbers and cumulative social impact of the new arrivals, not only from the West Indies, now became inescapable. Under the American McCarran-Walter Immigration and Nationality Act (1952), a blanket quota system came into force which dramatically cut the number of West Indians allowed into the United States, but Irish immigrants also found passage to America severely restricted; in the decade between 1951 and 1961, 409,000 emigrated from Southern Ireland to Britain.

Poles numbered about 135,000 in 1960; the combined West Indian and South Asian population rose from less than 80,000 in 1951 to about 500,000, or one per cent of the population, by 1961.[13] West Indian arrivals peaked in the second half of the 1950s in anticipation of the British Commonwealth Immigration Act (1961), which introduced new restrictions, though not on the Irish, from 1962.[14] While London became the major settlement area for all immigrant groups, 33,000 of the 140,000 Poles were in Greater London by 1951 for example, both Europeans and 'non-Europeans' settled all across the United Kingdom: Glasgow, Edinburgh and Dundee; Cardiff; Belfast (and Dublin); Liverpool, Manchester, Birmingham, Nottingham, Bradford, Leeds, Leicester and Wolverhampton among other places.[15] In social contacts, black immigrants were often treated with indifference, if not outright hostility; in finding accommodation the chronic housing shortage together with the abolition of controls under the Rent Act (1957) allowed landlords to exploit tenants, not least in heavily populated black districts such as Notting Hill. In Lewisham, Thelma Perkins observed the affluent suburban streets around Tressilian Road, Wickham Road and Breakspears Road as they were increasingly sub-let, as black faces and street life began to appear towards the end of the 1950s.[16] Cloran Singh came from Jandialy to Gravesend in 1954. By 1957, the group of South Asians living and working in the district had gathered enough funds to set up a proper temple, a house in Edwin Street, where the Sikh scriptures could now be held.[17]

For some groups, religious practice provided familiar routine and community focus in strange surroundings. Yet as Sam Selvon (1923–94) shows so eloquently in *The Lonely Londoners* (1956), his fictional account of the postwar Caribbean immigrant experience, customs, values and even the routines of everyday life often remained mutually incomprehensible for both native and immigrant, a source of tension and misunderstanding. Donall MacAmhlaigh too, just arrived from Galway in 1951, was depressed by the sight of Rugby station as he sat waiting for his train to Northampton, and bemused by the early-morning commuters. 'Everything looked so foreign to me there. Round about six o'clock hundreds started pouring into the station, pallid pasty faces with identical lunch boxes slung from their shoulders . . . God save us, I murmured to myself as I thought that nobody in Ireland would be even thinking of getting out of their beds for another couple of hours yet!'[18] If Northampton commuters appeared strange to an Irishman, Caribbean fashions were conspicuous to the English. When Dr Beryl Gilroy arrived in England from Guyana in 1952 for instance, she sported a black-and-white checked woollen coat, scrim and velvet hat, a plastic 'mock crock' bag, and a cotton mix two-piece suit. Run up from American fashion magazine photographs by a local dressmaker, her wardrobe also included knee-length breeches, 'pedal-pushers', as well as a variety of bright colours that were unlike the more staid local style.[19]

Visible difference as well as perceived disadvantage in housing and employment became the pretext for open hostility in August 1958 in the Chase district of Nottingham and in Notting Hill, West London. In the St Ann's Well Road area in Nottingham recession concentrated resentment, a knife fight outside a pub led to the injury of eight white people, a crowd of between 1500 and 3000 began to attack the black population and burn down their homes. The following day,

24 August, and the next weekend there were fire bombings as well as mob attacks on individuals, groups and houses in London's Ladbroke Grove and Shepherd's Bush.[20] Colonial tensions over Kenya, South Africa and Suez highlighted 'race' sensitivities; youth violence and crime were already subjects of intense public interest; newspaper reports exaggerated events as well as emotions. Sociologist Ruth Glass interpreted the riots as an expression of unease and division within British society, of an inability to confront native intolerance except among a few delinquent 'Teddy boys', whereas in reality racism was 'latent in all social strata'.[21]

In the wake of the 1958 disturbances came the killing of Kelso Cochrane on 17 May 1959 on what local people alleged were racial grounds. In response to the 'all-pervasive British ambivalence towards colour' came a more vocal opposition and active organization among the black community. The *West Indies Gazette* had already been set up in March 1958; a prototype Caribbean Carnival took place in January 1959.[22] Thelma Perkins and her friends in Lewisham had already established a social scene in the basement clubs of the district, where they drank Cherry B and Babycham, listened to Blue Beat and Ska. In Willesden a Congregational Minister who helped many new arrivals settle began to hold additional mid-week meetings, an 'Evangelical Service' with a 'testimony time' and a small orchestra of guitars, tambourine and trumpet. 'The rhythm at times would be particularly hot,' said the minister, '. . . the type that "send you" '.[23] Between leaving her English boarding school and starting university, Simi Bedford, born in Lagos in 1941, began to meet with her cousins in London to attend Nigerian dances, concerts and parties at the High Commissions. Around the same time Simi noticed that she was acquiring a new, fashionable cachet. She attributed this partly to the rise of young, elegant female stars such as Sandra Dee, as well as to the success of black, female soul groups, especially The Ronettes. Another pleasing surprise greeted her on arrival at college. 'By the time I went to university in 1960, black was where it was at. All that soul music. Then there were these fine art students at Durham University who were into Benin bronzes and African masks and tall thin women and suddenly here were all these people saying, "You are a great beauty," I thought, "This is all right then." ' [24]

String tie, check shirt, duffle coat

The fine art students who came to admire Simi Bedford were part of the middle class bohemia which developed through the 1950s and which was symbolized at the decade's end, at least in its more politicized wing, by the duffle-coated marchers with the Campaign for Nuclear Disarmament (CND). Attending an Aldermaston anti-nuclear march Lou Taylor wore a camel coloured duffle, which matched the CND colours, a wool, ex-naval sweater, wool skirt and stockings and black leather lace-up shoes. 'The clothes were absolutely not an end in themselves,' she later commented. 'No one discussed them or seemingly took any interest in them. We wore practical cheap and comfortable clothes for active campaigning. We wore very little make-up and eschewed conventional notions of young women in the 1950s . . . it did not take much then, either in dress or political terms, to cause a public shock.'[25]

The rise of youth as dissident, as consumer and as object of moral concern was charted uneasily by the media throughout the decade from the first appearance of the Teddy Boy with his distinct crepe-soled shoes, long-tailed waist jacket and string tie; through the commercialization of the mid-1950s 'skiffle' music craze, at which time musicians and audiences imitated American folk styles. Girls wore black jumpers, black stockings and loose hair; boys fringe beards and open-necked check shirts. If most in their teens were not 'teenagers' as defined by policy makers, academics or journalists, not promiscuous, criminal or subcultural, engaged in hobbies rather than flamboyant youth cults, they were almost invisible. Magazines, advertisements and pop songs, as well as lurid newspaper reports, animated youth as avid consumer or as cat-torturing Teddy Boy who 'stalked like some atavistic monster through much of the otherwise prosaic newspaper reporting' of the time.[26] While some among the older age group, the manufacturers of clothes, magazines and music, gradually grasped the nature and size of the youth market, others worried about unmarried mothers under the age of 15, whose number doubled between 1945 and 1959: the wartime and postwar generations seemed to have less and less common ground.

Teenage romance comics, 'werewolf' movies and Little Richard came to represent the apparently increasing dominance of American popular culture in the United Kingdom and, according to their critics, to erode 'native' culture and debase the taste and morality of their consumers. Similarly as the younger generation began to express its own values, it appeared, either by accident or design, provocatively 'uncultured'. Describing the reception of the play that first defined the generational shift in theatre, John Osborne's *Look Back in Anger* (1956), Christopher Logue notes how extraordinary it seemed that 'a discourteous, loud-mouthed boor should be allowed to appear at all, let alone to rant about *class*, *money* and *sex*, while bursting with rage at the habits of the society that had borne him and scorning – it seemed – the values of the men and women who died in the Second World War'.[27] Such spleen expressed through the middle-class medium of theatre was nonetheless more acceptable than the working-class subcultural style of the spivs or the Teddy Boys. Early school leavers in their teens, poorly educated or skilled, the Teds' appearance displayed conspicuous consumption of a kind unthinkable among the same age group in earlier generations:

> Essentially the dress consisted of a long, narrow-lapelled, waist jacket, narrow trousers (but without being 'drainpipes'), ordinary toe-capped shoes and a fancy waistcoat. Shirts were white with cutaway collars and ties were tied with a 'windsor' knot. Headwear, if worn, was a trilby. The essential changes from conventional dress were the cut of the jacket and the dandy waistcoat. Additionally barbers began offering individual styling, and hair length was generally longer than the conventional short back and sides.[28]

In their spiv-like concern for smart appearance and disregard for convention if not the law, the Teddy Boy image became shorthand for the new generation of youthful rebels and law-breakers; while the original south London Teds flourished from 1954 until just before the arrival of rock'n'roll in 1956, it still seemed credible, almost, to blame them for the Nottingham and Notting Hill 'race' riots of 1958.[29]

'Angry Young Men' were a related symptom of the new welfare state to their critics; again the term was most widely employed by journalists. Initially it described a group of novelists, playwrights and thinkers, among them Kingsley Amis (1922–95), John Osborne (1929–94) and Colin Wilson (b.1931), mostly aged between 20 and 30, non-metropolitan, from lower middle- or working-class background. By extension the term came to mean almost anyone who openly attacked, disparaged or mocked contemporary society. Reviewing *Look Back in Anger* in 1956, theatre critic Kenneth Tynan (1927–80) was in no doubt that Osborne and his peers mirrored accurately the mood, voice and behaviour of postwar youth, whose qualities included an instinctive leftishness, outright rejection of 'official' attitudes, surreal humour, casual promiscuity, rejection of 'good taste', refusal of class or leaders.[30] Furthermore, 'the salient thing about [*Look Back in Anger*'s main character] Jimmy Porter was that we – the under thirty generation in Britain – recognized him on sight. We had met him; we had pub-crawled with him; we had shared bed-sittingrooms with him. For the first time the theatre was speaking to us in our own language, on our own terms.'[31] While 'anger' was not new then, Osborne and his contemporaries caught the mood of the postwar generation. They were further fired by the Suez crisis of 1956, which was seen to expose the hollowness of Britain's continued imperial posturing, and by the nuclear arms race, which seemed to threaten civilization in the name of its preservation. Rejecting tradition and conformity, they brought together the like-minded of a generation, but the new consumerism of the mass media also assisted their rise to fame.[32] The Angry Young Men were the arts wing of the new youth consumer boom.

After 1956 – the rock'n'roll riots which accompanied showings of Bill Haley's film *Rock Around the Clock*; the Suez crisis; the invasion of Hungary, which destroyed the faith of the old political Left; and the arrival of the 'Angries' in the media – the new clash of generational values was played out as street theatre. The rituals of Saturday night out described by Keith Waterhouse (*Billy Liar*, 1959) or Colin MacInnes (*Absolute Beginners*, 1959), or the new popular music club scene of the Cavern (Liverpool) or the Two I's (Soho, London) dramatized how far and how fast consumerism had changed the values and outlook of the young. Among the 'instinctively left' identified by Kenneth Tynan the most pressing issue was 'the bomb'. 'The real benefit of the left-wing zeal was finally not felt in the society but in the practitioners themselves,' argued Jeff Nuttall (1933–2004), experimental poet as well as author of *Bomb Culture* (1968). 'They had developed in their own minds an idealism which acted as an antidote to the sickness attendant on living with the bomb.'[33]

In the anti-nuclear movement many disenfranchised, disaffected groups found a common cause. Though relatively few were prepared to engage as political activists, many supporters adopted it as a badge of their discontent. Word of mouth promoted large crowds for the inaugural meeting of the organization, a meeting at Central Hall, Westminster on 17 February 1958, the first Easter protest march to the Berkshire village of Aldermaston, site of an atomic weapons research establishment, was quickly organized. In the event, six or seven hundred determined to follow the entire route. They were students and youths, women and men, mostly from London and surrounding areas, some foreigners, others from elsewhere within the country. The description of one participant captures well the oppositional atmosphere:

> Having survived all the flattening speeches and all the brassy stupid attempts to make political capital of one kind or another out of the March, having come through it all with sore feet and maybe a slight ringing in our ears, one felt a sudden sense of relief that afternoon at Falcon Field . . . These marchers had done something which belonged to *them* and they knew that it was, beyond questioning, good and right. The spiritual success transcended the immediate political futility of what a contemptuous Tory onlooker called 'Khrushchev's Bunion Derby'.[34]

Lou Taylor wore her camel duffel coat, other shoppers in the army surplus stores of the late 1950s preferred black: the predominant colour of the new cultural and political 'beatniks', the colour of youth, of mourning and of anarchy.[35]

Regarding modern life

Living in an age of mass media, organizing their symbols and campaigns – the CND logo, the protest march – to best profit from public exposure, anti-nuclear protesters understood how public affairs and political debate had been transformed by the new broadcast technology in the postwar years. Visual artists, critics and curators had to respond to the new mass society too, to rethink the role of the fine arts within the new age of mass communications. Lawrence Alloway (1926–90), critic and commentator, argued that the rise of popular culture was a telling, irreversible transformation. 'Sensitivity to the variables of our life and economy enable the mass arts to accompany the changes in our life far more closely than the fine arts which are a repository of time-binding values . . . the new job of the fine arts is to be one of the possible forms of communication in an expanding framework that also includes the mass arts.'[36] Artists responded by exploring these new visual idioms, as well as by inventing their own: by decoding the myths and symbols of *High Noon*; by constructing abstract, diagrammatic analogues of the experience of modern living; by casting a searchlight on to the apparently prosaic lives of province and sub-let.[37]

It was again the generation that came of age as the war ended who embraced change. Meeting at the Institute of Contemporary Arts in the early 1950s a small group of practitioners and critics were among the first to seriously examine the new aesthetic of sci-fi illustration, car design or movie superstar looks. Their number included Eduardo Paolozzi and Lawrence Alloway; Richard Hamilton (artist), as well as Alison Smithson (1928–1993) and Peter Smithson (1923–2003, architects), joined them. Against the notion of universal laws which could define beauty and proportion, they argued that within the new visual environment of modern mass culture a classical statue and a *King Kong* movie poster were now both to be seen as rich, vibrant art objects.[38] Paolozzi explored further in 1952 with a slide show at the ICA using advertisements, comic book and horror movie images; he developed his interests in sculptural form too, for instance by pressing everyday objects – a rubber dragon, clock parts, a bent fork

– into plaster, making waxcasts, and building them into mythical, alien heads and creatures such as the *Japanese War God* (1958). Just as low-budget horror films told of sensations and emotions beyond the reach of traditional art forms, he argued, so the chaotic beauty of everyday life could be exposed through what the artist called the 'metamorphosis of everyday things'.[39]

The *This is Tomorrow* exhibition brought together twelve groups of collaborators: an architect, sculptor and painter in each. Futuristic, fantastic and everyday aspects of design connected the various exhibition areas as they explored advertising, technology and lived environments. Catching the attention of journalists and the imagination of the public, *This is Tomorrow* attracted almost 20,000 visitors to the Whitechapel Art Gallery over the summer of 1956.[40]

The majority, seven of the twelve groups in *This is Tomorrow*, were not affiliated to the ICA or 'Independent Group' of Paolozzi, the Smithsons and their associates. A parallel response to the reinterpretation of 'fine arts' was the development of a visual dialect that described the essence of form without representational reproduction. Lawrence Alloway was involved here too as he documented and promoted the movement beginning with the publication of *Nine Abstract Artists* (1954). Both the ICA 'Independent Group' and the abstractionists shared a conviction that the older generation of neo-Romantics were now irrelevant, that the inward language of landscape had served its purpose by evoking a reverence and loyalty of place. Becoming part of an influential postwar avant-garde in the process, what the new abstract artists particularly stressed, Patrick Heron (1920–99) and Terry Frost (1915–2003) among them, was the encounter of artistic imagination with materials: brush, oils, canvas. As both were associated with St Ives, there was too an inescapable sense of rootedness in response to space and place, in the very particular town and landscape in which they lived and worked. Another group of abstractionists, many London based, took a more 'analytic' approach: less 'a man swinging out into a void', as Roger Hilton described the abstractionist vocation, than measuring points of take off and landing, speed, angle and trajectory.[41] Victor Pasmore, who exhibited with Ernö Goldfinger and Helen Phillips (1913–95) on his *This is Tomorrow* exhibit, constructed near colourless reliefs; intricate patterns of rhythm and space, as in *Relief Construction in White and Black, Maroon and Ochre* (1956–7).

From January 1956, when the first Abstract Expressionist paintings were shown at the Tate Gallery's *Modern Art in the United States* exhibition, affinities with and respect for the American scene strengthened. Rethinking his view of Jackson Pollock, David Sylvester asked 'What must I have been using for eyes?'[42] Sylvester was responsible too for labelling those who responded to their times with careful consideration of the everyday: domestic interiors, suburban scenes and the lives that were lived within them. For the 'neo-' or 'kitchen sink' realists as the art critic described them, the spaces for cooking, sleeping and eating, the dining room table, clothes, bedding and washing that were the surroundings for daily routine, were not necessarily 'political', but could be a worthy object of attention. And such attention was engrained in the postwar concern to celebrate and explore the lower middle- and working-class lives of the mass population. Among the artists associated with these preoccupations was John Bratby (1928–92). Yet while works such as *Still Life with Chip Frier* (1954) or *Sarah*

Dressing (1958) appear to fulfil all the criteria laid down by Marxist critic John Berger for a realist, cause-driven art, *Four Lambrettas and Three Portraits of Janet Churchman* (1958) hints that no artist's expressive world lies within critically imposed criteria.[43] Bratby's intense colours, thick application of paint and more affluent surroundings might also be read as a celebration of the world of sensual, material pleasures.

Certainly the inclusion of Lambretta motor scooters, a representation of youthful prosperity and of the wider influence of Italian arts and design on British consumers, was remote from the increasingly austere forms of welfare public art. While Giacometti inspired many artists in Britain, Paolozzi and William Turnbull among them, it was the Olivetti typewriter and the Gaggia chrome coffee machine, as well as the Lambretta motor scooter, that now became necessary mass pleasures. By contrast the rebuilt Coventry Cathedral, consecrated on 30 May 1962, with its sculpture of *St Michael and Lucifer* by Jacob Epstein, and its tapestry of *Christ in Glory* by Graham Sutherland, appeared as a last blossoming of the welfare state's 'arts for the people' vision.

A children's uprising

The new mood of the mass entertainment and media age was nowhere better caught than in the world of popular music, which was increasingly associated with youth culture, particularly after the arrival of Lonnie Donegan's 'Rock Island Line' and Elvis Presley's 'Heartbreak Hotel', both of which reached number one in the British charts in May 1956. British youth and American popular music formed a new alliance in this moment; to many older people the jangling guitars and frenetic dancing of the new pop scene made it a rebellion by the nation's youth.[44] One astute observer of the pop scene was film music composer Frank Cordell. Writing in 1957 he noted that popular song was as subject to collective behaviour, approval and taste as comic strips, advertisements or movies, that the new pop star was a product to be consumed as personality rather than appreciated as artist or craftsman.[45]

It was exactly for these reasons that an intoxicating pop culture now began to brew. The arcane rituals and obsessions of the traditional jazz revival just after the war had already shown the potential appeal of fresh musical styles, while the small group of modern jazz and bebop fans of the early 1950s was among the first to affect the cool, ironic subcultural style of 'dark glasses and the hip stance'.[46] Critics and some audiences continued to stress the superiority or authenticity of acoustic blues singers from the deep South or Gaelic musicians in the west of Scotland, but the newly aware and enthusiastic consumers of pop had their own tastes. It was this audience that made Johnnie Ray, named for his weepy delivery 'the nabob of sob', one of the most popular acts in Britain through the decade. 'Emotional, rather effeminate in appearance, liable to burst into tears,' George Melly wrote, 'he nevertheless succeeded in provoking a near-orgasmic effect on large audiences of young girls. He was a forerunner of the pop hero proper.'[47]

American-born Ray's theatrical delivery and showmanship was accompanied by a less glamorous home-grown style, loosely based on American folk, known as skiffle, of which Lonnie Donegan (1931–2002) was the leading British performer. With its strongly acoustic sound and its borrowings from the American ballad tradition, skiffle was as revivalist as trad jazz, as ethnic as folk, but, with common roots in black musical genres, particularly when accompanied by electric guitar rather than washboard, as energetic as rock'n'roll. Its prominent folk music tradition meant skiffle thrived in Scotland, so it was no accident that Donegan's hit, 'Rock Island Line', was 'riveting in its powerful, ongoing drive . . . delivered in a rich southern states accent quite amazing to hear from a Glaswegian'.[48]

The British fascination with American folk and jazz styles that fuelled the early postwar jazz boom subsequently set off the skiffle craze led by a band of enthusiasts including Ken Colyer, Chris Barber and Lonnie Donegan. Initially they were concerned with the reinterpretation of the blues and protest songs of Leadbelly, Big Bill Broonzy or Woody Guthrie. Listening to Library of Congress recordings at the American Embassy, Colyer and his peers were drawn to the hobo life of freight train travel and casual labour, singing in coffee houses and jazz club basements. The first folk club in Scotland was set up at Allan Glen's Secondary School for Boys in Glasgow in 1953; by the mid-1950s Glasgow folk concerts had begun to incorporate both jazz and native piping.[49] Enthusiasm for the style spread across the UK and peaked around 1957 when there were thousands of groups, many in schools. While skiffle was not rock'n'roll, it was nevertheless exploited commercially and had a presence in the imagination, advertising and entertainment of the nation: at holiday camp there were skiffle band competitions, cereal packets contained free 'skiffle' whistles and how to hold the perfect skiffle party was the subject of an article in *Woman* magazine.[50]

Like many showbusiness acts of the mid-1950s, Donegan's performances and choice of material were rooted in the variety and music hall tradition too: he performed in pantomime over Christmas 1957, he also recorded novelty songs such as 'My Old Man's a Dustman' and 'Does Your Chewing Gum Lose its Flavour', which reached number three in the hit parade of February 1959.[51] For all its limitations, skiffle was the first native form of postwar pop, adapting and selecting material, reworking themes and styles to suit the tastes of the native audience: a unique response to the mood and opportunities of the new commercialism. As interest in skiffle faded through 1958–9, the movement had already spawned two new native enthusiasms: for rock'n'roll, and for folk. The affinity with folk and native tradition which had shaped skiffle now re-enthused both audiences and performers with an interest in indigenous songs of Scotland, Ireland and Wales. The preoccupations of the new folk scene are well illustrated by the remarkable career of Ewan MacColl (1915–89), whose Scottish background and socialist upbringing drew him to a vision of folk music unsullied by business or media influences.

After the arrival of Elvis, and Lonnie, the British pop scene moved on quickly. The 'rock'n'roll riots' of September 1956, when crowds danced and shouted outside the Gaumont cinemas in East London's Dagenham, Leyton and Stratford as well as elsewhere, showed the potential commercial appeal of the new music. Over the next few years Larry Parnes used that appeal as he became manager of many native rock'n'roll stars with names like Johnny Gentle and Marty Wilde. Parnes was manager too of the first real British rock'n'roll idol, Tommy Steele (b. 1936), whose 'Singing the Blues' was a number one hit in February 1957. Wolf

Mankowitz retold Steele's rise to fame as a satirical short story. 'Expresso Bongo' (1960) charted the rise of Bongo Herbert through the cynical voice of his manager:

> The picture in the fan-mag showed this gangly kid in jeans and a sweat shirt, his face contorted, mouth wide open, beating with both hands on a bongo set round his shoulders, over the headline BONGO SCORES AT TOM-TOM. The same terrible stuff, but this time it was good, because it was me who dropped the dead-beat drunk columnist a fiver to run it. Because this boy Bongo Herbert, playing nightly for the past week in the Tom-Tom expresso back of Frith Street, is under contract to nobody but me. Half of everything he beats out of those little bongos for the next three years comes to me.[52]

Despite its mix of show business and awkwardness, British rock'n'roll still inspired devotion among its fans. Listening to American music brought to Liverpool by seamen, Ronald Wycherley, renamed Billy Fury, became one of the best remembered stars. His 1960 ten-inch LP *The Sound of Fury* effected a powerful mix of American-style vigour with native vulnerability, for example on the ballad 'You Don't Know'. Here the new pop which critics such as Richard Hoggart saw as a distortion of communal tradition, and as a degrading influence, might better be understood as testimony to the resilience of cultural traditions which continually shaped the interpretation and understanding of the newly imported musical styles according to local conditions.[53] The variety show and music hall directed British pop as much as developments in Memphis. American popular styles broadened the musical possibilities of the British scene, became rooted in it and renewed native styles. As if to prove the point, one skiffle group, The Quarrymen, Liverpudlians like Ron Wycherley, and with an equally keen ear for American sounds, went on to become Britain's best-selling export of the mid-1960s.

What song are we to sing?

The shift in critical, artistic and cultural values in the mid-1950s registers in film too. In January 1957 the young documentary film-maker Lindsay Anderson (1923–94) joined dissident figures such as playwright John Osborne and Colin Wilson in condemning what he saw as the complacent values of British society. The particular object of Anderson's attack was the war film. 'Chasing the *Graf Spee* again at the Battle of River Plate, tapping our feet to the March of the Dam Busters, we can make believe that our issues are simple ones – it's *Great* Britain again!' 'If "Land of Hope and Glory" is to be decently shelved,' he continued, 'what song are we to sing?[54] Anderson and his associates in the new Free Cinema movement perceived an artistic crisis; studios and theatre managers were faced with a more tangible fall in attendance. In 1950, weekly audiences averaged 30 million but by 1960 the figure had fallen to ten million. While there were 4500 cinemas at the beginning of the decade, by its end there were only 3000.[55] As living conditions improved, cinemas were no longer warmer or more comfortable than homes, and the weekly trip to the pictures lost its charm. The Newcastle area commercial TV channel for example, Tyne Tees, began broadcasting in January 1959: five cinemas closed down in 1958–9, 14 in 1960–1.[56]

While commercial cinema did not necessarily comment directly in social change or uphold a distinct aesthetic, it nevertheless reflected the society from which it emerged; its subject matter and critical perspective shifted through the decade. While Dirk Bogarde had appeared as lawless hoodlum in *The Blue Lamp*, he reinvented himself as a vulnerable yet capable romantic lead in *Doctor in the House* (1954); while *The Dam Busters* (1954) celebrated wartime courage and endurance, *Orders to Kill* (Anthony Asquith, 1958) or *Yesterday's Enemy* (Val Guest, 1959) were evidently in the aftermath of Britain's defeated imperial pretensions following the Suez crisis. Both *The Quatermass Experiment* (1955) and *Quatermass II* (1959) questioned national self-satisfaction in contrast to wartime unity, and doubted the apparent benefits of scientific and technological progress.[57] Film historian Charles Barr interprets one of the box office successes of 1955, *The Ladykillers* (Alexander Mackendrick), as an explicit critique of Britain ten years after the war's end. A group of oddly matched classical musicians, including an intellectual leader, Professor Marcus (Alec Guinness), and a youthfully naïve teddy boy, Harry (Peter Sellers), move into the house of Mrs Wilberforce, an elderly lady nostalgic for the Victorian age and empire. In truth these supposedly cultured gentlemen are criminals planning a robbery at King's Cross Station. When landlady Mrs Wilberforce discovers their plot they set out to murder her but are instead killed off, one by one, in the process. Barr's argument is that the 'criminals' bear a more than passing resemblance to the Labour administration of 1945, Mrs Wilberforce to the 'natural' aristocratic elite of the nation, and the gang's downfall parallels the fate of the government. They are helpless in the face of internal quarrels and opposition from the ruling classes.[58] Certainly Mackendrick was discontented with the nostalgic, parochial mood in the early 1950s, which developed against the backdrop of new material well-being.

The social and artistic upheaval at which Mackendrick hinted in *The Ladykillers* took a more radical form in Lindsay Anderson's own early film-making career. Involved with documentary work from the late 1940s, it was only with the Free Cinema manifesto, which accompanied screenings at the National Film Theatre 5–8 February 1956, that the new aesthetic attracted wider attention. 'These films were not made together; nor with the idea of showing them together' wrote signatories Lorenza Mazzetti, Lindsay Anderson, Karel Reisz (1926–2002) and Tony Richardson (1928–91). 'But when they came together, we felt they had an attitude in common. Implicit in this attitude is a belief in freedom, in the importance of people and in the significance of the everyday . . . No film can be too personal. The image speaks. Sound amplifies and comments . . .'[59] These themes were apparent in the contribution by Karel Reisz and Tony Richardson, *Momma Don't Allow* (1955), which observed without judgement the shop girls and Teddy Boys of suburban London as they enjoyed their Saturday evenings at the Wood Green Jazz Club. *Together* (Lorenza Mazzetti, 1956) was described in the programme as above all 'a poetic film', not so much concerned with the disabilities of its two main characters, deaf-mute labourers in the London docks, as with their isolation. Anderson's *O Dreamland* (1953) drew support, but was also reviled for its depiction of seaside holidaymakers at a Margate funfair as they enjoyed crude pleasures such as a 'Torture Through the Ages' exhibition. While Anderson was keen to visualize working-class culture, he was also unsparing, and some reviewers understood his film as a commentary on the 'savage' quality of popular entertainment.[60]

For critic Calvin Lambert writing in spring 1956 Anderson's work made the lives of working people newly visible, yet encompassed 'the most rigorous, difficult and austere kind of compassion'. In 1958, discussing Anderson's film on the Covent Garden Fruit and Vegetable Market *Every Day Except Sunday* (1957), Rudolf Arnheim highlighted the director's poetics. The film 'added up to an even texture of unceasing disorder cut from the loom of time more or less at random, and thus directly related to the abstract paintings of the Jackson Pollock school'.[61] Anderson's refusal to compromise either his artistic or social agenda made both his Free Cinema documentaries and his later feature films both distinctive and idiosyncratic.

In line with David Sylvester's characterization of postwar British culture as 'smooth' or 'textured', and in view of his belief that certain artists constituted a 'kitchen sink school', a grittier reality now showed itself in film-making. The Free Cinema's documentary poetics continued for several years and produced, for example *We Are the Lambeth Boys* (Karel Reisz, 1959) and Anderson's own *March to Aldermaston* (1959). Popular features now gave increasing attention to the everyday and the ordinary lives of men and women too. *Woman in a Dressing Gown* (J. Lee Thompson, 1957), for instance, describes the dilemma of a husband as he contemplates leaving his partner of twenty years for a good looking, respectable younger woman, but finds himself unable to do so; while class and the struggle for material success are the themes of *Room at the Top* (Jack Clayton, 1959). Rather than turn to dramatic realism in the later 1950s the Boulting Brothers produced a series of satires on national institutions including *Private's Progress* (1956), which examined the absurdity of army life, *Brothers in Law* (1957) on the legal profession, and *I'm All Right Jack* (1959) on industrial relations and especially on the 'Napoleons of the shop floor', Shop Stewards.[62] One further sign of the changing tastes and preoccupations of audiences was the fall in popularity of Kenneth More, archetypal wartime movie hero of the mid-1950s, or rather his eclipse in 1959 by the rise to stardom of Welsh actor Stanley Baker. While More was vigorous and cheerful, Baker played a complex, flawed hero. In *Hell Drivers* (1957) his time in prison enabled Tom Yately to successfully negotiate the unglamorous, not to say treacherous, world of the lorry driver. In *Hell is a City* (1960), prided by its director Val Guest for the realism of its Manchester crowd and street scenes, the actor portrays an aggressive, confused policeman.[63] Baker's achievement was to represent credibly and entertainingly how 'ordinary men, doing ordinary jobs, can be exciting and often are'.[64]

Timeline 1: 1945–59

───────────────────────────1945───────────────────────────

SOCIETY: Family Allowances Act; *Planning Proposals for the Belfast Area*. **February:** Yalta Agreement. **May:** VE Day, Germany surrenders; Labour Party leaves coalition; Churchill forms 'caretaker' government. **July: General Election**, gives a huge Labour majority; Clement Attlee becomes PM in the first Labour government. **August:** Hiroshima and Nagasaki destroyed by atomic bombs; Japanese surrender ends war. **October:** Lend-Lease finishes and Britain takes emergency powers. **December:** loans offer from United States.

ARTS: TV, theatre, film: David Lean, *Brief Encounter*; Michael Powell and Emeric Pressburger, *I Know Where I'm Going*; Gabriel Pascal, *Caesar and Cleopatra*. **Visual:** Francis Bacon exhibition, Lefevre Gallery; Picasso and Matisse exhibition, Victoria and Albert Museum. **Musical:** Benjamin Britten, *Peter Grimes*; American dance bands arrive, starting a postwar craze; George Webb's Dixielanders sign to Decca. **Written:** Henry Green, *Loving*; George Orwell, *Animal Farm*; Evelyn Waugh, *Brideshead Revisited*.

───────────────────────────1946───────────────────────────

SOCIETY: New Towns Act; National Insurance and Industrial Injuries Acts; Manchester Corporation Act introduces pioneering smokeless zone legislation; *Report of the Royal Commission on Equal Pay*; John Bowlby, *Forty-Four Juvenile Thieves*; Police Act; Trade Disputes and Trade Union Act (1927) repealed. **March:** nationalization of the Bank of England; Churchill's 'Iron Curtain' speech. J. C. Spence, *The Purpose of the Family*. **July:** nationalization of the coal industry. **November:** National Health Service Act, effective from July 1948.

ARTS: foundation of the Arts Council; Third Programme begins broadcasting. **TV, theatre, film:** Ivy Compton Burnett, *Daybreak*; David Lean, *Great Expectations*; Terence Rattigan, *The Winslow Boy*. **Visual:** Robert Colquhoun, *Woman with a Bird Cage*. **Musical:** decline of big band groups; Benjamin Britten, *The Rape of Lucretia*. **Written:** Keith Douglas, *From Alamein to Zem Zem*; Henry Green, *Back*; Philip Larkin, *Jill*.

───────────────────────────1947───────────────────────────

SOCIETY: Town and Country Planning Act; nationalization of London transport, docks, road haulage and railways under the Transport Act; Agriculture Act; National Service Act; first British nuclear reactor built at Harwell; *Report on the Ulster Countryside*; partition of India. **February:** Indian independence announced by the government. **April:** fifteen becomes the new school leaving age. **June:** US aid for Europe, the Marshall Plan, announced. **July:** Commonwealth Relations Office established. **August:** nationalization of the electricity industry; first Edinburgh Festival.

ARTS: TV, film, theatre: David Lean, *Brighton Rock*; Robert Hamer, *It Always Rains on Sunday*; Herbert Wilcox, *The Courtneys of Curzon Street*; Ken Annakin, *Holiday Camp*. **Visual:** Eduardo Paolozzi, 'I was a Rich Man's Plaything'; Robin Ironside, 'Painting since 1939'. **Musical:** The Ink Spots in London; beginning of the trad jazz craze, led by Humphrey Lyttelton. **Written:** G. D. H. Cole, *The Intelligent Man's Guide to the Post-War World*. Robert Graves, *The White Goddess*; Malcolm Lowry, *Under the Volcano*.

──────────────────────**1948**──────────────────────

Society: National Health Service comes into operation; The Children's Act; Criminal Justice Act; Commonwealth citizens given British subject status under the British Nationality Act; Council of Wales established; wage restraint agreement between government and TUC; *Regional Plan for Central and South-East Scotland*; Olympic Games in London. **January:** nationalization of the railways. **February**: British troops finally leave India. **April:** Marshall Plan funds to Britain; Organization of European Economic Cooperation established. **June:** arrival of the *Empire Windrush* at Tilbury Docks. **July:** end of bread rationing; Monopolies and Restrictive Policies Act establishes Monopolies Commission. **December:** Republic of Ireland Act passed.

Arts: TV, theatre, film: David Lean, *Oliver Twist*; St John L. Clowes, *No Orchids for Miss Blandish*; Ken Annakin, *Here Come the Huggetts*. **Visual:** B. Brandt, *Camera in London*; Joseph Hermann, *Evenfall, Ystradgynlais*; Henry Moore, *Family Group* at Stevenage New Town. **Musical:** release of Leonard Bernstein's *On the Town* on film; Humphrey Lyttelton begins jazz club residency in Leicester Square. **Written:** T. S. Eliot, *Notes Towards the Definition of Culture*; Graham Greene, *The Heart of the Matter*; F. R. Leavis, *The Great Tradition*; Evelyn Waugh, *The Loved One*.

──────────────────────**1949**──────────────────────

Society: Ireland Act; National Parks and Access to the Countryside Act; Royal Commission on Divorce Report; Royal Commission on Population Report; *Clyde Valley Regional Plan*; Lord Montague opens Beaulieu. **January:** execution by hanging of Margaret Allen. **March:** clothes rationing ends. **April:** NATO established; formation of the Commonwealth; the Irish Free State becomes the Republic of Ireland. **September:** sterling devaluation from $4.03 to $2.80.

Arts: TV, theatre, film: Henry Cornelius, *Passport to Pimlico*; Robert Hamer, *Kind Hearts and Coronets*; Carol Reed, *The Third Man*; T. S. Eliot, *The Cocktail Party*. **Visual:** Jacob Epstein, *Lazarus*; C. Jones, *Sawdade*; Graham Sutherland, *Somerset Maugham*. **Musical:** Billy Cotton Band Show begins on BBC radio. **Written:** Roy Fuller, *Epitaphs and Occasions*; George Orwell, *1984*; R. Lewis and A. Maude, *The English Middle Class*.

──────────────────────**1950**──────────────────────

Society: New peak of 17 million on the sale of daily newspapers; Britain officially recognizes communist China. **February: General Election:** Labour majority sharply reduced. **May:** petrol rationing ends; common French and German coal and steel authority proposed by Robert Schuman. **June:** outbreak of the Korean War. **September:** British troops in Korea to support the United Nations operation. **December:** removal of the Stone of Scone from Westminster Abbey; suspension of Marshall Aid.

Arts: TV, theatre, film: Basil Dearden, *The Blue Lamp*; Charles Crichton, *Dance Hall*; Herbert Wilcox, *Odette*. **Visual:** David Jones, *Flora in Calix-light*. **Musical:** London Jazz Club opens; William Walton, *Violin Sonata*. **Written:** William Cooper, *Scenes from Provincial Life*; Doris Lessing, *The Grass is Singing*; Angus Wilson, *Such Darling Dodos*.

──────────────────────**1951**──────────────────────

Society: 300,000 homes per year pledge by new Conservative Government; J. Bowlby, *Maternal Care and Maternal Health*; defection of Burgess and Maclean; opening of the Lansbury Estate in East London; Coventry establishes the first smokeless zone. **January:** GBP 4700m rearmament programme announced. **April:** introduction of prescription charges; establishment of the European Coal and Steel Authority. **September**: ANZUS Pact established Pacific security between USA, Australia and New Zealand. **October: General Election:** majority of 16 for the new Conservative government; Churchill becomes Prime Minister.

ARTS: Festival of Britain. **TV, theatre, film:** Charles Crichton, *The Lavender Hill Mob*; Alexander Mackendrick, *The Man in the White Suit*; Roy Boulting, *High Treason*. **Visual:** Lucian Freud, *Interior near Paddington*; William Gear, *Autumn Landscape*. **Musical:** Kay Starr, 'Rock and Roll Waltz'; Eagle Jazz band, formerly the Canterbury Jazz Appreciation Society, begin performing in public. **Written:** Graham Greene, *The End of the Affair*; Anthony Powell, *A Question of Upbringing*.

---**1952**---

SOCIETY: first production of the contraceptive pill; conviction of Derek Bentley for murder; construction begins on Cwmbran New Town in South Wales; Gatwick Airport development approved; beginning the Mau Mau rebellion in Kenya; McCarran-Walter Immigration and Nationality Act (USA, 1952). **February:** accession of Elizabeth II following the death of George VI. **October:** Monte Bello Islands, Western Australia – the first British atomic weapons test.

ARTS: TV, film, theatre: Charles Crichton, *Hunted*; Ronald Neame, *The Card*; film version of *Singing in the Rain* released in Britain. **Visual:** Independent Group begins meeting at the Institute of Contemporary Arts, London; John Berger organizes the first 'Looking Forward' exhibition at the Whitechapel Gallery. **Musical:** first 45rpm single released; *New Musical Express* begins a singles chart; *Hit Parade* TV show; early chart success for Johnnie Ray with 'Here Am I – Broken-Hearted'. **Written:** David Jones, *The Anathemata*; Dylan Thomas, *Collected Poems, 1934–52*; Evelyn Waugh, *Men at Arms*.

---**1953**---

SOCIETY: Press Council established following recommendations from the Royal Commission on the Press; Armistice in Korea; government of British Guiana overthrown after intervention by British troops. **March:** denationalization and establishment of the Iron and Steel Board under the Iron and Steel Act. **April:** road transport denationalized under the Transport Act. **May:** Everest ascent by Hillary. **June:** coronation of Elizabeth II. **September:** sugar rationing ends after fourteen years.

ARTS: TV, theatre, film: Lindsay Anderson, *O Dreamland*; Charles Crichton, *The Titfield Thunderbolt*; Charles Frend, *The Cruel Sea*. **Visual:** Patrick Heron exhibition, Hanover Gallery, London; 'Parallel of Life and Art' exhibition, Institute of Contemporary Arts, London; Jack Smith, *Mother Bathing Child*. **Musical:** first Scottish folk club established at Allan Glen's Secondary School, Glasgow. **Written:** Samuel Beckett, *Watt*; L. P. Hartley, *The Go-Between*; Ian Fleming, *Casino Royale*; John Wain, *Hurry on Down*.

---**1954**---

SOCIETY: Independent Broadcasting Authority established to run commercial television under the Television Act; crime at its lowest rate since the war; media coverage of Teddy boys begins; predictions that Britain will double its standard of living in the next 25 years; railway 'rationalization' and allocation of funds to replace steam with diesel and electric engines. **July:** food rationing ends. **September:** South-East Asian Treaty Organization (SEATO) formed. **December:** Associate membership of the European Coal and Steel Community for Britain.

ARTS: TV, theatre, film: Anthony Asquith, *The Young Lovers*; Ralph Thomas, *Doctor in the House*. **Visual:** Peter Blake, 'Children Reading Comics'; John Bratby, *Still Life with Chip Frier*; David Sylvester coins the term 'kitchen sink realism'; Lawrence Alloway, *Nine Abstract Artists*. **Musical:** Alma Cogan's first chart success with 'Bell Bottom Blues'. **Written:** Kingsley Amis, *Lucky Jim*; William Golding, *Lord of the Flies*; Dylan Thomas, *Under Milk Wood* (radio production); J. R. R. Tolkien, *The Lord of the Rings*.

———————————————————————1955———————————————————————

Society: increase in West Indian immigration; major industrial unrest; London declared a smokeless zone. **April:** Eden becomes PM following the resignation of Churchill. **May:** Conservatives gain a majority of almost sixty in the **General Election.** **June:** proposal for further European integration at the Messina Conference. **July:** British dock strike ends after a month. **September:** first commercial TV broadcast. **October:** balance of payments crisis and autumn budget.

Arts: Malcolm Muggeridge's *New Statesman* article on the Monarchy; concept of 'the Establishment' revived. **TV, theatre, film:** Alexander Mackendrick, *The Ladykillers*; Karel Reisz and Tony Richardson, *Momma Don't Allow*; Hammer films begin production with *The Quatermass Experiment.* **Visual:** first Mary Quant fashion boutique, Bazaar, opens on the King's Road, London; Edward Middleditch, *Dead Chicken in a Stream.* **Musical:** pop music slowly begins to be broadcast on television, *Music Shop.* **Written:** Samuel Beckett, *Waiting for Godot*; William Golding, *The Inheritors*; Philip Larkin, *The Less Deceived*; Evelyn Waugh, *Officers and Gentlemen.*

———————————————————————1956———————————————————————

Society: Royal Commission on Marriage and Divorce Report; suppression of anti-Soviet revolt in Hungary; first anti-nuclear demonstrations; widespread dissatisfaction with Prime Minister Eden; sharp rise in crime rates; Frank Cousins new general secretary of the Transport and General Workers Union; the coffee bar craze begins. **July:** Suez Canal nationalized by Nasser. **August:** Britain, France and the USA declare against Egypt's decision; Restrictive Trade Practices Court established. **September**: first commercial television broadcast. **October:** Anglo-French invasion of Suez. **December:** evacuation of troops from Suez; Britain borrows GBP201m from the IMF.

Arts: TV, theatre, film: first Free Cinema programme organized by Lindsay Anderson at the National Film Theatre; John Osborne, *Look Back in Anger*; *Rebel Without a Cause* (1955) makes James Dean a cult hero; Lewis Gilbert, *Reach for the Sky.* **Visual:** Richard Hamilton's 'Just what is it that makes today's homes so different, so appealing?' is the catalogue cover to 'This is Tomorrow' exhibition, Whitechapel Gallery; *Modern Art in the United States* Exhibition. **Musical:** rock'n'roll craze; screenings of *Rock Around the Clock*; Elvis charts with 'Heartbreak Hotel'. **Written:** Simone de Beauvoir, *The Second Sex* (English trans.); Alva Myrdal and Viola Klein, *Women's Two Roles* Robert Conquest (ed.), *New Lines* poetry anthology; Colin Wilson, *The Outsider.*

———————————————————————1957———————————————————————

Society: abolition of rent controls for 810,000 houses under the Rent Act; Macmillan 'liberalizes' Conservatism; 'Never had it so good' speech in Bedford; Windscale nuclear plant suffers major radioactive leak. **January:** Macmillan becomes PM following Eden's retirement. **March:** Ghana, formerly the Gold Coast colony, granted independence from Britain; European Economic Community established under the Rome Treaties. **April:** announcement to discontinue National Service after 1960; Labour opposed planned hydrogen bomb testing. **May:** first British hydrogen bomb test. **September:** *Wolfenden Report on Prostitution and Homosexuality.*

Arts: 'short' skirts become fashionable. **TV, theatre, film:** Lindsay Anderson, *Every Day Except Christmas*; Terence Fisher, *The Curse of Frankenstein*; David Lean, *The Bridge on the River Kwai*; John Osborne, *The Entertainer.* **Visual:** Lawrence Alloway, 'The Arts and the Mass Media'; Victor Pasmore, *Relief Construction in White and Black, Maroon and Ochre.* **Musical:** the skiffle craze reaches its peak; Tommy Steele's 'Singing the Blues' reaches no. 1 in the charts; Lonnie Donegan plays a two-week run at the London Palladium; *Oh Boy!* TV Show; live edition of the teenage music show *Six-Five Special* from the 2-Is coffee bar in Soho. **Written:** John Braine, *Room at the Top*; Richard Hoggart, *The Uses of Literacy*; Wolf Mankowitz, *Bongo Express*; Tom Maschler (ed.), *Declaration.*

---1958---

SOCIETY: property boom begins, and the first high-rise flats appear in London; 'race' riots in Notting Hill, London; television begins broadcasting nationwide; Conservative revival begins; 'affluence' widely discussed; Claudia Jones and Frances Ezzrecco set up the Coloured People's Progressive Association. **February:** Britain agrees to US missile bases; CND established with Earl Russell as President. **March:** *West Indies Gazette* begins publication. **April:** first CND protest march to Aldermaston. **July:** resumption of British nuclear testing announced; first life peers announced.

ARTS: TV, theatre, film: *Monitor*, TV arts programme presented by Huw Weldon; Samuel Beckett, *Endgame*; *Krapp's Last Tape*; Shelagh Delaney, *A Taste of Honey* debuts at the Stratford East Theatre; Harold Pinter, *The Birthday Party*; *Carry on Sergeant*; Terence Fisher, *Dracula*; Anthony Asquith, *Orders to Kill*. **Visual:** John Bratby, *Four Lambrettas and Three Portraits of Janet Churchman*; Eduardo Paolozzi, *Japanese War God*; **Musical:** Alma Cogan, 'She Loves to Sing' EP; beginning of Cliff Richard's career. **Written:** Kenneth Allsop, *The Angry Decade*; Alan Sillitoe, *Saturday Night and Sunday Morning*.

---1959---

SOCIETY: 'Tendency to deprave and corrupt' becomes the test of obscenity under the Obscene Publications Act; Britain's first motorway, the M1, opens; a new peak in consumer spending; the best summer of the century thus far; Macmillan becomes 'Supermac'; Caribbean Carnival at St Pancras Town Hall organized by *West Indies Gazette*. **May:** death of Kelso Cochrane, allegedly on race grounds. **October: General Election** returns the Conservatives with a majority of 100. **November:** UK among several European nations to sign up to the European Free Trade Association (EFTA).

ARTS: TV, theatre, film: Woodfall Films begin production; John Boulting, *I'm All Right Jack*; Basil Dearden, *Sapphire*; Karel Reisz, *We are the Lambeth Boys*; Tony Richardson, *Look Back in Anger*; John Arden, *Sergeant Musgrave's Dance*; Keith Waterhouse, *Billy Liar*; Arnold Wesker, *Roots*. **Visual:** *The New American Art* – an abstract expressionist exhibition – at the Tate Gallery, London. **Musical:** *Juke Box Jury* TV show; Billy Fury's first chart hit 'Maybe Tomorrow' reaches no. 18 in February; film version of *Expresso Bongo*. **Written:** Eustace Chesser, *Is Chastity Outmoded?*; Colin MacInnes, *Absolute Beginners*; Alan Sillitoe, *The Loneliness of the Long-Distance Runner*; Keith Waterhouse, *Billy Liar*; Vladimir Nabokov's *Lolita* (1955) published for the first time in Britain.

PART II
Pop Protest, Pop Arts

CHAPTER 4

Britain's Breakup

Willie Ross, dead loss

'The old British state is going down,' wrote Scottish nationalist and political commentator Tom Nairn in 1977. 'But, so far at least, it has been a slow foundering rather than the *Titianic*-type disaster so often predicted.'[1] Prompted by the rise of nationalist sentiment across the United Kingdom from the mid-1960s, *The Break-Up of Britain* was Nairn's attempt to explain why the stricken ship of state had stayed afloat so long, and why the prospect of secession had proven more popular than collective mutiny in the ranks. The ending of the colonial era, which decreased the mutual benefits of United Kingdom membership; the increasing intrusion of central government which accompanied postwar welfare; and the fading memory of collective wartime unity: all contributed to the feeling that the interests of the UK's constituent states might better be served by localizing political power. What might replace this system remained uncertain. The Northern Ireland referenda in 1973 and 1975 did not register any wish for change because they were boycotted by catholics; the Scottish and Welsh plebiscite defeats of 1979 were frustrated, partly due to political machinations at Westminster.[2] If nationalist allegiance was sufficient to register in the actions of a protesting voter, or even a bomber, it was insufficient to persuade the majority that their interests were best served by moving away from the institutions of the British state, and towards a more close-at-hand administration.

Local sensitivities across the United Kingdom were fuelled by economic change and government policy. Consumerism, liberalism and modernization brought new self-confidence; the 1973 oil crisis, the subsequent economic slump, the alarming escalation in prices and unemployment led to anger as well as frustration. Prime Minister Harold Wilson's (1916–95; Prime Minister 1964–70 and 1974–6) non-devolutionist regional policies seemed provocative too because local concerns and interests were often apparently dismissed. When, in November 1967, Winnie Ewing won the former safe Labour seat of Hamilton for the Scottish National Party (SNP) the Government's loss could not be so easily dismissed. In England, where no such nationalist movement existed, dissatisfaction at economic downturn and political volatility was displayed rather as anti-immigration feeling, in public demonstrations, in private speech. Among certain sections of the population Enoch Powell now became less a disgraced MP with unacceptable views than a symbolic figurehead, the mention of whose name was enough to strike a political pose, to describe a critical politics of race and nationhood.

Even before this the fabric of postwar society, which had often been patched

Illustration 4 The search for a model community: Seafar residential estate, Cumbernauld, Scotland, 1967

up through the first full decade of the postwar age, began to appear threadbare. One wear point showed up especially clearly: the chaffing constraints of class deference and 'the establishment'. The removal of these restrictions made it easier and more acceptable to voice certain discontents; in this respect the satire movement of the early 1960s licensed new thoughts from the new society. As television audiences rose dramatically – up to thirteen million sets were in use by the middle of the decade – in November 1962 the BBC launched a Saturday night current affairs sketch show which became one of its best remembered programmes. One teenager of the time recalls the show's impact. 'I was barely 14 years old when *That Was The Week That Was* began, but my parents allowed me to stay up to watch it. I was too young to understand the jokes in detail, but I remember the tremendous sense of excitement each week as the programme began – who would be the targets of the satire this week? I don't remember my parents being shocked, but they were sometimes surprised at just how daring the programme could be.'[3] A more serious expression of willingness to confront contemporary issues was Jeremy Sandford's (1930–2003) television play *Cathy Come Home* (Ken Loach, 1966), which addressed the continuing problem of homelessness. Less often discussed than other aspects of British social life in the 1960s and 1970s, poverty was a persistent preoccupation among researchers and journalists, and a subject of public concern, as shown by the formation of charities like the housing pressure group Shelter (1966) and the Child Poverty Action Group (1965). Two sociologists, Brian Abel-Smith and Peter Townsend, 'rediscovered' poverty with the publication of *The Poor and the Poorest* (1965). It was this study which helped establish that the most appropriate measure of poverty was relative rather than absolute within the new expectations of welfare society, and that 'quantitatively the problem of poverty among children is more than two-thirds the size of poverty among the aged.'[4] Shockingly in an age that seemed to have conquered want, three million from a population of around fifty-two million lived below the minimum standard in early 1960s' Britain.

Poverty, homelessness and housing were among the policy issues where national and local interests did coincide, where there was a willingness to pursue common goals. Twenty years after the war there were substantial improvements in the housing stock, and a new enthusiasm for public building programmes. More, if not always better, private and local authority housing was built, yet in the rented sector protective regulations for tenants were still poorly enforced. It was not until 1965 that landlords' abuse of the existing rules was controlled by the Rent Act (1965); nor were fair rents for subsidized housing properly set in place until the Housing Finance Act (1972). Consequently the elderly and the poor as well as tenants in the private sector of the housing market had little protection against overcrowding and insanitary conditions. It was these conditions which caught the attention of the new campaigning, investigative media, especially television and newspapers. Hence *The Times*' interest to establish housing as a vital issue within the public sphere; likewise reporting on the launch of Shelter in 1966 the *London Illustrated News* described why adequate accommodation was so urgently needed in cities such as London, Glasgow, Birmingham and Liverpool. 'Three million families in Britain today live in slums, near slums or in overcrowded conditions . . . The strain imposed on a family washing, dressing, eating, sleeping, and playing in one room may lead to it breaking up and to crime and juvenile delinquency.'[5]

Public housing sector building and slum demolition programmes were actively promoted in Scotland to prevent such ills. In the early 1960s, Glasgow's Housing Committee Convenor, David Gibson, was convinced high blocks in the modernist style were the best solution to shortages and insanitary conditions and began a building programme across the city. Meanwhile, between 1964 and 1966, Dundee saw the construction of its Ardler multi-storey complex: six, seventeen-storey slab tower blocks, each block consisting of 300 dwellings.[6] The solution itself turned to troublesome blight: as maintenance failed, walls dampened and heating ceased; as communities collapsed, residents were left in isolated, vandalized properties; as planning flaws came to light the distress of a lift too small for stretcher or, worse still, coffin became horribly, laughably real.

On irrefutably common causes such as poverty reduction or slum eradication, the 1960s Labour Governments found it easier to downplay national issues; social divisions were not confined within national borders, they argued, but they did require urgent attention. Where common interests were less obvious, for example in programmes of investment and modernization, this approach became more divisive: the national collective good did not always favour local requirements; the question of Home Rule was entirely sidestepped. Regional investment, communications systems and new facilities were nevertheless to be promoted by the Scottish Office and by the newly established Highlands and Islands Development Board. As the Premiership of Harold Wilson progressed, it became increasingly clear that new businesses such as electronics, which employed 30,000 people in Scotland in 1969, would be inadequate replacement for heavy industry. To prop up the older ways of life there was heavy state investment in Scottish manufacturing and agriculture: 9.3 per cent of the British labour force was in receipt of 15 per cent of all subsidies.[7] Moreover in the second half of 1966 an economic crisis, which forced deflationary measures and a six-month wages freeze, checked implementation of the reform-minded *Plan for Scotland* (1966). Nor were all districts of Scotland equally convinced by the latest government plans. On a visit to Orkney in 1967, Secretary of State for Scotland (1964–70 and 1974–6) William Ross, who oversaw the institution of the Highlands and Islands Development Board, as well as substantial increases in public aid and expenditure from central government, was not warmly greeted. Locals especially resented their possible incorporation into the Highlands and Islands Development Authority as well as the prospect of a merged police service incorporating Shetland and Caithness. Responsibility was never publicly claimed for the publication of a pamphlet by the Independent Orkney Party, which called for the return of the Islands to Norway and Denmark on the grounds that they had belonged there until 1468. Yet the St Andrew's Cross at half mast, the minister hung in effigy from a lamp-post, and the cries of 'Willie Ross – Dead Loss' were clear indication that beneath their rough good humour some felt local interests had been marginalized. Within two months the newly formed Orkney branch of the Scottish National Party had over 200 members.[8]

Forty-six Scottish Labour MPs were returned at the March 1966 election; the peak of support for the Scottish National Party came in February and October

1974 when respectively seven and then eleven party MPs were elected. North Sea oil, discovered in the meantime, may not have been responsible for this change of mood, but assisted in the temporary conversion of cultural pride into protest vote. Politics and locality were connected in the career of John McGrath (1935–2002), who adopted Scotland as his home although he was born to Irish Catholic parents in Liverpool, and whose play *The Cheviot, the Stag and the Black, Black Oil* (1973) catches the traditions and values of Scottish life as well as the mood of the time. Based around a Scottish ceilidh, the play tells of Scotland's land exploitation from the time of the Highland Clearances to the oil boom. In 1973 McGrath's cooperatively organized 7:84 (Scotland) Theatre Company took the production on tour from Edinburgh to Aberdeen, through many parts of southern Scotland and through seven crofting counties, travelling 17,000 miles in all.[9] Journalist Troy Kennedy Martin witnessed one performance. 'The entire population of Kyle had turned up at the hall to see the latest show, which was to include fiddle-playing and songs as well as a ceilidh . . . They sat patiently through the political bits, heads bowed as the actors denounced, years ahead of their time, the dangers inherent in globalization. Then the play continued . . .'[10] McGrath's intention was to reflect on working-class realities and history in front of audiences from the same background: village destruction and pollution, health and safety, the impossibly high cost of post oil-boom Aberdeen housing: all were among his subjects. In its concern with social conditions and working-class lives, though not in its form, *The Cheviot* is not so far removed from Jeremy Sandford's *Cathy Come Home*, and indeed it was filmed for BBC television in 1974. The message which resonated with audiences was that the oil barons of the late twentieth century were a far greater threat than the land barons of the early nineteenth century.

One of McGrath's achievements was the incorporation of Scottish performance traditions into his theatre even as it warned of the dangers of 'globalization'. His disquiet reflected a wider fear that local communal values kept alive in neighbourhood, regional or national traditions would be diminished in the movement towards post-industrial society; that consumer goods and mass media would regularized landscape and thinking.[11] In this view the loss of industrial labour – 10,000 jobs disappeared per year 1965–75 – signalled the decline of earlier communal traditions and work patterns. Likewise religious practice as registered in church attendance or divorce figures – a 400 per cent increase in the number of divorces 1961–74 – shifted towards the norm for England and Wales. Despite such worries the distinctiveness of local culture and community was not erased. The concern with Orkney fishing facilities did not lessen, though tourism increasingly became a rival source of income. The acerbic, sceptical, anti-authoritarian and adversity-hardened humour of Glasgow remained undiminished. 'Stopping by a pub to ask a local man to mind his load a carter is told, "My man, do you realize I'm a Bailie [magistrate] of the City of Glasgow". "Aye, okay, but surely to God I can trust you wi' my horse." ' The intellectual and social tradition of left-wing thinking rooted powerfully in Scotland's past thrived not least in the polemical writings of Tom Nairn, whose *The Break-up of Britain* reflected a revised, realistic aspiration to national self-determination.

The discovery of oil resources in what became known as the Piper field 100 miles east of Wick highlighted this conflict of local and global interest in

Scotland.[12] The viability of such fields was assisted by the economic crisis of 1973 – following an Arab boycott after the Yom Kippur War, oil prices quadrupled – but the knock-on economic effects of the crisis were at the same time felt world-wide, not least in Scotland. New fields became economically viable, but national economies began to falter, suffering increased prices and unemployment. These conditions stressed also the varied difficulties Scotland faced: the long-term loss of skilled jobs and local employers; the limits on control of local affairs; the persistence and renewal of industrial conflict, as in the reorganization of Clyde shipbuilding which was also under way in the early 1970s.[13] The ironic contrast between nearby wealth on the one hand, and low wages or unemployment among the Scottish population on the other, not surprisingly produced a new surge of local feeling and national Scottish sentiment.

Labour's hold on power following the two elections of 1974 was less and less secure. Struggling to maintain authority and a grasp on spiralling economic deterioration, trade-offs with allies became a necessity; with the rise in support for the Scottish National Party in the same elections one political issue that now had to be addressed was devolution. In 1978 Parliament finally passed a Bill for Scotland and Wales. Success would be hard-won though, as it included the proviso of 40 per cent support from the total Scottish electorate. In the event the referendum, on 1 March 1979, saw 33 per cent vote 'Yes', 31 per cent vote 'No' and 36 per cent abstain, and a failure to clearly endorse the policy. The rural districts of the Borders or Orkney and Shetland, despite some support for the SNP, remained largely sceptical of centralized political control, either from Lowland Scotland or from London. In some quarters the defeat was greeted with bitter disappointment, '. . . in the office [of the *Scotsman* newspaper], the sense of failure was suffocating,' wrote Neal Ascherson.[14] Yet he also records the mood of his flatmate:

> . . . Tom [Nairn] was astonishingly cheerful. He pointed out that where the working class had voted, they had voted for the assembly: this was very clearly in evidence from people who had been inside the counts at local level. It was the middle class who had ratted. And this also ensured that when self-government did come, it would be in a more radical form, not merely a painless removal of the Establishment into a new building.[15]

Pragmatic regional and community concerns for industry, facilities and quality of life were not easily pushed aside by generalized national sentiment; as yet neither global economic interests nor political nationalism was able convincingly to answer the needs of local populations.

How free is free Derry?

Sitting at home one spring evening in 1976, Dervla Murphy was gripped by a despair darker than that among Neal Ascherson and his fellow-journalists, her mood a reflection of the intricate, entrenched and contradictory claims to political power and territory in Northern Ireland. As she listened to a heated wireless discussion between two particularly 'bone-headed' politicians from the North, a thought formed. 'Why don't the Brits get out and let them all slaughter each other if that's how they feel? There's nothing to choose between them. Why did we ever long for a united Ireland?'[16] Murphy subsequently travelled around Northern Ireland in an attempt to understand the Province and recounted the journey in *A Place Apart* (1978). In the event there were no simple explanations, yet there were many opportunities to register the paradox of place, the contradictions of disputed history and locality, beginning with 'Derry'.[17]

'Derry' to descendants of the old Gaelic and Catholic natives is 'Londonderry' among descendants of seventeenth-century English and Scottish settlers. As Murphy notes, in protestant memory Londonderry is home to the last walled city built in Europe, which dates from 1614, and which subsequently became the site of two famously resisted sieges in 1649 and 1688–9. Catholic memory, by contrast, recalls the Derry of the civil rights march on 5 October 1968, which turned to violent confrontation with the Royal Ulster Constabulary, and the events of 30 January 1972, when British soldiers killed 13 demonstrators. Collective occupation and belief had nevertheless built a common heritage, even if irreconcilable claims to territory were now heard, '. . . one quickly becomes aware of Derry as a city where . . . strands within Irish Christianity have in some subtle way become interwoven'.[18] In the late 1960s the city drew world attention as a result of the protests against its housing policies. Allocation of a house meant enfranchisement. City authorities therefore sought to maintain the long-established *status quo* of protestant control by allocating families to districts where the overall electoral balance could not be shifted. With unemployment around ten per cent in 1966 and a population expansion rate of 21.2 per 1000 – four times higher than in England and Wales – the problem of adequate living conditions was worsening. The city seemed everything the Civil Rights movement wanted to change.[19] Centre to some of the most violent confrontations of the late 1960s and early 1970s, by the time Murphy arrived Derry looked battered and mutilated. The three years to 1974 saw the destruction or severe damage of 5200 houses, as well as of 124 business premises such as offices and shops; and claims made to the government amounting to £30 million for damages and injury.[20] As she explored it in 1976, the author was struck by the city's attractive setting and by its squalid environs:

> Slowly cycling into the Bogside I saw a huge proud notice: YOU ARE NOW ENTERING FREE DERRY . . . Many new rows of houses or blocks of flats already look irreparably neglected or vandalized and much black paint has been thrown at their walls – sometimes to deface large, carefully painted tricolours . . . painted in large letters across the front wall of the Bogside Inn – the main Provo pub – are the words INFORMERS WILL BE KILLED. For a moment I took this casually, just as another bit of swaggering adolescent graffiti. Then, with a chilly feeling inside, I realize that the slogan is nobody's sick joke. It is a statement of fact. How free is Free Derry?[21]

In the early 1960s Prime Minister Terence O'Neill's (1914–90; Prime Minister 1963–9) answer to this question was that Londonderry and Northern Ireland might be released from the constrictions of history and sectarian faction by modern development and, despite his unionist pedigree, by better relations with the Republic. Efforts to improve employment and infrastructure meant seven industries had set up in the town by the mid-1960s, Du Pont having already arrived in 1960 at the Maydown industrial estate; high flats were built on Rossville Street in 1966 to ease the housing crisis with allocation to catholic families. Central Government also provided regional assistance: Northern Ireland's first 'New Town' (1965), Craigavon – named after the first prime minister of Northern Ireland – was created from the union of Lurgan and Portadown. There was support too for industry including the failing Belfast shipyards, and encouragement for new investment. In the opinion of one observer, J. C. Beckett, it seemed possible, though not likely, that O'Neillism might succeed in its plan for gradual reform. That possibility was quickly destroyed by changes in the political situation towards the end of 1968, especially 'the early renewal of violent agitation, the growth of sectarianism, the lack of agreement within the Unionist Party'.[22] Following the confrontations of October 1968, the People's Democracy march from Belfast to Derry in January 1969, and the widespread violence from 12 August 1969, when arson attacks destroyed thousands of mainly catholic houses leaving many families homeless, British troops were sent into Northern Ireland. Their stated intention was to restore and maintain order.

The arrival of British troops sharpened tensions within Northern Irish society. Both sides were now trapped in a duel over a shared terrain. Both sides aggressively patrolled the boundary of their social and geographical territories, which despite competing claims were nevertheless inextricably, tragically bound. In 1968 the rise of the Northern Ireland Civil Rights Association (NICRA) alarmed some protestants. Their fears found voice in the words and actions of the Reverend Ian Paisley's (b.1926) particular blend of loyalism and faith: in 1969 Paisley stood against Terence O'Neill in the Bannside, North Antrim constituency taking 24 per cent of the vote compared to the Prime Minister's 29 per cent. Shortly after O'Neill resigned.[23] As a young protestant minister, R. G. Crawford noted the particularities of Northern Irish loyalist place. In the Shankill Road district of Belfast, where he had earlier held his first assistantship, Crawford noted that the South, and England, were equally objects of deep suspicion. In County Armagh he immediately recognized the familiar Ulster sentiment of 'no change' when a prominent church expressed strong views on where the church pulpit should be situated. 'Put the Irish way, he "didn't mind where it was as long as it was in the centre" '.[24]

As the Government of Ireland Act (1920) gave legal expression to the political and territory oppositions of the day, so it shaped ethnicities and outlook: protestant evangelicalism became 'the core of ethnic identity, the guarantor of the ethnic group', while catholic belief was 'expressed functionally through a rejection of, and abstention from, the unionist regime'.[25] Individuals were as contested as places. In the early 1960s St Patrick's Day, 17 March, was dropped as a state-sanctioned school holiday in Northern Ireland, though there were still ecumenical gestures such as an invitation for the Archbishop of Canterbury to visit Downpatrick. In 1974 the Falls Road, Belfast held a St Patrick's Day Parade; in 1977, after a break of twenty-five years, the Parade was revived too in Londonderry.[26]

Moods of reconciliation and opposition were absorbed into the figure of St Patrick in the 1960s and 1970s, but as tempers hardened and violence worsened, fractures and cracks grew visibly in Northern Irish society. After the arrival of British troops in August 1969 the most divisive turning point was the Derry killings ('bloody Sunday') in January 1972, which was quickly followed by direct rule from Westminster from 1 April 1972, and the appointment of William Whitelaw as Secretary of State for Northern Ireland (1972–3). The withdrawal of power from Stormont regional Parliament was followed by increased sectarian violence, including murder, by the establishment of 'no-go' districts, and by terrorist bombings in England. At the same time loyalist authority was diminished; the principle of equal access to power was established; employment practices were revised into the Fair Employment Act (1976); university education was expanded to allow the possibility of catholic employment and a greater share in Northern Irish society.

While no immediate conflict resolution seemed possible, non-sectarian activities such as public health campaigns gradually provided a new structure for contact between formerly segregated factions.[27] In the ten or so years after the flare-up of the Northern Ireland conflict, slower processes of change also began. Among the most important was the formation of the Housing Executive in May 1971, which was intended to take housing decisions away from the politically charged atmosphere of local government and to relocate them under the professional control of a more neutral body. The urgency of this requirement was underlined by the knowledge that 72 per cent of protestant homes had hot water, fixed bath or shower, or inside WC, but only 63 per cent of catholic households. While such conditions persisted it was impossible to overcome sectarian division. Hence even a non-sectarian peace movement, the Peace People, which was begun in 1976 when a gunman's car struck and killed three children, which briefly attracted tens of thousands of supporters, and which won for its West Belfast founders the Nobel Peace Prize before it collapsed, could not bring lasting reconciliation.[28] The 1973 referendum, boycotted by catholics, served only to show protestants were overwhelmingly in favour of Northern Ireland remaining a part of the UK rather than a part of the Republic of Ireland: 57.5 per cent of the electorate (591,820) as opposed to 0.6 per cent (6463).[29]

The complex weave of interconnections between territory and identity in Northern Ireland was displayed in arguments over political boundaries, housing disputes and conflicting claims to the past. As in Derry/Londonderry, it was apparent too in placenames. The province itself is one of four within Ireland. Six of Ulster's nine counties are contained within the modern political unit of Northern Ireland – Down, Armagh, Antrim, Derry, Fermanagh and Tyrone. A further three, Donegal, Cavan and Monaghan, are in the Republic of Ireland. A further dispute arose during the local government reorganization that took place throughout the United Kingdom in the early 1970s, which shifted ancient boundaries, consolidated administrative districts and abandoned the official use of many local placenames. In Northern Ireland 26 districts were put in place in the six counties: Moyle, Ballymena and Newtownabbey were among the districts into which Antrim was split. Counties subdivided traditionally into Parishes and then into Townlands. First recorded in the twelfth century, though long predating

Anglo-Norman times, the largest Townland was Slievedoo, Co Tyrone which covered 1840 hectares; the smallest by contrast was Acre McCricket in Co Down, at 1.6 hectares. It was these Townland names which came under threat of admin-istrative reorganization. 'Myroe, Crindle, Culmore, Ballyhenrey, Ballycarton, Glebe, Oughtymoyle, Ballymultimber, Ballyscullion, Drumavally, Lenamore, Clooney, Aughil, Ballymaclarey, Benone, Umbra, Downhill, Dunboe, Liffock, Exorna, Dartness, Articlave, Blakes Lower, Lower Quilley, Upper Magherawee, Drumaquill and Castletoory.'[30] The politics of place entered even into ancient, native knowledge. While these local names were not erased entirely, their survival was now in doubt, ensured only by associations with family and neighbourhood history, by personal life experience and collective memory.

The Sleeping Lord

At the end of his life distinguished Anglo-Welsh artist and poet David Jones (1895–1974) turned too to the re-naming and re-imagining of his nation in his long poem *The Sleeping Lord* (1974). Here technology and material advance draw vitality from the land, humanity from the people; ancient language and culture is pitted against the ephemera and instability of modern life; extinction competes with the possibility of resurrection. 'Does the land wait the sleeping lord/or is the wasted land/that very lord who sleeps?'[31] Tom Nairn's dissection of Britain viewed Wales as a nation divided too: a secondary centre of the European indus-trial revolution, underdeveloped, depopulated, culturally oppressed as well as social fragmented. Likewise the Welsh nationalist movement centred on 'a battle for the defence and revival of rural-based community and traditional identity – an identity evoked overwhelmingly by literary and musical culture, and having as its mainspring the language question'.[32]

Political and poetic scrutiny both centred on language as a symbol of national development and revival; the renewal of Welsh nationalist feeling connected cultural to secessionist self-definition. The drop in Welsh language use was now alarming; the Tryweryn incident continued to rankle as an indication of outside indifference; the number of communities where 80 per cent of the population spoke the language fell from 279 in 1961 to 66 in 1981.[33] Early on indifference gave way to the impassioned appeal of writer and Welsh political activist Saunders Lewis (1893–1985) in 1962 as he called for national renewal through language revival. The fate of the language now became the fate of the nation.[34] From this appeal came Cymdeithas yr Iaith Gymraeg (the Welsh Language Society); the sit-down protests and tax form boycotts for equal language rights; the blanked out English language placenames on Welsh road signs. Eventually the Welsh Language Act (1967) granted equal legal status to both languages, and with offi-cial standing came new social status, the thought of better national fortunes.

In the mid-1960s, at the same time as local Welsh feeling became a force in British politics, industrial and economic prospects remained hopeful. Steel and tinplate production was strengthened by the development of Shotton and Ebbw Vale as well as the great Llanwern plant, completed in 1962; the Welsh consumer boom thrived on profits from industry. Yet the signals remained mixed as both agriculture and the North Wales slate industry were in decline: as new methods in farming made the industry less dependent on labour intensive tasks numbers working on the land fell from 33,385 (8.2 per cent) in 1951 to 11,257 (4.5 per cent) in 1971; likewise the number of farms fell from 40,000 (1945) to 20,000 (1971).[35] The number of men in slate production, meanwhile, fell steadily from more than seven and half thousand in 1939 to less than a thousand by 1972, not least because in 1969 and 1970 two major quarries, the Dinorwic and the Dorothea, were closed down.[36] The Labour government handled dramatic change in the mining industry tactlessly. Extensive pit closures in 1958 were a severe blow to the British industry as a whole while in Wales initial hope for better prospects when Labour was elected in 1964 was short-lived. Refusal to promote the industry from 1966 in particular was viewed as the rejection of a long, honourable alliance between coal and the Labour movement. With planned production cuts came pit closure and transfer, loss of skills and established working practices, and the gradual disintegration of social welfare structures as well as community support systems. 'You get used to a colliery,' said one man, 'you know which parts are dangerous and what to look out for, you can feel when something is going to happen. At Cefn Coed it was strange, I didn't know anything.' Another miner was made redundant twice within two years, at Nine Mile Point where he had worked for twenty-five years, and again at Risca. 'After being a skilled worker all those years and earning a wage, to work outside your mining skills means nothing – it's only labouring jobs offered . . . I received my first pay from Switchgear which amounted to £10 16s. 0d. after stoppages – this amount to keep my family, I could get more if I was unemployed.'[37] As in Scotland, voters switched when a living wage and a secure future could not be guaranteed by old alliances. In this light, the historic election of writer and Welsh political activist Gwynfor Evans (1912–2005), as the first Plaid Cymru candidate to be successfully elected as a Member of Parliament, at Carmarthen in July 1966, was a vote of no confidence in Labour as well as a statement of nationalist intent. Yet its effect was to embolden Welsh language and nationalist activists as further strong shows of support, though not outright victory, followed for Plaid Cymru in Rhondda West (1967) and Caerffili (1968).

Though not necessarily translated into political activism, Welsh national feeling grew through these years as it focused on territorial rights and cultural heritage. With decreasing employment on the land as well as depopulating out-migration came large numbers of English newcomers; with widespread property purchases came large numbers of English-only speakers whose presence disrupted former Welsh-speaking communities. The coastal counties of Caernarfonshire, Denbighshire, Merionethshire and Cardiganshire were among the most affected, particularly in the north-east seaside districts and Anglesey.[38] New patterns of home ownership, car ownership and mobility also began to change Welsh society from the early 1960s. The number of licensed cars went up by more than 576,000 over the decade; the number of new homes being built per year hit a record high of 19,524 in 1965.[39] Shopping became a less intimate, communal activity as self-service stores, supermarkets and hire purchase all altered patterns of social interaction as well as attitudes towards money. In other respects Welsh society remained stable. Extended families continued to exert a powerful force, as in Swansea where one 1965 study showed that 70 per cent of married sons and 80 per cent of married daughters lived in close proximity to their parents, while more than half of all daughters had seen their mothers in the previous twenty-four hours. Similarly the average age of marriage remained low, 22 in 1975.[40] Asking Welsh women about their experiences of the 1960s, one researcher found the common response was 'Well, it wasn't swinging around here. Perhaps in London.'[41]

Central government policy did on occasions cause specifically political resentment, even if temporarily. In the case of the Aberfan disaster in 1966 for example, when a huge slag heap collapsed, engulfing a school, killing 116 children and 28 adults, local opinion was that the National Coal Board had not managed the site properly. Following a special Tribunal however, the then Chairman was allowed to remain in post. Worse still George Thomas, Secretary of State for Wales (1968–70), announced that rather than taxpayer or NCB money, funds from the charity set up to assist families connected to the disaster would be used to pay for the removal of the remaining tips. Thomas was representative too of anti-nationalist opinion and policy within the Labour government at this time. Thus while there was substantial support within Wales for the elaborate investiture ceremony of Prince Charles (b.1948) as Prince of Wales, which took place on 1 July 1969, the event also highlighted differences between the non-secessionist mainstream and the moderate as well as more extreme pro-Welsh groups: Plaid Cymru, Cymdeithas yr Iaith Gymraeg, as well as the amateurish but violent protesters of Mudiad Amddiffyn Cymru (the Welsh Defence Movement). The intense opposition aroused by the investiture in some quarters became evident when two members of this group were killed by a premature bomb explosion at Abergele while apparently preparing an attack.[42]

Regional development policy was also a continuing cause of discontent. South Wales drew most industrial investment, the north-east of the country was a lesser beneficiary, central districts struggled with poor communications, gradual decline in the wool industry, falling birth rates and the continual drain of out-migration. The largest town in the mid-Wales district, Aberystwyth, had a population of 10,690 in 1971, while the overall population of mid-Wales had fallen from 278,000 in 1871 to 204,000 in 1971.[43] In 1977 the Development Board for Rural Wales was established by the Development of Rural Wales Act (1976), but it was a predecessor organization, the Mid-Wales Development Corporation, which had overseen the planning of Newtown as a central hub in the district and as a means to revive its fortunes. Located 32 miles (51km) from Shrewsbury, it did achieve some success, though early on facilities for sports or recreation were sparse. Critics nevertheless accused successive governments of inadequate commitment to mid-Wales:

It is questionable whether so small a town [as Newtown] is, in the long term, socially satisfactory. We believe that the government should be far more imaginative and embark on a much more ambitious programme, designating a group of new towns with target populations in the region of 30,000 to 40,000. This would enable the provision of much more comprehensive facilities for the people and, providing the towns were located in reasonably close proximity, major undertakings such as a sports arena and arts centre could be shared.[44]

During the unstable economic times from 1973 onwards, though, other priorities seemed more pressing.

The fate of British Steel, which had already suffered a dramatic fall in demand, and which effectively collapsed between 1973 and 1975, illustrates the economic and political crisis of the mid-1970s. Coal, by contrast, appeared more competitive as oil prices rose and government increased funding. Yet miners and other trade unionists, for example in the Glasgow shipyards, continued to argue for higher wages to keep up with or exceed dramatic rises in inflation, to assist in their crusade for greater equality within British society. As the South Wales Area President of the National Union of Mineworkers put it. 'Why should men who risk their lives through injuries and disease, who work physically hard, who produce a commodity which is essential to British industry not be paid accordingly? And if the answer is that society cannot afford it, then my reply is that society must be changed so that it can afford it.'[45] But society was not changed. A series of confrontational, nationwide pay strikes between 1972 and 1974, largely a response to the economic instability of the moment, established the miners as the nation's highest earners. Within a year they had fallen back to eighteenth place as ever increasing wages and falling productivity squandered potential gain.

Yet Wales' social fabric was not entirely rent even in the crisis years of the mid-1970s. Peter Townsend's pioneering *Poverty in the United Kingdom* (1979) illustrates this by recounting the life and circumstances of 76-year-old Mr Morgan. A miner for twenty years, he was forced to retire from the industry after an injury, but without any compensation or pension, he then went on to work as a foreman in a company that built luxury coaches, and eventually retired at the age of 72. While his life in retirement did not allow a summer holiday, he remained energetic and kept in close contact with his married son and daughter who lived nearby, often having daily meals with them. By pooling income Mr Morgan and his wife lived in comfortable retirement, although their six-roomed terrace house only had a small backyard and 'there was a foul smell sometimes from a neighbouring oil works' depending on the direction of the wind.[46] Mr Morgan seems not to have been overly bothered by such inconvenience.

It seems unlikely in any case that he would have believed a better life might come from a devolved Wales. When, on St David's Day 1979, the referendum on Welsh devolution finally took place, distaste for the British political system was not strong enough to provoke complaint among a significant section of the population: on a turnout of 58.3 per cent of the electorate a majority of four to one was against the proposal. As in Scotland, devotees of the national cause were dismayed at the result. Historian Gwyn A. Williams, writing in the early 1980s, for one. 'The Welsh electorate in 1979 wrote *finis* to nearly two hundred years of Welsh history. They rejected the political traditions to which the modern Welsh had committed themselves. They declared bankrupt the political creeds which the modern Welsh had embraced. They may in the process have warranted the death of Wales itself.'[47] Prospects looked all the more bleak because as a small nation Wales was dependent on British, European and worldwide conditions beyond its control.

'Greensleeves' at half-tempo

Welsh, Irish and Scottish national sentiment expressed itself in the explicit call for political autonomy, in the requirement for imaginative self-expression unfettered by the external controls of the British state. England meanwhile, demographically, politically and economically at the heart of the United Kingdom, had no such possibility. Nevertheless, subject to the same cycle of consumerist expansion and post-oil crisis collapse, and in the face of political as well as artistic redefinitions elsewhere, the largest nation within the United Kingdom did lay claim to territorial sovereignty, expressing it indirectly through the extended, angry debate on immigration. The rise and fall of the immigration debate, and most particularly of the National Front, uncannily matches that of other nationalist movements at the time, beginning explosively in the late 1960s, becoming a significant political force during the mid-1970s and collapsing by the end of the decade. England's resurgent nationalist movement fought over the territory staked out by Conservative MP, distinguished scholar and soldier, Enoch Powell (1912–98) in his notorious 'Rivers of Blood' speech on 21 April 1968, which called for immigrant repatriation, and which had the much wider effect of sanctioning anti-immigrant feeling. Powell's sentiments found immediate support among London's dockworkers, after he was sacked from the Shadow Cabinet on 23 April for example, when two thousand staged a walk-out in protest.[48] Hostility towards immigrants and minorities now became more open in other parts of the country, too, including such major urban centres as Birmingham and Manchester. While neither English pride of place nor other nationalist movements within the United Kingdom were necessarily allied to racist sentiment, the effect of Powell's comments, whatever his intention, was to hitch the two together in acrimonious marriage for a decade or more.

Regret at the passing of the industrial age, of older farming and country ways of living, was a powerful sentiment at this moment too, expressed in a non-political territorialism that gave loyalty to particular places and ways of life. Writing in 1979, poet Ted Hughes (1930–98) was acutely aware of changes in both the country and the city as he observed the landscapes of industrial Yorkshire, west of Halifax, in the Calder Valley. 'Throughout my lifetime, since 1930,' he wrote, 'I have watched the mills of the region and their attendant chapels die. Within the last fifteen years the end has come. They are now virtually dead and the population of the valley and the hillsides, so rooted for so long, is changing rapidly.'[49] Likewise another poet, Roy Fisher, provided an elegy to the fading urban landscapes of the industrial Midlands in *City* (1961). 'Brick-dust in sunlight. That is what I see now in the city, a dry epic-flavour, whose air is human breath. A place of walls made straight with plumbline and trowel, to desiccate and crumble in the sun and smoke. Blistered points on cisterns and girders, cracking to show the paint . . . Wharves, the oldest parts of factories, tarred gable ends rearing to take the sun over lower roofs. Soot, sunlight, brick-dust; and the breath that tastes of them.'[50] As MP for a Midlands constituency in Wolverhampton, Powell saw failure and loss in change, Hughes recognized its inevitability, Fisher's tribute to the physical traces of the past in Birmingham and North Staffordshire allowed the possibility of future renewal.

In the event the diverse immigrant populations of the English Midlands, from the Republic of Ireland, from Pakistan, would become remarkably assimilated into the native population. The 1981 census showed 36.6 per cent of babies born in the district were children of black, Asian, 'non-European' couples or mixed unions; 14.8 per cent of the million plus population in the Birmingham Metropolitan District were in households headed by a person of recent immigrant background.[51] Similarly Bedford, a small county town in a population of 70,000 around 1970, had nearly fifty nations among its population, including Italians, Indians, West Indians, Pakistanis, Poles, Yugoslavs, Germans, Latvians, Hungarians and Chinese.[52] Coexistence rather than active community, however, as yet remained the basis of their common life. Away from the Home Counties meanwhile, in the more pressured atmosphere of inner-city London, there was little possibility of neutral coexistence. Anti-immigration rhetoric was one response among the East London dockworkers; Joy Hendry's work as a health visitor in Hackney brought her to a different understanding of ethnic and cultural difference. Interpreting her role as broadly as possible, Hendry sought to promote 'optimum health' by ensuring that those on her patch had adequate access to housing, education and a stable income. As she dealt with families from different backgrounds she became aware of how issues related to health and to living conditions could be culturally inflected. She recalled particularly a series of visits to the house of a recently arrived Indian woman:

> I accept far more how people are than when I came. A lot of it has been just learning about different people's lifestyles . . . I remember going to a house and having to sit on the floor and being given glass after glass of a peculiar lime drink. I didn't know what the hell it was. I thought the house was incredible. It was completely disorganized. They couldn't speak English and I couldn't speak their dialect. We just sat and smiled at each other, drinking this lime juice. I used to go there quite often. The woman there was in a terrible state because in India she'd had help in the house. Somebody in a lower class had come in and done it for her . . . Then I introduced her to an Indian neighbour and she learned how to cope.[53]

In human connections and shifting attitudes such as these the possibility of a more cooperative multi-ethnic society began to slowly emerge; similarly, in response to the growth of the National Front from the end of the 1960s came the politicized youth movements of the late 1970s. In the Greater London Council elections of May 1977, the National Front reached the peak of its electoral success when the party took 17.4 per cent of the vote with strong support in the East London districts of Hackney, Bow and Poplar; on 30 April 1978 a Rock Against Racism/Anti-Nazi League carnival at Victoria Park in London drew an estimated audience of 80,000.[54]

Such developments within the major urban centres were one part of a longer cycle of change across the English regions which profoundly altered the social mix as well as the everyday feel of lived-in landscapes. In inner-city areas such as Hackney, demolition of older housing districts and replacement with low- or high-rise blocks continued, as in Clapton, where an area of five streets know as

The Island was demolished in 1970 to make way for the Borough Council's Landfield Estate. The houses of The Island were 'two up, two down' terraces with small yards or gardens and little decoration. While they were plainly built for working people, so that outside toilets and a front door onto the street were standard, the community, according to one former resident, was lively and self-sufficient. Carol Morris (b.1948) recalled the early 1960s. 'The music was mainly records but at Terry Jennings's parties they had a fellow with a banjo. It was fantastic, that kept the whole place alive . . . Terry Jennings used to go with the motorbike boys. There used to be ten or twelve motorbikes roaring up outside the house about midnight, nobody complained, they were all motorbike mad around there.'[55] While the Landfield estate of red brick houses and flats and Hackney Borough Council's housing policy made the move out of The Island relatively painless, more generally across London inner-city districts now divided into hazardous if gradually better regulated private, rented rooms; run-down council estates; poor working-class districts of mixed ethnic makeup; and better off owner occupier areas. The incoming middle classes engaged in refurbishment and 'gentrification' now gradually edged out the poorer inner city populations. Jonathan Raban observed the process around 1970, in a square where he lived on the border of Islington and Holloway:

> it was by no means a complete takeover; people still repaired old cars from front rooms along the square, and on the unreclaimed east side, the houses seemed to actually swell with the influx of the displaced and very poor . . . On the far side, the sunny side, of the square, these unluckier migrants could see a future of a sort; a future of Japanese lampshades, *House and Garden*, French baby cars, white paint, asparagus tips, Earl Grey tea and stripped pine stereo systems – the reward of success is the freedom to choose a style of elegant austerity.[56]

In Birmingham the growing immigrant population concentrated in the 'ring road' of late Victorian and Edwardian housing that was too new to be affected by slum clearance and of little interest to the middle-class population, who now began to commute from outside the central city districts. New town development away from Birmingham also arrived in the early 1960s with the establishment of Telford in 1962 and Redditch in 1963.[57] In the Garden City district of Wythenshawe, Manchester, where owner occupation was as low as five per cent in some areas, crime was relatively rare, but violence and vandalism were to grow through the 1970s. Light and service industries came under threat from financial takeovers and strikes. Popular entertainment thrived at the Golden Garter night-club, a converted bowling ball alley with a fifty foot bar and retractable stage which hosted cabaret singers, comics and TV personalities: Ronnie Corbett, Val Doonican, Ken Dodd, Harry Secombe, Cleo Laine and Johnny Dankworth, and Frankie Vaughan.[58]

While planned urban expansion such as the new town schemes eased the accommodation of new populations and the changing requirements of a partially affluent society, social and industrial relations were persistently troubled. In 1979 trade union membership accounted for 55 per cent of the employed workforce;

as inflation and strikes multiplied from the late 1960s, attempts to contain union power or limit pay increases were subject to constant dispute. The Trades Union Congress refused to cooperate with the implementation of the Industrial Relations Act (1971) for instance during the premiership of Edward Heath. In 1978, when James Callaghan was Prime Minister, efforts to limit wage rises to five per cent were similarly rejected by the unions, leading to extensive strike action among some of the poorest paid state employees, including refuse and hospital workers. While the trades union movement fought a rearguard action against loss of job security and earnings there were other indications of change in the industrial landscape that could not be resisted by strikes or protest marches. It was clear in 1969–70 for instance that the London docks had ceased to function as viable industry: overseas competition grew, post-colonial ties withered, the Port of Rotterdam expanded. All of this worked against the Port of London.[59] A glimpse into the future came with the redevelopment of St Katherine's Dock after 1969, which preserved its warehouses while creating a marina, shopping facilities, housing and a large hotel, but which did nothing to reduce the waiting list for council houses, 6000 names in 1973, in Tower Hamlets.[60] During the war Bristol had suffered bomb damage and consequently, in the postwar era, a housing shortage; by the early 1960s facilities and communications were much improved with the new motorway network that extended east to London, north to the Midlands, south to Devon and Cornwall. The British Aircraft Corporation factories at Filton helped the economic prospects; the inner city riots in the predominantly black district of St Pauls were to show up the tensions within the city in 1981.[61] By contrast, partly because several well advanced projects were cancelled by the Wilson administration following the election of 1964, Coventry's aircraft industry effectively ceased to exist between 1962 and 1967. The loss of 11,000 jobs followed. The pattern of development within the city was by now becoming a familiar one: after postwar boom and population expansion, by 1966 50 per cent of Coventry's employment was in metal working industries; by the early 1970s however the car industry too began to collapse with redundancies at Rolls Royce. In June 1980 46 per cent of all the city's 14 to 18 year-olds were in search of work.[62] Unusually, Teesside thrived as an industrial heartland through the 1970s: British Steel and ICI were leading employers in the area, and among the world's leading companies in their field. Yet here too while regional development policy assisted economic growth, domestic recession and pressure from international competition inevitably led to industrial collapse and job losses.[63]

Zeal for tower block development had fallen before four residents were killed in the partial collapse of a 27-storey building in Islington, Ronan Point, in 1968. Nevertheless, the decayed mass housing development, with its failed facilities and broken community, became an iconic symbol of the lost hopes for prosperity and a new society. Jonathan Raban described one such development:

> Four miles to the west of Southampton city centre, they built a housing estate called Millbrook, a vast, cheap storage unit for nearly 20,000 people. Laid out on a sloping plain, it has fifty acres of grassland at its centre, a great, useless, balding greenspace of sickly turf of . . . purely symbolic value. What one sees first are the tower blocks, twenty-four storeys high, of pre-stressed

concrete and glass, known, I am told, as 'slab block/scissors-type', should anyone order more. The roads are service roads; they loop purposelessly round the estate in broad curves that conform to no contours. There is no street life on them: an occasional pram pushed by a wind-blown mother, a motorbiking yobbo or two, a dismal row of parked Ford Anglias, an ice-cream van playing 'Greensleeves' at half-tempo, a mongrel snapping at its own tail.[64]

The downbeat mood of Millbrook was not the only musical expression of English life in the mid-1970s: in response to their troubling times the Sex Pistols composed a personal, passionate, chaotic and ironic anthem: 'God Save the Queen'.

CHAPTER 5

Limited Freedoms

Touch me if I want you

Women's situation in that most mythic of all decades, the 1960s, may be said to flicker between defeat and optimism, between the mixed fortunes of two power-ful fictional figures of the time: Jo, who is awkward, gauche, yet defiant, constantly struggling, with limited hope of success, towards self-realization; and Diana, who is glamorous and emancipated, yet still sometimes troubled, reaching for acceptance, security and fulfilment.[1] Neither picture captures the complexity of everyday social experience, nor the changeability or gradations of women's social roles as they are lived and imagined. Nevertheless, these two models hint at the range of human possibility in an age of newly liberated values as well as the continuing constraints of convention, at aspiration towards a new society expressed in popular music or state legislation, and at the harsher limits imposed by personal finance and national economy.

Surface and style were preoccupations of the age. Hyperbolic self-promotion competed with an idealistic critique of social mores, inherited models of behav-iour and traditionally established relations between women and men. With the idea that femininity and motherhood were learned and perpetuated roles came the belief an actor might rewrite or even improvise her character as she played it day by day. Fashionable designer and successful businesswoman Mary Quant (b.1934) used her clothes to strengthen these ideas for women of the baby boom generation. Libertarian, market-oriented and unconventional, Quant had set up shop in Chelsea and established her business in the mid 1950s, expanded to America by 1962 and received an MBE in recognition of her marketing skills and fashion verve by 1966. Interviewed in *The Guardian* in 1967, she described her cut-out, see-through dresses, her liking for 'good' pornography – 'erotic but pleasing' – and her designs for body stockings with plastic soled feet.[2] In conver-sation with journalist Alison Adburgham a revealing tension emerged between, on the one hand the still widely held feminine ideal of romantic love and domes-tic security, and on the other hand the prospect of social and sexual liberation. While Quant praised permissiveness, the right to creativity and eroticism, the constructive anarchy of the hippies, Adburgham stressed the new 'brutal' quality which had emerged in fashion as it had in architecture and theatre. While Quant also connected fashion to personal creativity and freedom, social commentator and fiction writer Angela Carter (1940–92), meditating on the possibilities of dress as play and as statement of intent, added that clothes could signal too a provocative misinterpretation of conventional social roles.[3] To illustrate how this had already happened Carter imagines a young woman dressing up for a party in

Illustration 5   The artist as celebrity: David Hockney, *c*.1969

the late 1960s who might wear a Mexican cotton dress, grandmother's button boots, mother's fox fur and a Faye Dunaway style beret as seen in *Bonnie and Clyde* (1967). By her mixing and matching, Carter argued, by wearing her clothes in unexpected ways and situations, the woman not only redefines the meaning of her garments, she freely tries out for size unconventional gender and class styles, traverses the traditional social and historical boundaries of conventional living, signals alternative aspirations. A Union Jack becomes a designer jacket; an op art painting an angular hairstyle; and a military uniform an emblem of peace.

Quant and Carter saw clothes could be liberating, creative, and a potential force for control and freedom, an expression, in Carter's words, of 'touch me if I want you'.[4] Yet while fashion styles became less elaborate and class-bound, and models such as Jean Shrimpton more 'girl-next-door', it remained difficult for women to control how they were seen. In his definitive article on 'swinging London', for instance, American journalist John Crosby stressed the 'deluge of pretty girls' in the capital who were 'young, appreciative, sharp-tongued, glowingly alive'.[5] Such alternative patterns of thought and models of behaviour as there were spanned the political spectrum and saw women gradually take a greater role in public life. In the Labour governments of 1964–70, for example, Barbara Castle (1910–2002; Secretary of State for Employment and Productivity, 1968–70; Secretary of State for Social Services, 1974–6) was a prominent figure. After working on development, transport and employment policy, she also attempted to reshape industrial relations as Minister for Employment and Productivity in 1969. Non-Parliamentary activists included Mary Whitehouse (1910–2001), teacher, leader of the right-wing moral rearmament movement and leading critic of permissive society. In 1965 she founded the National Viewers and Listeners Association, which campaigned to increase women's support for Christian values. The NVLA attacked the BBC and other broadcasters for promoting what the organization saw as low moral standards in broadcasting, and targeted public figures such as the liberal theologian John Robinson and the anti-censorship lawyer John Mortimer.

Others turned to women as a subject of both academic study and underground polemic. Sociologist Hannah Gavron (b.1936) argued that ideas of intensive childrearing, together with the relocation of working-class women in new housing, often in high-rise blocks, left them isolated and frustrated; Germaine Greer's (b.1939) counter-cultural critique saw the oppression of women as symptomatic of a corrupt society. Where Gavron advocated community provision, education and employment opportunities, Greer looked to the radical overthrow of political structures.[6] Liberal legislation also reflected the changing consensus of opinion within British society: the Abortion and Family Planning Acts (both 1967) allowed limited termination of pregnancy as well as contraceptive advice from local authorities; the Divorce Reform Act (1969) allowed legal separation on grounds of 'irredeemable breakdown'; the Equal Pay Act (1970) aimed to prevent unequal pay for equal work. While concern for family breakdown or fatherless families continued, legislation reflected a less prescriptive recognition of social reality, as in the discussion on the NHS Family Planning Bill (1967):

[Such] Marriages are founded not on mutual love but on a momentary and, perhaps, bitterly regretted impulse. Children, the innocent victims, are resented and even rejected. Illegal back-street abortions occur in squalor and misery. These are the tragedies of infatuation gone sour, and we see the legacy in divorce and the desolation of the children affected.[7]

Divorce rates increased from around 40,000 per year during the earlier postwar period to almost 80,000 per year by 1971, especially as a result of the Divorce Reform Act (1969).[8] The obligation to family stability gave way to the requirement for individual fulfilment; the institution of marriage began to matter less than the quality of respect and love within a relationship.[9]

With release from the constraints of an unhappy, legally defined union came greater freedom to experiment with different relationships; with partial exemption from conventional social roles came uncertainty too. 'We and our brothers are born with the same adventure potential,' wrote journalist Irma Kurtz in 1968, 'but rarely does either sex explore it.'[10] After completing her education at the University of Glasgow in the mid-1960s, Liz Heron felt unpoliticized and classless, a reader of de Beauvoir but as yet unconnected to feminism, 'a bit less naïve than when I started, and a lot more confused'.[11] While idealization and a superficial libertarianism, sometimes sexual, was often associated with women at this time, a surer gain was to be found in the clear-eyed observation of how women lived and spoke from day to day. Hannah Gavron's sociology of the housebound mother is one example. Another is *Up the Junction*, Nell Dunn's imaginative recreation of the conversations and lives of a group of hands, mostly young, in a south London sweet factory, their affairs, anecdotes, boyfriends and work:

> Flecks of soot, large as pennies floated down on the hot afternoon.
> 'What you doing tonight, Rube?'
> 'I've got a date with two ginks in a van, but I'm not going.'
> 'Why not?'
> 'Can't be bothered. Has Dave kissed you yet?'
> 'No.'
> 'You want to get hold of him. This is Dave.' She runs her fingers up and down her legs. 'Look, she's getting all worked up. Aren't Chelsea blokes sexy?'
> 'No,' says Sylvie. 'They lost their knackers in the Flood.'[12]

Up the Junction was remarkable in 1963 for its mundane dramatic incident – a newborn infant's death, a fatal motorbike accident – it was memorable too for the snatches of pop song and conversation which drift through its pages to evoke the incidental and communal life of south London. A measure of how attitudes changed through these years may be that while the unvarnished thoughts and voices of Rube and her friends seemed shocking when Nell Dunn published her novel, five years later *Up the Junction* (P. Collinson, 1968) could be made into a popular film.

Citizens, second class

While women such as those described by Nell Dunn, and many others besides, were relatively poorly paid and educated, as well as unregarded socially, state intervention and gradually shifting attitudes held some promise of better opportunities. Yet expectations of change, opportunity and achievement were mostly unfulfilled among immigrants, who signally failed to experience "the sixties". Postwar political and other exiles established a community life, but were disadvantaged by their immigrant status. The Polish population reached around 135,000 in 1960 and numbers fell thereafter to 88,000 by 1981; there were similar falls among other postwar refugee and ethnic groups including Hungarians and Czechs.[13] Immigrants and minorities were nevertheless still increasing in number and visibility. The second, larger phase of Chinese immigration came in the 1960s. Likewise the Caribbean and South Asian populations increased from 500,000 in 1961 to 1,500,000 in 1971, a rise from roughly one to three per cent of the total population.[14] The individual circumstances of the new arrivals could be trying. Lagos-born Buchi Emecheta, for example, who arrived in London in 1960 with her husband at the age of 16, used personal experience as the starting point for her novel *Second Class Citizen* (1974).[15] In it she describes the difficulties of adapting to a new climate, living conditions and language, to the general contempt of her adopted homeland as well as the neglect of her husband. Beyond such personal stories the collective condition of the new immigrants, especially their exploitation as tenants following the introduction of the Rent Act (1957), came to the attention of the wider public. This was particularly true during the Profumo scandal of 1963, in which the notorious London slum landlord Peter Rachman was entangled. It also brought unwanted attention to two West Indians, Johnny Edgecombe and Lucky Gordon, both of whom had been involved with another of the main protagonists, Christine Keeler.[16] Some positive changes resulted. A Rent Act (1965) was rushed through Parliament with the express intent of protecting tenants from 'Rachmanism'; the Race Relations Act (1965) outlawed public, though not housing or employment, discrimination. Yet the wider anti-immigration mood persisted in the two Commonwealth Immigrants Acts (1962 and 1968) as well as in events outside Parliament.

The experience of racial 'difference' could be especially difficult for children who were first generation arrivals. A Bradford man (b.1954) from Punjab, India, one of the increasing number of South Asians in Britain, recalled an incident which took place when he was about 12 years old:

> there was some discussion started by a teacher, or the teacher was pointing to somebody, and she was trying to convince the pupils, or try to tell them that all human beings are the same, and they shouldn't have these prejudices and if you think they smell, Japanese people think we smell of meat because we eat meat. And it's . . . and I became conscious then actually, you know, I felt embarrassed, and I felt very conscious that somehow I was different. You know . . .

Not until then?

No, not until then.[17]

While this local attempt to promote better understanding between immigrant and host community foundered, more concerted efforts to improve relations gradually appeared. The need for such initiatives was highlighted by the successful anti-immigration election campaign of district politician and headmaster Peter Griffiths in the Smethwick constituency of Birmingham in 1964. Griffiths' election came not long after an increase in the number of Commonwealth arrivals in anticipation of the strict limits put in place by the Commonwealth Immigrants Act (1962). His success was all the more disturbing because he defeated senior Labour MP Patrick Gordon Walker, who was widely expected to become Foreign Secretary in Harold Wilson's new Labour government. In light of such events ethnic minority groups now began more actively to promote their rights. Since 1958 representation of immigrant interests had mainly been through the West Indian Standing Conference. After Martin Luther King preached at St Paul's Cathedral in 1964, during a stopover on his way to collect the Nobel Peace Prize in Stockholm, wider campaigns began. The year 1965 saw the establishment of new organizations, both voluntary and state sponsored: the Campaign Against Racial Discrimination, which fought for fairer treatment of minorities, and the Race Relations Board, which investigated complaints of discrimination.

Agreement that minorities deserved an equal place in British society was not universal, nor was there consensus on practical issues. Nineteen sixty-eight saw the introduction of a new Commonwealth Immigrants Act for instance, which deprived East African Asians of the right to stay in the United Kingdom. Similarly, just as the Race Relations Act was being extended to include employment and housing, education and services, and at the same moment the Community Relations Commission was set in place, the campaign for immigrant repatriation was extending its grip among certain sections of the population. The far right National Front Party, formed in 1967, advocated an end to 'coloured' immigration and voluntary repatriation; one effect of Enoch Powell's campaign, promoting much the same line, was the loss of government popularity in Midlands constituencies. The anti-immigrant cause had gathered such support that Powell's expulsion from the Shadow Cabinet caused affront among many thousands of potential Conservative voters.[18]

Race relations now worsened. Immigrants and minorities often mistrusted the permissiveness and liberal values for which the era is best recalled. Yet they were not outside their times. Discussion on the presence and role of immigrants and ethnic groups within British society came increasingly into the public sphere. The 1969 life peerage awarded to Sir Learie Constantine, the West Indian cricketer, demonstrated some sense of ethnic equality and citizenship. At the same time an increasing awareness of exclusion and isolation pushed the new communities away from mainstream society and back towards ethnic identity and language. Insensitive community policing in the West Indian settlement district of Moss Side, Manchester, and the continued support for repatriation, delineated acceptance and integration.[19] While radical separatism had been advocated by Michael X in London in the mid-1960s, and while Malcolm X had visited London in 1965, it was again only towards the end of the decade that radical political groups grew in number and popularity, including the Black Unity and Freedom Party and the British branch of the Black Panther Movement.[20]

Despite the efforts of the British state then, which were at best contradictory, notions of ethnicity and nationhood were little altered since the war's end. For the ethnic minorities and immigrants of the United Kingdom, cultural revolution remained elusive.

Students, students! Ha! Ha! Ha!

While immigrants and ethnic minorities were neither substantially beneficiaries of the new consumerism, nor necessarily sympathetic to the new permissiveness, eastern 'mysticism' as well as the music and fashion of West Indian popular culture now gradually became fashionable among young people. Collectively youth was well placed to take advantage of the new mood of liberalism and consumerism. The commercial success and fashionability of popular culture appeared on the TV pop show *Ready, Steady, Go!*; self-expression and the counter-culture showed off in the shop windows of trendy boutiques such as Granny Takes a Trip or Dandie Fashions; musical art and pop art fused in Beatles' albums. By the mid-1960s too there was an alternative 'establishment': pop stars, including John Lennon (1940–80), Paul McCartney (b.1942), Brian Jones (1942–69) and Mick Jagger (b.1943); artists, including painter David Hockney (b.1937) and photographer David Bailey (b.1938); as well as fashion models such as Twiggy (b.1949) or Jean Shrimpton (b.1942), all of whom had achieved recognition in the media and in London society. Release from the perceived constraints of province and background was a defining features of the new, young, alternative establishment. Respectable youth, however, both working- and middle-class, remained in the majority: according to one 1964 account upwards of 65 per cent.[21] For those not able to make a spectacular leap into the alternative establishment the outlines of a less class-bound society emerged more gradually with the expansion of higher education recommended by the Robbins Report (1963).[22] Even slower to change was life in the suburbs and provinces, which during the early 1960s meant Saturday night dances, bowling alleys, cigarettes and peppermint chewing gum, Babycham for girls and beer for boys. As this world was caught by the photojournalists of the time, John Bulmer and Don McCullin among them, it was by turns gritty and glamorous. Bulmer's photograph 'Man About Town', for example, taken in January 1961, pictures a teenage boy sitting alone in a coffee bar in Nelson, Lancashire. Pensive, self-conscious and cocky, wearing an oversized sheepskin coat, he peers out uncertainly across a smoke-filled room.[23]

The mood of this photograph, part resentment at the past's disappointment, part pleasure in the future's promise, part living simply in the moment, illustrates the pressures which many young people felt, as one teenager explained in 1964. 'Me, I failed the 11-plus, and I felt bitter, my parents were disappointed in me and instead of getting the bike I was promised, I was bagged for the next six weeks.'[24] Yet the censure of elders and parents, who often seemed constantly critical of teenagers' chewing gum, hairstyles and blaring transistor pop, now became increasingly inefficient as a constraint on thought or behaviour.

The 'Mod' style reacted violently against the frustrations of youth, asserting instead a desire for self-definition through clothes, music and speed. Mary Quant was associated with the craze by her attention to taste and detail; newspapers and public were against the teenagers for their Vespa-riding, gang-fighting and seaside holiday-disrupting bank holiday riots at Margate, Brighton and Clacton in 1964. At Clacton locals anticipated charges of assault and loitering with intent as they publicly posted their sentiments: 'Teenagers, go home.' In their investigation into the lives and thoughts of early 1960s' youth, an attempt to explore what lay behind the sensational newspaper headlines, the authors of *Generation X* (1964) describe a complex world of creative fashion and taste. Among Mods there was a general dislike of The Beatles, for instance. They loathed too the style and music of Elvis as his look and sound had inspired their motorbike-riding rivals, the Rockers. Boy Mods wore small 'blue beat' hats, smart suits with three-button jackets, 17-inch trouser bottoms and round-toed imitation crocodile boots; they read, or admitted to reading, spy and detective stories by Ian Fleming or Mickey Spillane. Girl Mods wore shift-style dresses with round collars, white stockings with stacked shoes, or stretch slacks, tweed coats and pink or blue combinations; they read, or admitted to reading, love stories, pop and women's magazines. Everyone danced to Jamaican tunes like Prince Buster's 'Madness'.[25]

A symbolic connection between Mods and their middle-class peers was the common use of the round CND sign, one group from political conviction, the other from a fondness for badges, labels and emblems such as the Union Jack. While the subcultural Mods drew on the newly available styles and sounds of the Afro-Caribbean immigrant, the more self-consciously subversive, counter-cultural Beats and their successors followed an existentialist creed of creative self-expression. Born and educated in Glasgow, Alexander Trocchi (1925–84), who moved to Paris in the early 1950s and then on to West Venice, California, was one of the founders of the Beat movement. By their rejection of standardized and customary morals, their jazz and avant-garde aesthetic, and their dedication to intellectual and artistic endeavour, the Beats found a strong following in Britain, and rooted the counter-cultural movement of the later 1960s. Trocchi's best-known work is his remarkable account of heroin addiction, *Cain's Book*.[26] The hedonism of the drug scene, disaffection with conventional politics, work and marriage, sexual revolution to liberate humanity: these ideals were soon accompanied by a more commercialized expression of youthful hippie community. London in 1968 saw both the American Embassy anti-Vietnam war demonstrations in Grosvenor Square and the Pink Floyd's free concert in Hyde Park. Richard Neville, editor of the underground magazine *Oz*, gave full expression to the anti-establishment ethos in his 'hippie bible' *Powerplay* (1971):

> 'Project London' ['a survival manual for full-time drop-outs'] is published on the principle that the best things in life are free, if only you have the necessary information to obtain them. The morality of the booklet is the morality of the underground – minus the profit motive. The Deviants, a London rock group, sing 'Let's Loot the Supermarket' and many fans ask 'Why stop there?' The world is over-producing already . . . and everyone, except the Underground, seems embarrassed by it.[27]

The ethical niceties of shoplifting were lost, though, on some of Neville's less idealistic contemporaries. During the Grosvenor Square demonstrations, a group of about two hundred skinheads taunted the anti-war protesters with chants of 'Students, students! Ha! Ha! Ha!'[28] Their angry heckling, well aimed at the more absurd pretensions of the better off, was an echo of the sentiment Enoch Powell tapped into: a call to traditional values, local community and native territorialism.[29] Despite their differences, both the youthful middle-class 'counter-culture' and their skinhead counterparts continued to attend closely to dress and music. In the case of the skinheads by a variation on the Mod uniform: short, cropped hair, Ben Sherman shirts, narrow denim trousers, Army greens and braces, donkey jackets and steel-capped work boots. In his 1970s *Skinhead* trilogy – a staccato terrace-chant of praise to teenage yobbism – Richard Allen describes why to his fictional anti-hero, Joe Hawkins, the boots mattered above all. 'Without his boots, he was one of the common herd – like his dad, a working man devoid of identity. . . . His were genuine army-disposal boots, thick-soled, studded, heavy to wear and heavy to feel if stamped against a rib.'[30]

The skinheads made an early appearance at the Grosvenor Square demonstrations, but soon caught wider public attention as the fans of London football teams including Tottenham Hotspur, West Ham and Chelsea. Commenting on his first sight of four thousand such fans at a match, one supporter said, 'They all wore bleached Levis, Dr Martens, a short scarf tied cravat-style, cropped hair. They looked like an army and, after the game, went into action like one.'[31] Unlike the more art school-oriented Mods of the later 1960s, among them Pete Townsend (b.1945), Marc Bolan (1947–77) and David Bowie (b.1947), who became flamboyant and dandyish, the skinheads turned self-consciously proletarian and thuggish: 'soft' Mods became hippies; 'hard' Mods became skinheads. If the early skins had admiration or respect for anyone, it was the physically tough, street-hustling Jamaican Rude Boys. They took pleasure too in the black dance music played in the dancehalls and pub back rooms of south-east London, northwest Kent and inner-city pubs, for instance, in Brixton. In this respect, if not in their ugly intolerance and thuggery, skins were an 'underground scene' as they danced to the songs of Desmond Dekker or the Upsetters, from Kingston, Jamaica, as they listened to eulogies to drink and drugs, stories of imprisonment and outlaw heroes.

My Marilyn

A mythic world of tragedy and deity appears in the visual arts too, where, as in contemporary photojournalism and film, the 'kitchen sink' style was gradually glamorized. Where John Bulmer and Don McCullin prized photography as documentation, for example, of the disappearing northern industrial landscape, Terence Donovan or David Bailey favoured the fashionable gloss of *Vogue*, or the new Sunday newspaper supplements such as the *Sunday Times* 'colour section', introduced in 1962. 'The fifties were grey – the sixties were black and white,' said Bailey.[32] British artists, by turns analytic, critical, nostalgic, took a similar approach to working-class and popular culture, say, in their various considerations of actress Marilyn Monroe, who died in 1962. Peter Phillips' *For Men Only, Starring MM and BB* (1961), with its board game layout and pin-up subject matter, views the American film star as a familiar object in the everyday landscape of British society. Pauline Boty's (1938–66) *The Only Blonde in the World* (1963) comments on the hypnotic, debilitating effects of stardom. Richard Hamilton recreates the snaps from a photo shoot, where the actress has picked out and marked her own 'best' image', in *My Marilyn (paste up)* (1964). This last picture especially lays bare the tiers of artifice and commerce in shooting and posing: the photographer's act of directing the actress; the actress's self-conscious control of her public image; and beyond these, the reproduction and framing by the painter.

This variety of Marilyns reflects the still-growing visibility of popular culture, not least American popular culture, within British society, and the rapidly shifting visual surroundings which British artists now urgently sought to explore.[33] Many of the younger artists who took an interest in such subjects made their debut at the Young Contemporaries exhibitions, held annually at the Whitechapel Gallery. Derek Boshier (b.1937), Patrick Caulfield (1936–2005) and David Hockney (b.1937), for instance, who were near contemporaries at the Royal College of Art in 1960. Boshier's paintings of airmail letter envelopes, or of toothpaste container-like tubes offset abstraction with graphic precision, as in *First Tooth Paste Painting* (1962), to describe a humanity folded and squeezed by its own technological and commercial ingenuity. Caulfield's use of illustrative techniques, schematic, diagrammatic outlines as well as the visually overfamiliar, as in *Artist's Studio* (1964), drew on the language of advertising, comic and illustration to make the everyday unfamiliar. Hockney became a celebrity in his own right, associated with the 'new aristocracy', and photographed by Lord Snowdon in a gold jacket, shopping bag in hand. Moreover, this social liberation was accompanied by an artistic openness that expressed itself in his *Tea Paintings* (1960–1), in his use of words on canvas to narrate the human presence, or in *The First Marriage (A Marriage of Styles 1)* (1962).[34] While the 'Young Contemporary' artists attended to the packaging, wording and imaging of mass society, sculptors associated with the 'New Generation' exhibition (1965) and movement turned to the girders, bolts and plastics of the mass constructed age.[35]

The fusion of popular culture and fine arts is one of the remarkable features of this period. In 1967, for instance, Peter Blake created the cover for The Beatles' *Sergeant Pepper's Lonely Hearts Club Band*, dressing the four members of the group in elaborate, colourful outfits reminiscent of both military and musical band uniforms. He surrounded them with pictures of film stars, writers and musicians, placed them within an artistic and historical context where creativity flowed freely across boundaries of time and space, framed them within a new mental and musical picture. Blake's interest in pop music and comics, in lapel badges and film stars, seen in his painting of American guitarist *Bo Diddley* (1963), expressed a wish to remodel art into a new folk culture outside the old constraints of class or taste. Remaking technique to match the contemporary, he worked in collage and assemblage. In the mixed media relief *Toy Shop* (1962) – complete with near full-size door and painted, metal plate advertising sign – the shop window displays flags, masks, circular practice targets, toy balls, space ship and aeroplane models, pictures of fashion and pop star pin-ups. Richard Hamilton moved freely too in the worlds of popular music and popular culture, designing the blind, embossed cover to The Beatles' double LP (1968) that became known as *The White Album*. The original packaging included as well a free give-away print, also Hamilton's work, based on personal photographs donated by members of the group and worked up into a collage. In *Swingeing London '67* (1968–9), John Twine's *Daily Sketch* photograph of Mick Jagger and art dealer Robert Fraser arriving at the Rolling Stones' drug trial in June 1967 is used by Hamilton to illuminate the attraction and repulsion of publicity – disgust too at the abuse of personal liberty the case represented.[36]

One of Hamilton's greatest passions as an artist was the work of Marcel Duchamp. In 1966 art establishment and underground came together at the Tate Gallery's Duchamp retrospective and at the unsubsidized Destruction in Art Symposium (DIAS). Thereafter the subversive element in contemporary art, the challenge to the art object, and to the separation of art and society, was increasingly sighted. The business of pop, with its newly successful entrepreneurs, channelled funds towards the unexpected and experimental at the Arts Laboratory, the Indica Bookshop and *Oz* magazine. As the press release for DIAS articulated it, openness to new possibilities was the essence of art. 'This exhibition will deal with . . . destruction used as a form of political and religious protest and agitation throughout the world . . . [the public] will also be invited to take part in some sessions.'[37] Predictably, DIAS was not everywhere well received. 'They will exhibit photographs of men sitting in the dripping blood of eviscerated animals, which is said to be art,' reported the *Guardian* on 9 September 1966, the eve of the Symposium. 'Some of them would like to stamp on frogs or crucify a lamb. They have smashed up a piano, though Laurel and Hardy used to do it better.'[38] Likewise John Latham (b.1921), one of the organizers of DIAS, who had worked with burned, torn and painted books in his *Burial of Count Orgaz* (1958) assemblage, attracted police attention when he set light to his 'skoobs' – towers of books – in public spaces about London, as part of his own contribution to the proceedings. Latham subsequently lost his job at St Martin's School of Art after organizing a meeting to chew up pages from *Art and Culture* by the renowned American art critic Clement Greenberg.[39]

As with Latham and DIAS, many artists working at this time sought to manipulate or reorient vision through the creation of a dramatic space or encounter, for one Bridget Riley (b. 1931). Explaining her use of abstract combinations of colour, light and space, an attempt to draw attention to the role of both viewer and artist through a confrontation with the mechanics of seeing, she said: 'I feel my paintings have some affinity with happenings where the disturbance precipitated is latent in the sociological and social situation. I want the disturbance or 'event' to arise naturally, in visual terms, out of the inherent energies and characteristics of the elements that I use.'[40] While Riley scanned the borders of the mental state, defining its moments of calm, fear and disorientation using non-representative colour and texture, Allen Jones observed a world of seduction and absurdity. A contemporary of Boshier at the Royal College of Art, and expelled in 1960, Jones moved to America to further test the bounds of free expression. In 1969 he produced *Table Sculpture*, *Hat Stand* and *Chair*: three female models in painted fibreglass, each fixed in a provocative, sexualized posture. Drawing on fetish magazines, Jones comes deliberately to voyeurism and guides the viewer's attention directly to the mass-produced, artificial quality of consumption. Once the mind's eye of the artist had consumed the everyday and the objects of its desire, the mood, tempo and values of imagination, in music as well as in visual arts, veered towards the fantastic.

Twenty clowns, sculptors and some girls who defy description

That proletarian, down-at-heel Liverpool, with its seaport heritage of industry and immigration, should have produced one of the world's most successful musical groups also gave an air of fantasy to the early 1960s. By 1964 The Beatles were reputedly earning £6,250,000 per year, whatever their actual earnings, they were certainly giving a Royal Variety Performance in front of the Queen, and expanding into the American market to become, as one British diplomat said, 'superb ambassadors' for the country. In their wake came a great wave of other 'beat' groups including Manfred Mann, The Animals and The Kinks. As in the visual arts, new developments were greeted with some scepticism. Journalist Paul Johnson, writing in *The New Statesman* in 1964, was one disbeliever. The Beatles were, he argued, an 'apotheosis of inanity'. 'The young,' he believed, had become 'enslaved to a commercial machine' that dictated their wants; intellectuals, in the meantime 'sat in damp, cavernous jazz clubs listening to the monstrous braying of savage instruments' in order to be thought 'with it'.[41] Johnson, the select intellectual and social elite he supported and the cause of high culture that he promoted, were as powerless as the parents of a Mod to prescribe the tastes of the new mass culture.

The roots of the musical renewal which was now taking place, and which was in many respects less inane or primitive that Johnson imagined, were in American tradition, in country, blues and folk. It remained relatively uncommon for US acts to tour the UK. For this reason Muddy Waters' performance in the late 1950s, playing raw, amplified blues guitar, echoed all the more loudly in the ears of devotees. As director Mike Figgis realized while making his film on the history of the British blues movement, *Red, White and Blues* (2004), few UK fans saw such concerts, so, like jazz followers, they mostly learned and were inspired by the recordings. 'It was all about listening to albums – whether it was in London or Birmingham or Newcastle or Manchester. They all got together in a house, smoked some dope or drank some beer or whatever, and listened to albums all night.'[42] By 1961 fans around the country were turning themselves into musicians, beginning to form electric blues bands: Alexis Korner's Blues Incorporated was among the first, but other fan-musicians included Van Morrison, Bert Jansch and Eric Burdon.[43] One impromptu concert at the Ealing Club in west London in March 1962 included Alexis Korner, Cyril Davis and Charlie Watts; other regulars were Keith Richards, Brian Jones, Jack Bruce and Graham Bond, all of whom became successful, professional pop musicians. Nor was blues the only influence as various musical traditions competed for their audiences' ear. Skiffle faded; r'n'b, calypso and soul grew in popularity; the Graham Bond Organisation brought electric jazz to pop. From this scene various other groups emerged including The Rolling Stones, The Detours, who later became The Who, and The Yardbirds.

By the middle years of the decade the mood had shifted towards a broader eclecticism and a more adventurous, self-conscious experimentalism. One expression of this came with the release of The Kinks' *Face to Face* (1966), an album which was unusually long at around sixty minutes, and which consisted of twenty-one pieces spliced together with connecting sound effects. Leader of The Kinks Ray Davies used the album to express his unease at the trappings of pop stardom, yet the clubs and discotheques where the younger musicians, artists and actors gathered also became a source of the new counter-cultural hybridity. The Beatles' *Revolver* (1966) hints at this new fusion of expression, too, with its ad-mixture of pop-like songs, close to the group's earlier successes, and the less conventional experiments with tape loops, sound effects and reverse speech. Performance, art and theatre spaces gradually ceased to be distinct social or imaginative areas as clubs such as the UFO or the Spontaneous Underground combined musical, visual and theatrical elements into a single 'happening', on 29 April 1967, for example, during a series of simultaneous performances at the Alexandra Palace known as the '14-Hour Technicolor Dream'. At the Spontaneous Underground, the attractions included, according to one advertisement, 'poets, pop singers . . . 20 clowns . . . sculptors . . . and some girls who defy description'.[44] The clothes of stars and fans flaunted the same mood. Fads changed quickly, new colours and cuts could be bought easily and inexpensively; new images could be created in Chelsea boutiques, high street stores and flea markets. 'The first hippie clothes weren't just bells and beads,' said music promoter Jeff Dexter, 'they were very smart military uniforms. Robert [Albag] dressed Jimi Hendrix – that beautiful red Guards jacket – and that became the uniform of the period.'[45] As Julie Christie or Rita Tushingham wandered the cinematic streets staring at the pedestrians, investigating the shop windows and backroom corners, so, now, any such walk to a record store, bookshop or discotheque might be embellished with whimsy or with a play of colours.

The diversity of influences and openness to the eclectic extended to other areas: the new pop was both metropolitan and regional, embracing The Rolling Stones (London), The Hollies (Liverpool), The Animals (Newcastle) and Them (Belfast); it involved and coexisted with folk and avant-garde styles; its listening patterns were less constrained than in north America by ethnicity. British fans of blues, jazz or soul absorbed, interpreted and re-exported the music to Stateside audiences, thereby advancing the reputation and sales of such idols as B. B. King.[46] The restricted flow of traffic between Britain and America, long established among music fans, now entered broader channels. Led by The Beatles, British artists 'invaded' America between 1963 and 1966. Thereafter America revisited Britain. The stories of two among the best known musicians from this time, John Lennon and Jimi Hendrix, illustrate this trading of ideas and styles.

Lennon's encounter with America at first shocked and then politicized the musician. Though the early concerts, in New York's Shea Stadium for instance, were hugely successful, when Lennon went to Memphis, Tennessee in 1966 he faced the hostility of Christian believers who baulked at his observation that The Beatles were more widely recognized than Jesus. Moreover, his exposure to the race politics of the South, the struggle for civil rights, the anti-Vietnam war movement and the artistic as well as political underground led Lennon into sympathy with various radical groups and towards greater musical experimentation.[47] Travelling in the opposite direction across the Atlantic, also in 1966, Jimi Hendrix moved from New York to London. By March 1967 he was playing on a show business-style variety act tour along with The Walker Brothers, Cat Stevens and Engelbert Humperdink. In the downtown Manhattan district of Greenwich Village, New York, he had begun to discover avant-garde blues rock, and to encounter British groups, including The Who; as a performer the guitarist participated in and stimulated the British capital's music scene.[48] 'Hendrix came to London,' said Robert Wyatt, member of the influential jazz-rock band The Soft Machine, 'and musically that was tremendously important for a lot of people.'[49] He played at the jam sessions of jazz and pop musicians in London clubs; living and working in Britain he was able to establish a reputation, set up recordings and return as a success to the USA. Musical creativity at least seemed to transcend the boundaries of genre, nationality and race.

Alfie Boy and Darling Girl

The confidence and eclecticism that spread through the visual arts and popular music scene was paralleled by a shift of focus, form and content in cinema. Julie Christie, who became a film star with her first major feature *Billy Liar* (John Schlesinger, 1963) and enhanced her reputation with *Dr Zhivago* (David Lean, 1965) described the change. 'Suddenly naturalism – or realism – came in, just as it had in Italy in the neo-realist cinema after the war, and I was lucky enough to be part of that. It was also the subjects of the films and the way we were allowed to behave. Suddenly we were able to challenge audiences to accept us – which they did . . .'[50] Accepting 'us' for Christie may have meant engaging more fully with the new attitudes of the young, not least young women. The challenge for audiences was also to consider life outside the metropolis, especially in the north of England: the aspirations and dissatisfactions of the factory worker, the borstal boy or the teenage mother. Following the concerns of the Free Cinema movement and a wider interest in working-class life, especially as it was altering under the influence of American popular culture and increasing consumerism, a series of 'new wave' films considered their protagonists' frustrated or compromised search for freedom from interfering authorities, be they parents, bosses or police, for material success, for a better life.[51] Among the most important of these films were *Saturday Night and Sunday Morning* (K. Reisz, 1960), *A Taste of Honey* (T. Richardson, 1961), *The Loneliness of the Long-Distance Runner* (T. Richardson, 1962) and *This Sporting Life* (L. Anderson, 1963). While the rusting industrial landscapes of Manchester or Nottingham appear romanticized, the women marginalized, a genuinely broader vision of national life was nevertheless now set before audiences.[52] Factory worker Arthur Seaton, matching his movements to an unrelenting machine tool's requirements, stands all day in a noisy workshop reciting his credo, 'What I'm out for is a good time, all the rest is propaganda.' Youth offender Colin Smith, caught between the competing ideologies of his liberal social worker and his authoritarian borstal warden, refuses to win the race which will supposedly be his salvation, continuing instead to blame 'the bosses' for the work-related illness and death of his father. Pregnant teenager Jo and her mother are 'enjoying themselves' as they shout and argue with one another and are forced together to confront their respective responsibilities of parenthood.

The artistic and critical recognition of the 'new wave' was not, though, matched by commercial success. Musicals films, among them *Summer Holiday* (S. Furie and P. Yates, 1963), The Beatles' *A Hard Day's Night* (R. Lester, 1964), or *Oliver!* (C. Reed, 1968) drew greater box office crowds. James Bond films, released annually from *Dr No* (T. Young, 1962) to *Thunderball* (T. Young, 1965) were such successes that they upped the presence of American production companies and finances on the British film-making scene for several years.[53] The use of outdoor locations, the attention to social conflict and the guarded optimism of the 'new wave' films, was augmented by new interests. *The Day the Earth Caught Fire* (V. Guest, 1961), for instance, shot among the atmospheric locations and eccentric characters of London's newspaper district, Fleet Street, carried an anti-nuclear message. Here political leaders are the same as 'the bosses' attacked by Arthur Seaton or Colin Smith; in Guest's film, though, they control not only life chances, but also the survival of life itself.[54] Subsequently various of the 'swinging sixties' films, including *The Knack* (R. Lester, 1965), or *Poor Cow* (Ken Loach, 1967), married a realist aesthetic to a critique of the pressure towards peer group conformity, the failure of intimacy and affection in relations between men and women.

Peter Stenning, the journalist at the centre of *The Day the Earth Caught Fire*, is not a class rebel, but he does share with other males a cockiness fashionable to 1960s' screen heroes. A closer assessment of the see-sawing balance of control in male–female relations comes with *Alfie* (L. Gilbert, 1966). Sexual profligacy, and an abortion, discretely signalled, were among the subjects of careful negotiation between the film-makers and the British Board of Film Censors while *Alfie* was in production. BBFC advice could be remarkably detailed leading to recommendations like 'Ruby's costume should be adequate and not transparent.'[55] While the censors were able to advise on the language, sexual content and morality of this populist, mid-1960s film, they had less control over the shifting values and tastes of filmgoers. Satisfying the newly acknowledged liberal tastes of audiences became a lucrative business; in its marketing and artistic choices, a film like *Alfie* recognized the new mood's commercial possibilities. Michael Caine's reputation as one of the talented new screen idols of his generation increased with *Alfie*; Julie Christie achieved much the same when she starred in *Darling* (John Schelsinger, 1965). Taken together, the main characters of these two films show the pleasures and limits of freedom as seen by mass audiences. Both characters are 'liberated', but while Alfie is cynical and charming, Diana is fickle and restless; their fates, in both cases failed attempts at more ambitious, advantageous relationships, call the reality of libertarianism into question. Alfie finds himself outwitted by an older woman whose values mirror his own. As Diana moves through the worlds of media, advertising, high society and politics, she is a diverting plaything to those who encounter her, and finally at the mercy of forces beyond her control.[56] Finally both Diana and Alfie emerge as stylish, self-created and trapped within their own self-interest.

Towards the end of the 1960s the values of the avant-garde and the underground began to appear before wider film audiences; experimental and populist fused in a blend of formal play and commercial appeal. Antonioni's *Blow-Up* (1966) is one example, with its acutely observed account of the London world of trendy fashion models and photographers, and its metaphysical exploration of reality, illusion and 'seeing'. Roeg's *Performance* (1970) plays a variation on another contemporary topic: how apparent opposites – good and evil, male and female, sanity and madness – may only be as restrictive as human convention. Two of the most successful directors of the moment made anti-war features in *How I Won the War* (R. Lester, 1967) and *The Charge of the Light Brigade* (T. Richardson, 1968), the former combining a satirical onslaught against both armed conflict and the class system. One of the most controversial film-makers of the time was Lindsay Anderson, who by the early 1960s had moved from documentaries to features. *This Sporting Life* (1963) is typically hard-edged in its characterization, and features elaborate flashbacks as well as a startling, bleak existentialism in its final sequence. *If . . .* (1968) combines formal experiment and radical political content as it creatively switches between black and white and colour segments to make an avowedly 'anti-establishment' tale.[57] Set in a public school, *If . . .* considers the meaning of resistance and repression, conformity for the common good and rebellion for private gain. Despite the opposition of a few boys, who are viciously beaten for their dissent, the authoritarian, repressive school government remains unchallenged. Finally, the schoolboy rebels take revenge by gunning down parents and staff at a Founders Day celebration, which becomes an unwinnable pitch battle.[58] Inevitably, though perhaps misleadingly, the film was read as a symbolic representation of contemporary society. By the end of the 1960s that society was changing quickly: the British film industry lost American partnerships and finances; admissions plunged from 327,000 (1965) to 193,000 (1970). Anderson persisted with his anti-realist, counter-cultural approach to film-making in *O Lucky Man!* (1973) and *Britannia Hospital* (1982), though audiences were increasingly reluctant to follow. Opportunities for such anti-establishment experimentalism, as well as for the idealism that underpinned them, were increasingly reined in.[59]

CHAPTER 6

UK Anarchy

Passionate Eve and the Bondage Babes

Wedged between the years of relative optimism and confidence before 1973, and the rise of populist Conservatism after 1979, the 1970s, as recorded in Jonathan Coe's fictional account *The Rotters' Club* (2001) say, is a time of strikes, political violence and racism. While this reflects popular memory as it has been distorted by the Tory ascendancy that followed, the sense of unpredictable times, of stagnation, of events unravelling at unprecedented, alarming speed, was nevertheless powerfully present through these years.[1] Yet new thoughts accompanied the failure of old certainties. In *The Passion of New Eve* (1977), for example, Angela Carter imagines a band of women freedom fighters who reconceive relations between the sexes: they transform Evelyn into Eve, their call becomes 'Time is a man, space is a woman'. Man is identified with the stiff, upward trajectory of space rockets, with the efficient prosecution of warfare; woman, by contrast, is identified with the fabulous envelopment of cycles and replication.[2] Both identities are invented, both require continual, self-conscious remaking. Carter's novel was one of many possible re-workings of male–female relations to emerge in the previous few years, but a notable one because of the author's playful treatment of gender conventions and restrictions. In the day-to-day world women also took new roles: as trade union membership peaked at the end of the decade, South Asian factory worker Jayaben Desai became a national figure in the predominantly male world of trade unionism.[3] She led a two-year long strike at the Grunwick film processing and mail order plant in London, beginning in August 1976, where about 500 mainly immigrant workers were employed. While the strike to establish basic union rights faltered eventually, Desai nevertheless saw positive effects. 'The dispute is bringing up so many good things. Before the mass picketing began in June the issue was not so clear in our community, it was misty before. But now the Asian community sees what we are fighting for. And before the trade unions in this country were feeling that our community was not interested.'[4]

Desai's engagement was not guided by the radical activism of the women's movement, which was rooted in one wing of the counter-culture at the end of the 1960s; nor was it connected, at first, to the traditional Labour and trades union movement, which remained relatively unsympathetic to both minorities and women. Rather, it pushed forward alongside the wider move towards equal rights and opportunities promoted since Harold Wilson's first premiership of 1964–70, especially by Barbara Castle during her time as Secretary of State for Employment and Productivity (1968–70). The result of these initiatives included the Equal Pay Act (1970), which came into force on 1 January 1976, and the Sex Discrimination

Illustration 6 Era of unrest: striking miners facing a coal lorry driver, Dover, 1972

Act (1975), which led to the institution of the Equal Opportunities Commission to promote its provision. The Grunwick dispute was a vivid illustration too of the difficult truth that even with the Employment Protection Act in force, which established a clear legal requirement for equal pay, even with better pension rights or the promise to reject discrimination, regulatory control could not direct attitudes and behaviour.[5]

Critical investigation into the social situation in which women found themselves as well as into the social institutions within which they functioned, particularly the family, continued through this volatile period. Here too there was a refusal to accept unquestioned contemporary convention or inherited tradition. Ann Oakley's remarkable series of sociological studies from this moment includes *The Sociology of Housework* (1974) and *Women Confined: Towards a Sociology of Childbirth* (1980). In *Housewife* (1974), Oakley interviewed Juliet Warren, a middle-class mother frustrated and depressed by the relatively unusual move, for the time, from challenging career to full-time parent. In her description of everyday chores Warren expresses her social situation: 'My standards have definitely dropped since I've been doing housework all the time. I suppose it's because I really cannot do anything uninterrupted and I still can't get used to that . . . Anyone listening to that recorder will probably think the place is a pigsty which, you can see, it isn't. I'm very aware that there are little jobs I ought to do.'[6] Towards the end of the decade, as economic and political uncertainties peaked, one women's liberation group brought into question the legal, social and parental role of married partners in their 'Why be a Wife?' campaign, arguing that 'love and the care of children should cease to be synonymous with a dependent and unequal status of women.'[7] 'Why be a paid employee?' would have been an equally valid question. The number of women in paid work increased from less than 25 per cent in 1961, to over 50 per cent by the end of the 1970s, yet the wages and life circumstances of many women were not improved. The hourly rate of pay for women both before and after the Equal Pay Act was around 75 per cent of men's wages. Outside the workplace, as life expectancies rose by more than 20 per cent, middle-aged women were more often faced with the double task of raising children and caring for elderly relatives.[8]

The state was also able to mediate between the sexes: first, in the Divorce Reform Act (1969), second in the Domestic Violence and Matrimonial Proceedings Act (1976). Divorce rates dramatically rose between 1970 and 1979: triple the number for those up to 25 and double the number above that age. By the end of the decade one in three marriages was ended by divorce.[9] How common physically abusive behaviour was in married relationships remains difficult to judge, but according to one estimate between one third and two thirds of all divorced relationships was to some degree violent. The 1976 Act certainly seemed to answer an existing need as shown by the growth of the women's refuge movement, and by the issuing of 3000 court restraining orders in 1976 against violent partners.[10] Most women did not reject the family; relationships between the sexes nevertheless became less traditional. One example of this social repositioning was the more aggressive, confrontational attitude of the young singers, and of the fans that supported them, in the punk bands of 1976–9. Jordan, for instance, the first vocalist with Adam and the Ants, or Siouxie, of Siouxie and the Banshees, provided new models of behaviour and appearance for younger women. In the same year as she published *The Passion of New Eve*, Angela Carter commented on the punks' new dress code:

> It seems only right and proper that a mute sartorial response should surface as black shiny plastic slit-sided dresses; camouflage combat trousers, as if either you do not know there was a war on or else an ironic comment after the fact that nobody else seems to acknowledge there is a war on; chains everywhere, as if you had not been born free; and blouses printed with excerpts from dirty books.[11]

Pressure

Twenty-five years on from the arrival of the *Empire Windrush*, second generation immigrants, often British by birth, were also acutely aware of how their lives were constricted. Within the school system, for example, a disproportionate number of children of West Indian background were judged 'educationally subnormal' and placed in Special schools: according to one 1971 estimate, 40 per cent in the London district of Lewisham.[12] Five-year-old Nathan George, for instance, was sent to a Special school, based on a judgement that was later revoked; until he was ten his parents were caught up in a dispute over his best interests with the local educational authority. According to his mother, the school did not help Nathan. 'You could watch,' said Mrs George. 'The child was learning nothing. I mean a well-behaved child you sent out to school, and he is coming back disruptive . . . they seemed to have no control over the situation.'[13] As Nathan and his peers grew up and were schooled in Britain, they found themselves isolated by background or prejudice from their white peers, and by experience as well as education from their parents' generation. In *Endless Pressure* (1979), a study of West Indians in Bristol, one interviewee, Danny, describes these degrees of separation:

> Well, with me now, my father – and my mother too – think I'm just bad – because my dad, he really think the white people dem are good people, and he don't like me to talk anything bad about the white people . . . But he isn't getting the problem that we younger guys get in our struggle with the white people. As for the older folks . . . They are out of touch with our problems, whereas I can talk from experience.[14]

Linton Kwesi Johnson (b.1952) was among those in the younger generation who reacted to these conditions by attempting to establish a new, distinct cultural presence. 'I realised that black people were in this country to stay and we had to accept that we weren't going anywhere . . . we had to build our own independent institutions here.'[15] Raised within the Caribbean oral tradition, with the literary heritage and imagery of the Bible, by the early 1970s Johnson was recording his poetry backed by reggae musicians. In 'Five Nights of Bleeding' (1973), he describes an incident where gang violence led to a confrontation with the police: 'two rooms packed an the pressure pushing up/hot. Hot heads. Ritual of blood in a blues dance/broken glass'.[16] Many of Johnson's contemporaries were also drawn to Rastafarianism, a movement which provided a critique of material, western values, as well as a distinctive music and street fashion. For Johnson this was one step in the struggle to establish a vital communal presence within Britain, as was his development of individual and collective artistic expression through performances and workshops, and through his journalism and editorial work with the *Race Today* collective.

Patterns of immigrant arrival also continued to change as new groups settled. Following the fall of Saigon, 20,000 arrived in Britain from Vietnam as political refugees. While poor knowledge of English and inadequate work skills meant that employment was initially concentrated in the catering trade, overall the Chinese were the most successful of ethnic groups, both socially and financially.[17] Britain's South Asian population, from India, Pakistan and Bangladesh, was also increasingly rooted after the arrivals of the 1960s, while the settlement of English-speaking Asians from East Africa pushed the population up to over 200,000 by 1973.[18] Working in small businesses, often aspiring to middle-class financial security and educational achievement, and aware that high costs and competition could cut profits, South Asians tended to move to the less expensive districts both inside and outside the capital, to Leicester or Birmingham in the Midlands, and further north to Leeds or Bradford. In these close-bound communities religion, culture and family assisted the process of cultural transition, which often meant a move from a rural farming life to inner-city shift work. In her study of one immigrant family, sociologist Ursula Sharma found family obligations, for example towards the older generation, could be an additional difficulty under these changed circumstances. 'The old people get bored and lonely here, too. It is hard enough for us to learn a new language and adjust to new ways, but they are past the age when they can adapt easily . . . I can get a baby-minder for my baby, but where could I leave my poor old father-in-law?'[19]

Relations between police and ethnic groups, not least West Indians, were also increasingly strained: the Notting Hill Carnivals of 1976 and 1979 provided vivid, damaging pictures of violence on television and in the newspapers. In 1976 there were 1600 policemen in the district when the Carnival took place; by 1979 almost half of the entire London force, around 10,000 officers, was present in what had by now become a ritual confrontation.[20] Such flashpoints developed from the 'mugging' scare, a crime which newspapers associated especially with young black men; from high unemployment among young black school leavers, who became very visible on the streets of London, Bristol and Liverpool; and from the persistent stop and search or 'sus' policy used by the police between 1978 and 1980, in which searches, raids and crowd control techniques seemed to be targeted aggressively and particularly against West Indians. Ethnicity was similarly divisive in South Asian districts. 'By 1978 it had become impossible for anyone living or working in the [London] E1 area not to have witnessed the provocations: doorstep and bus-stop abuse, the daubing of menacing graffiti, the window-breaking and air-gun pot shots, the stone and bottle-hurling sorties on Sundays, and the threatening atmosphere around certain estates and tube stations which produced a de facto curfew.'[21] The result was shocking, if predictable: in May 1978 a Bengali tailor in Whitechapel, East London, Altab Ali, was murdered.

The artistic and social responses among ethnic minorities and immigrants to this hostile mood gradually grew more confident and varied. Horace Ové (b.1939) produced the first feature-length film by a black director in Britain, *Pressure* (1975), which described generational differences, the effects of the 'sus' laws and gradual politicization as seen by one black teenager in Ladbroke Grove, West London. Similarly, *A Private Enterprise* (P. K. Smith, 1974) was the first film on Asian immigrant experience in Britain. According to Ken Pryce's study *Endless Pressure*, the stresses of daily experience among the black residents of Bristol in the mid-1970s provoked two main social response, two styles of life. Some, whose acute sense of educational and employment exclusion meant they were often judged 'at risk' in the community, became disreputable 'hustlers' in their teens or early twenties. By contrast the law abiding 'saints', as the name suggests, often actively engaged in the church, and believed compliance rather than confrontation would eventually bring an improvement. Nevertheless, both groups shared the times' difficult living and employment conditions.[22]

Empty spaces

Two footballers, George Best (1946–2005), and Charlie George (b.1950), best illustrate the shift in youth culture and social conditions that took place alongside the growing conflict in race relations. Best had the charisma of swinging London's 'new aristocracy', a Mod-like interest in stylish clothes and fashionable women, but made little impression on the skinheads who massed on the terraces and ran the streets after the final whistle. Charlie George, a few years younger, less well groomed and less well behaved, was closer to the terrace crowds; obsessed by the game, abusive to opponent fans, as tense and angry as an argument in a petrol queue, an affray on the picket line or a racist threat at the National Front repatriation rally. Not only were sections of the young population defiantly nationalistic or aggressively proletarian, they often felt freest to reject whatever apparent symbols of decline came to hand: the pop music of teen idol Donny Osmond; the middle-class aspiration and supposed corner-shop deference of the Pakistani immigrant; the privileged idealism of an 'effeminate' hippie or student revolutionary. Chanting on the terraces, kicking on the streets, the football 'bovver boys' fought to defend an imaginary, collapsing past of local community, white territory and masculine supremacy.

Among the wider cross sections of youth, new privileges came with the reduction of the age of majority from twenty-one to eighteen, and, in 1972, the expansion of educational opportunities as the school-leaving age was increased from fifteen to sixteen.[23] At the same time, however, young people were among the first to suffer from the downturn in employment opportunities. Individual and collective self-esteem as well as any sense of security soon drained away. Families were disrupted too: by 1976, 33 was the median age of wives at divorce; by 1978, about four per cent of all families, three quarters of a million, had only one parent.[24] While Roger Mills (b.1954) had a stable family background, with poor school-leaving results he struggled to find anything other than dead-end jobs when he began searching in 1970. His first paid work, as a 'Messenger/Trainee' at a business firm in the City, involved practically no training. He resigned, was unemployed, travelled abroad for three months and then in 1972 began to look for another job:

> I was getting desperate for employment so I tried to get back into the advertising business. I had burnt any bridges behind me and I went to about a dozen interviews. All but one never even bothered to let me know if I had got it or not . . . I'd sit all day by the phone but they never rang, of course . . . I finally got a job, a paste-up man again, in a small design studio.[25]

Some young people were entirely absorbed in the struggle for work and pay, a number found vent for their restless insecurity as delinquents, while others escaped into apocalyptic imagery and fashion.

Images of lurid destruction, consumerism and paranoia constituted a critique of modern day reality for novelist J. G. Ballard. 'Across the communications landscape move the spectres of sinister technologies and the dreams that money can buy,' he wrote in an introduction to his auto-destruction novel *Crash* (1973).[26] Away from the fringes of the literary counter-culture, the destructive images and end-of-the-world fashions seen in Stanley Kubrick's film *A Clockwork Orange* (1971), as well as in David Bowie's Ziggy Stardust stage act, also attracted audiences. More popular still was the 'glam' style, which offered its own make-believe universe of decadent glitter and dance. One of its icons was pop star Marc Bolan. While less dedicated followers of fashion stayed with the urban hippie look of jeans, tie-dye T-shirts, cotton dresses, Mexican ponchos or Indian cheesecloth smocks, Bolan and his chic contemporaries were flamboyant, even caricatured. Glam's preference was for an afro hair style, an elaborate jacket with patterned collars and ruffs, a red feather boa, velvet trousers, and highly stacked platforms, or ballet shoes.[27] The 'glam' look was complemented by the dreadlocks and bright 'Ethiopian' colours of the Rastafarians, who now became much more visible on the streets; and by the smart dress of the dedicated, energetic club dancers, both black and white: at the All Nations Club, Hackney, East London; at the Northern Soul all weekend dances, Wigan Pier.

What a large segment of white and black youth shared was an absence of certainty that might allow life plans to be made or outcomes predicted. Writing a diary entry in 1975, future music journalist Jon Savage saw only 'London suburbia: sterility – cynicism – boredom'.[28] Savage describes the middle-years of the 1970s as especially bleak: dominated by an older generation wrapped up in its memories of wartime glory and keen to impose its traditions, while the young attempted to define their values and to achieve more mundane goals such as financial independence. The mood among a significant minority eventually turned to the tactics of shock and provocation, beginning in December 1976 when The Sex Pistols provoked public or at least journalistic outrage by swearing repeatedly during a live interview on Thames Television. As a movement though, punk was rooted in the counter-cultural radicalism of a small group interested in music hall political theatre, in cultural propaganda and cash profit. Bernard Rhodes, the manager of The Clash, was most engaged politically; The Sex Pistol's manager, Malcolm McLaren, and the graphic designer who created the group's album cover, Jamie Ried, rather tapped emotions than invented a movement.[29] Mockery of patriotism, and the incorporation of political symbols including the swastika, the Union Jack, and the Queen's head, served to underline the irrelevance of the 'British way of life'. With celebration of empire came the Notting Hill Festival riots; with the powerful folk memory of the Second World War, rerun each Sunday afternoon on television in triumphalist 1950s movies, came a dreadful nostalgia for better times; with celebration of the Royal Family came, worklessness and the iniquities of the youth job market. The contemporary truths were exactly these: unemployment or the threat of it, inner-city decay, above all tedium. Better to wear a string vest, ripped trousers and a dog collar to express this reality; better to embrace a world of plastic clothes and swastika armbands. 'Empty spaces seemed to embody an emotional truth,' wrote Savage, this time describing Notting Hill in 1975, 'this is what England is *really* like'.[30]

The sharp objection which punk and its associated styles stood for was blunted almost immediately. Ordinary teenagers who were neither avid glam rock or punk fans, who gradually altered and adapted their ideas and wardrobe as they passed through school and into the world of work or further education, soon moved on to the more commercial 'new wave' sound, to the reggae fusions of The Police, the 'literate' pop of Kate Bush, or the commercialism of disco. Yet, as the popular cultural and political landscape began to shift away from welfare and consensual collectivism, the prospects for children and young people were not improved. In 1979, 230,000 families had an income below the poverty line; 140,000 more were up to ten per cent above it; with state spending in sharp decline, 370,000 families were officially poor, the vast majority earning low or very low incomes.[31]

Art dematerialized

The condition of mass society, and the political radicalism of the counter-culture as well as the rebellions of 1968, also found displaced expression in the practice of artists. Donald Judd's claim that art was about a name, not an object, that 'if someone calls it art, it is art', was matched by Lucy Lippard's call for a 'dematerialized' art.[32] If the market, dealers and galleries compromised artists into supporting capitalist and materialist values, artists and critics now reasoned, the craft and object of art should be abandoned. The scrutiny of form and meaning might now be carried out by other means: by reducing to essential qualities, as in minimalism; by engaging in a process such as a walk or a street performance; by replacing an object with a concept. Traditional forms, established galleries, preconceived notions of training, elite critics, curators and audiences: all of these could now be disregarded. In their place came a new interest in consumerism itself, in the environment, and the place of particular social groups. For a collective Edinburgh exhibition in 1976, which included work by Victor Burgin, Hamish Fulton, as well as Gilbert and George, one version of this approach was described as follows:

> The photograph and the text have established themselves within the context of art. Outside of this context our experience of these media in newspapers, magazines, books, television, advertising etc. is a familiar part of our everyday lives . . . these works leave us with quite different impressions to the impressions we are used to getting from the mass media. They open up a distance between us and the sorts of ideas we get 'without a second thought'.[33]

Victor Burgin (b.1941) sought to provoke a 'second thought' by his initial attempts to minimize the art object, and then by using combinations of photography and text to reveal the 'meaning'-making procedures of the billboard or the magazine image. For the 1976 exhibition at Edinburgh Fruit Market Gallery, Burgin produced an advertisement-like photograph of an attractive, wealthy woman standing by a fast car and, in an inset photograph, a second woman in work clothes engaged in factory labour. 'Class consciousness,' the inserted text reads in part, 'you're nowhere without it'.[34] Bruce McLean (b.1944) took a similarly oblique and critical view of consumerism when he began to develop *Nice Style: The World's First Pose Band*, a collaborative project with Paul Richards and Ron Carra, which set out with satire and pastiche to explore the idea of 'impression management' as well as the everyday creation of 'persona'. *Nice Style*'s final show, *High Up in a Baroque Palazzo*, drew its title from an article in *House and Garden*, one of the many media sources the group studied for its preoccupation with appliances and layouts as images of perfection.[35] Abandoning the studio for 'throwaway' temporary pieces, for photography, performance, painting and ceramics, McLean's subsequent work, such as *The Masterwork: Award Winning Fishknife* (1979) pricks at the over-inflated in art, in bureaucracy and in politics.[36]

Where Burgin and McLean explore the exaggerated claims of capitalist consumerism, media and advertising, other artists looked again beyond the studio window to consider urban and rural environments. Rejecting the still powerful presence of Henry Moore in British sculpture for instance, Tony Cragg (b.1949) preferred to pile up the discarded odds and ends of the city street: cardboard, corrugated paper, felt offcuts, as in *Stack* (1975). City, not country, surroundings enclosed the majority of the population, Cragg argued, and the broken, corrupted artefacts which float within this world could be recycled, re-sited and re-seen. Cragg took to metal and plastic fragments and created object silhouettes, but he also 'recycled' video and photographic images, again to prompt a new view or thought, or to draw attention to the everyday 'unseen'.[37] Where Cragg amassed the abandoned litter of the city, Richard Long (b.1945) began with *A Line Made by Walking* (1968), travelling and recording in words and photographs his treks over the British Isles as well as Asia, South America and the Arctic Circle: 'A walk is just one more layer, a mark, laid upon the thousands of other layers of human and geographic history on the surface of the land. Maps help us show this.'[38] Like the Boyle Family or Hamish Fulton, Long drew attention to 'environment' and 'nature' and the effects on it of human proximity. His interventions were deliberately slight too, as environmental scrutiny was now unavoidably coloured by concern for the loss and damage humans might inflict.

Another aspect of this reconceptualization of art and the everyday more directly questioned social positions and roles. Arriving in Britain from Pakistan in 1964 for example, Rasheed Araeen (b.1935) found himself marginalized and politicized by his new life, and in response began to explore the social and artistic situation of the 'Afro/Asian' artist. Describing the most overtly political phase in his career, during which he wrote *Preliminary Notes for a Black Manifesto* (1975) and produced such works as *For Oluwale* (1973) and *'Paki Bastard.' Portrait of the Artist as a Black Person* (1977), Araeen stated '. . . my concern remained the pursuit of a critical language that would articulate my aesthetic experience as well as my social experience of living in a society which continued to aspire to its imperial past, and whose institutional structures or intellectual discourses remained trapped in the legacies of colonialism.'[39] Mary Kelly's (b.1941) *Post-Partum Document* (1973-9), by contrast, extended the radical feminist critique which was now emerging among women artists and critics, and which questioned both their role and their purpose. Documenting the relationship she had with her son from his birth onwards, recording exchanges, developments, the intake and excretion of solids and liquids, Kelly attempted to capture personality development and gender definition as they progressively emerged in child and mother, in the sexual division of childcare labour.[40]

Like peasants with free milk

Together with longing and affection, social displacement and critique became insistent themes in popular music; tastes remained volatile, even though the recording industry grew in size and became gradually more influential in defining styles and directing artists towards particular genres. David Bowie's early career illustrates the mix of influences and fashions through the late 1960s and early 1970s. On the one hand, he was rooted in art school and counter-cultural experimentalism, for instance, citing beat novelist William Burroughs as an inspiration; on the other hand, he achieved a commercial appeal that attracted younger teenage fans. By 1970 Bowie had become a successful pop singer with experience of acting and mime as well as an interest in the trappings of fame, glamour and gender. Between 1970 and 1973 he produced a sequence of albums (*The Man Who Sold the World*, 1971; *Hunky Dory*, 1971; *The Rise and Fall of Ziggy Stardust*, 1972; *Aladdin Sane*, 1973) that explored these subjects. Exploiting too his own jokey interpretation of the 'glam' look, 'Legs astride as wide as possible, his face painted incongruously to project a [female impersonator] Danny La Rue profile and a diction quite splendid,' as one reviewer reported, he swayed audiences, critics and other pop acts.[41] When Bowie created the Ziggy Stardust persona and album, which charted the fictional, apocalyptic career of an artist awaiting the world's end, fans copied the 'look' obsessively; the theme music from Stanley Kubrick's recently released film *A Clockwork Orange* was incorporated into the mock 'bovver boy' style and theatrical stage show of *Aladdin Sane*.[42]

Four years on, the Sex Pistols' single 'God Save the Queen', a vitriolic jab at the monarchy and the state it represented, went on sale just a week before the official Silver Jubilee celebrations of 6–13 June 1977. It had sold 200,000 copies by the time the street parties began. The sources of this primitive, aggressive new sound were not so far removed from glam: the British pub rock movement and the American club bands of the early to mid-1970s, especially The New York Dolls. Sex Pistols promoter Malcolm McLaren had managed both in his earlier career. Caroline Coon's description of the London band in 1976 as a 'positive reaction to the complex equipment, technological sophistication, and jaded alienation which has formed a barrier between fans and stars' accurately catches too the pre-punk sound of both London and New York.[43] As the younger British pub bands, Eddie and the Hot Rods, or Dr Feelgood for instance, searched for cheap, accessible entertainment and a more immediate music, they favoured a fast, simple style. It only required a little more aggressive edge, as provided by The Clash or The Damned, to become punk. The movement's symbolic beginning, though, may be dated from the September 1976 Punk Rock Festival at the 100 Club in London, where groups such as Siouxie and the Banshees, from the more affluent, suburban district of Bromley, began to define its look and sound for a wider audience.

Though there were social protest elements in the songs, it was the apolitical slogans, the rejection of consumerism and fashion, of the older generation's values, that stood out. To observers and commentators the movement looked like another of the social ills which blighted the country; to supporters it was an inept attempt to administer a cure. Punk's shifting lyrical preoccupations were largely negative: against youth unemployment and apathy; suburban as well as inner city living; the commercialization of music and fashion. 'Your future dream is a shopping scheme,' sang The Sex Pistols on 'Anarchy in the UK.' 'If you like peace and flowers, I'm going to carry knives and chains,' said The Slits. Rejecting 'bondage,' the X-ray Specs chanted 'chain store, chain smoke, I consume you all/chain gang, chain mail, I don't think at all'.[44] Within a few months the movement had rooted, and its spores gave rise to some livid, unlikely blossoms. Manchester, one of the early centres of punk, threw up Joy Division, while Mark E. Smith, quixotic, inventive leader of The Fall, began his career at the same time. 'In Lancashire . . . the scene started here / Then was America / We went there . . . / All English groups / Act like peasants with free milk,' he droned in one of his songs, describing the beginnings of the movement.[45] Punk's most powerful statement was *London Calling* (1979) by The Clash. Both political and hedonistic, mixing reggae, jazz and rockabilly, its sound was unmistakably a reflection of the West London social milieu from which it emerged.[46]

Glam and punk were among the more fashionable, spectacular styles. Yet teenage audiences still played out romantic fantasy with idol boy singers such as David Essex; students and those who couldn't dance listened to progressive rock groups like Yes; for disco dancers there was the soundtrack to *Saturday Night Fever* (J. Badham, 1977), a film which despite appearances provided a gritty account of blue-collar life in the American inner city. It was punk, though, that brought attention most directly to British inner-city life, and in doing so gave voice to the experiences and frustrations of a generation; it also highlighted the new hybrid culture in which white as well as black, fashion as well as music, were fused.[47]

As both groups felt the same pressures, many of the same experiences and values, it was natural that punk and reggae musicians should share the same performance spaces. Linton Kwesi Johnson continued to provide imaginative, powerful responses to constrained circumstances and hostile surroundings. He published *Dread Beat an' Blood* in 1975, and *Inglan is a Bitch* in 1980; he released *Forces of Victory* (1979) and *Bass Culture* (1980) on the same label that recorded Bob Marley's music, Island Records.[48] Marley, signed and promoted by the British company, sold 500,000 copies of *Exodus* (1977) in Britain and became one of the most successful black musicians of his day. Steel Pulse, who played on the same bill as punk group Generation X, named their 1978 album, *Handsworth Revolution*, after the district where they lived in Birmingham. Punk versions of reggae tunes by The Police or Elvis Costello popularized the style; the deaths of Sid Vicious (1957–79) and Bob Marley (1945–81) effectively ended its commercial run. One legacy of both movements was in the multiracial ska revival from the tail end of the 1970s, which mixed the ethnic background of groups and fans, and, in the sound of groups like The Specials and The Selecter, their musical styles.[49]

A different point of view

With its high production costs, huge potential profits and corporate aversion to risk taking, the movie industry in Britain was less able or interested in responding directly to close-at-hand social change. The failing economy immediately produced a sharp drop in box-office returns, television and other pursuits took precedence, financial support from US companies as well as from the National Film Finance Corporation collapsed.[50] The total number of British films registered fell through these years to 36 in 1981, whereas ten years earlier there had been 98.[51] Moreover, as uncensored features were increasingly shown in private 'clubs', actually public screenings where a nominal membership fee was due, censorship guidelines had to be relaxed to prevent the law falling into disrepute. The British film now faced a creative crisis too: in response to the rise of violence and sexually explicit content from Hollywood came TV spin-offs; mild, bawdy comedies; some low budget avant-garde productions; even the occasional would-be American blockbuster.

Such audiences as there were found refuge in the localized, familiar world of these home-made comedies and musical films. Pop singer David Essex appeared in a cycle of star vehicles including a rock'n'roll movie with Ringo Starr, *That'll be the Day* (1973); the long-running 'Carry On' series finally collapsed with the sex comedy, *Carry On Emmanuelle* (1978); the Who's rock opera *Tommy* (K. Russell, 1975) was given a working over. By the time he made *Tommy*, Ken Russell (b.1927) had become one of the most prolific and popular directors of his time. Beginning in BBC arts documentary in the early 1960s, and with a particular interest in music, both popular and classical, his films typically took biographical material, from the life of an artist, a composer or sculptor for instance, transforming it into fantasy.[52] While Russell was criticized for a visual flare which could appear crude and excessive, film critic Alexander Walker nevertheless saw the qualities of a film such as *Tommy*:

> Russell seized all the opportunities for visual wizardry: *Tommy* resembles a phantasmagoria of Dali, Bosch, Tanguy and Yves Fuchs. A skeleton crawls with slugs, lizards and snakes; the pinball machines which Elton John (in glitter specs and gargantuan bovver boots) bids to do his will like a Pop Messiah, throb with psychedelic razzamatazz; huge iron canisters litter the amusement park like the spawn of monstrous fishes . . .[53]

Russell's own statements on his visual style are reminiscent of Francis Bacon's attempts to remove the 'screens' of self-deception and inhibition from the eyes of viewers. 'There are certain points in every film I do, where I deliberately want to shock people into awareness . . . to turn everything upside down will make everyone, including myself, look at a situation from a different point of view . . .'.[54]

Russell's own *The Devils* (1970), a giddy jumble of sexual and religious hysteria, was one of several films that now tested the bounds of official regulation and public decorum. *Last Tango in Paris* (B. Bertolucci, 1973) for its explicit, compulsive and troubled couplings, and *Monty Python's Life of Brian* (Terry Jones, 1979) for its alleged blasphemy, were similarly contentious. Stanley Kubrick's version of *A Clockwork Orange* (1971) highlighted the censorship debate early on as directors argued they should make full use of less stringent regulation. Perhaps because it was sited in an identifiably British urban setting, the story of Alex DeLarge's career as leader of a gang of violent youths who indulged in terror, robbery and murder was especially disturbing to audiences. Following a vicious gang rape in a remote country house, and a subsequent murder, Alex is sent to prison and given the chance of 'aversion therapy', intended to inhibit his evil intentions before he can act on them once more.

Attempting to justifying the rape scenes in particular Kubrick argued that it was 'absolutely necessary to give weight to Alex's brutality, otherwise I think there would be a moral confusion with respect to what the government does to him'.[55] To sections of the press and public though, the argument that the violations of free will and rape were morally equivalent was less relevant than the apparent copycat attacks which followed the film and which caused Kubrick to withdraw it from circulation in the UK during his lifetime. Similarly Mike Hodges' film of the Newcastle criminal underworld, *Get Carter* (1971), was attacked for its 'pointless' violence and its seeming manipulation of the audience's emotions. In this case, the assassination of the main character in the final moments of the movie left less moral ambiguity.[56]

While the explicit or imagined violence of *A Clockwork Orange* or *Get Carter* felt uncomfortably close to contemporary British life for some viewers, similar themes in futuristic, science fiction or horror movies were somehow less threatening. Pastiche, mockery and nudity became a part of the horror formula. There were, though, still notable oddities and successes, including *Scream and Scream Again* (G. Hessler, 1970) or *The Wicker Man* (R. Hardy, 1973).[57] *Don't Look Now* (N. Roeg, 1973) was both artistic and commercial success as it became the biggest box-office hit of 1974. Like *The Wicker Man*, which portrays a policeman's investigation into a murder on a remote Scottish island as a lure that leads eventually to the policeman's ritual, pagan sacrifice, *Don't Look Now* describes a series of events, beginning with the accidental drowning of a young girl, which run unexpectedly and dangerously out of control. In both films the central protagonist is caught in an inexplicable, fatal web; remote and malignant forces draw their victim towards destruction.[58] *Don't Look Now* was also distinguished for its visual flare and its complex portrayal of a marriage in which the interior, mental and emotional world of the protagonists was reflected in their physical union. Roeg's explained:

> I didn't consciously set out to make it [an explicit scene] that way. It came out of the fact that their performances [Donald Sutherland and Julie Christie] were so wonderful. I gradually realized as we were shooting that, in reality, they were a young married couple with children and that in every scene they were rowing or something, and they were rather grumpy people . . . Sexual intimacy is part of love and marriage, closeness and oneness, and it was a very innocent shot . . .[59]

Likewise the horror and fantastic elements of the film, John's premonition of his daughter's death and his eventual murder in Venice by the red-cloaked dwarf, play out against a backdrop of convincing human relationships between the central protagonists.

The success of Roeg's film was insufficient, however, to revive the failing career of the British cinema industry. The major companies, Lord Grade's Associated Communications Corporation, as well as EMI and Rank, made a final, doomed attempt to reach the American market with blockbusters such as the $35m flop *Raise the Titanic* (1980). Younger film-makers, more interested in low budget and experimental production, were in any case by now moving in different directions. After a false start with *Bleak Moments* (1971), Mike Leigh worked in television through the 1970s and later revived his career as a cinema director; Derek Jarman, whose life as a film professional had begun with his set designs for Ken Russell films, began to display his vision in the dystopian, futuristic punk dream of *Jubilee* (1977).[60]

Timeline 2: 1960–79

1960

Society: CND popularity peaks; Polaris missiles to be stationed in the UK. **February:** Macmillan's 'wind of change' speech marks acceleration of decolonization; British Somaliland, Cyprus and Nigeria all achieve independence. **March:** government scraps Blue Streak missile project. **July:** Wolfenden Report, including liberalization of laws on homosexuality, rejected by Commons. **November:** *Lady Chatterley's Lover* (1928) published. **December:** refusal of independence for Buganda.

Arts: TV, theatre, film: Michael Powell, *Peeping Tom*; Tony Richardson, *The Entertainer*; Karel Reisz, *Saturday Night and Sunday Morning*; first episode of *Coronation Street*; Harold Pinter, *The Caretaker*; Peter Hall and Peter Brook appointed directors of the RSC. **Visual:** Bridget Riley, *Pink Landscape*. **Musical:** new 'trad jazz' boom. **Written:** Stan Barstow, *A Kind of Loving*; Robert Bolt, *A Man for All Seasons*; David Storey, *This Sporting Life*.

1961

Society: Yuri Gagarin's first space flight, American Alan Shepard follows within a few weeks; Conservatives begin to lose support; expansion of British universities. **May:** betting laws liberalized; British spy George Blake sentenced to 42 years. **July:** British negotiations to enter European Common Market begin. **October:** rise in Cold War tension after Russian explosion of a 60-megaton bomb; 'sit-down' demonstrations and mass arrests of the anti-nuclear Committee of 100 in Trafalgar Square.

Arts: TV, theatre, film: the rise of satire; Samuel Beckett, *Happy Days*; Basil Dearden, *Victim*; Tony Richardson, *A Taste of Honey*. **Visual:** David Hockney, *We Two Boys Together Clinging*; Peter Phillips, *For Men Only, Starring MM and BB*. **Musical:** the Twist dance craze; opening of the first discotheque; Benjamin Britten, *A Midsummer Night's Dream* (opera); Lionel Bart, *Oliver!* (stage musical). **Written:** Doris Lessing, *The Golden Notebook*; Muriel Spark, *The Prime of Miss Jean Brodie*; *New English Bible*.

1962

Society: Macmillan's government continues to lose support; 'What went wrong with Britain?' debate peaks; smog in London kills estimated 750 people; Cuban missile crisis. **March:** British applications to join the European Coal and Steel Community and the European Atomic Energy Community. **May:** consecration of Coventry Cathedral. **July:** Commonwealth Immigrants Act limits entry into Britain; Macmillan 'purge' of seven cabinet ministers to regain public confidence. **August:** Jamaica, Trinidad and Tobago gain independence.

Arts: TV, theatre, film: TV satire: *That Was the Week That Was*; *Z Cars*: realist TV police drama; David Lean, *Lawrence of Arabia*; Tony Richardson, *The Loneliness of the Long-Distance Runner*; Arnold Wesker, *Chips with Everything*. **Visual:** first solo exhibition by Bridget Riley; Derek Boshier, *First Toothpaste Painting*. **Musical:** The Beatles reach no. 19 in the charts on 8 December with *Love Me Do*. **Written:** Anthony Burgess, *A Clockwork Orange*.

———————————————— 1963 ————————————————

SOCIETY: Worst winter for 200 years; assassination of President Kennedy; Test ban treaty signed; Robbins Report recommends doubling of university places over next ten years. **January:** British EEC entry blocked by President de Gaulle. **February:** Harold Wilson elected leader of the Labour Party. **June:** Profumo scandal becomes public; USA and USSR agree on 'hotline' link. **October:** Macmillan resigns as Prime Minister, succeeded by Alec Douglas-Home.

ARTS: TV, theatre, film: National Theatre opens; Lindsay Anderson, *This Sporting Life*; Joseph Losey, *The Servant*; Tony Richardson, *Tom Jones*; Peter Yates, *Summer Holiday*; TV pop show *Ready, Steady, Go!* **Visual:** Pauline Boty, *The Only Blonde in the World*; Joe Tilson, *A–Z Box of Friends and Family*; Biba fashion stores open. **Musical:** Peter Yates, *Summer Holiday*, starring Cliff Richard; Beatles, first LP: **Written:** Nell Dunn, *Up the Junction*; Hugh MacDiarmid, *Collected Poems*; John A. T. Robinson, *Honest to God*.

———————————————— 1964 ————————————————

SOCIETY: major financial crisis within the first three months of Labour election victory; Campaign against Racial Discrimination established; launch of *The Sun*; *The Observer* and *The Daily Telegraph* introduce colour supplements. **April:** BBC2 begins broadcasting. **October: General election:** Labour government takes power with a narrow majority. **December:** loan of $100 million to steady the economy from IMF; Martin Luther King visits London.

ARTS: TV, theatre, film: Stanley Kubrick, *Dr Strangelove*; TV arts programme, *Monitor* ends its 7-year run; Peter Brook's 'theatre of cruelty'; Joe Orton, *Entertaining Mr Sloane*. **Visual:** New Generation exhibition, Whitechapel Gallery, London; Richard Hamilton, *My Marilyn (paste up)*; Ron Kitaj, *The Ohio Gang*. **Musical:** release of The Beatles' *A Hard Day's Night*; mods and rocker seaside riots; *Top of the Pops* begins on BBC TV. **Written:** Philip Larkin, *The Whitsun Weddings*; first tabloid newspaper: *The Sun*.

———————————————— 1965 ————————————————

SOCIETY: Race Relations Act and Race Relations Board; Rent Act; race riots in the Watts, Los Angeles. **January:** Sir Winston Churchill dies. **September:** discovery of North Sea Oil; major escalation of the war in Vietnam. **October:** House of Commons vote to abolish death penalty; anti-Vietnam War demonstrations in Britain and USA. **November:** death penalty abolished in Britain; Rhodesia declares unilateral independence.

ARTS: 'Swinging London'. **TV, theatre, film:** David Lean, *Dr Zhivago*; John Schlesinger, *Darling*; Silvio Narizzano, *Georgy Girl*. **Visual:** New Generation sculpture exhibition at the Whitechapel Gallery. **Musical:** Beatles LP *Help!*; The Beatles receive MBEs in Queen's Birthday Honours; Bob Dylan, *Bringing it All Back Home*. **Written:** B. Abel-Smith and P. Townsend, *The Poor and the Poorest*; M. Horowitz's *Poetry International*, Royal Albert Hall.

———————————————— 1966 ————————————————

SOCIETY: introduction of colour television; *Plan for Scotland*. **February:** proposals for what later became the Open University announced. **March: General election** Labour increases its majority from five at the last election to 97. **July:** England wins the World Cup; end of three month seamen's strike; announcement of deflationary measures including a six-month wages freeze; Gwynfor Evans, Plaid Cymru MP, at Carmarthen. **October:** Aberfan coal tip disaster in Wales kills 28 adults and 116 children.

ARTS: TV, theatre, film: Lewis Gilbert, *Alfie*; Joe Orton, *Loot*; Ken Loach directs acclaimed TV play by Jeremy Sandford, *Cathy Come Home*. **Visual:** William Turnbull, *5x1*. **Musical:** The Beatles, *Revolver*;

The Kinks, *Face to Face*. **Written:** Basil Bunting, *Briggflatts*; Seamus Heaney, *Death of a Naturalist*; John Fowles, *The Magus*; Paul Scott, *The Jewel in the Crown*; first issue of *International Times*.

1967

SOCIETY: Abortion Act and Family Planning Act; football violence and skinheads gain media attention; formation of the anti-immigration, pro-repatriation National Front. **March:** 120,000 gallons of oil spilt off Land's End in the *Torrey Canyon* shipping disaster. **April:** Conservative gains in GLC elections signal loss of support for Harold Wilson and the Labour government. **October:** Major demonstrations against the Vietnam War in European capitals and Washington. **November:** following withdrawal of British troops, Aden declares independence as the Republic of South Yemen.

ARTS: TV, theatre, film: Michelangelo Antonioni, *Blow-Up*; Terence Fisher, *Frankenstein Created Woman*; Richard Lester, *How I Won the War*; Joseph Losey, *Accident*; John Schlesinger, *Far From the Madding Crowd*; Tom Stoppard, *Rosencrantz and Guildenstern are Dead*. **Visual:** Anthony Caro, *Prairie*. **Musical:** The Beatles, *Sergeant Pepper's Lonely Hearts Club Band*. **Written:** first issue of *Oz* magazine.

1968

SOCIETY: Clean Air Act; Ronan Point tower block, London, collapses. **March:** Second Commonwealth Immigrants Act limits entry; Wootton Report recommends liberalization of drug use. **April:** anti-immigration speech by Enoch Powell. **May:** student movement peaks: protests at Essex, Hornsey, Hull and Birmingham. **August:** invasion of Czechoslovakia. **September:** abolition of theatre censorship. **October:** Northern Ireland conflict begins; clashes between police and demonstrators in Grosvenor Square; large anti-Vietnam demonstrations in Trafalgar Square.

ARTS: TV, theatre, film: Lindsay Anderson, *If . . .*; Edward Bond, *Narrow Road to the Deep North*; Peter Collinson, *Up The Junction*; Terence Fisher, *The Devil Rides Out*. **Visual:** Richard Hamilton, *Swingeing London 67 II*; Richard Long, *A Line Made by Walking*. **Musical:** Pink Floyd release *A Saucerful of Secrets* and play a Hyde Park free concert. **Written:** Cecil Day Lewis becomes Poet Laureate.

1969

SOCIETY: Divorce Act. **January:** Northern Ireland Protestant leader Ian Paisley jailed. **April:** British armed troops enter Belfast; Bernadette Devlin elected MP, aged 22; Children and Young Persons Act; Government White Paper, *In Place of Strife*, proposes mediation in industrial disputes. **July:** Armstrong and Aldrin land on the moon. **August:** British Army take over Northern Ireland police and security following Apprentice Boys March and three-day street battle in Londonderry. **December:** Free vote in the Commons abolishes death penalty.

ARTS: TV, theatre, film: Richard Attenborough, *Oh! What a Lovely War*; Ken Loach, *Kes*; Joe Orton, *What the Butler Saw*; first broadcast of *Monty Python's Flying Circus* and Kenneth Clark's *Civilization*. **Visual:** Allen Jones, *Table Sculpture*, *Hat Stand* and *Chair*. **Musical:** Rolling Stones play free in Hyde Park; Bob Dylan and The Band play at the first Isle of Wight Festival. **Written:** John Fowles, *The French Lieutenant's Woman*.

1970

SOCIETY: Equal Pay Act, to operate from 1975, intended to end pay discrimination between women and men; age of majority reduced from 21 to 18; establishment of Royal Commission on Environmental Pollution. **May:** Cancellation of South African Cricket tour to Britain due to opposition from apartheid activists. **June: General election:** Conservative government with a majority of 30; Edward Heath becomes Prime Minister; new application from Britain to join the European Economic Community. **October:** strike by London's refuse collectors.

ARTS: TV, theatre, film: Young Vic Theatre Company formed in London; R. W. Baker, *The Vampire Lovers*; Joseph Losey, *The Go-Between*; Nicolas Roeg, *Performance*; Ken Russell, *The Music Lovers*; *The Devils*. **Visual:** David Hockney, *Mr and Mrs Clark and Percy* (1970–1); **Musical:** Jimi Hendrix performs in front of 200,000 fans at the Isle of Wight pop festival. **Written:** Ted Hughes, *Crow*.

--------------------------1971--------------------------

SOCIETY: introduction of Family Allowance Supplement; abolition of free milk for school children; Misuse of Drugs Act; *Oz* trial; Immigration Act further limits entry rights. **January:** Divorce Reform Act. **March:** 1.5 million engineers go on strike against the Industrial Relations Bill. **August:** Conservative government introduces Industrial Relations Act; preventative detention and internment without trial introduced in Northern Ireland. **October:** Parliament votes in favour of joining the Common Market.

ARTS: TV, theatre, film: Stanley Kubrick, *A Clockwork Orange*; Richard Attenborough, *Young Winston*; M. Leigh, *Bleak Moments*; Nicholas Roeg, *Walkabout*; Peter Sykes, *Steptoe and Son*. **Visual:** M. Lancaster, *James Gibbs*. **Musical:** David Bowie, *Hunky Dory*. **Written:** Germaine Greer, *The Female Eunuch*; Richard Neville, *Powerplay*.

--------------------------1972--------------------------

SOCIETY: Ugandan Asians, expelled from Uganda, forced to settle in Britain; Housing Finance Act. **January:** power cuts and industrial action as a result of the strike by miners; 13 civilians killed by paratroopers in Londonderry on 'Bloody Sunday'. **February:** state of emergency and 1.5 million workers laid off as a result of the power crisis; IRA bombing campaign begins on mainland Britain, seven killed at Aldershot; direct rule introduced in Northern Ireland. **July:** national dock strike begins. **November:** government imposes a 90-day pay and prices freeze.

ARTS: TV, theatre, film: Tom Stoppard, *Jumpers*. **Visual:** Lucian Freud, *Wasteground Near Paddington*. **Musical:** David Bowie, *Space Oddity*; First Windsor Free Festival; Andrew Lloyd Webber's musical *Jesus Christ Superstar*. **Written:** John Berger wins the Booker Prize for *G*; Angela Carter, *The Infernal Desire Machines of Dr Hoffman*.

--------------------------1973--------------------------

SOCIETY: school leaving age raised to 16. **January:** Britain, Denmark and Irish Republic join the EEC. **May:** Select Committee hearing on Watergate begins in Washington. **July:** following pro-British referendum in Northern Ireland the first sitting of the new Northern Ireland Assembly breaks up in disarray. **October:** Arab–Israeli war begins, reduction of oil supplies to the west. **November:** OPEC announces major increases in the price of oil. **December:** fuel crisis in Britain; emergency measures including a three-day working week and 50mph speed limit.

ARTS: TV, theatre, film: Lindsay Anderson, *O Lucky Man!*; Alan Ayckbourn, *Absurd Person Singular*; Robin Hardy, *The Wicker Man*; Nicolas Roeg, *Don't Look Now*; **Visual:** Francis Bacon, *Triptych May–June*. **Musical:** Bob Marley, *Catch A Fire*; Roxy Music, *For Your Pleasure*; First Stonehenge People's Free Festival. **Written:** Martin Amis, *The Rachel Papers*; J. G. Farrell, *The Siege of Krishnapur*; John McGrath, *The Cheviot, The Stag and the Black, Black Oil* (BBC *Play for Today* adaptation, 1974); death of W. H. Auden.

--------------------------1974--------------------------

SOCIETY: February: Eighty-one per cent of miners vote to strike; **General election:** Harold Wilson forms a minority government. **May:** collapse of the Northern Ireland Assembly, return to direct rule. **June:** one person killed when National Front and opponents clash in Red Lion Square, London. **August:** President Nixon resigns. **October: General election:** Labour returned with a majority of three; IRA pub bombings in Guildford leave five dead and 70 injured. **November:** IRA pub bombings in Birmingham leave 21 dead and 121 injured; Anti-Terrorism Bill extends police powers.

ARTS: **TV, theatre, film:** Tom Stoppard, *Travesties*; Michael Apted, *Stardust*; Don Sharp, *Callan*. **Visual:** David Hockney exhibition in Paris. **Musical:** David Bowie, *Aladdin Sane*. **Written:** David Jones, *The Sleeping Lord*; Buchi Emecheta, *Second-Class Citizen*.

1975

SOCIETY: environmental and conservation concerns prompt foundation of the Ecology Party. **February:** Margaret Thatcher becomes Conservative Party leader; London Tube train crash kills 35. **July:** inflation rises to 25 per cent; government limits pay increases. **October:** unemployment rises to over one million. **November:** £975m loan to Britain from the IMF. **December:** end of internment without trial in Northern Ireland; Sex Discrimination Act and Equal Pay Acts come into force.

ARTS: **TV, theatre, film:** Howard Brenton, *The Churchill Play*; Trevor Griffiths, *The Comedians*; first British feature film by a black director: Horace Ove's *Pressure*; Ken Russell, *Tommy*. **Visual:** death of Barbara Hepworth in St Ives; Rasheed Araeen, *Preliminary Notes for a Black Manifesto*; Tony Cragg, *Stack*. **Musical:** Bob Marley charts with 'No Woman No Cry'; Bay City Rollers reach no. 1 with 'Bye Bye Baby'. **Written:** Martin Amis, *Dead Babies*; Malcolm Bradbury, *The History Man*; Anthony Powell, *A Dance to the Music of Time*. Ruth Prawer Jhabvala wins the Booker Prize for *Heat and Dust*.

1976

SOCIETY: heatwave and drought throughout the summer; severe public expenditure cuts announced in response to economic crisis; Domestic Violence and Matrimonial Proceedings Act; Race Relations Act, and establishment of the Commission for Racial Equality; Fair Employment (Northern Ireland) Act. **April:** following the resignation of Harold Wilson, James Callaghan becomes Labour Prime Minister. **June:** European and American banks provide £3b loans for Britain. **July:** British Ambassador to the Irish Republic assassinated. **September:** disturbances during Notting Hill carnival, London.

ARTS: **TV, theatre, film:** Caryl Churchill, *Light Shining in Buckinghamshire*; Terence Davies, *Children*; Guy Green, *Luther*; Nicolas Roeg, *The Man who Fell to Earth*. **Visual:** Carl Andre's *Equivalent VIII* (1966) causes outrage when shown at the Tate Gallery. **Musical:** first album by The Clash; Rock Against Racism campaign begins. **Written:** Ann Oakley, *Housewife*.

1977

SOCIETY: Development of Rural Wales Act. **March:** Liberal–Labour pact prevents the Conservatives forcing a general election. **June:** Silver Jubilee celebrations in London mark the 25-year reign of Elizabeth II. **July–September:** Grunwick strike: police and mass pickets clash. **August:** new post-war unemployment peak of 1,635,800; violence during a London march by the National Front. **November:** firemen strike for a 30 per cent increase in wages; army deal with fires.

ARTS: **TV, theatre, film:** David Hare, *Plenty*; Mike Leigh, *Abigail's Party*; Lewis Gilbert, *The Spy Who Loved Me*. **Visual:** Rasheed Araeen, *'Paki Bastard': Portrait of the Artist as a Black Person*. **Musical:** 'God Save the Queen' reaches no. 2 for the Sex Pistols. **Written:** Angela Carter, *The Passion of New Eve*; Tom Nairn, *The Breakup of Britain*.

1978

SOCIETY: February: inflation below ten per cent for the first time since 1973. **March:** House of Commons consider stricter immigration controls. **April:** regular broadcasting from Parliament begins. **May:** murder of Attab Ali in East London. **July:** Devolution Bills for Scotland and Wales pass through Parliament. **October:** five per cent wage norm rejected by Unions. **December:** IRA bombing campaign; explosions in several cities including Manchester, London and Bristol.

ARTS: TV, theatre, film: John Guillermin, *Death on the Nile*; Don Sharp, *The Thirty-Nine Steps*; Derek Jarman, *Jubilee*. **Visual:** Lucian Freud, *Two Plants*. **Musical:** Steel Pulse, *Handsworth Revolution*; Anti-Nazi League festival in London. **Written:** Margaret Drabble, *The Ice Age*.

1979

SOCIETY: January: 150,000 laid off work in road haulage strike. **March:** devolution referenda: Wales votes against; and Scotland fails to reach the required majority. **April:** serious clashes between the National Front and the Anti-Nazi League in Southall, London, 1 killed, 300 arrested. **May: General election:** Mrs Thatcher becomes Britain's first woman Prime Minister, the Conservatives win a majority of 43. **December:** Employment Bill changes regulations on picketing, secret ballots and compulsory union membership; British Steel announces 52,000 job losses.

ARTS: TV, theatre, film: *Monty Python's Life of Brian*; Denis Potter, *Blue Remembered Hills*; Franc Roddam, *Quadrophenia*; Peter Shaffer, *Amadeus*. **Visual:** Mary Kelly, *Post-Partum Document*; Bruce McLean, *The Masterwork: Award Winning Fishknife*. **Musical:** New Romantics appear in London clubs; The Clash, *London Calling*. **Written:** Seamus Heaney, *Field Work*; P. Townsend, *Poverty in the United Kingdom*.

PART III

Post-empire, Post-aesthetics

CHAPTER 7

Communication Webs

A centre in the northern world

The collectivist ethos and welfare ideals of the postwar era were stretched to their furthest extent by the winter of 1978–9: health, welfare and education had improved immeasurably for the majority of the population since before the Second World War. Yet as the memory of military conflict and of factory production in the mass industrial age began to ebb, new tides caught the collective imagination. In Scotland, where unity, equality and labour remained powerful creeds, and where industrial development had profoundly affected ways of living, the passing away of heavy industry, and of the radical idealism that accompanied it, was often a cause of regret. Journalist Ian Jack, using his father's life story as a medium through which to trace wider social and urban developments, observed that by around 1985 the old collective routines and urban environs were almost lost. The house that Jack's father had grown up in was gone; in its place stood a traffic island; the school that had taught him such carefully sculptured handwriting was demolished, replaced by a supermarket; and the mine where he had spent much of his working life was covered over by urban grassland and carparks.[1] When Irish writer Colm Tóibín visited Glasgow in 1993 he discussed the city's political heritage with author Jim McCormack, whose father had travelled from Ireland in 1934. McCormack, by then in his fifties, still 'loved and respected the older men who tried to run a revolution in Scotland, men who spoke to Lenin'. He also saw the persistence of these values not so much in politics as in the arts: theatre groups such as 7:84 and the Citizen's Theatre, singers, poets and writers, whose activities became 'the flowering of the old socialist/communist world'.[2]

While activists and ideologues were only ever a small minority, the wider industrial culture of Scotland together with its urban and social landscape was now transformed. Between 1979 and 1987, 20,000 jobs were lost per year in manufacturing. The greatest losses were in the Borders, long associated with textile manufacture, and in the industrial heartland of the west of Scotland: in light industry the list of closures over the 1980s included, among many others, Singers (Clydebank), Goodyear (Glasgow), BSR (East Kilbride), and Rowntree Mackintosh (Edinburgh).[3] The most symbolic shut down was Ravenscraig Steelworks, which had stood for Scotland's industrial heritage and future for over thirty-five years until it was closed in 1992. Dundee had by now lost its long-established partnerships with jute and carpet manufacture as well as with Timex. The age of global competition arrived in the town in 1988 when negotiations for a possible Ford car plant were halted, as unions could not agree between themselves on a single deal with the company. Much to the chagrin of

Illustration 7 Downs and ups of the market: London Stock Exchange, 1987

the local population the plant was relocated to Portugal.[4] Such changes, and disappointments followed from wider national and international developments. Between 1981 and 1996 the twenty largest urban areas in the United Kingdom, including the West Midlands, Greater Manchester, Glasgow, Edinburgh and Cardiff, witnessed the disappearance of around half a million jobs. In the rest of the United Kingdom about 1,700,000 jobs were created. Those who were now expelled from the labour market were often unable to re-enter; many spent the remainder of their working lives claiming subsistence from the state.[5]

Some opportunities offered by the new Thatcher administration were taken up in Scotland. In December 1979, 1.07 million households were on council estates or some other kind of state housing and, as this public housing came up for sale, many tenants were happy to become owners, so that by December 1991 there were 243,000 less people in such subsidized accommodation.[6] Other measures also indicated a gradual increase in living standards: by 1981, 31 per cent of Dundee's council tenants and 41 per cent of home owners had their own cars; in more prosperous Aberdeen, which had benefited from the oil boom, 41 per cent of council tenants and 53 per cent of homeowners also possessed cars.[7] Nevertheless, damage seemed to outweigh benefit in the new political dispensation. Unemployment increased alarmingly through the first half of the 1980s, pushing up social security payments by a half; anti-union legislation and the miners' strike of 1984–5 were socially as well as politically disruptive. Public and private investment and redevelopment continued, but with less stress on collective welfare than on business promotion, enterprise and private profit. In Inverclyde and Tayside enterprise zones were set up and received financial incentives as well as concessions to encourage manufacture and commerce. In Dundee, the expansion plan for 1982–5 meant an investment of £18 million from the Scottish Development Agency, £6 million from the Tayside region and another £18 million from private business. Dundonians were sceptical of the designs for the new waterfront, however, as investors, among them Mecca Leisure and UGC Cinemas, planned the bay front to include a supermarket, a windowless cinema, a home improvement store and a thousand parking places.[8]

If it ever did become a coherent set of values or policies, Thatcherism's characteristic qualities only evolved gradually. If its motives and effects remained not entirely predictable, the coincidence with rising unemployment, the limited success of market exports and manufacturing, caused widespread resentments in Scotland, and thereby assisted a gradual return to the nationalist cause. From 1979 to the mid-1990s electoral support for the Conservatives was halved to around fifteen per cent: active dislike for the ruling party among the majority of the Scottish population steadily increased through their years in office.[9] The initial resistance of both sides: of Scottish voters to Thatcherite Conservatism, and of Conservatives towards Scottish fastness, caused each to redouble its efforts. Tories hoped for the conversion of votes; Scottish activists for the revival of politicized nationalist militancy. While this revival was slow to develop, a new assurance was displayed in the arts, as the values and culture of Scotland were re-imagined beyond the confines of the political union. Unaccountability, unpopular policies, centralization of political decision making outside the reach of Scotland's electorate: these became questions of collective value and moral weight, and an attack on community, on 'our distinctive systems of education and government'.[10] If the failure of North Sea Oil revenues to perceptibly advance the cause of Scotland during the painful years of deindustrialization was one symbol of how local interests felt marginalized, the Community Charge – the Poll Tax – provided the moment for a dramatic display of resistance.

With strong backing from Scottish Conservatives, and against the advice of Ministers in central government, the Scottish version of this Bill on new local taxation arrangements was passed in May 1987 to come into force in 1989, a year ahead of the Bill for England and Wales. The non-payment campaign was protracted and bitter in Scotland: only 76.5 per cent of revenue was raised by local authorities in 1991–2; 2.5 million summary warrants were issued for non-payment over the first three years of the Act. Significantly, it was less the Scottish campaign that destroyed the political resolve to retain the tax than the imminent prospect of electoral defeat for many Conservative MPs because the tax was so unpopular. The disorderly, headline-grabbing demonstration in March 1990 also helped destroyed the tax: a protest attended by around 300,000 people, and held in London.[11]

Together with these dramatic and ideological oppositions came patchy social change in both city and countryside. Attempts to reinvigorate the urban environment, especially the Glasgow Eastern Area Renewal Project, began to revive some of the poorest areas of the city, while central Glasgow became increasingly attractive and cosmopolitan. In the outer estates and peripheral districts, though, unemployment and social deprivation was more visible. During his travels around Britain in the mid-1990s journalist Nick Danziger explored many such places, and in Glasgow he spoke to Carol, one of whose daughters was a heroin addict subsequently killed by an overdose:

> I've often asked myself, where've I gone wrong. Six lassies had jobs, two machinists – the younger two – two girls in the carpet factory, two in a dispensary, they called it the Sannex factory. They got laid off, all six, in time all the factories closed down. Machinists switched to computers, only eighteen of them in it now, Sannex went into liquidation and the carpet factory moved to London. I really think that contributed to it. They started hanging around the street corners. Got fed up of sitting in the house.[12]

In the more elevated surroundings of the Queen Elizabeth Square project, in the immigrant district and poorest quarter of inner Glasgow, the Gorbals, hopes for a better future had also gone sour. It was here that Sir Basil Spence (1907–76) attempted to recreate working-class community in two huge tower blocks holding around two thousand people. Spence's vision was that his blocks should resemble the great ocean liners that had once been built on the Clyde. Like the shipbuilding industry itself, the development suffered both financial and human neglect, so that despite efforts to preserve the site as a monument to modernist architecture, it was demolished in 1993.[13]

Beyond the city limits too there was dramatic social and environmental transformation. In the early twentieth century the restructuring of agricultural labour and the decline in the rural populace foreshadowed the depopulation of the countryside. After 1945 these processes accelerated: jobs fell from 100,000 to 28,000 in the forty years to 1991 in the formerly vital industries of agriculture, forestry and fishing.[14] While rural life was not so obviously a wellspring of national values or traditions as in Wales, tourism and the heritage industry nevertheless both became major sources of employment as well as an increasingly important source of revenue, adding £2 billion per year to the economy by the mid-1990s. Nor was the decline of Scottish Gaelic, spoken by 65,000 in 1991, such a politically charged issue as Welsh language development, though much the same processes were at work. As communications to even the remotest districts improved, bilingualism, or rather the use of English among Gaelic-speaking populations increased, the contexts and purposes of Scottish Gaelic language use changed. The consequence of this linguistic 'colonization' was, to take one example, that 'Gaelic thins out in Mull earlier than in Tiree, in Skye sooner than in Harris, in Benbecula (with its airport and army camp) sooner than in South Uist.'[15] Yet with many Scottish nationalists in the Thatcher years, Orkney historian W. P. L. Thomson points out that 'end of the line' maps are not the only way to imagine local geography, that local identities, linguistic, cultural or political, do not have to view urban or governmental centres as the 'core' while all else remained 'peripheral'. The process may be reversed by, for example 'twinning Orkney with Hordaland, cooperation between the three Island Authorities, the activities of the Orkney–Norway Friendship Society, and attempts to revive sea links with Shetland' to promote the rediscovery of 'a central position in the northern world'.[16]

While Scotland's values and institutions long predated Thatcherism, and while a strong unionist tradition connected Scotland and England during the imperial age, the interests of the two nations were now seen to be steadily diverging: in England the 1983 election saw the Tories ahead of Labour by 17.5 per cent; in Scotland Labour led the Conservatives by 6.7 per cent.[17] In the wake of the 1979 devolution fiasco there was an attempt to describe the new cultural divide, the moral and social state of the nation, in theatre, music and literature. In *Poor Things* (1992) Alasdair Gray (b.1934) underwrites Glasgow's industrious, democratic impulse from the Victorian era; *How Late It Was, How Late* (1994) is James Kelman's (b.1946) attempt to recover and revalue the marginalized language and culture of his own working-class background. 'I wanted to write and remain a member of my own community,' he explained in 1992. 'In fact, as far as I could see, looking around me, it had never been done.'[18] The new, small presses such as Rebel Inc and Clocktower shared these interests; less established writers, among them Irvine Welsh (b.1961) and Janice Galloway (b.1956), used vernacular language and formal experiment to express peripheral lives. Galloway's *Foreign Parts* (1994) describes a blocked and broken journey as her two protagonists, Cassie and Rona, encounter 'abroad' and reflect on 'hame', Scotland. Welsh famously attends to the language and bodily needs of Edinburgh's drug addicts in *Trainspotting* (1993), but his wider body of work catches too the regional and class accents of Manchester, Somerset and the West Indies.

Not initially intended to snare any political prey, the gradually spun web of imaginative expression that developed after 1979, and particularly in the early 1990s, came to represent a new self-confidence. Eventually a more concerted effort to establish Scottish Home Rule emerged, for example in December 1992 at the European Union Summit meeting in Edinburgh, which prompted a supporters' march of 25,000. Following Labour's huge election victory in May 1997, a referendum on Scottish devolution was held in September and, unlike 1979, the answer was clear-cut: 1,775,045 (74.3 per cent) voted for a Scottish Parliament; 1,512,889 (63.5 per cent) for tax-raising powers.

Breakdown of Irelands

No such decisive solutions were available to Northern Ireland by 1997. Rather a process of complicating and making more intricate the claims and counter-claims of both history and territory was under way. Edna Longley, critic and essayist, suggested that artists, as in Scotland, now had an important role in the imaginative reworking of nationhood. In particular writers first and foremost felt the need to question, 'to explore and criticise language, images, categories, stereotypes, myths'.[19] Also as in Scotland, the pressure of political events gradually altered attitudes on all sides and slowly led to a potential redefinition of territorial claims, a possible redrawing of mental geographies.

Looking at Belfast with an outsider's eye in the mid-1980s, one observer saw no such possibilities but rather a city held in the affections of its inhabitants, and yet subject to destructive strains and contradictions. 'There was a Bacardi billboard showing Telly Savalas surrounded by love, heat and prosperity, itself perched in a heap of debris among buildings with bricked up windows. Lots of other buildings had cages around them, but the people were open and unprotected.'[20] In the summer of 1986, the year following the most concerted political initiative by British and Irish authorities to bring a peace settlement in the Thatcher years, the Anglo–Irish Agreement, writer Colm Tóibín walked the Irish border from Derry in the north west to Newry in the south east. At a moment of political tension, and surrounded by empty landscapes, Tóibín arrived at Enniskillen in South Fermanagh. 'History had made Fermanagh quiet; again and again I experienced the quietness of the streets in Enniskillen outside business hours. Nobody was on the streets. It was like a town in the early hours of the morning, before the milkman started on his round.'[21]

Relatively undamaged by violence, the killing of eleven civilians in Enniskillen during the Remembrance Day service in 1987 was an appalling moment which compelled some to search for a new end to violence. Escape from ideological deadlock and its destructive effect was barred in part by the continuing poor economic and social conditions that prevailed in Northern Ireland. As elsewhere de-industrialization took hold as shipyards, aircraft manufacturers and component factories were run down or closed down: from 25,000 employees in 1970 only 6000 remained at Harland and Wolff shipyard in 1983. Lack of outside investment or economic growth made the Province among the most disadvantaged districts within the European Union as unemployment, at around twenty per cent, was around double the UK average.[22] While regional aid in the form of state subsidy, private investment and the arrival of high-tech, as well as light, industry, assisted development, prospects remained poor. Additionally the number of farms fell steadily, from 47,000 in 1975 to less than 30,000 by the year 2000; the number of workers in agriculture over the same period declined from 72,000 to 58,000; while agriculture remained productive, a major export to mainland Britain, it no longer sustained a rural way of life for whole communities.[23] As global economies of scale came increasingly into play through the last two decades of the twentieth century, and as the Channel Tunnel opened in 1994, Northern Ireland was limited by its geographical and economic position.[24]

Improvement of housing conditions remained a vital issue, so that by the middle of the Thatcher era 8500 new homes were built in Belfast of which almost a quarter were in the core city.[25] Ethno-religious territorialism still made housing a geographic symbol of loyalties, and rebuilding the infrastructure of the inner city especially, as envisaged by the Belfast Housing Renewal Strategy (1982), was understood as a prerequisite to better communal relations. Such initiatives were not necessarily received with enthusiasm by all sections of the local population, reluctant as they were to move out of secure housing enclaves or into workplaces where they would represent a minority. Notions of equality and plurality never-theless gradually began to matter. Moreover, while during the earlier years of conflict, especially through the 1970s, it was believed that a 'silent majority' could be brought forward to shame and obstruct terrorists, events such as the Enniskillen bombing led to the thought that violence and difference might better be eradicated by other means.

The establishment of the Cultural Traditions Group in 1988 and the Community Relations Council, to encourage mutual concession and the accep-tance of both protestant and catholic festivals; the introduction of the Education Reform (Northern Ireland) Order (1989), which helped facilitate the establish-ment of integrated religious schools, thirty-two by 1996; and the Fair Employment (Northern Ireland) Act (1989), which established monitoring on religious grounds, and which was gradually accepted by both protestants and catholics.[26] All of these were seen as a part of the management of difference with the final objective of establishing a newly pluralistic Northern Irishness. The effects were seen, for example, in the official recognition of varied strands within northern Irish history, as was shown by official attendance at Remembrance services. While loyalties and allegiances varied in time and according to place, and while Irish and British remained mutually exclusive definitions for the majority, the early 1990s nevertheless saw an increasing, mutually inclusive recognition of local and regional affiliations.

In political affairs the late 1980s and early 1990s saw a new readiness to reach for common agreement, or, as was shown by the discussions between John Hume (b.1937), leader of the SDLP, and Gerry Adams (b.1948), President of Sinn Féin, at least the possibility of pragmatism. Yet while outsiders often commented on the stoicism and good humour of a people forced to make ordinary lives in troubled circumstances, these slight signs of movement were not yet sufficient to lift the stress of everyday uncertainties, as one Belfast doctor noted in 1994. 'The tension and fear of not knowing when the next killing will be drives people to drink if they can't get sedatives. There seems to be no answer for such widespread acute depression.'[27] By the end of August 1994, though, the Provisional IRA (PIRA) announced an immediate ceasefire; by February 1995, despite suspicion, cynicism and wariness among various governments and parties, framework negotiations to resolve the political conflict were under way; by the end of 1995 President and Mrs Clinton were visiting both parts of Ireland and the troubled process of arms decommissioning had begun. Support for Sinn Féin jumped in the May 1996 elections, yet local attacks and fatalities continued.[28] The months after the ceasefire began, in late 1994 and early 1995, were also a moment of genuine hope and careful reflection. As one observer commented in August 1995. 'Now, near the first anniversary of the ceasefire, Ulster has a strangely lulled feeling, I begin to think. The excitement of peace – palpable in the early months – is starting to ebb. Something is bottoming out, and now and then this lulledness infiltrates our talk and we fall silent. It's a bit like stopping halfway across a dried-up river-bed, or looking round the sides of a maybe extinct volcano.'[29] The collapse of the ceasefire following the bomb explosion at Canary Wharf, London on 6 February 1996, the explosion of a PIRA bomb in central Manchester on 15 June, which injured two hundred and twenty, and the confrontation and violence surrounding the Drumcree Orange Parades, near Portadown in County Armagh, early in the following month, made it all too apparent that the volcano was far from extinct.

For all the continual setbacks and reluctant negotiation, over arms decommissioning for example, the slight relaxation of ethnic tensions also began to allow a broader view of Irish identity to emerge. 'For as long as Irish people think of themselves as Celtic Crusoes on a sequestered Island,' one advocate of Irish 'postnationalism' argued in 1997, 'they ignore not only their own diaspora but the basic cultural truth that creation comes from hybridization not purity, contamination not immunity, polyphony not monologue.'[30] Perhaps unwittingly towards this end both the Republic of Ireland and Britain signed up to the Single European Act in 1988, which had among its provisions regional representation as well as the preservation of language, custom and minority rights. Awareness of pluralist sentiment was expressed too in an interest in the work of John Hewitt (1907–87), poet and curator at the Museum of Ulster, who stressed a diversity of histories and imaginative geographies. 'Ulster considered as a Region, and not as a symbol of any particular creed, can command the loyalty of every one of its inhabitants,' Hewitt wrote in 1949, because 'regional identity does not preclude, rather it requires, membership of a larger association.'[31]

Similarly by the mid-1990s commentators stressed both the distorting effects of 'cultural defence' on unionist and nationalist imagination of history, locality and ideology, and the mutual inability of these 'death-cult' belief systems to escape their oppositional stance. In this view the twin perspectives of transnationalism and localism offered a new insight into the ways in which territories and traditions overlap at the frontier zone. 'To admit a more varied, mixed, fluid and relational kind of identity would advance nobody's territorial claim. It would undermine cultural defences. It would subvert the male pride that keeps up the double frontier-siege. It would dismantle the dangerous ratchet that locks Catholic advance into Protestant demoralization and emigration. All this would be on the side of life . . .'[32] The difficulty of such processes can hardly be underestimated through these years. At a moment when all parts of the United Kingdom were looking back at the century about to end, considering their own national place within it, Northern Ireland's heritage remained one of deep division, where sense of place was intimately connected with religious and political allegiance, where the admission of 'outsiders' could only be interpreted as a sign of weakness. To protestant liberal Basil McIvor (1928–2004) any real coexistence would remain a rarity until a 'full deployment of material well-being' could be achieved, which was certainly not the case by the May 1997 local elections, when unionists stayed away from the polls, frustrated and alienated by political developments.

Such common ground as there was expressed itself in the usage by catholics (24 per cent, 1993) and protestants (11 per cent, 1993) of the term 'Northern Irish'.[33] McIvor's view was that in common with 'at least 40 per cent of Northern Irish citizens I have always regarded myself as Irish – not English – but within a tradition of Britishness'.[34] Writer Glen Patterson described a different feeling of his own northern Irishness at around the time of the Provisional IRA ceasefire in 1995. 'I have no sense of myself as a protestant. I do though have some sense of Northern Irishness of which I am proud – Northern Irishness free of political and constitutional absolutes – Northern Irishness in the way that I had Northern Englishess when I lived in Manchester.'[35]

Surviving a nightmare vision

Surveying the Welsh scene at the beginning of the 1980s, historian Gwyn A. Williams was sufficiently pessimistic to wonder if his own homeland could preserve any character or independence in the future. Following the defeat of the 1979 devolution referendum it was difficult to imagine what might persist of Wales' distinctive history or traditions, so that 'some looking ahead, see nothing but a nightmare vision of a depersonalised Wales which has shrivelled up into a Costa Bureaucratica in the south and a Costa Geriatrica in the north; in between, sheep, holiday homes burning merrily away and fifty folk museums where there used to be communities.'[36]

From a peak of 1,022,000 in 1979, employment figures dropped rapidly with losses in industry, manufacturing and transport, for instance, as well as slight gains in services; employing 65,981 in 1973, ten years later, following such sudden cuts as at Shotton, Ebbw Vale, and Cardiff, the British Steel Corporation's employees numbered only 19,199.[37] Women played an increasing role in the nation's economic life as unemployment particularly affected the heavy industries dominated by men; part-time work increased, but this was of little assistance to the young, who still had difficulty finding proper employment. One effect of the miners' strike of 1984–5, which was also a struggle to preserve the mining communities of South Wales and elsewhere, was to destabilize further relations between the sexes. As one woman in Maerdy, Rhondda, stated 'the women were reaching the ordinary man and woman in the street more than the men with their speaking about the day-to-day things of the strike. The men were a bit worried that we weren't going to be the same'.[38] While Welsh support for the Conservatives initially increased, reaching a peak for the century, fourteen seats, in the 1983 election, ten years later attempts to revive the economy still had limited effect. By 1993 male unemployment in Aberdare, Mid Glamorgan, for example, was 29 per cent, and in some areas it rose as high as 50 per cent.

After 1983 anti-centralist sentiment increased. While it was true that the Welsh

Office became more active, with the creation of Welsh language television in 1982, the transfer of varied aspects of administration such as agriculture, health and housing, away from central government and the energetic efforts of the Welsh Development Agency to improve material conditions, it nonetheless seemed that central government was out of step with local interest and opinion. The mining industry effectively collapsed after the strike of 1984–5 leaving only two pits open by 1993; Conservative support continued to fall at the 1992 general election; three successive English Secretaries of State for Wales collectively left the impression of a centralist state imposing its wishes on a satellite principality. From 1983 Wales split into three distinct political regions: the conservative eastern constituencies together with the southern coastal areas; the southern coalfields; and the Welsh speaking districts, notably Gwynedd (in the North-West) and Dyfed (West Wales). Those most affected by the threat of closures, as well as those most closely involved with the miners' strike, were in the southern valleys.[39] By the end of the 1980s there were more Welsh men working in banks than in mines.[40] Along with these pit closures came the loss of the minimum wage and the loss of earnings. Together with the Valleys Initiative, intended to revive the fortunes of de-industrialized districts, came efforts to renew urban areas. In Swansea for instance, the docks had fallen into disuse, the deep-sea fishing fleet no longer existed and with the demise of the coal industry the sea transport link also disappeared. The South Dock was turned over to the city council for redevelopment as a marine, leisure and residential area; likewise the Cardiff Bay Development Corporation proceeded with a huge project between 1987 and 2000.[41]

The thought that the distinctive patterning of Welsh community would be damaged, if not irreparably lost, was among the greatest fears raised by the economic and social changes of the Thatcher and Major years. In the summer of 1995 one researcher decided to retrace the steps taken by investigators thirty years earlier in the East-side neighbourhood of St Thomas, Swansea, in order to understand the actual rather than imagined extent of change within the neighbourhood.[42] Residents of St Thomas felt that they did not have the close-knit relations and extended families that had once been present. Better education had allowed the younger generation the option of study and work elsewhere, while new arrivals had also changed the community. Observing and participating in the Fiftieth Anniversary VE Day celebrations in the district, it was obvious, however, that there were still a number of families whose lineage went back several generations, that family feuds as well as common locality created a criss-cross of connections through St Thomas and that in a part of the town closely connected to dockworkers and seafarers, there had always been new arrivals.[43] Rather than a dissipation or 'dilution' of the community, then, local district social networks now functioned differently. Relatives no longer lived in such close proximity, in the same street, or in nearby roads, as had one family taking part in the mid-1960s study. Nor were face-to-face encounters within such groups quite so common. If relatives were spread across a wider geographical area, telephone and car nevertheless allowed communal, neighbourly and familial closeness to continue. 'Social structures of locality are not homogenous, static entities, but rather dynamic, constantly changing nuanced phenomena . . . local practice and tradition continue to shape specific family values and lifestyles. Locality continues to be defined by the individuals who live within it, and remain an important constituent of an individual's identities.'[44]

Countryside communities also faced dramatic change, and the question of whether the social networks of rural areas could carry on as before or whether they would be irreversibly fragmented seemed even less clear cut. Like other upland areas across the United Kingdom, and particularly across Wales, the quality of soil had never been favourable to large-scale agricultural development; climate, rainfall and high grazing areas meant farmers were generally less prosperous than their lowland English counterparts. As profit margins gradually narrowed, by the mid 1990s the land became one of several sources of income necessary for economic survival: land workers found supplementary employment and business activity. Welsh rural society, which was traditionally tied to small farms in family hands, and which was also contained by relatively enclosed social circles, appeared unable to hold itself together under such intense economic pressure. Moreover, the possible collapse of farming had symbolic significance as two per cent among the Welsh population as a whole was engaged on the land, but ten per cent of Welsh speakers.[45]

Rural life was further affected by complex migratory patterns: depopulation as employment prospects collapsed, outward migration of the young to improve both education and job opportunities; and inward migration by 'foreigners'. These developments had both social and linguistic effects. Welsh-born residency decreased between 1981 and 1991 from 79.4 per cent to 77.2 per cent. Over the same period English-born residency in Wales rose to one fifth of the total population: to 37.5 per cent in Clwyd, 22.1 per cent in Dyfed, 29.6 per cent in Gwynedd, 36.9 per cent in Powys.[46] Given the strength of long-running family and personal ties within such rural social networks these changes seemed ominous. Describing her family and community ties in a study of three settlements in south-west Wales – Llansteffan, Llandeilo and Llanybydder – one woman told how her grandmother, mother and she had become close friends with women of the same three generations of a neighbouring family. 'Our families are linked through the ages,' she said. 'I like that. It's nice, it's safe and familiar, to think that we've had a common link. They're not family but feel like it, they're an extension of my family.'[47] To incomers these inner circles were easy to admire but difficult to enter: everyday social encounters might as soon reveal differences as connections; eagerness to participate could be misinterpreted as 'interference'. Locals were sometimes intimidated too because of the perceived higher economic or social status of the new arrivals.[48] There was no simple solution to mutual misunderstanding or antagonism.

In Welsh-speaking areas alterations in rural life seemed a particular hazard. As the 1981 census showed and as broader patterns of bilingualism confirmed, better transport and communications, and the settlement of English speakers, directly affected the number of Welsh-language speakers. Thus while in some of the more remote districts the Welsh-speaking population might reach 90 per cent, and while concerted efforts to promote the language meant that younger people were more actively entering the community of Welsh-language speakers in the strongest areas such as Cardigan or parts of Gwynedd, the overall pattern was one of fragmentation and decline. By the early 1990s there was improvement as the range and status of the language expanded, in part from Welsh-language television, and as the number of young speakers increased from 18 per cent to 24.9 per cent.[49] Although there were initial doubts among Welsh-language campaigners as to whether it went far enough, on the one hand, and about whether its effects would divide artificially Welsh- and non-Welsh speakers, on the other, the introduction of the Welsh Language Act (1993) and the Welsh Language Board, founded to support and promote the Act's objectives, proved largely positive and inclusive. A further complication was added, however, as wider social and economic conditions affected language usage. One activist, Cefin Campbell of Llandeilo, Dyfed, who became involved in a Welsh Office initiative to promote the language in a semi-industrial valley on the border of West Glamorgan and Carmarthenshire, described the problem, stating: 'there's a lack of confidence amongst people [due to recession and unemployment] and that reflects itself in their [lack of] confidence in the language'.[50] A corresponding question arose as to how English-speaking Wales might distinguish itself culturally from England given that the industrial origins and communitarian creeds of Christianity and socialism had all but disappeared.

As in Northern Ireland, the demands of change forced redefinitions of nationhood and a sufficiently strong increase in nationalist feeling to register in the 1997 devolution referendum. While Plaid Cymru, the Party of Wales, grew increasingly attractive to voters through the 1990s, the decision to establish a Welsh Assembly was still only narrowly won. On 18 September 1997, 552,698 (49.7 per cent) voted against, and 559,419 (50.3 per cent) voted in favour: a majority of 6721 which was only achieved because of the large 'yes' vote in rural Carmarthenshire. Yet as one commentator noted, across the Principality, a new sense of Wales was emerging: its sources both localized and politicized:

> The 1997 devolution referendum resulted in the expression, *par excellence*, of the Welsh civic national identity: Welsh-speaking (agri)culture combined with destitute South Wales mining valleys to deliver a decisive verdict on what was effectively a referendum on the Thatcher–Redwood effect on their area of Wales. The subsequent electoral success of Plaid Cymru in the South Wales valleys added a further dimension to the political configuration, which has its roots in a distinctive social and economic history.[51]

Places changing

England, more particularly, the southern and eastern quarters of the country, provided the strongest support for changes that affected the whole of the United Kingdom through these years. Following the wider pattern, though, the effects of Conservative government were patchily beneficial at best. Attempting to sum up the changes in 1991, one survey picked out four locations: in the south, mid Bedfordshire, which represented London and the south east as one of the main beneficiaries of change; on the south coast, Worthing, which gained economically, but which by the 1990s, with its ageing population, partly retirement settlers, also had a high proportion of households without either children or incomes; in the north, Jarrow stood for those areas, among them Barnsley East or Birmingham Hodge Hill, where there was an above-average proportion of non-earners; finally, South Shields, which like Liverpool Derby West as well as Southwark and Bermondsey in London, had a proportion of non-earning households above the national average and a lack of increased participation in the workforce since the 1970s.[52] It was difficult to remain neutral or indifferent to the new England that was emerging; along with variable circumstances came extremities of attitude. Describing the excitement and energy of the new business culture, especially the 'Big Bang' in October 1986 when the new electronic stock exchange system amalgamated the division between jobbers (sellers) and brokers (buyers), creating in the process around 60,000 new jobs in the financial sector, style columnist Peter York commented. 'The city wanted you young . . . because that meant you'd be more likely to have a degree . . . or young because you were straight out of Hackney Downs Comprehensive and you were sharp as a tack . . . *and* you have the energy to work like a maniac, ten hours a day at the dealers' screens, for the next eight years.'[53] Describing his arrival a few years later in the West End of Newcastle, one of the most deprived, run-down districts in the country, Nick Danziger was unprepared for what he encountered. 'When the bus deposited me at the desolate crossroads I felt the same adrenalin rush of fear as I had when covering a war zone. Do I proceed? Without a car, or the protection of a guide who knew his way round, what were the odds of being robbed? I carried what was for many people more than a lifetime's savings in camera equipment tucked into my shoulder bag.'[54]

Existing fissures within British society, including that between south and north, were deepened by the new political dispensation.[55] Based on a belief that the promotion of business would revitalize all sectors of society, that state welfare and development was less desirable than private enterprise and that debilitation and dependency flowed from state assistance, Conservative policy centred on the reduction of state expenditure, the end of universal benefits as well as the extension of markets and privatizations. While these policies succeeded spectacularly in certain areas, they also produced political as well as social disenfranchisement. By 1989 incomes were 20 per cent higher in the south-east, and 30 per cent higher in London, than in the remainder of the country; the housing stock was newer, and investment in repairs and infrastructure greater; while 25 per cent of the population had degrees in London, in the north-east the figure was only 10.4 per cent.[56] While these divisions did produce an artistic, intellectual and eventually political reaction against Conservatism in Wales and Scotland, in the non-affluent areas of England, say, the north-west, there was no regionalist campaign.

To its beneficiaries, the appeal of the new money-oriented business culture was obvious – London's John Vallance (b.1953), for instance, who worked as a trainee draftsman in 1968, who then went on to construction and engineering workshops as a planning engineer and who finally set up his own company in 1985. His income immediately increased from £9000 to £28,000 per year. Vallance's conversion to Conservatism came from the new freedoms he was allowed as an employer, especially from the trades unions. 'The magic thing that Mrs Thatcher's done, which has affected the quality of my life, and of most people's lives, is to deal with trade unionism . . .' he said. 'A handful of people were able to manipulate millions. She changed all that . . .'[57]

One piece of architecture which may be taken as a symbol of the new mood Vallance represented was the Lloyd's Building (1978–86) in London, which made every effort to stress its newness as permanency rather than as novelty by placing escape stairs and service pipes on the outside walls, by allowing light in from above rather than through conventional windows.[58] Yet the sheen of architectural revitalization that now swept across London, for example at Canary Wharf, and the closeness too, alluded to by Peter York, between city, docklands and eastern districts, also inspired an entirely different reinvention of the metropolis. One such remaking of the city was by novelist, essayist and book dealer Iain Sinclair. In *Lights Out for the Territory* (1997), Sinclair set off on a series of walks across London following its underworld of historical, social and occult associations. Alert to the atmospheric and imaginative resonance of his surroundings, the author follows the major arteries of the city, its roads, its dilapidated shopping arcades, its criss-cross of histories and footpaths as they parallel and traverse the Thames. On 24 October 1994, for example, he walked through the north-east of the city inwards, headed for the financial district:

> Dalston Town Centre, I love the chutzpah of that. Can a ghost have a centre? Dalston, coming into its pomp after a railway carve-up, as an alternative for those who couldn't afford a trip 'up west', has all the buzz of a J. G. Ballard traffic island squatted by cowboys. Everything-Under-A-Pound bazaars rub shoulders with embattled chemists, off-licences, and the famous eel and pie shop with its blood smeared slab. LARGER EELS IN STOCK. PLEASE ENQUIRE . . .[59]

In northern England too the spectral presence of past community was in the street, sometimes with the same chaotic energy of Dalston, but more often remote from the centres of business, finance and industry. Teesside, with its huge industrial developments of the 1970s and its leading world companies such as British Steel and ICI, had greater opportunities, a better chance of survival, than other industrialized districts. Certainly in the fifteen or more years before Thatcher came to power the indications of rapid economic growth and prosperity were partly fulfilled. Yet by 1987, when Teesside formed an Urban Development Corporation, levels of unemployment, which in Cleveland County and Teesside now reached 20 per cent, stirred memories of job insecurity and of low pay, of the interwar slump.[60]

Changed regulations on the role of the unions, on pay and on working hours were set to increase business opportunity and economic growth; while the larger global corporations sometimes stayed, where skills and profits allowed, the United Kingdom was now viewed as one of many possible locations. Lower costs and financial benefits were increasingly found outside the industrialized west of Europe and the USA. In Sunderland too the end of shipbuilding led to unemployment and social decay, while resurgence was partly brought about by the arrival of car manufacturers Nissan from July 1986, and by expansion from the early 1990s to 3500 employees. By 1998 the company was the largest car manufacturer in the UK.[61]

Imaginatively, southern and northern England were connected in the nineteenth century by values of industry, enterprise and self-improvement; by the end of the twentieth century these values were reversed. Southern visitors writing on the north were sometimes unable to see anything more than a region buried beneath the rubble of collapsed community and economy. Mark Hudson, for example, describing the former mining community of South Tyneside in 1994:

> It was Friday evening and one could sense the incipient energy of the lads and lasses preparing for their respective nights out. The last-minute crimping of perms, the queuing up for bathrooms; and outside, the little gangs gathering on street corners, by the bins or the garages, in the doorways of derelict buildings. And far away, in the faint distant haze of the sea's edge, standing up like a pin-head, the winding gear of Westoe Colliery – virtually all that remained of the old industries – the heavy industries – that had created the character and culture of that part of the world.[62]

As in the 'new wave' cinema of the 1960s the midlands and northern 'provinces' represented whatever was to be escaped from; the metropolis, whatever hopes or aspirations might exist for the future. The nearest northern equivalent to Iain Sinclair's remaking of London in his own image was Paul Driver's *Manchester Pieces* (1996): a rare attempt to convey the complexity and energy of contemporary northern life, to explore its lived as well as its imagined landscapes, for example its city parks, and to imagine the dying thoughts of painter L. S. Lowry. *Manchester Pieces* records too an insider's unpunctuated, free flowing, associative history of the city. A 'financial info-technological and educational city with its distinctive pop and classical culture and glamorous facilitation of sports its clean scrubbed architecture and even a loosening of the old licensing laws so that the spectre of the Temperance movement may at last be exorcised'.[63]

Farming and rural life were subject as well to the new political and economic conditions, but were also imagined differently: the traditional heartland of the nation now became 'the environment'. While the industrialization of food production was nothing new, the competitive pressure to lower costs, to increase crop areas, production and profits, increasingly raised ecological and health concerns. Farming techniques, multinational corporations such as ICI, Deloitte and Touche Agricultural, Bayer and the supermarket chains, all required huge crop areas. In turn this meant the removal of hedgerows as well as the intensified use of artificial, chemical fertilizers, weed killers and herbicides.[64] Describing the changes that had taken place in Barton, Cambridgeshire, Robin Page notes the rise of 'prairie fencing', the disappearance of the small Holly Blue butterfly and harvest mice, and the decline in the number of partridges. With Barton's new railway connection came commuting to London and Cambridge, and city newcomers, who were alarmed when locals greeted them; with longer residency the better-established 'newcomers' who had lived in the village for around twenty years were judged 'almost' acceptable to older residents.[65] While the 1980s saw the construction of a four-lane motorway nearby, a rise in the number of cars and lorries passing through and, following the construction of Stansted Airport, the number of aeroplanes, there was also the reappearance of willows and yellow water lily as well as, most gratifying of all to Page, frogs.[66] Environmental anxieties gradually expanded from questions over the preservation of rare plants and animals to food standards issues such as chemical residues or BSE ('mad cow disease'), to animal welfare protests. Moreover, much of the most visible political activism since the miners' strike of 1984–5 surrounded such questions. Concern with the lack of adequate health regulation led in 1997 to the establishment, rather after the fact, of the Food Standards Agency; Wildlife Enhancement Schemes promoted efforts at nature conservation as almost 4000 Sites of Special Scientific Interest had been designated by 1995–6.[67]

By the middle of the 1990s, with the growing confidence of political opposition to the Conservatives, the shrinkage of support for the government to its core supporters and the collapse of old political values, it was clear that many of the collective certainties which had underpinned British life since the Second World War were vanishing. The better education, health and welfare that were enjoyed by the generations of the welfare state years were for historian Paul Addison less an enduring structure than a Ministry of Works prefab 'bulldozed away in spite of many pleas to preserve it as a memorial to a more civilized era'.[68] The eagerness of the demolition crews was also literal as the high-rise blocks and estates built as an intended answer to the chronic housing shortage of the postwar years were now blasted away at an unprecedented rate as they had come to symbolize all that was unsuccessful in collective, state and social planning.[69] For many of that generation raised with the hopeful vision of an end to avoidable sickness and poverty, the inheritors from their parents of the folk memory of the slump, these changes were unnerving, even distressing. Describing his personal journey through the postwar years, his teaching, writing and sympathies, partly drawing on his own background and memories of growing up surrounded by the shoemaking trade of Northampton, Jeremy Seabrook saw the continuing need for the ideals on which the welfare state was founded. 'The values borne of the shoemakers are not extinct. Their radical dissenting sensibility lives on within their scattered descendants . . . I am glad now that their influence was not so easily left behind. They have bequeathed us their sceptical, critical spirit, that flame of dissent which burns so low in these times of gaudy conformism . . .'[70]

CHAPTER 8

Fractured, Rearranged

Top girls

In Caryl Churchill's play *Top Girls* (1982) a group of women from throughout history gather to celebrate the promotion of Marlene as Managing Director of the Top Girls job agency. Among them is Dull Gret, who in Breugel's painting heads a charge into Hades; the apocryphal Pope Joan, stoned to death as, during a procession, she gives birth to a child; also Patient Griselda, submissive wife in Boccaccio, Petrarch and Chaucer; and Lady Nijo, member of the thirteenth century Japanese court, subsequently a wandering Buddhist nun.[1] To Marlene all these women are sources of strength for her own success, but as their over-lapping stories are told the collective mood darkens. In each case, their achieve-ment is at great personal cost; Marlene herself has a disowned daughter. *Top Girls* is less a political commentary than an observation of human experience. Nevertheless, Churchill's (b.1938) play expresses a vivid awareness of social opportunity and disadvantage, of the world women found themselves in by the early 1980s.

The person of Margaret Thatcher (b.1925; Prime Minister 1979–90) was also a powerful representation of the freedoms and constraints that now, gradually, emerged. As the first woman prime minister of Britain her continuing success and recognition as a world leader showed what might be achieved; as a politician, she did little to improve the rights or conditions of women's lives. Profits and promo-tions might be increasingly available to some women; keeping wages low and promoting the traditional values of family life were also a priority. The first woman editor of a national newspaper was appointed in 1987, yet only 41 women MPs from a total of 650 were elected in the same year's General Election.[2] The paradox of the post-1979 years was that while the postwar political consensus was ended and the welfare state was increasingly destabilized, the values of liberalism articulated so powerfully in the social legislation of the 1960s could not easily be rescinded. Women's progressive roles and values were to some extent expressed in the work of successful businesswomen such as Anita Roddick (b.1942), owner of Body Shop, or fashion designer Vivienne Westwood (b.1941). Counter-cultural feminism resurfaced with the planned posting of Cruise and Pershing II nuclear missiles at American airbases in Britain, which led to a prolonged women-only protest camp at Greenham Common RAF Camp from 1981. The equally extended, violent conflict between miners and the government also drew women in first as supporters and then as political activists defending families and mining districts through the strike of 1984–5.[3] Local government initiatives in many parts of the country now actively promoted women's rights and opportunities. In

Illustration 8 Alternative society: New Age travellers' camp at Otterbourne, Hants, 1992

this respect the Greater London Council, led by Ken Livingstone (b.1945), which established a Women's Committee with a budget of £90 million as well as 96 members of staff, has been described by one historian as 'the greatest experiment in "municipal feminism" in modern times'.[4] Opposition to this and other locally based, municipal initiatives led to the Local Government Act, enforced in 1985, and the abolition of the Greater London Council as well as the six metropolitan county councils.

Neither social protest groups nor local government initiatives could, however, change either the fact that both in the kinds of work they were able to take and in the wages that they were paid, women continued to be treated unequally. In 1979, the Equal Opportunities Commission found their wages to be 73 per cent of men's earnings; in 1982 another survey found 60 per cent of women believed men's job prospects remained better.[5] Government and employers effectively used female workers as a reserve 'pool' of temporary, low-paid labour, as if earnings were supplementary to the family economy.[6] Moreover, as Conservative policy was the reduction and restraint of wages and the limitation of union power, and as women were often in the vulnerable part-time employment sector, such security of employment, conditions and wages as existed was increasingly difficult to maintain. One study of a hosiery factory in 1980–1, just at the moment when industries were closing in large numbers and job opportunities were fewer, illustrates many of these developments. Based in an unnamed English industrial town with a large immigrant population, StitchCo produced socks, tights, sweaters and cardigans on mechanical knitting machines. Already running short of work, one employee at the factory described the insecurities of the trade:

> The hosiery industry is in such a bad state that the employers haven't got money for rises, and if the gaffers haven't got any money then we certainly won't get any. It's this bloody Thatcher. The companies can't afford to pay off their loans and all companies have to borrow to invest. Then they get to the point where the money coming in won't meet the money going out and they're stuck. That's what happened to the company I was working for when I was made redundant.[7]

The supply of work was not enough to guarantee bonus earnings through the summer of 1980; the rising cost of living was not met by increased wages; male trainee knitters grossed £58 per week at the age of 18, while female trainee machinists earned £35 per week at the age of 16.[8]

Furthermore, while the European Commission directive on equal pay was introduced in 1986, other changes in the law reduced access to equal pay protection (Wages Act, 1986) to maternity rights (Social Security Act, 1986) and to social security claims (Social Security Act, 1988). The long-cherished belief that state benefits could assist the promotion of family life was also called into doubt.[9] By contrast, and despite the vocal support given to 'traditional' family structures and values, opinion on many social questions did not alter. Renewed debate on abortion did not result in substantial change (Abortion Reform Bill, 1987), divorce became easier (Family Proceedings Act, 1984), legal recognition of childbirth outside of marriage was expanded (Family Law Reform Act, 1987) and the autonomy and rights of minors were extended (Children Act, 1989).

Under the influence of Thatcher, and especially after the increase in Conservative support that came with the 1983 election, political policy and economic prospects began to affect many social interests within the United Kingdom, including the interests of women. Single-issue politics seemed increasingly less relevant than the broader challenge to postwar consensus values. Caryl Churchill's work took on the new political and economic culture in *Serious Money* (1987), which acknowledges in its complex plot centred on intrigue in London's financial district, and in its citation of Thomas Shadwell's *Volunteers, or The Stockjobbers* (1692), that there is nothing new in the compulsion to 'turn a penny', that legality and public service are often and easily relegated to second place. At the same time the play celebrates the possibilities of the newly emerging global age, of the diverse flows of capital through Europe, Africa and America, of the newly pertinent questions of sex, race and class distinction still to be addressed.[10]

A kind of distorting mirror

Like Caryl Churchill, Salman Rushdie (b.1947) was a sharp observer of the British social scene through the Thatcher years, not least in his sensitivity to questions of ethnicity and immigration. At around the time he was awarded the Booker Prize for *Midnight's Children* (1981), Rushdie examined the powerful strain of racism that persisted within British society, arguing that it was a symptom of the nation's own uncertain place in the modern world. A fixation with past imperial greatness, as expressed in the Falklands War of 1982, signalled growing 'cultural psychosis' in inverse proportion to actual decline; the absence of any bitterly fought war of decolonization such as the French experience in Algeria meant in politics and in the legal system that the crippled language of imperial domination still circulated freely, unchallenged and unrecognized.[11]

Certainly the new government seemed unsympathetic to further immigration as the British Nationality Act (1981) restricted entry rights in general, while the right to entry for family members was limited in particular. Like others in part-time or low-paid employment, ethnic minorities were vulnerable to the consequences of economic downturn and changes in employment practice: black and Asian workers, for instance, earned 15 per cent less than their white male peers; by the end of the decade unemployment levels were at 14 and seven per cent respectively, while black unemployment reached 19 per cent in London, 20 per cent in the north and north-west, and 23 per cent in Yorkshire and West Humberside.[12] Job security, pay and conditions grew worse for many of those who were employed within the National Health Service, for instance, where black women especially had worked in significant numbers since the 1950s. Pay, increased privatization and the introduction of an Ethical Code, whereby nurses were required to empty bins, serve meals, do porters' work or ancillary and domestic duties, were vexed topics. One nurse gave an example:

> If you're asked to lift a patient and you don't feel you can do it without damaging your back – and this often happens – you can refuse to do it and call a porter and tell the Sister . . . A lot of auxiliary nurses are practical nurses, bedside nurses, and the can't get out of it without giving themselves a record. They've got all the arguments to contend with about, 'Look, you're meant to be a nurse and your role is to care and put the patients' needs before your own.'[13]

One cause of further resentment and frustration for the Afro-Caribbean community in 1981 was the apparent indifference or even apathy of the police. Following the death of fourteen young people in a south London fire for example, the unsympathetic reaction of media and police to what many saw as a racist fire bombing led to a large protest march, the Black People's Day of Action, on 2 March; similarly, a stop and search campaign by the police from 6 April 1981, which saw 943 people questioned and 118 arrested, was background to the most severe riots of twentieth-century Britain in Brixton, but also Bristol and Liverpool.[14]

The fortunes of other immigrant groups varied. With the failure of the southern Irish economy in the mid-1980s for example, net emigration reached 75,300 for the 1981–6 period, although there are no figures for the numbers arriving in mainland Britain. There was also an increase in the number of protestants moving out of Northern Ireland.[15] Like the young, well-educated Irish who now travelled across the Irish Sea, the new Polish immigrants now crossing the Channel, who amounted to a net gain of around 6000 over the 1983–9 period, were often highly schooled and skilled. The British government remained wary because of the Communist regime's policy of exporting 'criminals'; in doing so it lost the benefit of skilled workers.[16] One development now began gradually to affect ethnic and immigrant groups: as earlier notions of 'multiracial' harmony seemed inadequate to limit the destructive effects of racial intolerance, local government initiatives in Birmingham, London, Coventry and elsewhere became more actively anti-racist. The 1987 General Election also saw the beginning of greater ethnic representation in Parliament with the election of Diane Abbott (b.1953), Paul Boateng (b.1951), Keith Vaz (b.1956) as Members of Parliament, and, from 1985, of Bernie Grant as Leader of the Haringey Council. South Asians in Britain were also increasingly present in local politics, representing both Labour and the Conservatives.

Questions outside the existing realm of party politics were raised, though, with the controversy surrounding the publication of Salman Rushdie's *The Satanic Verses* (1988), which provided a focus for resentment against discrimination within British society, and which began to change attitudes on all sides. An expansive, ambitious novel, *The Satanic Verses* refers in part to the early history of Islam, and among its themes seeks to view religious history within its cultural context, as well as to create a speculative, questioning vision of the Muslim faith comprehensible to non-believers and secular Muslims such as its author. Fantastic in form and content, for example when a group of prostitutes use the Prophet's wives' names hoping to attract more clients, Rushdie defended his work saying: 'I wanted to make these two worlds [sacred and profane] so similar. First of all, the talk about the strange echoes of sexuality and sexual politics . . . Secondly, in order to make a kind of distorting mirror between the world of licentious, degraded secularist Jahilia and the new power, which is the religion I call "Submission".'[17] When British Muslims sought to ban the book and to prosecute Rushdie, Home Secretary Douglas Hurd told them that as they were members of a minority faith Britain's blasphemy laws were irrelevant. Liberal, secularist Britain stirred uneasily at the Bradford burning of copies of *The Satanic Verses* in public on 14 February 1989, and at the death sentence passed on Rushdie by Iranian cleric Ayatollah Khomeini. Both acts appeared unprecedented and dangerous. Media coverage was as hostile to Muslim protesters in 1989 as it had been to the Deptford Fire protest marchers in 1981. Multiculturalism had reached its limit.[18]

In the investigation that followed the 1981 riots in Brixton, Lord Scarman rightly stressed the corrosive effects of unemployment: the resentment and envy that it produced within an overtly materialistic society. He argued too that the prerequisite for communal stability was 'useful, gainful employment and suitable education, recreation and leisure opportunities for young people, especially in the inner city'.[19] Such good intentions, it now became clear, were difficult to practise while the British superiority complex, which extended from its colonial heritage to its limited tolerance of ethnic minorities, remained unchallenged. Moreover, immigrants and minorities now became increasingly unwilling to content themselves with whatever aspects of British life were deemed accessible to them. Rather than being the centre of a worldwide empire that viewed the rest of the globe and its inhabitants as 'foreign', it now became possible, revealing even, to view Britain itself as a nation of strange natives and exotic customs. South African Christopher Hope:

> Britain was a deeply foreign country, populated by the most unruly natives. A very strange and turbulent place . . . Your exoticism was a wonderful thing to behold in the eyes of your neighbours. But it wasn't their recognition of our foreignness that struck me, rather it was the other way round: to me their foreignness was so profound and disturbing and was made worse by the fact that I spoke the language. I had felt that I was at least a little bit English, and I discovered painfully, over a period, that I wasn't.[20]

Dressing up, dressing down

In some respects, British society was becoming strange to itself too. The post-punk world of fashion and style magazines, of peacock display nightclubs and 'post-industrial' music for example, was seemingly far removed from the fanzine recession chic or the anti-fascist benefit concerts of the late 1970s. Yet the connection may be traced, say, through *i-D* magazine, founded by Terry Jones (b.1945) in August 1980, which declared its fascination with fashion and style in Issue no. 1. 'Style isn't what but how you wear clothes. Fashion is the way you walk, talk, dance and prance.'[21] Featuring articles on King's Road street styles and Brighton rockabillies, the first punk fanzine-like issue of the magazine consisted of 40 stapled pages; by 1986 *i-D* was transformed into a monthly with a circulation of 45,000, and an 'alternative' presentation style which gave as much weight to layout and 'attitude' as it did to text. Fashion too reflected this gradual move away from proletarian severity, the collapse of subcultural pasts and future certainties, and towards ironic mockery, exaggerated quotation, the mixing and matching of long-gone and contemporary styles. Describing a nightclub in 1980 for example, one journalist saw:

> A young man with a Ted's quiff extended to baroque proportions and dressed in a satin jump-suit which looks like the product of an imaginative sci-fi movie designer, were it not for the addition of Elizabethan cuffs, stands drinking with someone whose clothes are half '30s Mafioso, half '60s boot-boy and who is sporting a semi-shaved Mohican Indian haircut. They are surrounded on all sides by a casual array of slightly askew cinematic stereotypes.[22]

Describing the rise of the new pop which accompanied this scene through the career of Boy George (b.1961), who himself made an early appearance in *i-D*, music writer Dave Rimmer noted that the street styles and poses of punk now appeared forgotten and irrelevant. Yet the bonfire blaze of punk did shoot out stray sparks, and from these came the smokescreen of new pop.[23]

If the distance between 'do-it-yourself' punk and the new art-pop world of style and design was small, entry was nevertheless restricted. School-leavers and the young had thrived through the years of economic growth and relative stability following the Second World War. Now patterns of youth employment changed. Apprenticeships and clerical posts took up 25 and 20 per cent of the youth job market respectively around 1970, but ten years later job opportunities were far fewer as university graduates competed with 18-year-old school leavers, and 18 year olds with those who left age 16. By 1986 almost 727,000 (nearly a third of all young people between the ages of 16 and 24) were unemployed.[24] Evidence from the Scarman Report of 1981 showed that over-representation in vulnerable occupations, language and cultural difference, and employer discrimination, conspired to place young black men at a particular disadvantage: 55 per cent were registered unemployed in Brixton under the age of 19.[25] Equally young people who were able to make the transition into the new service industries, into banking, business or tourism for instance, had easy access to the profits of consumption.

The fashion and values of the young now followed these alternative trajectories: at one extreme those drawn to the counter-cultural tradition, some of whom became 'travellers'; at the other, those who embraced consumerism and celebrated its values, for example the 'casuals'. Travellers were drawn from varied backgrounds: some were unemployed by choice or circumstance; others were homeless; and another section included allies of political causes such as environmentalism or the peace movement. Though relatively few in number, travellers now came to represent the growing oppositional feeling among sections of the young towards the new social values in general, and the political mood in particular.[26] Living in buses and caravans, often throughout the year, one focus of activity was the free summer festival season, and especially the Stonehenge Free Festival, where crowds reached 50,000 by 1984. Following the introduction of the Public Order Act (1986) and the efforts of politicians and police to eradicate the movement, rather than disintegrate, it was radicalized: committed especially to symbolic causes including squatting, animal liberation and ecology. 'At the heart of the [later] road-protest movement,' wrote one participant, 'are all those travellers that the government tried to stop travelling.'[27] Attempting to explain why they had drawn nationwide attention, both avid support and vitriolic opposition, one newspaper saw them as 'the spiritual heirs and witnesses of [seventeenth-century English radical] Gerard Winstanley and all the deluded and humiliated utopians' whose chosen task was to set an example, to live 'free from the state, money and the nuclear family'.[28] Among more affluent, mainstream youth were the 'casuals', who followed in the Mods' natty footsteps: they were neat, even fussy, they had a fondness for Italian movie and fashion house influences, and they displayed a particular weakness for expensive sports wear and designer label leisurewear.[29] Popular in some of the better off areas of southern England, in Manchester and Liverpool too, the casual style particularly drew football fans who often travelled in Europe, knew its clothing styles, and adapted them as both a celebration of, and a warped misinterpretation of contemporary consumerism.[30]

By the latter part of the 1980s, the ideals of prosperity, enterprise and entrepreneurship took a hedonistic turn among the young. Those who wanted to create a controlled consumer society and an affluence tied to particular moral values discovered the bounds of social engineering as clothes and drugs, music and alcohol once again became a source of media and political moral panic. While heroin, 'crack' cocaine and AIDS had all caused media hysterics in the early and mid-1980s, towards the end of the decade it was Ecstasy, mostly associated with the 'Acid House' club music scene in 1988 and 1989, which now attracted attention. It is difficult to know what the true levels of drug use were, but just as the alcohol companies now targeted 18–24 year olds with theme pubs and marketing campaigns, so the use of drugs seemed to become more visibly popular. According to one source for 1990 'Every weekend in the North West of England, an estimated 20 to 30 thousand people go to House music clubs and parties, known as "raves". Several thousand take drugs such as cannabis, ecstasy, amphetamine, and/or LSD.'[31] Once the British tabloid press began to publicize the social scene and to stress the dangers of drug use as well as the involvement of criminal drug gangs, government and police responded with punitive policies and campaigns. The result of this public pressure was that ravers – by now a diverse group of travellers, football supporters and older participants in the counter-culture – were not diminished as a movement, but instead further unified and driven underground.

The fashionable, commercial and political responses of the young gradually shifted through the 1980s then. The frustration of being excluded even from the most basic material benefits of mainstream society lay in part behind the Brixton riots of 1981. The push of advertisers and manufacturers who fed young people's enthusiasm for alcohol or designer labels was matched by the pull of style, taste and spending power. Pressure to conform to fashionable models of taste in music or clothing or 'lifestyle' was funnelled for the new young generation through the appeals of advertisers or the admonitions of style-watchers. The results were not always predictable. Play-acting and consuming were dressed up; escaping and misbehaving were dressed down.

Inside is outside is inside

In his film journal for *The Last of England* (1987), Derek Jarman (1942–94) describes something of his own alternative values as a film-maker and as a creative visual artist. In doing so he echoes Salman Rushdie's view of 'hybridity' as well as the mix and match street styles of the new youth culture. 'My world is in fragments, smashed into pieces so fine I doubt I will ever reassemble them. So I scramble in the rubbish, an archaeologist . . .'[32] Partly an allusion to the 'rubble' aesthetic of *The Last of England*, and to *Jubilee* (1977), partly to the collage of fractured narratives, disrupted time sequences and anachronistic, superimposed objects which appear in his work, these comments express too Jarman's urgent effort to respond to his times. While not all artists were necessarily interested in such overt political or social commentary, many were sympathetic to his moral as well as formal use, as in *Caravaggio* (1986), of 'tenebrism': the dramatic contrast of darkness and light.

The content and context of art also responded to the business of art, to the culture of enterprise and commerce. The work of 'household name' artists, Van Gogh for example, made headlines with their record auction prices; the newly established British modern art award Turner Prize, which struggled for several years to achieve both public attention and a workable format, was established in 1984; the following year collector and patron Charles Saatchi (b.1943) opened his gallery in London. Design, style and fashion also began to draw greater attention in Terry Jones' *i-D* and in Neville Brody's work at the rival style magazine *The Face*; advertising agencies and campaigns as well as pop videos zigzagged between popular and high art sources; in 1989 the Design Museum opened in London. Likewise the wall between 'gallery' art and more accessible 'public space' art was gradually breached. Two artists whose work drew attention to their concern with the traditional subjects of landscape and the human body as much as for their use of new techniques and materials, were Andy Goldsworthy (b.1956) and Antony Gormley (b.1950).[33] Goldsworthy's art intervened in the landscape with 'natural' materials, bark, leaves, twigs as well as even less stable substances such as ice or snow. This impermanence, itself an integral part of the work, also means that many pieces are only available to viewers as photographs. Three overlapping prints which show blades of grass staved and splayed, as if a caterpillar or worm were wriggling across the bare soil beneath, make *Blades of Grass creased and arched, secured with thorns. Penpoint, Dumfriesshire* (14 August 1988). The artificial light of a camera flash here highlights the glowing sheen of living vegetation, as well as the decaying mulch of the earth into which it will sink. Gormley attended especially to the universal human quality of the body. *Sculpture for Derry Walls* (1987) took the form of 'three identical, cruciform, cast-iron figures, each composed of two body-casts joined back to back, and sealed except for the eye holes – which were placed at symbolic and politically sensitive points on the fortified walls of the Northern Irish town'.[34]

In the early 1980s a loosely associated group of sculptors came into the public eye.[35] Richard Deacon (b.1949), Shirazeh Houshiary (b.1955) and Anish Kapoor (b.1954) were connected, according to critic Lynne Cook, by a common concern with 'self-sufficient, relatively self-contained, fixed objects: objects which, moreover, were made by hand, and were fabricated rather than crafted from mundane, familiar materials'.[36] Contemporary materials now made it possible to shape a dialogue between artist and observer, to fabricate organic forms from metal girders for example, in Richard Deacon's *Two Can Play* (1983), or *Figure of Thought No. 1* (1987–8), a mass of interlocking, riveted aluminium air shafts which become an imagined or dreamed form, simultaneously mechanical and natural. The interests of Shirazeh Houshiary are still more remote from the material world. Connected to Islamic, Sufi, mysticism and to an amalgamation of her Iranian and British backgrounds, Houshiary's work expresses elements and energies. It is intent too on 'unveiling the invisible', as in *The Earth is an Angel* (1987), and to this end uses 'elemental' materials such as straw, tin and copper. Similarly Kapoor is engaged in the search for essential values and properties, for the bringing together of binary opposites: Asian and European, female and male, light and dark, presence and absence:

> I began to evolve a reasoning, which had to do with things being partially revealed. While making the pigment pieces, it occurred to me that they form themselves out of each other. So I decided to give them a generic title, *1000 Names*, implying infinity, a thousand being a symbolic number. The pigment works sat on the floor or projected from the wall. The pigment on the floor defines the surface of the floor and the objects appear to be partially

submerged, like icebergs. That seems to fit the idea of something being partially there.[37]

Kapoor was at this time working with brilliant, powdered pigments, particularly red, yellow and blue. In this sense his work has a surprising affinity to pieces by Gilbert and George (b.1943 and 1944). While the large photo works by the latter are entirely different in their surface qualities, especially their apparent reference to autobiographical and social matters, Gilbert and George nevertheless share with Kapoor an aspiration to make work that is at once symbolic and meditative.[38]

The imagined, animal and social experience of the human body was also an object of ambiguous scrutiny. Paula Rego (b.1935) moved from collage to acrylic canvases in the early 1980s, using themes and images from children's rhymes and stories, from *Alice in Wonderland,* or from Portuguese folk tales, to create frozen scenes from an unknown narrative. Her nursery rhyme series, including *Baa Baa Black Sheep* (1989) viewed childhood as unsettling and violent. *The Family* (1988) likewise forces difficult thoughts and uncomfortable questions as the onlooker observes a woman together with two girls pinning a startled man awkwardly against a bed.[39] The art of Helen Chadwick (1953–96) similarly provokes conflicting, contradictory sensations. Drawing close to the self as subject, using food, domestic cleaning liquids, dead vegetable matter, animal carcasses and meat, and her own body as sources, Chadwick saw humanity as flesh-bound, represented and imagined through bodily experience.[40] 'Inside is outside is inside' was the artist's comment on her own work.[41] The thought that beneath the skin of beauty lay the visceral body from which humans try to dissociate themselves is expressed in *Of Mutability* (1986). Photocopied images of Chadwick floating, naked, and around her images of dead yet seemingly alive animals; a column full of decaying animal flesh and vegetable matter which had been used for the first part of the piece:

> Of course, what happens is that one has to work quite rapidly because these things decay. I suppose just the business of the animals becoming more and more corrupted so I couldn't work with them any more, and the leaf matter shrivelling, I became interested in that passage. I wanted to produce a counterpoint for the delicious world of desire and the senses that was much more specifically to do with how frail things break and decay, and how they become foul.[42]

By her attention to the physicality of the emotions, the spirituality of the flesh, the brevity and uncertainty of life, Chadwick became one of the most influential artists of her generation.

Poses, threads and images

'My preference is for mongrels over pedigree dogs,' said Salman Rushdie in a discussion of *The Satanic Verses*.[43] Describing the Acid House scene of the late 1980s, one participant observed how this electronic dance music, both abstract and rhythmic, 'strips down, reforms, reconceives, fractures, twists, speeds up, slows down, disorients and rearranges, selecting and reselecting, redefining music according to mood . . .'[44] What these comments share, and what they have in common with Helen Chadwick's unusual materials, is a freshness of sources, a sense of the apt uses of hybridity, mixing and matching, collage. The thought was nothing new, but the use of varied styles, images and sources took on a new urgency and energy. Technology and recording history allowed musicians access to the equivalent of past literary, visual or clothing styles; the worlds of fashion, design and music were intimately connected. Punk turned pop star Adam Ant described in 1981 his influences. 'The influences on [guitarist] Marco and myself are very diverse but have a common filmic quality. We both like John Barry and Link Wray. But for the past two years I've been collecting albums from France . . . one of Pigmy music and others by Aboriginals which appeal to me at a structural level.'[45] Vaguely 'Native American' face stripes, tribal drum rhythms and fancy dress pirate outfits gave Adam and the Ants an unlikely, brief spell of chart success. As music technology and video became increasingly available the looks and sounds of the past were open to new uses and interpretations.

As well as allowing ever more access to the history of recorded music, new electronic technologies made synthesizers an increasingly versatile instrument in their own right. At this time they were used particularly to generate a uniquely brash, synthetic nightclub sound, balanced between the commercial and alternative ethos, by groups such as Depeche Mode, The Human League or Soft Cell; other bands, such as The Eurythmics or Culture Club used the same means to produce a calculated, mass market music. What these groups shared, for a peculiar moment, was an image draped in sexless androgyny. As music writer Jon Savage reported in 1983 in *The Face*:

> it was as heartening as it was amusing to see Marc Almond and Boy George mincing about all over the nation's TV screens – with as much courage as self-absorption – at a time when 'Our Boys' are warring with the 'Argies'. Small beer, yet their manifest camping was a relief from all the bellicosity that I, for one, refused to believe in. But they also hinted, in their different ways, at a pop perennial: the expression of divergent sexuality.[46]

On the less commercial edge of popular music, experimentation with synthesizer and sampler went much further, *My Life in the Bush of Ghosts* (1981) by Brian Eno and David Byrne, for instance, which used Latin and Middle Eastern ethnic music samples as well as electronic and conventional instruments. Other 'independent' musicians kept the traditional instruments and group format, but nevertheless were wary of the established record corporations, and advocated their own artistic freedom. For these bands, as well as in the more commercial groups of the early and mid-1980s, what punk passed on was an impulse to pursue both creative independence and profit. 'Among the cleverer artists,' wrote one music journalist, 'a consensus emerged around pop as the ethos to adhere to.'[47] An expression of this aspiration was the birth of the new, small record labels such as Factory Records, set up in Manchester around 1980, Postcard Records in Glasgow (1980) and Creation Records in London (1983). It was here that many of the new bands now began their careers.

By 1985 the music scene was a mix of independent and popular mainstream acts, experimental and commercial styles. Among those rooted in the late 1970s and still successful were ska, reggae and two-tone influenced bands such as The Specials and Madness. Equally unconventional in their musical and lyrical content were The Smiths, who signed to another independent label, Rough Trade, and whose most successful album, *Meat is Murder*, was released that year. Mainstream popular music now appeared to be bigger business than ever: a multi-media monster that devoured influences and quotations from film, art and literature and spewed them out again as mass market commodity. 'In keeping with its escalating, almost rapacious profile around the world', writer Dave Hill claimed in 1986, contemporary pop 'draws its inspiration from anywhere and everywhere . . . poses, threads, and images as well as tunes are lifted wholesale . . .'[48] Pop was assisted in its swift transition from subculture to mainstream by a global media event in the universal language of music, for an irreproachable issue of world political concern: the Live Aid concert of 13 July 1985. Yet an undertow of political resistance still persisted. Billy Bragg, who described himself, in a reference to one of the most revered punk bands, as a 'one-man Clash', brought together a left-wing alliance of artists and performers in 1985 who became known as Red Wedge. Their objective, only partly realized, was to draw press attention, provoke discussion and raise awareness of the political process.[49]

What characterized the latter part of the 1980s after the fracture of music into endless constituent subcultures was the new flux of constantly changing scenes and styles. Dance and disco music were associated with synthesizers from the 1970s for instance, and as new varieties of electronic disco filtered in from the USA they fed into the sound of the 'industrial' avant-garde and various versions of black styles including hip-hop and soul. Likewise, the new dance influences were quickly taken up by the post-punk travellers of the later 1980s, now known as 'crusties', by squatter and anarchist bands, by experimental and political artists such as the Mutoid Waste Company.[50] From around 1988 this new dance scene was accompanied by its own drug, Ecstasy, and by various studio-based groups, including M/A/A/R/S and S-Express; often one or two people manipulating electronic equipment and samples, first to serve the club scene, and second, to produce possible chart hits, as with 'Voodoo Ray' from A Guy Called Gerald. The new dance craze peaked in 1988 and 1989; the drugs associated with the scene quickly attracted the attention of media, politicians and police; in late 1989 a new political movement emerged, the Freedom to Party Campaign.

As well as the studio-based DJ style of dance music, some of the old-style guitar bands now added or mimicked synthesizers, samples and dance rhythms. Based particularly in Manchester and Liverpool one such style, scallydelic, so called because of its references to the 1960s and its northern English origins, exactly synthesized dance and rock:

> You can see them all over the North-West, drifting through Manchester's arcades doing the swim-dance in the high-tech Hacienda, travelling *en masse* to tribal events such as the recent Stone Roses' concert at Spike Island on the Mersey estuary: groups of young men and women wearing floppy fringes and

baggy, Day-glo clothes; 24-hour party people chasing the Great God Now in a millennial hedonism . . .[51]

As when the Beatles emerged, when punk dominated, and again in the dance craze of the late 1980s and early 1990s, northern England now made its own statement for a distinctive, influential, regional culture.

Slightly different worlds

Right through the Thatcher years too British cinema, often obliquely and some-times directly, questioned and depicted competing visions of both regional and national tradition, of distinctive value systems and ways of living. Describing the creation of his dystopian fantasy *Brazil* (1985), for example, director Terry Gilliam made reference to his earlier work on the Monty Python films. 'Comedy seemed to play better,' he said, 'especially political comedy or things that we were trying to say that would bother a lot of people – if you place them in a slightly different world. It would be funny if we put on funny costumes and said the lines . . .'[52] Not all film-makers wanted, needed or felt able to use comedy. However, there was a new exploration of contemporary themes within the politicized atmosphere of the moment: the effects of state and financial power, notions of personal and collec-tive definition, gender and ethnicity, the relationship of past to present, the substance and consequence of modern-day morals. By picturing the slightly different worlds of a national past, an imagined future or an alternative present, increasingly self-conscious attempts were made to explore, define and expand the constituent parts of 'Britishness'. The financial equation faced by every British film-maker was, though, as difficult as ever to solve. Tax subsidies were withdrawn from the mid-1980s; ownership of cinema chains, as well as the financial backing which made the films possible, was increasingly from overseas; despite the success early on of films like *Chariots of Fire* (1981), independent production companies including Goldcrest, Handmade and Palace Pictures were unable to survive into the next decade.

Chariots of Fire (H. Hudson, 1981) set the mood for many of the historical dramas of this time: like *Gandhi* (Richard Attenborough, 1982), for example, it was an examination of Britain's past which also projected present-day values, and which served as a comment on past failings as well as successes. Set around the events of the VI Olympiad in Paris, *Chariots of Fire* follows an English Jew, Harold Abrahams, and a Scottish would-be missionary, Eric Liddle, as they prepare and participate in the sports competition of 1924, and as they struggle respectively for acceptance and recognition of individual conscience over collec-tive, conventional, patriotic sentiment. Though it won three Academy Awards, including Best Director for Hudson, the film was criticized for its seemingly simplistic celebration of national achievements. 'In a way it is pro-traditionalist and could be accused of being very conservative,' Hudson replied. 'And yet you have the two main characters fighting against various kinds of bigotry.'[53] *Gandhi*, which won eight Oscars, was both epic film-making in the tradition of David Lean's *Lawrence of Arabia* (1962), and a sympathetic portrait of the Indian strug-gle for independence, of the flawed British character on which the imperial project had been built. 'Heritage' cinema, as it now came to be know, was more clearly defined as a genre with literary adaptations such as *A Passage to India* (David Lean, 1984) and *A Room with a View* (Merchant and Ivory, 1986), where questions of class, tradition and ethnicity were still in the frame, albeit sometimes focused softly.[54]

The contemporary world was also explored in satirical social commentary and biographical films. The most direct of these films in its concern with pressing political and social questions was *The Ploughman's Lunch* (R. Eyre, 1983), written by novelist Ian McEwan, which examines the invention of the past: history as a tale of the present. Taking a self-consciously critical view of Thatcherism as a moral ideology, the film draws parallels between the Suez crisis (1956) and the Falklands War (1982): its protagonist, a BBC journalist, reshapes both the events of 1956 in his book, and the conflict of 1982 in his current affairs broadcasts.[55] Similarly, following their successful first collaboration on *My Beautiful Laundrette* (1985), Stephen Frears (director) and Hanif Kureishi (writer) went on to make *Sammy and Rosie Get Laid* (1987), a picture of the multi-ethnic, hedonistic, burnt-out landscape of London in the mid-1980s.[56] Biographical films tended to place central protagonists with identifiably contemporary attitudes in an unsympathetic past to better articulate and reinforce present-day values, for example by consideration of the formerly excluded or legally wronged. Both *Dance with a Stranger* (M. Newell, 1985) and *Scandal* (M. Caton-Jones, 1989) reinterpret the events surrounding well-known legal cases partly from the viewpoint of the women involved.[57]

Dystopias, both criminal and futuristic, provided another form of commentary in Gilliam's *Brazil* (1985) and Michael Radford's *1984* (1984), both of which present the struggle against authoritarian rule and collectivized mass society as lost, except for momentary, symbolic acts of resistance.[58] Yet while *1984* portrayed a defeated humanity, and while Gilliam insisted on the 'unhappy' ending he wanted for *Brazil*, the gangster film was less concerned with communicating a message than commenting on social mores.[59] The usefulness of the criminal underworld in this respect was established by *The Long Good Friday* (J. MacKenzie, 1981), in which an East End crook, Harold Shand, seeks to expand his 'corporation' by linking up with New York mobsters, showing them around his criminal empire and providing hospitality on his Thames river yacht. Harold's plans are ruined, however, by a series of inexplicable, violent attacks. In one view gangsterism and entrepreneurship become indistinguishable; in another variant, *Buster* (D. Green, 1988), lawbreakers are misunderstood folk heroes; even more critically the entrepreneur/master criminal becomes a symbol of greed and moral bankruptcy as in *The Cook, the Thief, his Wife and her Lover* (P. Greenaway, 1989), which was, according to one commentator 'symptomatic as much as analytic of Thatcherism'.[60] 'It's also an angry film,' said another. 'The 1980s' political situation that existed in Britain was of such extreme self-interest and greed, and there is a way in which *The Cook, the Thief* is a parody of a consumer society, personified by the Thief, Albert Spica. He has no redeeming features, and is consumed by self-interest and greed.'[61]

British cinema was a splintered mirror through which the fracture and fissure of British society through the 1980s could be observed. Like other aspects of society and the arts, it reflected backwards towards tradition, empire and the re-viewing of particular incidents; at the same time it attempted to picture the present, to clarify its defining images and values. Yet in this age of multiple images and blurred boundaries, self-definition was not easily pulled into focus: only now could attention turn more explicitly to questions of nationhood.

CHAPTER 9

Fragile States

Twenty houses here once

The paradox of the United Kingdom in the mid-1990s was that while 'Brit-' became a common prefix to describe whatever was new, youthful or innovative, the constituent nations were increasingly divorced from a collective British unity. The cultural roots of nationalist devolution were deeply set, yet in the new global age, the idea of nationhood was called into question. The symbols of twentieth-century national achievement, the Second World War in particular, were examined closely as a series of anniversaries came and went, yet there was recognition too of the decay to which collective memory was subject. Eco-protesters, Scottish nationalists and homeowners who defaulted on their mortgage repayments found, however, that the nation-state was not about to die away. Artists too questioned where and how to recall past lives. Sculptor Rachel Whiteread's answer was that the local and domestic provided as much of a clue as national symbols; that personal history mattered as much as the collective past. Describing her best-known piece, *House* (1993), Whiteread (b.1963) stated. 'Everyone has an experience of the fragility of life. There were 20 houses here once. Now there is one that cannot be lived in. By using a cheap building material, I was making a statement. I was not trying to make a pretty object – but I do think it is very beautiful. I chose the colour of the concrete: it is the same kind used to restore the white cliffs of Dover.'[1] By spraying concrete into the interior walls of a derelict residential terrace in East London, filling the 'cast' and then removing the exterior, Whiteread pictured otherwise invisible interiors. As in her earlier work, which made, remade and meditated on the artefacts and structures of domestic life: mattresses, sinks, the area beneath chairs, *House*, among other things, observes a 'feminine' domain. It outlines the patterns of movement through space which make up daily routine – sleeping, working, eating – and in doing so acts as a memorial to the fragility and temporality of the human state.

That Whiteread was the first woman to win the Turner Prize, and that relatively little attention was paid to the fact, may be taken as vindication of earlier campaigns by women for full, equal participation in society. For activists, the pressing concern was a more integrated sexual politics of particular issues, among them the treatment of breast cancer or the casualization of labour.[2] Despite this the question of how far and how fast women had moved towards equality of choice and opportunity remained open. In *Because of Her Sex: The Myth of Equality for Women in Britain* (1994), Kate Figes put the case for continuing 'sexual apartheid': while 72 per cent of all working women were in paid employment, many of these worked part time; while a few had made spectacular

Illustration 9   A changed vision of Britain: Mandir Temple (Hindu), Neasden, north London, 1995

advances, women's earnings as a percentage of male income had risen by five per cent during 1980–91 to reach a high of 78 per cent; while women had made some progress in the professions, female obstetrics and gynaecological consultants still amounted to 12.5 per cent.[3] Education, campaigns for equal pay and equal rights and the move away from heavy industry towards new technology had altered the attitudes of women workers and their employers, yet the world of work was still in many respects structured according to male expectations. Equal relationships within marriage or family partnership made commensurate status in employment more achievable, yet by 1991, while 80 per cent of women aged 20–40 had children, among women managers in the same age group the figure was only 20 per cent.[4] Despite the limited expansion of state provision in 1992 intended to free women with school-aged children to return to work or enter employment, motherhood was still seen as a break in occupational and financial achievement.[5]

Acknowledging the constraints women faced, other commentators took a more hopeful view. Occupational segregation certainly continued; the growth of women's employment remained predominantly part-time, yet that small group of professional women who had entered the elite in medicine, science or the law was increasingly vocal in its advocacy of better promotion policies and organizational procedures.[6] Similarly, while the 1994 United Nations International Year of the Family provoked media discussion on the connections between crime, educational underachievement and the demise of the 'traditional' family, recognition of altered attitudes was still incorporated into the law. The Family Law Act (1996) thus extended the provision of the Domestic Violence and Matrimonial Act (1976) so that non-molestation exclusion orders would now apply not only to immediate family members, but also to various 'associated persons' such as parents or flatmates.[7] Advances in education perhaps provided the most positive evidence, as the summer of 1994 was the first year girls achieved a higher over-all success rate at 'A' level examinations than boys, though older women remained generally less well qualified than their male peers.[8] Changes in house-hold structure, education and employment in this view amounted to a dramatic long-term shift in gender relations not just in Britain, but throughout the west-ern world: the proportion of women aged 18–49 who were married fell from 74 per cent (1979) to 57 per cent (1994); lone-parent families increased from 8 per cent (1971) to 23 per cent (1994); less well-off financially, women were never-theless more independent.[9]

While her appeal was eminently resistible to some, and while she was hardly representative of any aspect of British society, Lady Diana Spencer was nevertheless among the most widely known women of the 1990s. Royalty had reached a peak of popularity with the wedding of Prince Charles and Diana in July 1981; in 1993 the debate over tax payments by the Queen and expenditure of the royal household demonstrated a less sympathetic mood. The response to Diana's death in late August and early September 1997, like the rest of her story, had an oddly mythic quality. The Queen's distant inability to respond to public feeling; the scenes of mass grief and banks of sickly-sweet smelling flowers; and the home-made posters and manifestos put up in their thousands. One observer of these scenes on The Mall was struck by the sight of 'an elderly black woman singing hymns in a cracked voice without regard for anyone else.'[10] The royal family's fail-ure to sense the lessening deference of British society, or to allow for the shifted balance between individual happiness and duty to the common good, eventually gave the Diana saga a wider significance. 'Diana's struggle within the royal family resonated with the stuff that British society was also trying to sort out . . . a new settlement between men, women and children'.[11]

Ain't going nowhere

Another unexpected death, a murder, also forced sections of the public and some institutions within British society to rethink the situation of immigrants and minorities within British society. On Thursday April 22 1993, 18-year-old Stephen Lawrence was standing at a bus stop in Eltham, south-east London, with his friend Duwayne Brooks. A group approached, Stephen was stabbed fatally, the group making their escape. The killers were never prosecuted. In February 1997 an inquest jury, abandoning normal procedure, decided the attack amounted to an unlawful killing, adding that it was also an unprovoked racist attack. A govern-ment inquiry into the murder between March and July 1998 came to the conclu-sion that the police had within its ranks a powerful strain of 'institutional racism': 'a collective failure to provide an appropriate and professional service to people because of their colour, culture or ethnic origin'.[12] This statement was an impor-tant achievement in the struggle by Doreen and Neville Lawrence, Stephen's parents, to find and convict their son's killers. When the Crown Prosecution Service case, and a subsequent rare private prosecution, both failed, 19 Members of Parliament together with the Campaign for Racial Equality, stated that the justice system, by simple fact of not having brought forward a successful conviction, was also racist. Like the Rushdie affair a few years earlier, the Lawrence case raised doubts about Britain's supposedly integrated society. While the borders of assimilation were not necessarily extended, there was now, at least, a willingness to confront this failure in public discussion, to name the deep fissures which existed, though such recognition would never raise the dead. Majority white society and its ethnic groups coexisted, it now became publicly clear, in separate worlds. The real questions of multi-ethnic accommodation had yet to be faced.[13]

The Stephen Lawrence case was remarkable not only for the family and legal drama that gradually emerged, but also for the public debate it engendered, which highlighted once again the persistent victimization that at times could isolate both long-standing minorities and recently arrived immigrants. Afro-Caribbeans were the most likely to be attacked bodily, Bangladeshis most likely to suffer an attack on their property. About half of all those who complained to the police were dissatisfied with their response, citing indifference, hostility or siding with the assailant as the most common failings.[14] Greater willingness to confront such inadequacies, and to report incidents of abuse or violence, was partly the result of a changing population profile. South Asians rather than Afro-Caribbeans now became the largest ethnic group; 35 per cent of South Asians were under 16 in 1994, most of them were British-born.[15] The difficulty for young people in particular remained the best way to pursue the delicate, unending negotiations that continued in order to breach different generational and cultural values. Shaheena Begum Mossarib, a second-year law student who gave up her literary studies at university to be able to assist members of her own community, described her own situation:

> So far I have talked about the difficulty of growing up with peers who have either totally accepted or totally rejected our ways, however I realize that there are now more women like me, who accept some of the traditional ways, but who feel restricted . . . The truth is that I feel closer to girls from my own culture, because I feel defensive about our cultural differences with non-Bengali friends, whether they are white, black or other types of Asian.[16]

Coping, or failing to cope, with the pressures of cultural difference and minority status took varied forms. Talking was one solution, but not one available to everybody: alcohol related problems among men especially, including admission to psychiatric hospitals for alcohol abuse, continued to trouble both South Asian and Afro-Caribbean communities.[17]

While the difficult realities of everyday life for ethnic minorities and immigrants showed little sign of diminishing, while black athletes or football players could represent the nation, but Afro-Caribbean men remained 17 per cent of the prison population, there were nevertheless some signs of reconciliation and mutual acceptance. Birmingham musician Steven Kapur, who grew up in the working-class immigrant district of Handsworth, with its Jamaican and Indian population, promoted raga, a music style that mixed reggae, dancehall and hip-hop influences with South Asian bhangra. He became a successful pop star under the name Apache Indian.[18] Within the wider community of ethnic groups and immigrants, education again provided the most positive indications of social integration and advance. Three quarters of all South Asian men were fluent in English by the early 1990s; Chinese, Asian Africans and Indians had the best educational qualifications; second generation Afro-Caribbean men had made the greatest progress, Bangladeshi men the least. Young black women saw the opportunities for mobility and autonomy that education offered and by the mid-1990s within the 16–24 age group, at least 77 per cent had achieved 'A' level or lower level school exam pass results.[19]

In London the largest group of the non-British population according to the 1991 Census was the Irish (214,000) followed by Indians (151,619); these were followed by Jamaicans (76,445), Kenyans (56,993), Bangladeshis (56,567), Cypriots (50,684) and Pakistanis (44,741); while German and Italian populations both exceeded 30,000.[20] As a matter of instinct, survival or compulsion, what immigrants and ethnic minorities often expressed from within these communities, in London as elsewhere, was their need not to be parted from that which was least visible within the host community, namely cultural tradition and upbringing. In 1991 Mrs Stanowska (b.1929), whose brother died in a labour camp during the war, whose father was in the Polish army stationed in Scotland during the Second World War, and who arrived in Britain in 1948, described her relationship to the past and her homeland. 'I think about those days all the time. As I grow older I think about them more. I remember people's faces and what I did and saw as if it were yesterday. I think about it and talk about it with others who were there. Is that young girl me? Is she me?'[21] For Muhammad Ali (b.1942), from Kashmir, who arrived in England in 1969, the struggle for acceptance within British society came eventually to seem futile. Ten years after leaving school he met up with some of the Asian and Muslim boys he had known. 'At least two had grown beards, become very religious and were completely involved in the Asian community. I asked them why. They said that they had tried their best to mix with the white community, but they had given up . . . When it really came down to being accepted as part of English society, it was impossible, and they found a lot more security in their community.'[22] Describing the changes that had taken place during his own lifetime Mike Phillips (b.1941), who arrived from Guyana with his father in 1956, took a broader view:

> What interests me now is the sense in which blacks and whites in England, and especially in London, are coming to share a difficult identity, an identity which is difficult and which has to be constantly negotiated . . . When white people say derogatory things about London, the inner city problems and so on, what they're really talking about is the black community. And what I say is 'Bugger their luck' – because we ain't going nowhere.[23]

Spiral Tribes

Public and media discussion of the Lawrence case took place against a background of concern over apparent rises in criminal activity, and this alarm extended too to the new counter-cultural youth movements. John Major's comment in 1992, 'New Age travellers. Not in this age. Not in any age,' expressed the confrontational deadlock and hyperbole of the time as counter-culturalism and criminality came to seem inseparable. Major perhaps had in mind groups such as the Spiral Tribe, a west of England dance party 'sound system' founded in 1991 and based on the 1960s' idealism – psychedelia, spirituality and egalitarianism – of Timothy Leary and Ken Kesey. Like their forebears, Spiral Tribe had a well-established network of connections and a well articulated set of values. In 1992 they staged the largest festival in the country for six years, which was a week long and attended by 40,000 people. This strong statement of counter-cultural values, associated as it was with drugs, noise and litter, and possibly with various forms of political protest too, was viewed unfavourably in governing circles. The Criminal Justice Act (1994) included provision to curb such events in the future; once again a broad coalition of opposing groups came together with the common cause of resistance.[24]

The association between criminality and the dance scene was part of a far broader stigmatization that was now attached to youth by both media and politicians. Reduced opportunities for school leavers, unemployment at 7.9 per cent between 1989 and 1996 and the journalistic 'discovery' of drug and later gun-related activity all contributed to this attitude. So too did a sequence of events. In September 1991 disorderly crowds caused disturbances which led to dozens of arrests in Cardiff, Tyne and Wear and Oxford for example, partly associated with race tension, and partly related to the 'ram raiding' craze where cars were stolen and driven into stores or warehouses, then goods looted. In February 1993 two ten-year-old boys abducted and beat to death a two year old whom they came across in a Liverpool shopping mall. From such tales photographers, film-makers and journalists now created a composite picture of disturbed youth gangs stalking a post-industrial landscape, 'groups of aimless boys in baggy jeans and hooded tops in the foreground; or run-down council estates, graffiti-ridden, with burned-out cars and again the obligatory aimless boys'.[25] Actual evidence as to whether crime rates among the young were increasing remained uncertain; nevertheless, strong anti-delinquency measures became the policy of both major parties. This 'criminalization' of youth offences was extended in the wake of the Liverpool abduction case by additional measures in the Criminal Justice Act which increased the variety and length of custodial sentences, and which allowed for the punishment of 10–13-year-old children.[26] Spirals of crime, violence, drugs and moral panic now seemed to dominate the public debate; underneath these dizzy signs of change were the values of consumption and consumerism so carefully bred and nurtured through the Thatcher years. The new cultures of youth could now be evoked in a shorthand list of desires that might consist in 1990, say, of 'beachwear, Lucozade, fluorescent paraphernalia'; or a few years later of 'sportswear, football, Britpop, Britfrocks, Alcopops'.[27]

The new discussion on the family that now emerged was part of a tradition that dated back to the Second World War and earlier, but it took place in a dramatically changed public and moral landscape. Social explanations of criminal behaviour were replaced by stress on personal responsibility; the safety net of welfarism was withdrawn, prompting fears of a newly stricken, potentially unruly underclass. While there was open debate and some overreaction to the mistreatment and abuse of young people, and recognition of the stress they now experienced in the increased rates of suicide among young men aged 15–24 for example, which tripled between 1982 and 1995, moral censure was attached especially to the debate on teenage motherhood.[28] From the early 1980s stories of teenage mothers in receipt of council housing and comprehensive welfare benefits were cited as examples of abuse within the welfare system. That such mothers were discouraged from marriage by inadequate partners, that the social pressures on working-class or non-professional women encouraged motherhood rather than deferred gratification, that despite welfare and housing support such women struggled to establish themselves but nevertheless were in the main able parents: none of this drew much attention in public discussions.[29] Likewise while public debate stressed fraud, criminality and anti-social behaviour, Donovan Wiley's remarkable 'Losing Ground' project (1993–5) documented in photographs the effects of the Criminal Justice Act on a group of 'New Age' travellers. In doing so Wiley revealed something of the brittle personal histories that had led one group of young people away from conventional society and towards their predictable loss of ideals in the face of poverty. In part this account follows the story of Julie, in her late twenties with two young sons, who like many of her peers had a background of family neglect or abuse, educational failure and poor material provision. When Wiley met with Julie in 1996, some two years after their initial contact, the new legislation had curtailed rural travel and a permanent caravan park in London had become home. 'The sense of optimism and collective protection I had caught in Gloucestershire had been brief. For the group, perhaps inevitably, it had turned out to be a misplaced ideal.' Wiley continues: 'It was irredeemably sad. The group were much more dependent on drugs, begging and welfare payments. Vodka and heroin had invaded all their lives, and Julie had aged considerably. Her children had their heads shaved to prevent lice infestation. They could not read or write.'[30]

The wider counter-cultural dance and eco-protest movement was more successful in drawing attention to its causes and beliefs, and in projecting a powerful image of its idealism and tenacity. Conventional pressure group politics and more alternative counter-cultural beliefs united after 1992 with the Twyford Down protests against a motorway link near Winchester, Hampshire, which was planned to cross a designated Site of Special Scientific Interest.[31] Protests took on the character of festivals, not least with the formation of the Dongas Tribe – the name derived from a Matabele word for ancient route or pathway, and used by teachers from the nineteenth century at the nearby Winchester College to describe Twyford Down's mediaeval criss-cross of countryside pathways – a loose association of activists and protesters. One of the Dongas Tribe was Fraggie, who designed and made her own outfits. Her favourite, which she had worn to her first festival, Stonehenge 1989, was a 'composite of bright layers of second-hands and customised clothing . . . hand-made socks and crafted accessories'.[32] She wore too a red and black hat, cotton and lycra dress, an Indian cotton and wool embroidered waistcoat and a wooden spoon ocarina; she carried her own wooden crochet hooks, liquorice stick and velvet pouch.

Such outfits may be taken as a statement of beliefs: self-sufficiency, creativity, regard for nature and for the values of indigenous peoples. Describing the objectives of the Dongas and other protesters, another activist argued their political significance was far wider than merely stopping the construction of a particular road. Rather, it was the '*creation of a climate of autonomy, disobedience and resistance* ... simultaneously a *negative* act (stopping the road etc.) and a *positive pointer* to a kind of social relation that could be ... a community of resistance'.[33] While varied groups were drawn together in opposition to road construction and the Criminal Justice Act, as Donovan Wiley's project hints, its underlying causes and consequences were less the stuff of headlines. Inevitably, too, the movement appeared to lose momentum and direction, to spin off without remaining a collective cause.

Yuk, phew

The thought of simultaneously destructive and constructive acts was also present among the younger generation of British artists whose work drew public attention in the early 1990s. Rejecting traditional notions of high culture as well as the pretence of the art establishment, some instead constructed a deliberately 'juvenile' approach in the conception and execution of their work. In 1997 art critic Matthew Collings noted how many of these so-called young British artists, some trained at Goldsmith's College, London in the latter part of the 1980s, had been drawn towards 'half coherent illiterate rambling thoughts that the young artist just writes down in biro or in clumsy typewriting, and somehow it's art. Cartoony doodles and scribbles, thought balloons, biro ventings saying I am a cunt.'[34]

Evading the constraints and exclusivity of the gallery system by setting up their own exhibitions in East London Docklands warehouses, modernizing through their acute awareness of popular culture, mass media and the techniques of commercial self-promotion, they now built on the work of earlier movements: the St Ives artists, the Independent Group, or the Royal College of Art school of pop practitioners.[35] These younger artists, who first drew public attention in 1988 with the 'Freeze' exhibition, curated by Damien Hirst (b.1965), became associated with the patronage of advertising magnate Charles Saatchi, but also received funding from the National Lottery. Their public notoriety peaked with the Saatchi collection exhibition of 1997. The excitement and vilification that *Sensation* aroused now signalled the emergence of new intellectual and generational values; their arrival could hardly have been more dramatic against a background of dreary political stasis.[36] What gradually emerged through the early 1990s, too, despite a sturdy tabloid tradition of mocking the apparent absurdities of contemporary art, was a new audience, which willingly stepped back from Britain's predominantly literary culture.

Conceptual, video and installation artists tended to grab the headlines; a less noted but nonetheless invigorating aspect of the new movement was its reinvention of painting. Jenny Saville (b.1970) for example, absorbed herself in the textures and tones of female flesh: indented by the elastic pressure marks of undergarments (*Trace*, 1993–4), inscribed by contour lines or writing scratched through pigment (*Propped*, 1992; *Plan*, 1993), or compiled into a composite body of mismatched fleshtones. Richard Patterson (b.1963) painted canvases of toy figures moulded from plastic (*Blue Minotaur*, 1996) and model motocross riders. His attention to the visual effects of photographic imagery, fascination with the minutiae of mass production and culture and his portraiture of the mundane objects and backgrounds of modern living describe the common imaginative landscape of his generation. Fiona Rae (b.1963) expressed her own awareness of the tenuous status of painting most directly. 'Painting is an unsolicited activity . . . Why paint? What kind of painting?'[37] Her reply was that painting invents its own language of signs and symbols that borrow from, reflect back and review the contemporary act of looking to incorporate both MTV and MOMA. In early paintings, such as *Untitled (yellow and black)* (1991), drips and scribbles give a cartoon-like energy to the struggle between communication and incoherence. *Untitled (Sky Shout)* (1997), a series of target-like circles within circles overlaid by interlocking areas of 'dragged' paint, by the blurs and smudges of making, leaves the viewer unanchored in a universe of chaotic, vivid symbols where no common agreement on meaning seems possible, and perhaps none is necessary.[38]

Damien Hirst became the best known and most notorious of the new artists. He provoked widespread public discussion as winner of the 1995 Turner Prize, especially for *Mother and Child, Divided* (1993), which played on his reputation for asking childlike questions that were at once innocent and provocative. While *The Sun* dismissed contemporary art in general and Hirst's piece in particular as 'garbage – and now dead animals', Hirst defended his approach by quoting Brancusi. 'When we are no longer children, we are already dead.'[39] A necessity to evade analytic interpretation in favour of instinct and emotion; an acute awareness of the contradiction between an impossible desire for immortality and the inevitable approach of death; and a skill for the production of clarifying, simple objects which serve as representation of an idea: all of these led to four containers, crate-like, with glass sides and top, containing cow and calf, each sliced longways into two. Equally discussed was Hirst's earlier *The Physical Impossibility of Death in the Mind of Someone Living* (1991), more widely known as the 'shark in formaldehyde'. The sources for this kind of work were, for Hirst and his contemporaries, taken from whatever forms seemed compelling:

> Sitting there, looking at 5 × 4 images of paintings, that was the world I grew up in . . . At the same time, though, I spent a hell of a lot of time talking about commercials when I was at art school, conversations like, 'My God, did you see the Coalite advert when the dog kisses the cat and then the cat kisses the mouse? Fantastic!'[40]

As inheritors of the commercially minded 1980s' generation, Hirst and others made use of such 'high impact' images, and benefited too from a training in self-promotion and marketing, from corporate funding. It is no surprise, then, that Britart, as it became known, was promoted abroad, especially in US shows such as *Brilliant! New Art from London* (1995–6).[41]

Despite the growing audience for contemporary art, sections of the public, the media and the art world remained sceptical. Attempting to explain this reluctance to admit the legitimacy of contemporary visual expression, one critic argued there was a general 'fear of feelings (yuk) and a corresponding reluctance to articulate them' which sprang from the belief that if something is not art, its challenge need not be taken seriously: '(phew) you are safe from that.'[42] The popularity of the new art in Britain may be taken as an indication of fresh willingness to confront difficult subjects and feelings, and as recognition of the unique imaginative and emotional power possessed by visual exploration to chart the troublesome realities of human existence. As Cornelia Parker put it, it was both possible and desirable to make 'something visible that everyone recognises to describe the indescribable'. In *Embryo Firearms* (1995) Parker created two fused metal fragments from a gun factory to express both the vulnerability of life and its potential for destruction; in *60 Minutes Silence* (1996), Gillian Wearing's video portrait of 26 men and women dressed as police officers, remaining more or less still for an hour, captures human energy, but also its restraint.[43]

Cropped hair, Sixties fashion, greasy spoon caff

With a less elitist image than the visual arts, popular music was an ideal commodity in the new age of worldwide consumption. Within Britain dedicated fans followed the intricate fragmentation of diversifying dance genres. Radio 1, though, the main pop music station of the BBC, was caught off guard: with falling audiences, ageing presenters and an unfashionable 'housewives' choice' image, it initially responded to acid house with a broadcasting ban. By 1994 however, the new styles had been added to playlists to draw back listeners.[44] On the wider music scene, media corporations now benefited from rapid transmission via MTV for example, and more generally from the thickening layers of financial and cultural connections that encircled the globe. One by-product of this was that while the nation-state remained central to legal, political and economic activity, for some it became less important in the creation of personal or collective forms of identification. Squeezed between the local and the worldwide, national belonging became an increasingly self-conscious act of imagination. Popular music became self-consciously nation-minded too, particularly resistant to the influence of American styles, and much more commercially minded: these developments were distilled in Britpop.

Dance music, in the meantime, especially acid house and techno, was one of the most successful styles of the early 1990s, worth £1.8 billion per year by 1993.[45] Beginning as subcultural alternative in the late 1980s, five years on corporate promotion and strategy had helped regulate the scene. Its style, though, nervy, euphoric, dominated by squeaks, rumbles and rhythmically patterned bleeps, was a chemically synthesized landscape of feeling rather than of formal musical structure. It could also achieve a state of blissed-out numbness which many participants felt entirely suited to the moment. By the mid-1990s the number and type of electronic and dance music styles was multiplying as quickly, and to similar effect, as the new cable TV channels that were starting up. Each sub-genre provided an increasingly predictable style that could be picked out by its label: 'downbeat', which reacted against acid house and techno with slower tempo; 'drum'n'bass', which could be groovy and uplifting or abstractly ethereal; 'ambient', which provided 'chill-out' atmospheres and soundscapes.[46] Ethnic and folk styles also took on a new relevance as a 'pure' uncommercialized musical expression, as a hybrid form which added ethnic complexity to traditional pop songs, and as an expression of artistic and social fusion within Britain's new multi-ethnic society. Jungle, for instance, was a fusion of dance, hip-hop and reggae styles.[47]

Stylistic and formal developments, as the connection between Ecstasy use and the dance scene showed, were not beyond the wider sea-change within British society. In particular, drug use, and the profiteering drugs and crime gangs associated with the music scene, drew increased attention. Drug seizures by police and customs doubled between 1991 and 1997, while the number of people imprisoned on drug related offences tripled between 1990 and 2000.[48] Within the harsher economic and social environment, and with the increased association between wealth, glamour and cocaine use for instance, despite its destructive effects, drug use was increasingly 'normalized'.[49] Drugs and crime also became inseparable from the dance scene. 'What was being played out in the clubs in the early 1990s seemed like the chaotic result of attitudes that had prevailed for the best part of a decade,' wrote one journalist, describing Manchester in 1992, 'trickling down from a Government that had prized the individual above the community'.[50] The growth of gang activity may be seen too as partly the result of youth unemployment, of the growing club scene and of potential profits. For police in the Manchester area, as elsewhere, clubs seemed less legitimate businesses than possible sources of vice and disorder, hence the quarter of a million pounds spent on covert monitoring by the Greater Manchester Police in 1997.[51] Recognition or, rather, acknowledgement of shifting attitudes towards drugs, of the rise of a social underclass and of the new critique of Britain's materialistic values, came with the film version of *Trainspotting* (D. Boyle, 1996), which centred on a group of dysfunctional heroin users, but which also provided one of the most successful club music soundtracks of the era.

Profit and cartoonish parody were characteristic, too, of the other major movement in 1990s' pop: Britpop. First used in an article in the *New Musical Express* in early 1995 to describe a loosely connected set of images and interests, the leading groups identified with the term, willingly or not, included Blur, Oasis and Elastica. Quickly 'cropped hair, charity shop clothing . . . [and] publicity shots in a greasy spoon caff' became essential to the many copycat bands that followed.[52] Yet Britpop was not so much about Britain as the outer metropolitan suburbs; not so much about multi-ethnic fusion as white rock segregationism; not so much a reflection of everyday life as of the express desire to escape limiting circumstances, for example Oasis' Gallagher brothers, who were raised in Manchester's outer suburbs.[53]

What these groups shared, too, despite their different social backgrounds, was a common sense of brash purposefulness also present among the 'Freeze' artists; Damien Hirst was symbolically as well as socially connected to Graham Coxon and Alex James of Blur as they were contemporaries at Goldsmith's College, London. 'Francis Bacon would certainly be going round with Damien Hirst and the guitarist from Blur', wrote Matthew Collings in 1997, 'if Francis Bacon wasn't dead, and if Blur weren't out.'[54] Yet while Blur in particular created an oddly nostalgic pastiche of past references, they were entirely contemporary in their ambition to communicate with the largest possible audience, and to create for themselves a global brand name. The same was true of The Spice Girls, who achieved huge, worldwide popularity in 1996, and whose press officer breathlessly explained their attraction. 'The Girls epitomised glamour galore, they were complete motormouths with an exuberant propensity towards a classic soundbite and they had become role models for at least half of the British female population.'[55] Though there was little to differentiate their view of the music business or their role as pop artists, The Spice Girls were unusual for their vocal admiration of Margaret Thatcher. By contrast, while Blur and Oasis became commercial rivals as they simultaneously released singles in the summer of 1995, in 1997 both groups willingly endorsed the most dramatic political shift of the decade with the election of Tony Blair's first New Labour government.[56]

Locality redefined

'Britflicks', like 'Britart' and 'Britpop', were engaged in re-creating national image as saleable commodity. Though such labels were more marketing ploy than cultural groundswell, there were common characteristics in these movements, not least aspirations towards worldwide audiences and profits, usually based on local, low-key financing. While British funding bodies were few – British Screen, Channel Four, ITV and to some extent the National Lottery – and while the European Union provided structural funds to aid redevelopment through film production, it nevertheless became increasingly difficult to identify clearly what might even qualify as a British film, or whether such categorization mattered any more.[57] Anthony Minghella's *The English Patient* (1996) echoes this theme both in its story, which describes in part the mutilation caused by national definitions and identifications, and in its production. Michael Ondaatje, whose background was Sri Lankan of Dutch Indian origin, wrote the novel on which the film was based, Italy and North Africa were among its locations, the financial backing was American, both director and cast were mainly British. If not all films had such internationally based content and production values, global business strategy was certainly now the business of the media corporations. For the population of the United Kingdom this meant changed viewing habits: multiplex cinemas revamped the movie-going experience and revived flagging attendances; by 1992 the rise of the multiplex had increased British exhibition market audience figures, but 92 per cent of the films on offer were American; digital terrestrial television started up following the Broadcasting Act (1996).[58]

Despite the limitations of the British film industry there was a revival of verve and imagination in native film productions, so that the number of films with some UK financial involvement increased steadily from 60 in 1990 to a peak of 128 in 1996. Audience figures also increased, from 97.37 million in 1990 to 139.90 million in 1997.[59] Heritage films broadened in scope to incorporate varied aspects of the national life, often with a strong historical perspective, but sometimes in a contemporary setting. In this respect heritage cinema, a label which in any case had outlived its purpose by now, resembled expatriate recollections of home: selective, idealized and bound by the expectation of outside observers. The literary eminence of an E. M. Forster or a Jane Austen was no longer essential;

the boundaries of the genre expanded over time, though some literary link either in the content or in the origin of a story often remained: *Orlando* (S. Potter, 1993) was by Virginia Woolf; *Carrington* (C. Hampton, 1995) was set within the artistic milieu of Bloomsbury; *Regeneration* (G. Mackinnon, 1997) was based on a prize-winning novel and concerned two First World War poets. *Four Weddings and a Funeral* (M. Newell, 1994) also deserves to be included in the heritage category for its fascination with the more ceremonial and aristocratic aspects of British life, and for its purposeful Anglo-American casting, 'set in the present, but sharing with English country house costume dramas much of the same iconography and many of the same character types'.[60] *Four Weddings* also shared another characteristic that appealed to audiences, namely the ability to display in an attractive and surprising light the characters and qualities of national life. In this sense heritage and other film-making of the time shared with art and popular music not so much an anti-Americanism as a fusion of belated English cultural nationalism with American-style business instinct.

If there was a cinematic genre that closely matched the always slightly absurd 'Brit-' epithet it was within the 'realist' tradition, dating back in part to the New Wave cycle of the late 1950s and early 1960s, which one critic described as 'Brit-grit'.[61] The claim that a new realism had emerged was based on the appearance of films such as *TwentyFourSeven* (S. Meadows, 1997) and *Nil by Mouth* (G. Oldman, 1997), which portrayed life in poor inner-city districts: the crime, poverty, inarticulacy and wish to escape among their inhabitants, as well as the constant, wearing struggle to survive such circumstances. The revival of this New Wave mood was clearly prompted by greater awareness and concern at such circumstances, perhaps now more urgent, as the early northern romanticism of the Woodfall films had been replaced by harsher landscapes of social and industrial collapse. Yet such searches for native authenticity were as constrained, by their domestic settings, by their search for a new arena of male activity, as the heritage vision. The persistence of interest in these extremes of the social spectrum only confirmed too that the majority belonged within the enlarged 'middle' class. Two film-makers who had managed to remain within the 'realist' vein for three decades, and whose work linked the New Wave to the 'Brit-Grit' revival, were Ken Loach (b.1936) and Mike Leigh (b.1943). Leigh's *Naked* (1993), for example, centres on Johnny (David Thewlis), as he wanders through the city day and night encountering the conflicts and human waste of modern-day society. Johnny fulminates at the stupidities and unfairness of his times, but finally limps away down a street, himself clueless as to any future direction or destination. Loach's *Riff-Raff* (1991), one of the first and most powerful portraits of modern working-class experience under the Conservative consensus, also gave expression to the new sense of lost certainties. As Stevie (Robert Carlyle) works with a building gang to convert a former hospital into an exclusive housing complex, he is divided between self-interest and the collective struggle for survival. Hoping to become a successful businessman by selling boxer shorts, bitter with his employers at what he sees as their exploitation of both him and his workmates, he eventually takes revenge.[62]

While Leigh and Loach had well-established bodies of work and were directors well qualified to handle such issues, other film-makers of the time also looked past regional accent and backdrop to less predictable subjects. Among the films they produced were *Trainspotting* (D. Boyle, 1996), *Twin Town* (K. Allen, 1996), *Brassed Off* (M. Herman, 1996) and *The Full Monty* (P. Cattaneo, 1997). Respectively set in cities that had close connections to Britain's collective industrial past, Edinburgh, Swansea, 'Grimly' and Sheffield, these films traded on the past to create a collective future. Each owed its production in part to funding initiatives that were intended to revive local arts and media with financing from the Glasgow Film Fund, the Welsh Film Commission, the Yorkshire Media Productions Agency and the Yorkshire Screen Commission.[63] Each evaded obvious symbols of national or local identification too in an attempt to reinvent place in the light of new times. Both Scotland and Wales in this respect had the advantage of nationalist movements to energize such reinvention, as in such comments as 'Ah don't hate the English . . . Ah hate the Scots,' or 'Daffodils. Sheep shaggers. Coal. Now if it's your idea of Welsh culture, you can't blame us for trying to liven the place up can you?'[64] Northern English industrial collapse by contrast was viewed as a failure that no plot contortions could alleviate. If there were a southern English equivalent to these regional accounts of the new Britain it might be found in *Fever Pitch* (D. Evans, 1996), which centred on a football supporter's obsessive relationship with his team, Arsenal, but which also describes the changing cultural landscape from the 1970s towards the 1990s. What Evans's film most expressively set out was the new social consensus of 'middle England'. Not a world where criminal gangs, drug subcultures or unemployment were the norm, nor necessarily one where most of the population was absorbed in football. Rather a state of affairs where distinctions of low and high culture or class mattered less, where affluence and peace were not able to exempt the individual from the struggle for maturity or integrity, where relations between women and men had entered a new stage of instability and continued debate.[65]

Timeline 3: 1980–97

1980

SOCIETY: council tenants given the right to buy their homes under the Housing Act; school governing bodies required to have participation of parents under the Education Act. **April:** riots in the St Paul's district of Bristol. **May:** Iranian Embassy siege in London ends as SAS forces storm the building. **August:** unemployment passes 2m. **November:** six per cent pay limit imposed by the government; Michael Foot elected Labour Party leader.

ARTS: TV, theatre, film: Jack Hazan and David Mingay, *Rude Boy*; Nicolas Roeg, *Bad Timing*; Julien Temple, *The Great Rock'n'Roll Swindle*. **Visual:** Gilbert and George, *England*; first edition of *i-D* magazine. **Musical:** Lynton Kwesi Johnson, *Inglan is a Bitch*; Postcard Records (Glasgow) and Factory Records (Manchester) established. **Written:** Howard Brenton, *The Romans in Britain*; William Golding wins Booker Prize for *Rites of Passage*.

1981

SOCIETY: British Nationality Act; Greenham Common Peace Camp established January; Deptford fire kills fourteen black youths; formation of the Social Democratic Party. **April:** riots in the Brixton district of London; Scarman Inquiry follows. **May:** IRA prisoner Bobby Sands dies after 66 days hunger strike. **July:** riots in Toxteth, Liverpool, and Moss Side, Manchester as well as several other towns and cities; the Prince of Wales marries Lady Diana Spencer.

ARTS: TV, theatre, film: Bill Forsyth, *Gregory's Girl*; John MacKenzie, *The Long Good Friday*; Hugh Hudson, *Chariots of Fire*; Karel Reisz, *The French Lieutenant's Woman*. **Visual:** Antony Gormley, *Bed*. Musical: launch of MTV. **Musical:** Brian Eno and David Byrne, *My Life in the Bush of Ghosts*. **Written:** Alasdair Gray, *Lanark*; Ssalmon Rushdie, *Midnight's Children*; D. M. Thomas, *The White Hotel*.

1982

SOCIETY: Belfast Housing Renewal Strategy. **January:** unemployment passes 3m. **April:** Argentina invades the Falkland Islands and South Georgia. **July:** surrender of the Argentine forces in the Falklands; IRA bombs in Hyde Park and Regent's Park kill 10 soldiers and injure 50 others. **December:** estimated 30,000 women demonstrate outside Greenham Common air base against siting of American Cruise missiles.

ARTS: TV, theatre, film: Richard Attenborough, *Gandhi*; Steven Berkoff, *Greek*; Alan Bleasdale, *Boys from the Blackstuff*; Caryl Churchill, *Top Girls*; Michael Frayne, *Noises Off*; Peter Greenaway, *The Draughtsman's Contract*; Terry Johnson, *Insignificance*; Mike Leigh, *Home Sweet Home*. **Visual:** Gilbert and George, *Youth Faith*. **Musical:** The Hacienda club established in Manchester. **Written:** Angela Carter, *The Passion of New Eve*; Timothy Mo, *Sour Sweet*.

1983

SOCIETY: recommendation from the Report of the Royal Commission on Environmental Pollution, that lead-free petrol be adopted, is taken up by the government. **June:** general election: Conservatives win 144 seat majority. **October:** Neil Kinnock elected leader of the Labour Party. **November:** first Cruise missile arrives at Greenham Common. **December:** IRA car bomb at Harrods kills six and injures 91.

ARTS: **TV, theatre, film:** Alan Bennett, *An Englishman Abroad*; Richard Eyre, *The Ploughman's Lunch*; Bill Forsyth, *Local Hero*; Sally Potter, *The Gold Diggers*. **Visual:** Tony Cragg, *Taxi!*; Richard Deacon, *Two Can Play*. **Musical:** Crass, an anarchist music collective, release their protest single against the Falklands War, 'How Does it Feel (To Be the Mother of a Thousand Dead)?'; Creation Records (London) established. **Written:** Anthony Burgess, *The End of the World News*; Salman Rushdie, *Shame*; Graham Swift, *Waterland*.

──────────── **1984** ────────────

SOCIETY: **March:** National Union of Mineworkers all-out strike. **May:** Orgreave coking plant nr. Sheffield: disturbances during mass picket by striking miners; MP Tam Dalyell accuses PM of lying over sinking of *The General Belgrano*. **September:** Kinnock supports miners but condemns violence. **October:** IRA bomb wrecks the Grand Hotel, Brighton, where Mrs Thatcher and Conservative leaders are staying. Five killed and several senior members injured. **November:** flotation of British Telecom shares; beginning of major 'privatization' programme for public corporations.

ARTS: **TV, theatre, film:** Alan Bennett, *A Private Function*; James Ivory, *Heat and Dust*; Marek Kanievska, *Another Country*; David Lean, *A Passage to India*; Pat O'Connor, *Cal*. **Visual:** Malcolm Morley wins the Turner Prize; Bill Woodrow, *Sunset*. **Musical:** three number one hits for Frankie Goes to Hollywood. **Written:** Martin Amis, *Money*; J. G. Ballard, *Empire of the Sun*; Julian Barnes, *Flaubert's Parrot*; Angela Carter, *Nights at the Circus*; James Kelman, *The Busconductor Hines*.

──────────── **1985** ────────────

SOCIETY: Local Government Act abolishes the Greater London Council and six Metropolitan City Councils; riots in predominantly black districts of Brixton, Handsworth and Broadwater Farm. **March:** miners vote to end strike. **April:** riots by Liverpool football supporters at Heysel Stadium, Brussels, 38 dead and 150 injured following collapse of part of the stadium; rise of the football casuals. **June:** government begins reform of pensions and welfare benefits system. **November:** Anglo-Irish Agreement. **December:** mass resignation of Ulster MPs resulting in 15 by-elections.

ARTS: **TV, theatre, film:** Alan Ayckbourn, *A Chorus of Disapproval*; Stephen Frears, *My Beautiful Laundrette*; Peter Greenaway, *A Zed and Two Noughts*; *The Belly of an Architect*; David Hare and Howard Brenton, *Pravda*. **Visual:** Howard Hodgkin wins the Turner Prize; Tony Cragg, *Plastic Palette II*. **Musical:** The Smiths, *Meat is Murder*; Live Aid; Stonehenge Free Festival ends in the 'Battle of the Beanfield'. **Written:** Peter Ackroyd, *Hawksmoor*; Caryl Phillips, *The Final Passage*; Jeanette Winterson, *Oranges are Not the Only Fruit*.

──────────── **1986** ────────────

SOCIETY: Lloyds building in London completed. Signing of the Anglo-Irish Agreement; US bases in the UK used for bombing raids on Libya; parliamentary enquiry into AIDS; Public Order Act; undercover police investigations into football hooliganism. **February:** agreement to build the Channel Tunnel. 'Big Bang' in the City of London introduces computerized trading; *Spycatcher* case. **December:** government failure to agree on entry to the ERM results in sharp fall in sterling.

ARTS: **TV, theatre, film:** John Akomfrah, *Handsworth Songs*; Alan Cox, *Sid and Nancy*; James Ivory, *A Room with a View*. **Visual:** Gilbert and George win the Turner Prize; Richard Deacon, *Tooth and Claw*; Helen Chadwick, *Of Mutability*. **Musical:** The Communards, 'Don't Leave Me This Way'. **Written:** Kingsley Amis wins the Booker Prize for *The Old Devils*; Kazuo Ishiguro, *An Artist of the Floating World*; Timothy Mo, *An Insular Possession*.

1987

SOCIETY: government announces major reforms in education; reopening of the Birmingham Six case; violent clashes at News International premises in Wapping; opposition to poll tax and privatization of water and electricity. **March:** *Herald of Free Enterprise* car ferry capsizes killing 184 at Zeebrugge. **June:** General election: Conservatives win 102 seat majority. **October:** 18 killed in severe storms in the south of England. **November:** Remembrance Day bombing in Enniskillen, Northern Ireland.

ARTS: TV, theatre, film: Alan Bennett, *Talking Heads*; Steven Berkoff, *Sink the Belgrano*; Stephen Frears, *Prick up your Ears*; John Godber, *Teechers*; Peter Greenaway, *Drowning by Numbers*. Derek Jarman, *The Last of England*. **Visual:** Richard Deacon wins the Turner Prize; Anthony Gormley, *Sculpture for Derry Walls*; Shirazeh Houshiary, *The Earth is an Angel*. **Musical:** Ibiza starts the new dance scene. **Written:** Margaret Drabble, *The Radiant Way*; Ian McEwan, *The Child of Time*.

1988

SOCIETY: Kinnock retains leadership of Labour following a challenge by Tony Benn; attacks on Labour from radical left, unions and Scottish nationalists. **January:** first of two major conferences in London confirms the serious threat posed by AIDS. **March:** three members of the IRA shot dead by British Secret Servicemen in Gibraltar. **December:** 36 people killed and more than 100 injured in the Clapham train crash.

ARTS: TV, theatre, film: Alan Bennett, *Talking Heads*; David Hare, *The Secret Rapture*; Mike Leigh, *High Hopes*; Tom Stoppard, *Hapgood*. **Visual:** Tony Cragg wins the Turner Prize; Anish Kapoor, *Mother as a Solo*; Damien Hirst, *Freeze* exhibition. **Musical:** Acid House popularized in London by nightclubs such as Schoom, Spectrum, and The Trip. **Written:** Peter Carey, *Oscar and Lucinda*; David Lodge, *Nice Work*; Salman Rushdie, *The Satanic Verses*.

1989

SOCIETY: Children Act; Community Charge introduced a year in advance of England and Wales, in Scotland; Fair Employment (Northern Ireland) Act; Education Reform (Northern Ireland) Order; rapid changes in Russia and Eastern Europe. **February:** public protests against *The Satanic Verses* in Bradford. **April:** 95 Liverpool fans killed in Hillsborough stadium disaster, Sheffield. **June:** bus, tube and rail workers on strike. **October:** Appeal Court finds Guildford four, found guilty of IRA public house bombing at Guilford and Woolwich in 1974, innocent. **November:** Berlin Wall breached by tens of thousands of East Germans.

ARTS: TV, theatre, film: Kenneth Branagh, *Henry V*; Michael Caton Jones, *Scandal*; Peter Greenaway, *The Cook, the Thief, his Wife and her Lover*. **Visual:** Design Museum opens in London; Richard Long wins the Turner Prize; Antony Gormley, *Field*; Paula Rego, *Baa Baa Black Sheep*. **Musical:** The 'Second Summer of Love'; 'Freedom to Party' campaign starts; Andrew Lloyd Webber, *Aspects of Love*. **Written:** Martin Amis, *London Fields*; Julian Barnes, *A History of the World in $10\frac{1}{2}$ Chapters*; Kazuo Ishiguro, *The Remains of the Day*; James Kelman, *A Disaffection*; Graham Swift, *Out of This World*; Jeanette Winterson, *Sexing the Cherry*.

1990

SOCIETY: re-unification of Germany; Gulf War improves John Major's image. **February:** Britain and Argentina resume diplomatic relations. **March:** anti-Poll Tax demonstrations in London and Nottingham. **May:** France leads call for a ban on British beef imports into Europe. **December:** critical resignation speech by Sir Geoffrey Howe provokes the end of Mrs Thatcher's premiership; election of Major as new Conservative leader.

ARTS: TV, theatre, film: Brian Friel, *Dancing at Lughnasa*; David Hare, *Racing Demon*; Ken Loach, *Riff-Raff*; Peter Medak, *The Krays*. **Visual:** Fiona Rae, *Untitled (purple and brown)*; Rachel Whiteread, *Ghost*.

Musical: Entertainments (Increased Penalties) Act attempts to outlaw acid house. **Written:** A. S. Byatt wins Booker Prize for *Possession*; Hanif Kureishi, *The Buddha of Suburbia*; Ian McEwan, *The Innocent*.

─────────── 1991 ───────────

SOCIETY: end of the Soviet Union; Yugoslavia slides towards civil war; increased concern over youth crime and disturbances in Cardiff, Birmingham, Oxford, Tyneside and Manchester. **January:** Operation 'Desert Storm' for the liberation of Kuwait begins. **February:** Kuwait re-entered; Gulf War ends. **December:** collapse of the Maxwell publishing empire; Maastricht Treaty negotiations, leading to the establishment of the new European Union in 1993.

ARTS: TV, theatre, film: Alan Ayckbourn, *The Revengers' Comedies*; Kenneth Branagh, *Dead Again*; Isaac Julien, *Young Soul Rebels*. **Visual:** Anish Kapoor wins the Turner Prize; Lucian Freud, *Naked Man*; Damien Hirst, *In and Out of Love*; *The Physical Impossibility of Death in the Mind of Someone Living*. **Musical:** Primal Scream, *Scream*; Massive Attack, *Blue Lines*; **Written:** Martin Amis, *Time's Arrow*; Pat Barker, *Regeneration*; Angela Carter, *Wise Children*; Janice Galloway, *Blood*; Ben Okri, *The Famished Road*; Timothy Mo, *The Redundancy of Courage*; Ian Sinclair, *Downriver*.

─────────── 1992 ───────────

SOCIETY: protest against the Twyford Down extension to the M3 motorway. **April:** General election: Conservatives win a majority of 21; large IRA bomb explosion in the City of London. **July:** John Smith elected leader of the Labour Party following the resignation of Neil Kinnock. **October:** severe reductions in the mining industry. **November:** Church of England votes for the ordination of women priests. **December:** separation of the Prince and Princess of Wales.

ARTS: TV, theatre, film: Alan Bennett, *The Madness of King George*; Terence Davies, *The Long Day Closes*; Neil Jordan, *The Crying Game*; Mike Newell, *Into the West*. **Visual:** Greville Davey wins the Turner Prize; Jenny Saville, *Branded*. **Musical:** Castlemorton Free Festival; *Paul Weller* (solo album). **Written:** Peter Ackroyd, *English Music*; Julian Barnes, *Porcupine*; Alasdair Gray, *Poor Things*; Ian McEwan, *The Black Dogs*; Graham Swift, *Ever After*; Jeff Torrington, *Swing Hammer Swing!*

─────────── 1993 ───────────

SOCIETY: Trade Union Reform and Employment Rights Act; 'Back to Basics' campaign launched by the Conservative government; James Bulger murder case. **January:** Unemployment reaches 3m. **April:** killing of Stephen Lawrence in East London. **May:** resignation of Norman Lamont as Chancellor of the Exchequer following Britain's withdrawal from the ERM.

ARTS: TV, theatre, film: Steven Berkoff, *Dog*; Antonia Bird, *Priest*; Gurinder Chadha, *Bhaji on the Beach*; Mike Leigh, *Naked*; Ken Loach, *Raining Stones*; Sally Potter, *Orlando*; Tom Stoppard, *Arcadia*. **Visual:** Rachel Whiteread, *House*: winner of the Turner Prize; Damien Hirst, *Away from the Flock*; Derek Jarman, *Sightless*; *Dizzy Bitch*; Jenny Saville, *Prop*. **Musical:** Blur, *Modern Life Is Rubbish*. **Written:** Peter Ackroyd, *The House of Doctor Dee*; Roddy Doyle, *Paddy Clarke Ha Ha Ha*; Will Self, *My Idea of Fun*; Vikram Seth, *A Suitable Boy*; Irvine Welsh, *Trainspotting*.

─────────── 1994 ───────────

SOCIETY: **May:** poor local election results for the Conservatives; Death of John Smith and election of Tony Blair, aged 41, as new leader of the Labour Party. **August:** IRA ceasefire. **October:** Labour Party promises a Freedom of Information Act and support for the European Social Chapter. **December:** worst Conservative by-election loss for fifty years in Dudley, West Midlands.

ARTS: TV, theatre, film: Mike Newell, *Four Weddings and a Funeral*; Caryl Churchill, *The Skriker*; Kevin Elyot, *My Night with Reg*. **Visual:** Antony Gormley wins the Turner Prize. **Musical:** Criminal Justice Act outlaws acid house parties; Blur, *Parklife*; Tricky, *Maxinquaye*. **Written:** Peter Ackroyd, *Dan Leno and the Limehouse Golem*; Alan Bennett, *Writing Home*; Jonathan Coe, *What a Carve Up!*; Alan Hollinghurst, *The Folding Star*; James Kelman, *How Late It Was, How Late*; Salman Rushdie, *East, West*; Iain Sinclair, *Radon Daughters*.

––––––––––––––––––––––––––––––––––– 1995 –––––––––––––––––––––––––––––––––––

SOCIETY: January: daylight patrols by British troops in Belfast cease. **May:** Conservative lose 2000 of total 11,000 seats in local government elections; celebrations on fiftieth anniversary of VE Day. **July:** John Major calls an unexpected leadership election and is reappointed as head of the Conservatives. **December:** link revealed between BSE in cattle and CJD in humans.

ARTS: TV, theatre, film: Danny Boyle, *Shallow Grave*; David Edgar, *Pentecost*; John Godber, *Lucky Sods*; Terry Johnson, *Dead Funny*; Sarah Kane, *Blasted*; Mike Newell, *Four Weddings and a Funeral*; Tom Stoppard, *Indian Ink*. **Visual:** Damien Hirst wins the Turner Prize; Tracey Emin, *Everyone I Have Ever Slept With 1963–1995*; Cornelia Parker, *Embryo Firearms*. **Musical:** Tribal Gathering Festival attracts 25,000; Goldie, *Timeless*; Pulp, *Different Class*. **Written:** Kazuo Ishiguro, *The Unconsoled*; Hanif Kureishi, *The Black Album*; Martin Amis, *The Information*; Ben Okri, *Astonishing the Gods*; Salmon Rushdie, *The Moor's Last Sigh*.

––––––––––––––––––––––––––––––––––– 1996 –––––––––––––––––––––––––––––––––––

SOCIETY: Family Law Act. **January:** IRA bomb explodes in the Docklands district of East London. **March:** British beef banned in Europe. **May:** by-election losses leave the Conservatives with a one-seat majority. **June:** IRA bomb explosion in Manchester injures 200. **August:** British forces begin final exit from Hong Kong. **October:** proposal to ban handguns in Britain. **November:** Stone of Scone placed on view in Edinburgh Castle.

ARTS: TV, theatre, film: Danny Boyle, *Trainspotting*; Mike Leigh, *Secrets and Lies*; Anthony Minghella, *The English Patient*; Michael Winterbottom, *Jude*; Globe Theatre opens in London. **Visual:** Douglas Gordon wins the Turner Prize; Chris Ofili, *Afrodizzia*; Richard Patterson, *Blue Minotaur*; Gillian Wearing, *60 Minute Silence*. **Musical:** Spice Girls single 'Wannabe' reaches no. 1; largest symphony orchestra in the UK performs in Birmingham. **Written:** Paul Driver, *Manchester Pieces*; Jeff Torrington, *The Devil's Carousel*; Pat Barker wins the Booker Prize for *The Ghost Road*.

––––––––––––––––––––––––––––––––––– 1997 –––––––––––––––––––––––––––––––––––

SOCIETY: January: a survey reveals that just under 50 per cent believe Britain will be a Republic within 50 years. **May: General Election:** New Labour wins an overwhelming election victory: Labour 418; Conservative 165; Liberal Democrats 46; Nationalist/Other 30. **June:** final handover of Hong Kong to China. **July:** new IRA ceasefire declared. **August:** Princess Diana killed in a car crash. **September:** constitutional referenda in Scotland and Wales and votes on devolution. **December:** beginning of the Kyoto Climate Conference.

ARTS: TV, theatre, film: Peter Cattaneo, *The Full Monty*; nine Oscars for *The English Patient*; Gary Oldman, *Nil by Mouth*. **Visual:** Gillian Wearing wins the Turner Prize; *Sensation: Young British Artists from the Saatchi Collection*. **Musical:** Spice Girls win the Brit Awards. **Written:** Iain Sinclair, *Lights Out for The Territory*.

PART IV

Re-locating, Re-imagining

CHAPTER 10

Millennium Life

Creating multicultures

Historical navigation is most difficult in the immediate past. Many possible sources such as unwritten memoirs are not yet on the horizon; some, including government papers which will be long outside the public domain, stay invisible below the waterline; others, private papers, news sources or official reports, are so vast that they remain uncharted seas. While what follows can only be a rudimentary mapping of coastlines and cape tides, the salient features remain those explored throughout this study, namely the remaking of identities in aspects of locality, society and the creative imagination. Three particular landmarks stand out on the horizon at this moment: the effort to renew nationhood in the light of devolution; the attempt to leave behind the age of post-industrial 'lost certainties', especially by redevelopment and urban renewal; and the creation of a new imaginative consensus, a reworked version of the post-1945 'fair shares for all' ideal based on the model of multi-ethnic cultures.

The revival of nationhood was most positively stated in Scotland, where the referendum of 1997 gave nationwide support for a Parliament, although Dumfries and Galloway, as well as Orkney, expressed reservations on raising taxes. The Scotland Act (1998) devolved various powers to the new legislature and in May 1999, on a decidedly un-historic turnout of 59 per cent, voters elected 129 Members of the Scottish Parliament (MSPs) into office. Following its opening in 1999 the new legislature moved into its purpose-built premises, opposite the Palace of Holyroodhouse in Edinburgh, in 2004.[1] With certain caveats, foreign affairs, defence and national security for example, which were policy areas reserved by Westminster, legislative rights and the limited tax-raising powers were handed over to Edinburgh. First Minister Donald Dewar was charged with the difficult task of matching high expectation with the practicalities of limited if real self-government and with wider local civic sentiment. Unionists, devolutionists and nationalists all had to negotiate their position in the light of constitutional changes in the United Kingdom state; Scotland's history as a part of Britain, and its future within the European Union could now be rethought. Likewise, the effects of the continuing United States-led economic, political and media global expansion for Scotland, as for the rest of the United Kingdom, could now be seen in a new light.[2]

Modern urban developments such as the Scottish Parliament building, designed by Catalan architect Enric Miralles, or the earlier New Building of the National Museum of Scotland, both in Edinburgh, symbolized regeneration, but regeneration at a high cost, and still against a background of abandonment and shrinkage in less fortunate localities. Across the UK where postwar social housing

Illustration 10   Global sounds for a global age: rave dance party, c.2000

had relieved the most severe shortages, whole districts became derelict, steel or plywood shutters appeared on the doors and windows of terrace and semi-detached council estates, large areas in Glasgow, Liverpool, Newcastle and Manchester were 'tinned up':

> It has to be seen to be believed, though, and even then it's not quite believable. Great patches of urban fabric, entire streets of terraced houses and blocks of flats, pavements, little corner shops, all built for people and their doings, now deserted, with the process of abandonment sometimes taking less than a couple of years . . . I had seen dereliction on that scale only once before and that had been 20 years earlier when, as a student summering in the USA, I had visited the South Bronx.[3]

In response, Scottish urban renewal policy now stressed the connections between central, regional and local government, funding for area development and the cultivation of local, community initiatives together with citywide strategy. Hence the development of the North Lanarkshire area, based on financial service companies, call centres and biomedical businesses for instance; or the north Edinburgh waterfront regeneration project, which set out to transform an eight mile stretch of shoreline and its surrounding inner-city environs.[4] Despite, or arguably because, only two of Scotland's cities, Edinburgh and Glasgow, compared in size and density to major English urban centres, the quality of Scottish life advanced in a variety of ways. There were falls in unemployment, in Glasgow, for instance, from 9.4 per cent (1996) to 4.6 per cent (2004); excepting Edinburgh, house prices were less than in the major English cities; low-cost air carriers partly improved communications across the UK, in English cities such as Liverpool as well as Dundee and Prestwick. At Prestwick passenger numbers went up by 225 per cent between 1996 and 2003.[5]

Away from the cities, small town and rural development was given new emphasis too with the appointment to the Scottish Executive of a Cabinet Minister responsible for smaller communities and less populated districts such as Dumfries, or Shetland. Decline in services, schools or post offices, increased commuter populations, the 'privatization' of leisure, and increased car ownership: all led to continuing concerns that neighbourhood community life was threatened. The establishment of the University of the Highlands and Islands (UHI Millennium) Institute, the active maintenance of leisure services, the promotion of tourism and Gaelic language institutions were put forward as ways to maintain and promote cooperative, communal values.[6] The support of Scotland's minority language, spoken by 92,396 (1.9 per cent) aged two or over at the 2001 Census, was also a priority, with the expansion of Gaelic-medium teaching, and £0.4 million allocated for its promotion in preschool education. Such policy-led attempts to promote diversity and equality of local cultures, to advance 'social inclusion' and cohesion, could only express a little of the everyday experience that informed national and communal belonging. A collection of personal statements published in 2002 reflected on the more intimate aspects of 'Scottishness'. The strong sense of social unity and locality described by so many, the editors concluded, was cause rather than result of the devolution process. Places, landscapes and social networks were important; being 'not English' was for many a part of the definition too. An awareness of racism, the persistence of poverty and unimpressive economic performance nevertheless muted self-satisfaction.[7] Ginnie Atkinson, Managing Director of the Edinburgh International Film Festival, described her own sense of urban belonging:

> Being Scottish is about ancestors from the glittering granite city of Aberdeen, laughing at the difference between east and west, liking vinegar on your chips outside the city wall. It's about cities being places of education. It's about castles in the middle of the town, about seeing Edinburgh anew after two years away and being gobsmacked at what a spectacle is in our front gardens. It's about a wee lassie behind the bar of a Glasgow bistro asking for a coffee, then saying, 'Aye, the kettle's just on.'[8]

*   *   *

While Scotland's new constitutional settlement and progressive civic nationalism were the fulfilment of a collective Scottish will, Northern Ireland's Belfast Agreement of 1998 was both a dramatic breakthrough, and a more limited success. Beginning with the Downing Street Declaration (1993) inclusive peace negotiations became a possibility. The 1998 Agreement itself set in place a series of checks, balances and mutual promises intended to counter the oppositional thinking that had long blocked resolution between unionists and nationalists.

Nationalists admitted a united Ireland would require majority consent, unionists agreed to cooperation between North and South, the Republic of Ireland renounced its claim to territorial unity established in the 1937 constitution. By allowing that all groups, no matter how contradictory their claims or concerns, had common territorial interests, it became possible to set up interlocking institutions within which power could be shared: the North–South Ministerial Council to coordinate between the Northern Ireland Assembly and the Irish Parliament; the Northern Ireland Assembly, which could only operate at the same time as the Ministerial Council; and the British–Irish Council, which drew together British and Irish government representatives with members of the devolved Scottish Parliament, the Welsh and Northern Ireland Assemblies.[9] Moreover, by stressing human rights, mutual trust, tolerance and reconciliation, all parties attempted to enter into a radical new multiculturalism.

A referendum in Northern Ireland on 22 May 1998 approved the Agreement by 71.1 per cent, and another in the Republic of Ireland gave 94.4 per cent backing. With elections to the 108-seat Assembly on 25 June 1998 pro- and anti-Agreement unionists of various parties were equally balanced, while the Ulster Unionist Party were the single largest group (28 seats). The nationalist vote, meanwhile, went mainly to the SDLP (24 seats) and to Sinn Féin (18 seats).

Under the provisions of the Agreement the Northern Ireland Executive was to be composed of ministers allocated places according to party strengths in the Assembly.[10] The movement towards human rights and inclusivity promoted in the Good Friday Agreement was also based on 'parity of esteem'; the difficulty of implementing the Agreement lay in reconciling contradictory identities. On the one hand, unionism: 'a shared psychological bond and a history of triumphs and sacrifices shared with the rest of the people of the United Kingdom'; on the other hand the Northern nationalism of those who 'saw themselves denied full membership to society and forced by an alien and alienating state into permanent dissent'.[11] One example of parity of esteem was the successful campaign by Unionists to have the status of Ulster Scots incorporated into the Belfast Agreement as a counter to the Irish language movement of the previous two decades. Nevertheless, both sides laid claim to a particular mental geography; both saw place naming as a powerful expression of cultural heritage. While the enlargement of the Unionist middle class meant the Scots language tradition in Ireland was the fastest growing cultural movement of 2002, its status as a dialect rather than language revealed, above all, the politicization of the spoken word. As a result loyalists attempted to remove Ulster-Scots road names in the mistaken assumption that they were Irish.[12]

Social, economic and infrastructural alterations accompanied political and constitutional change. Birth rates notably increased, for example, reaching 22,318 in 2004, an increase of 3.1 per cent (670 births) on the 2003 figure; similarly the number of registered deaths in 2004 was the lowest on record in Northern Ireland. While changes in the death rates may be explained by better medical care and increased health awareness, changes in the number of births reflected trends not confined to Northern Ireland. Birth rates remained substantially less than ten or twenty years earlier as many women now put careers before marriage and family; the rate of births outside marriage steadily increased from one in five

(1994) to one in three of all registered births (2004) with altering social conventions. Yet in other respects moral and communal custom remained powerful: over the same period the number of births to teenage mothers remained stable at around 1500 per year.[13] The same pattern of patchy change could be discerned in the economy: job places continued to fall in manufacturing, but increased, together with productivity, in service industries and especially in construction. Estimates for tourism showed a rise of 14 per cent in holiday visits and a six per cent rise in the total number of visits to 2,059,000.[14] Considering longer-term development, and despite limitations of geographical and economic position, over 200,000 jobs had been created during the twenty years to 2004. Compared to other parts of the United Kingdom Northern Ireland was now a region of economic growth, its unemployment rate now much closer to the average.

Urban and rural regeneration proved more difficult to integrate into processes of constitutional or cultural change. Between July 2001 and March 2002, for example, social and sectarian unrest caused the vacation of 136 houses in Belfast, while surveillance cameras, security gates and zones of influence were still strictly enforced. Furthermore, the promoters of public and private investment in regeneration, as in the Foyleside Shopping Centre (Derry) or the Custom House Square (Belfast), tended to stress how urban renewal could transform old allegiances, while in truth urban planning continued to 'float free from underlying cultural identity conflict, having long ago, as in many other cities, cast off its moorings from the city of lived experience'.[15] The lived experience of the countryside and smaller communities, meanwhile, sustained its communal character through community organizations and churches; commuter occupation, unemployment and trade liberalization nevertheless all made the rural economy difficult to sustain, more difficult as a way of living.

Under the provisions of the Good Friday Agreement, and in line with the new stress on cohesion and equality, difference and human rights, efforts were now made to reform policing, a symbolic and a substantial block to conflict resolution, by implementing the recommendations of the Patten Report (1999). Similarly the Mitchell Review (1999) sought to break the deadlock over PIRA weapons decommissioning. Eventually the failure to resolve these questions sapped support for the Executive and the Assembly, both of which were suspended in 2002. In late 2004 concerted efforts to overcome mutual suspicion and mistrust failed as Democratic Unionist leader Ian Paisley demanded the destruction of PIRA weapons be recorded for review at a later date. In the UK General Election of May 2005 the joint architect of the Good Friday Agreement and leader of the Ulster Unionist Party, David Trimble (b.1944), lost his majority in the Upper Bann constituency as unionists expressed their frustration at the failure of the 1998 settlement to bring lasting peace. By this stage, in any case, two thirds of all protestants and a half of all catholics were frankly indifferent to the Stormont Assembly.[16]

The achievements and legacy of the Good Friday Agreement were nevertheless remarkable. By stressing diversity within Irish society, by acknowledging varieties of religious thinking as well as ethnic and social interests beyond the traditionally dominant nationalist and unionist framework, by attempting to replace sectarian conflict with a politics of mutual justice, duties and rights, a new avenue of discussion was opened. David Trimble gave one expression to this new approach from a unionist perspective:

> One should not try to blend together traditions that are essentially different. We may disagree as to the extent of these differences, but there is little to be gained by trying to meld things together. Instead, our objective should be to find a way in which diverse traditions can be affirmed and enjoyed. We should not be afraid of difference.[17]

*   *   *

The Welsh assent to devolved political power and revised constitutional arrangement was much narrower than in either Northern Ireland or Scotland. While this may be taken as confirmation of the civic nationalism which remained so characteristic of Wales, of its greater stress on linguistic and cultural difference, the narrow majority indicates too a situation unlike that in the other devolving nations.[18] The most immediate reason may have been that Scotland had established its Constitutional Convention in 1989 and won support for a Scottish Parliament from the Labour Party in 1994. By contrast the Welsh reforms were proposed from within the Labour Party and were still subject to change a year or so before the election of 1997. Moreover, Wales remained a divided country: as Welsh language speakers gave substantial support to Plaid Cymru; as almost a quarter of the population was born outside its borders, most particularly in England; as Welsh national feeling was not tied to any particular set of constitutional arrangements, 'Welsh' Wales supported devolution in the referendum while 'British' Wales remained doubtful or clearly opposed.

Following the referendum the Government of Wales Act (1998) was passed, then the National Assembly for Wales (Transfer of Functions) Order (1999) and finally the first elections were held 6 May 1999. The results of these elections suggested that, despite divisions, a broad alliance of interests, one not confined by language or cultural background, might emerge. Plaid Cymru won 17 seats (29.5 per cent), Labour 28 seats (36.5 per cent), Conservatives 9 seats (16.2 per cent), and Liberal Democrats 6 seats (13 per cent).[19] While the Assembly was limited to 60 members, while it had decision-making powers in such areas as education, health, housing, conservation, transport and agriculture, and an annual budget of £7 billion, its role was to encourage civic nationalism rather than follow the lead of popular sentiment.

As a heartland of 'Old Labour', welfarism and heavy industry, Wales only gradually expanded its programme of redevelopment and its new sense of nationhood. Notions of social hybridity, the progress of the post-industrial economy and the programme of urban regeneration gradually led the way beyond oppositional definitions of nationhood, either political or cultural. After the institution of the new Assembly change quickened, unemployment fell from 6.4 per cent (1997) to 4.6 per cent (2004), slightly below the UK average rate of 4.8 per cent; European Union funding over the period 2000–6 was almost £1.5 billion; Structural Fund programmes, when added to the various other public, private and voluntary sources, amounted to over £3.2 billion.[20] In the first flush of New Labour modernization, *Time* magazine reported excitedly to its readers on British development, singling out Cardiff:

> Missions from post-communist Central and Eastern Europe regularly visit to pick up tips. They find a vision of the future taking place in docklands; smart housing projects, a vast Japanese-owned glass factory making screens for TV sets and monitors, office blocks, a science discovery centre, parkside restaurants that include a converted lightship and a deconsecrated old white Norwegian church once used by sailors. With a tunnelled road link to the new motorway system and a $300 million dam to keep the mudflats flooded at low tide, the project is still a work in progress.[21]

Subsequently large-scale developments, such as the Wales Millennium Centre at Cardiff Bay, which cost over £100 million and which became home in 2004 to the Welsh National Opera and the BBC National Orchestra of Wales, provided a new focus for some aspects of Welsh life. The Welsh Development Agency provided too for many smaller projects throughout the country. These included in 2003–4 the Llys Ednowain project, which transformed a derelict building in the village of Trawsfynydd, Gwynedd, into an interpretation and community centre. Meanwhile the Welsh Assembly funded other major public projects such as the new Sail Bridge in Swansea.[22] The quality of everyday life was not necessarily improved by such changes. A survey in 2004 for example noted the rise of 'clone towns' across Britain, where the narrow range of global brand name stores squeezed the local character of city centres out. Ralph Lauren clothes stores and Starbucks coffee houses in wealthier districts, Nando's chicken restaurants or Ladbrokes bookmakers in less well-off areas. Moreover, a successful project such as the Big Pit, the National Mining Museum of Wales in Blaenafon, South Wales, which won the Gulbenkian Prize for Museum of the Year in 2005, gave due recognition to a powerful social and industrial heritage, with a distant echo, by now, of Gwyn Williams' prediction that the future held for Wales 'fifty folk museums where there used to be communities'.[23]

Following Williams' moment of post-industrial pessimism in the early 1980s Wales had rethought its own past and present so that a museum of national heritage was no longer a symbol of loss. Within this new context, and as patterns of inward migration from around the globe became more complex and varied, new questions were raised about how Wales might expand its multiculturalism, what Welsh society might now become and how it treated its own minority groups. While the Welsh public, unlike the media, reacted moderately to the arrival of 700 asylum seekers in Wales under the Immigration and Asylum Act of 1999, for instance, only one per cent of the new 600 strong Welsh political class was from the ethnic minority population. Among some African groups in Cardiff unemployment ran at 90 per cent.[24] Resolving the question of how minorities are treated became part of the transition process in Northern Ireland, and Scotland or Wales, as nationalist-oriented oppositional politics was replaced by a sturdier local civic culture.

Wales' post-devolutionary future remained an open question, at least a half-open question. 'Everything is half-done, half-undone, mainly by us. That door is only half-open, or only half-shut,' art critic Ivan Bala's argued in 2003.[25] Conquest and colonization were jumbled into the nation's history; institutions tended to collapse from within; Wales was continually over the horizon but never achieved. One representation of nationhood and locality, present and future in 'postcolonial' Wales emerges from the work of Tim Davies (b.1960). For his 'Postcard Series II' (2002) Davies collected holiday greetings cards from junk shops picturing women dressed in the traditional Welsh national costume. By cutting out these figures, whose apparel was an invention of the nineteenth century age of nation-making and nationalism, Davies left the viewer to contemplate an empty silhouette and surrounding landscape, or, when the cards are reversed, a disrupted, partial message. While questioning the meaning of national symbols, and the tourist's gaze, Davies also asks what might remain once such symbols and acts were removed, and with what they might be replaced. One reply was that:

> it [Wales] is a complex of living thought and feeling, of myth, history and transmitted custom, of inherited character and trait. Its mental landscapes may compare to its variegated topographies: they are inscribed with the lineaments of a complicated spirit, shaped by powerful imaginative impulses, shadowed in bitterness . . . It is in its arts and learning, its chairs, books, theatres, its schools, universities and libraries, churches and chapels, its pubs and its playing fields that its distinctiveness is to be savoured.[26]

*   *   *

While Wales, alongside Scotland and Northern Ireland, had historically invested nationhood with local symbols, heroes and pasts variously adapted to suit their needs and preoccupations, the English nation had additionally subsumed itself into a collective British nationhood. Excluded from the vote on devolving central powers, the largest nation of the United Kingdom now had no choice but to redefine itself, at least in part, by giving away limited political powers, by altering the conditions on which the United Kingdom was established. In the post-devolution moment, England began a fuller reconsideration. Initially Englishness remained troubling for its associations were with extreme right-wing nationalists and racist intolerance. In 2005 MP, David Blunkett (b.1947; Home Secretary 2001–4 and Secretary of State, 2005) argued for a broader definition, citing country and urban landscapes, the sea, poetical tradition, folk music and carols, democratic values, radicalism and sense of humour as characteristic features.[27] Such lists mainly served to stress that as the dominant partner within the United Kingdom, England had not until now found it necessary to produce any definitive account of itself.

Regional assemblies across England were promoted by central government as a further step towards the extension of democracy and the devolution of central authority, but the initiative failed in November 2004 when a referendum in the North-East rejected the proposal by 696,519 to 197,310.[28] The question remained as to where nationhood might reside, whether the search for essential qualities was merely a sign of new insecurity, or whether a failure to discover or invent such features might not undermine community or promote lawlessness and intolerance. While David Blunkett's list of quintessential English features illustrated that the countryside retained an imaginative hold on many people, around 90 per cent of England's population lived in urban areas with a population of over 100,000 by the early twenty-first century.[29] Media comment and public debate on countryside, moreover, from where most people derived their information and opinion, tended to favour drama and crisis. The vivid image of burning animal pyres during the foot and mouth crisis of early 2001, populist campaigns against conditions of animal testing or transportation, and at the other extreme the prolonged and determined resistance to the ban on fox hunting, all brought attention to rural issues. Urban, metropolitan government and population now perceived 'the countryside' as a part of 'the environment', though, and as such saw it as a cause of anxiety. Not so widely discussed were the less dramatic changes such as the chronic shrinkage of woodland, lowland wet grassland, marshes and fens as well as meadows and hedgerows.[30]

As elsewhere in the United Kingdom, urban regeneration was promoted as a means to improve quality of life and support civic society. In 1999, for example, Manchester became a beneficiary of the new government zoning policies, while it had previously gained from the Urban Development Corporation fund from the late 1980s. One result was the new Bridgewater Concert Hall, which replaced the city's earlier symbol of civic pride and achievement rooted in the nineteenth century, the Free Trade Hall. In Hulme, a troubled district of inner-city Manchester, major programmes of housing, economic and social provision were introduced, and after the demolition of nearly 3000 1960s 'deck access' flats, a building and renovation scheme was enacted to provide the area with adequate housing.[31] Major new art galleries such as The Baltic, previously a grain warehouse on the Gateshead bank of the River Tyne, or the Tate Modern, a former power station in London on the south bank of the River Thames, symbolized emergent urban modernity. Town and city centre redevelopment improved the Bullring shopping centre in the central Digbeth district of Birmingham; as in Manchester, Leeds demolished its unfashionable 1960s architectural heritage to make way for commercial redevelopment in 2004. In 2005 plans were put forward by Frank Gehry, architect of the Guggenheim Museum in Bilbao, for two 120-metre towers on the south coast seafront at Hove designed to resemble crumpled Victorian dresses. While some schemes had benefits, such as the Hulme redevelopment, in other cases the question remained as to how far unemployment, poor health or deprivation might be improved by such profit-driven entrepreneurial activity. Out-of-town 'supertanker' shopping malls such as the White Rose (1998), which served the Leeds area, or Bluewater (1999), near Dartford in Kent, raised the same issue. With 13,000 parking spaces and 320 retail outlets, the Bluewater had three vast department stores, one at each corner of its triangular layout, which constituted 'the Holy Trinity of this awesome cathedral of consumption'. With their use of theming as well as 'retail-to-leisure' facilities such as cinemas, restaurants and food courts, the new malls showed how fully American ideas might now be adapted to Britain.[32] While giving space to the transnational corporations' retail outlet stores such as Warner Brothers and Pizza

Hut, and while promoting consumption as the highest form of citizenship, the Oracle shopping complex in Reading too announced itself as an enhancement of the town's profile and of the local community.[33] Though regulations discouraged such 'off-centre' developments from the mid-1990s, the conflict of interest between town centre shopkeepers, who needed a livelihood, and the retailers as well as developers, who wanted the advantage of car-borne customers and cheap land away from city centres, was unresolved.[34]

Material conditions may have been the precondition to social inclusion; integration required more direct reform. Lord Bikhu Parekh's *Report of the Commission on the Future of Multi-Ethnic Britain* (2002) recommended more appointments from ethnic minorities as mortgage and financial advisers and as bank managers; greater encouragement in business activities; and additional research on the contribution of minority groups to the UK Gross National Product. While these were positive recommendations, the violent confrontations between South Asian youths and police in the northern English towns of Oldham, Burnley and Bradford from April to July 2001 underlined the severe restraints that minority status placed on parts of the British population. Most heavily represented in these events were second and third generation Pakistanis and Bangladeshis who felt themselves outside British society, isolated by unemployment and aggressive policing.[35] Suggestions that the 'Leicester model' of civic multiculturalism could be exported turned out on closer inspection to be not entirely convincing. While Leicester adapted to and integrated with its minority groups, the city's success lay in enabling the choice, rather than the compulsion, of varied community groups living 'parallel lives'. Moreover, the economic success of all sectors of society, which was fortunately present in Leicester, was not available in Oldham or Bradford. Support for Labour among South Asian groups itself eventually proved conditional, ebbing quickly in the May 2003 local elections, which came in the wake of the second Gulf War.[36] The multicultural model was at best, then, only a partial solution. The procedures of constitutional devolution allowed power to move partially away from Westminster; for minorities and immigrants, parity of esteem remained an unachieved ideal.

Moreover, the many conflicting version of Englishness remained to be articulated and reconciled. While associations with imperial control both outside and within Britain may have been somewhat diminished, urban and rural landscapes and histories served as a reminder that corporate, global and financial interests were at work reshaping the local economic and social environment, not always in the interests of individuals or communities. The achievement of civic regeneration, it was clear, required consensual, collective participation and the establishment of common goals. In this respect the new metropolitan government of London, with Ken Livingstone as the Mayor since his popular re-election in 2000, offered new possibilities: all planning applications were now required to include 50 per cent 'affordable housing'; the introduction of a road congestion charge in central London and the upgrading of public spaces often improved the quality of community life; public events such as the Notting Hill Carnival, and poorer districts of the city, were given new priority. Yet even here large-scale public initiatives like the redevelopment of Elephant and Castle or King's Cross tended to exclude the concerns or interests of poorer districts. Nonetheless, the search for a more inclusive version of English nationhood might itself yield possible gains:

> Encouraging people to feel pride in the affirmative aspects of their history makes it easier to get them to accept the wrongs that have been carried out in the name of that heritage. If we start to tackle Englishness, we may find a way of dealing with the difficult situations that are arising around the country; white middle-class flight into the safe English arms of Norfolk and Somerset; the surge of secular parents sending their children to Church of England schools; the foolish policies that deny mixed-race children their English background.[37]

The personal and the global

By the early years of the twenty-first century, the role and status of women within British society was greater than at any time during the postwar years. In work and pay inequities persisted; in policy, legislation and often in the private opinions of both women and men, the ideal of equality was a high priority. The career of film director Gurinder Chadha showed that gender, or ethnicity for that matter, had become a lesser bar to professional success. Born in Kenya and raised in the predominantly South Asian district of Southall, West London, Chadha's early drama-comedy feature *Bhaji on the Beach* (1993) dealt with the connections and rifts that followed from Britain's colonial legacy and postcolonial ethnic communities as they were seen by a group of women taking a seaside trip. In 2002 *Bend it Like Beckham*, a story partly set in the British Asian community which centred on two aspiring players in a women's football team, became a surprise, worldwide hit. Subsequently Chadha produced a version of Jane Austen's best-known work, called *Bride and Prejudice* (2004), which played on the conventions of Indian popular cinema with songs, extravagant dance routines, as well as rapid location shifts between the subcontinent, London and Los Angeles.[38] Chada's strength as a director was that she valued her own background but also went beyond the interests of a particular social constituency to address wider themes: the complexity and diversity of human relations, the struggle for acceptance as well as opportunity, and the constraints of social position and viewpoint. A group of women, meeting in Nottingham in the late 1990s to discuss and write about their experience, described something of the same hybrid experience:

> As British Asian women our identities need not be shaped by some imaginary past, fixed in history by our connections with the Indian subcontinent such that we (and our children) remain defined as 'foreign' to the country in which we live. We may be proud of being Pakistani, or Indian, perhaps feeling lucky to have links to another culture outside Britain, but this need not give us cause to devalue our uniquely British lives and experiences.[39]

The personal consequences of change, of shifting migration and settlement patterns, or of cross-cultural creative forms such as *Bride and Prejudice*, also affected patterns of work and home life among the wider population. Among well-educated professionals, business executives or managers for instance, the gender pay gap narrowed from 38 per cent (1990) to 8 per cent (2000). The highest paid jobs were in information technology and management services; over 60 per cent of managers in personnel were women; 54 per cent of management positions belonged to women in actuarial, insurance and pension group work.[40] Positive employment policy, the wider process of gender redefinition and the benefits of attachment to national or transnational corporations assisted certain sections of society; the rise in part-time and casualized labour, the persistence of low pay and job insecurity as well as the absence of child-friendly working arrangements were still unwanted constraints. Women's average pay in 2001 remained 79 per cent of men's earnings. The intensity of national and global economic competition within the national market limited the earning power as well as the prospects of, for example, supermarket or call centre employees. Yet continuing inequalities reflected too the low value placed on work by women: part-time, low paid and unskilled employment was what the market, and to a lesser extent home circumstances, made available, not what employees, women or men, preferred.[41]

Family and home life continued to alter. Cohabitation rather than marriage, single person households and single-parent families became increasingly common; marriage rates were at their lowest since the First World War. The reasons for these changes, which amounted to a broader definition of the family rather than its demise included: belief in the independence, especially financial, of women; changing attitudes towards sex, contraception and abortion; an increased premium on personal happiness and fulfilment; and alterations in the job market.[42] However, since nearly one half of poor children lived in households headed by a single parent, and 9 in 10 lone parents were women, deprivation remained part of many women's lives. Divorce rates and the levels of teenage pregnancy rose in tandem; an estimated 2.7 million children were living in poverty in 2005. Moreover, all of these rates were among the highest in the industrial world.[43] The British Crime Survey (1997) estimated 835,000 incidents of domestic violence per year; children living in such households often suffered neglect and abuse. Some women from all social backgrounds continued to believe that their first right and responsibility was to raise children, that they were best qualified for the job; government policy now stressed the 'dual role' of both work and home life.[44]

The high rates of teenage pregnancy continued to cause worry, not to mention outrage, in public debate, for example in 2005 when a Derby family found itself with three mothers-to-be all under the age of 20. Earlier the government had set up a Teenage Pregnancy Unit intended to halve the number of such cases given that in 2003 there were 8000 among the under-sixteen age group alone. The continuance of education and training as well as efforts to ensure employment took priority; payable state benefits were cut to help achieve the government's target, which was 70 per cent of all single parents in work by 2004.[45] While the government viewed teenage motherhood as a lost opportunity, it appeared that those girls who were most likely to become pregnant were in reality already boxed in by circumstances: low educational aspiration and low achievement, limited literacy and a record of disorderly conduct were all likely indicators. Yet though they were often found wanting by their elders, young mothers and their partners were not always irresponsible. Ursula and Ryan, she of mixed-race origin but white in appearance, he black, both born in the early 1980s, and together inter-viewed in 2003, commented on the attitudes they commonly encountered. Ryan:

> If you only ever show the bad, it's a stereotype. All young mothers are all bad cos they all have children young. Even the sound of it is repetitive. It's hard for people who aren't living this generation, who aren't doing it for them-selves, to understand, because the times that they lived aren't the same as the times are now.[46]

*   *   *

Immigrants and ethnic minorities were equally subject to a confusing mix of support with hostility; public attempts to praise and promote minorities could barely be reconciled with the often wary antagonism displayed towards asylum seekers. When, in 2003, he was offered an Order of the British Empire (OBE) award for his services to literature for example, poet Benjamin Zephaniah rejected it on the grounds that reference to the British Empire reminded him of slavery, of the brutal treatment handed out to his ancestors and of those other writers, pop musicians and business successes whom he felt had been compro-mised by royal patronage.[47] Debate on the arrival of new and varied immigrant groups, often illegally, and often from countries with no historical or other connection to the United Kingdom, was especially vexed. According to Malcolm Stuart, Director of the Medical Foundation for the Care of Victims of Torture, the Nationality, Immigration and Asylum Act (2002) instituted a policy of 'destitution by design' which meant rehabilitation of torture victims could not usefully begin without first battling to claim benefits, to meet the basic material needs of this most vulnerable group.[48] On the particular issue of illegal immi-grants regulations remained tight. On the wider subject of recognition and equality there were some signs of increasing acceptance of multi-ethnic society. Despite gross misrepresentation in public debate when it was first published, many of the recommendations of the *Parekh Report* on criminal, immigration and asylum as well as employment policy had been implemented by 2004; a 2005 ICM research survey of 500 ethnic minority respondents indicated that there was limited trust of politicians (9 per cent expressed 'a lot of faith'), the media (17 per cent) or the police (23 per cent); race and gender discrimination were seen as equally wrong.[49]

The presence in the United Kingdom of Muslims from varied national back-grounds was signalled by events in 2001. First by the civil disturbances of May to July in Leeds, Oldham and Bradford, and second, following the terrorist attacks on New York and Washington in September, by concern at the potential presence of extremists which led to surveillance, stop-and-search campaigns as well as arrests in 2002–3. Yet the Muslim presence had been growing since the 1960s, and by 2002 had spread right across the UK. The majority were from Pakistan (700,000), Bangladesh (300,000) and India including Kashmir (240,000). Belfast had 10 mosques and a 4000-strong presence; Cardiff had 11 mosques

(5000); Glasgow and Edinburgh combined had 30 mosques (48,000); spread across the country from Bradford and Leeds to Oldham, Birmingham, Leicester and London, England had 218 mosques and a Muslim population of 1,322,750. Despite this long-established presence, efforts towards intercommunal dialogue made little headway, and the opportunities for Muslim involvement within mainstream society were now increasingly curtailed by mutual suspicion, not least among those who believed the Anglo-American campaigns against Afghanistan and Iraq to be misguided.[50] The aftermath of the US terror attacks revealed too the divergent schools of thought on what exactly it meant to be a British Muslim: some wished to follow traditional, fixed values; others saw adjustment as inevitable, a necessary step towards effective settlement. In the 2005 General Election four Muslim MPs were returned, and while younger voters rejected the Labour Party, the older generation remained loyal supporters.[51] The London terrorist attacks of 7 July were all the more shocking when it emerged the perpetrators were British Muslims; closer consultation, understanding and integration between minorities, state and citizens now resulted from a common cause: threat to the collective community.

In addition to the Muslim population, the broader group of 'British Asians' included other religious affiliations, particularly 600,000 Sikhs and 400,000 Hindus, as well as varied linguistic and geographical backgrounds. Moreover, just as the political affiliations among the young did not necessarily match those of earlier generations, so earlier images of the Asian population were superseded. Hanif Kureishi (b.1954), whose reputation as a novelist and scriptwriter was established from the mid-1980s, became the 'literary godfather' to a generation of British Asian writers including Monica Ali (b.1967), author of *Brick Lane* (2003), and Meera Syal (b.1962), whose scripts include *Bhaji on the Beach* and who worked on the BBC comedy series *Goodness Gracious Me*. Syal's standing was furthered when in 2005 her second novel, *Life isn't All Ha Ha Hee Hee* (2000), was produced as a TV series. The new visibility of British Asians was noticeable too in the pop world, where musicians such as Nitin Sawhney, and groups including Cornershop, Fun-Da-Mental and Asian Dub Foundation melded themes, styles and voices to evade ghettoizing 'Asian' or 'ethnic' categorization.[52]

As with the popularity of reggae in the 1970s and 1980s, however, interest in music or comedy television, or novels, could not put right the social inequalities and injustices to be found within the immigrant and ethnic populations. Killed in November 2000 as he returned home, the death of ten-year-old Damilola Taylor, who was recently arrived in England from Nigeria, served as a sharp reminder of continuing violence, racial or otherwise, and of the strong correlation between poverty and crime. The number and the treatment of black and Asian men, especially young men, in mental health institutions; the rights of potential immigrants and asylum seekers, including the right to efficient, fair treatment and family reunion; the continuing, discriminatory stop-and-search policy employed by the police beginning after September 2001: all remained causes of public concern. Yet those who managed to gradually negotiate their place within British society showed integration without eradication of background or tradition might be possible; equally, how diversity could become an enriching, accepted aspect of society. As Hanif Kureishi said in 2004, finding a place had been possible 'not because of the generosity of the ruling class, but because we fought for representation. I don't think about my own identity any more. I'm very secure.'[53]

*　*　*

The death of Damilola Taylor and the street violence in Oldham and elsewhere also fed into another contemporary preoccupation, youth lawlessness and violence. The difference between reported and actual crime rates made it difficult to judge levels accurately. The major sources of data, first from the British Crime Survey, second from those crimes reported to the police, pointed in opposite directions. Nevertheless, there was a clear perception among the public of rising rates of criminal activity. There were 97 firearms-related killings in 2001–2, for example, more than double the figure for the second half of the 1990s, and often these were drug-related incidents where victims as well as offenders were young, black males. Between 1997 and 2004 the number of violent crimes recorded by the police trebled, and exceeded the one million mark for the first time.[54] One incident that further strengthened the association between crime and youth took place on New Year's Eve 2002 when two teenagers, Charlene Ellis and Letisha Shakespeare, were killed by gunfire as they momentarily left a party. Subsequent media comment concentrated on the potential influence of violent movies and video games as well as rap song lyrics, while the generation of teenagers born in the 1980s was condemned as more dysfunctional and potentially dangerous than those of earlier years.

Some media commentators and politicians took eagerly to 'kidbashing', other studies revealed a more nuanced picture. Nick Barham, for instance, toured mainland Britain in 2003 speaking with young people, considering their views, experiences and activities in an effort to discover if they matched the current public image of the young. His impression after a year was of an independent-minded, freethinking generation. '. . . there were few signs of moral ambiguity or destructiveness. The majority of people I spoke with were more conservative than I had expected. They were decided on a set of personal moral codes, and were judgemental of people who acted differently.'[55]

Barham's most significant observation was that, as watchers of the media and the political classes that so freely attacked them, young people were deeply sceptical and often disengaged from wider society or political affairs. Finding themselves alienated or excluded by those who criticized them out of hand, by the corporate strategies that sought to manipulate their behaviour and taste, they turned to local and personal activities, to spheres of interest where their energies and enthusiasms might more positively be engaged: among others, computers, music, driving. Similarly a sociological study of youth, ethnicity and class in the late 1990s which concentrated on the formation of gender and race attitudes found social background, home and community neighbourhood particularly influential, while anti-racism was a matter of common conviction and communal support in school.[56] Finally, in a study of youth and crime in the inner city, the same impression of morally coherent worldviews among the young emerged. Cannabis use was to a large extent 'normalized', as indicated by widespread references within popular culture, while a clear distinction was made with 'class A' drugs such as crack cocaine or heroin, which was widely condemned. In a media and advertising saturated environment, where acquisition and ownership as well as material success were constantly emphasized, the trade in stolen goods such as TVs, videos or hi-fi systems was seen as a necessary profit-making activity when other employment was unavailable, as a way to access consumer goods that were not to be gained by more conventional or legal means. While such criminal activity was not to be condoned, it nevertheless created a 'beneficial network of sociocultural resources'.[57]

Such networks persisted in part because, as noted earlier, an estimated 2.7 million young people lived in deprived circumstances in 2005, because poverty and homelessness were a continuing part of many young lives. Sixty years after the introduction of the welfare state, the United Kingdom had one of the worst deprivation rates in the industrial world.[58] In 2004 the Joseph Rowntree Foundation established that nearly three quarters of the poorest children, those least able or likely to escape the cycle of poverty, were to be found in the wards of four cities. In Easterhouse, Glasgow, where more than 50 per cent of adults were long-term unemployed and infant mortality was 4.5 times the national average; in Harpurhey, Manchester, where there were above-average levels of child obesity; in Everton, Merseyside, where 37.8 per cent had no educational qualifications; in Tower Hamlets, London, where more than a half of all children lived in families receiving out-of-work benefit, and many pupils failed to reach minimum national English language standards.[59] Such children, among the most vulnerable in society, and likely themselves to become homeless in their teens or early twenties, were among the estimated three quarters of a million aged 17–25 living in squats, bed-and-breakfast accommodation or sleeping rough. Like other young people, this group was also subject to moral disapproval and 'zero-tolerance' punitive legislation.[60]

A final piece of evidence supporting the view that media and political censure as well as attempts at corporate and commercial influence tended to push young people away from wider social engagement came from a study of urban nightlife in Leeds, Bristol and Newcastle. As local authorities promoted investment, deregulation and surveillance, as alternative, independent and community-based spaces were pushed out of inner-city centres, so urban nightlife was subject to a standardizing 'McDonaldization'. Not surprisingly, young people turned to the fashion and musical styles they felt better represented their personal experience:

> I listen to my music because I think what they are talking about is important. It's like Eminem, everyone says Eminem fuck this, fuck that, but Eminem speaks absolute truth. If you watch the film *8 Mile*, it's his life, it's his own life. This is how he's trying to put across how he's been in his life and for us not to go that way. All this shit that says about Eminem is a bad influence, he's not.[61]

*   *   *

Changing and confrontational attitudes were visible too in the art world; the cynicism or ignorance of conservative critics, news or sections of the public was increasingly challenged by other voices, including public supporters and younger artists. The success of the Tate Modern, opened in May 2000 on London's South Bank, and of the Baltic, a second major new gallery, this time on the South Bank of the River Tyne at Gateshead, confirmed the public's fascination with modern art, particularly among the young. The beginnings of this interest may be partly dated to the revamping of the Turner Prize in the early 1990s, as well as to the decision to televise the annual awards ceremony by Channel 4. Ten years on, in 2001, the fashionable status of the new art was confirmed when Madonna came to London to host the awards ceremony.[62] Between the 1996 and the 1999 Prize exhibitions, the latter controversial for the display of Tracey Emin's piece *My Bed* (1998), the number of visitors to the exhibition more than doubled from 56,000 to 120,000. Similarly *Sensation*, the 1997 exhibition of work from Charles Saatchi's collection, was attended by 300,000, 80 per cent of whom were under the age of 30. Five years on from its opening, nearly 22 million people had visited the Tate Modern, 60 per cent of them under the age of 35.[63] While the era of the Young British Artist ended with the shutting down of Saatchi's St John's Wood gallery in 2003, London had become a major art centre to rival New York. If modernist art was now much more widely appreciated and accepted, it was nevertheless still viewed in the same light as the Turner Prize itself: simultaneously admired and mocked.

While there was no more direct link to the theme of nationhood among contemporary British modernist art than there was among participants in the 1951 Festival of Britain exhibition, there were common interests. Entrepreneurial self-promotion and corporate funding had allowed the new art movement to come into sight in the 1990s; a convinced self-confidence across a range of media gradually materialized too; 'the fine arts' as the preserve of a small class-based elite gave way to a more visible urgency to explore and convey human experience to a mass audience. One artist whose work followed many of these themes was Grayson Perry (b.1960). Working in embroidery, photography and especially pottery, Perry also exploited the performative possibilities of his transvestite alter ego Claire, as in *Claire's Coming Out* (2000), a performance where artwork and female persona combined in the presentation of an original, deceptively childish dress.[64] Evading confrontational 'big' statements, Perry addressed both personal and social themes engaging viewers with the seductive beauty of his objects, so that the more threatening and ideological elements within the work emerged gradually, to 'make something that lives with the eye as a beautiful piece of art, but on closer inspection, a polemic or ideology will come out of it'. In *We've Found the Body of Your Child* (2000), for example, the artist confronts one-dimensional and manipulative media images of paedophilia with the reality that parents were among those most likely to inflict violence on a child. Similarly *Village of Penians* (2001) creates 'a sort of fairytale Ruritanian kingdom – constructed completely from phallic imagery to depict a state in which phallocentrism determines how the world is seen and understood'.[65]

This outspoken approach, which some unsympathetic or bemused observers found difficult, was one of the new art's greatest strengths. While Perry charmed his audience, all the better to draw it into his complex, troubled and highly personal worldview, the Chapman Brothers' work seemed to cultivate offence, in their opinion to a purpose. According to Jake Chapman (b.1966) galleries and

the work they contain should not exist to promote established values, but to challenge conventions. 'Galleries should not seek to be redemptible spaces for bour-
geois people to pay their dues to culture ... Sometimes shock is merely a
Pavlovian response.'[66] Certainly the viewer might struggle against a queasy
mixture of fearful thrills, nausea and ethical quandary, when faced with the alarming inhabitants of 'Chapmanworld' in *Tragic Anatomies* (1996): genital-faced
children, naked but for sneakers, sprouting mutant heads, torsos and limbs.
Where Perry used the disregarded 'folk art' medium of a pot or a quilt to question the status of the art object, the Chapman brothers exploited their awareness
of past art to re-energize it, to question conventions of expression. *Hell*
(1999–2000) displays too, by its use of miniature action figures to convey an epic
scene, the often disregarded wit of the brothers' work. Using around 30,000 tiny
figures *Hell* presents a vision of the damned acting out a parallel world of destruction and suffering. *Works from the Chapman Brothers Family Collection* (2002),
likewise, displays 'primitive' carvings exhibited in the manner of an ethnographic
museum exhibition, all 'fake', and one carved wooden figure (*CFC76311561.1*,
2002) clutching McDonald's french fries and milkshake containers.[67]

The Chapman brothers emphatically rejected any possible autobiographical or
personal references in their work, yet display a carefully refined group of themes
and preoccupations, Tracey Emin (b.1963) began with funny, distressing or
unnervingly intimate confession, but had a broader ambition: to 'start with myself
but end up with the universe'.[68] Because of the confessional nature of her work,
the celebrity culture surrounding her rise to fame and the debate her art aroused,
Emin became one of the best known artists of her time. 'Mad Tracey from
Margate' to some, herself included, Emin's works, such as *My Bed* (1998) or
Everyone I Have Ever Slept With (1963–95) (1995), nevertheless demonstrated
how personal experience could be universal, how works could be constructed to
allow the individual observer an imaginative, interpretive space in which to create
narratives and meanings.[69] Similarly her 2005 show, 'When I Think About Sex',
with its etchings, sculpture and appliqué sewing, the latter bleached of colour,
showed in its best moments personal intensity in which any individual might find
relevance. 'People think my work is about sex', Emin said at the time, 'but actually a lot of it is about faith'.[70]

Bad faith was the accusation Emin made against journalists and reviewers alike
in the wake of the May 2004 fire at the Momart warehouse in East London, in
which several of her works including *Everyone I Have Ever Slept With (1963–95)*
were destroyed. While some seemed to take pleasure in the destruction of pieces
by a number of artists who became prominent in the 1990s, it only gradually sank
in that important art by many earlier postwar figures had also been lost, including works by Patrick Heron, Gillian Ayres, Paula Rego and Patrick Caulfield.
Without the achievements of the most recent generation such losses would probably have been less acknowledged among the wider media and public; without the
vision of earlier generations the work of the Young British Art movement would
never have existed.

*   *   *

While many British artists were realizing their intense, often misinterpreted visions, the music industry was engaged in its own obsessive struggle to adapt to the times, to match the taste of a far wider audience. As the downloading of digital music files became increasingly popular, as singles chart sales severely dropped, the search for mass, profit-making sales intensified. In the late 1990s for instance, boy bands became a new craze. While Boyzone, Westlife or Four-play had some commercial success, according to one music industry insider, Simon Napier-Bell, the manufacturing of such groups tended to depend on the same songwriters, video directors and marketing managers, so that all the groups quickly came to look and sound alike:

> A&R departments are no longer in the business of Artists and Repertoire. They have become high-level concept merchants who can't sell a new artist to their own record company unless there is a clear-cut marketing angle to be exploited . . . Now the tail is wagging the dog and the music is the last element of the equation to be put into place.[71]

'Alternative dance' groups such as the Chemical Brothers, or those groups who fused pop to dance styles such as Fatboy Slim, were to some extent successful, but a lower priority to record companies. Moreover, as computer-generated music and technology changed, the generation raised on digital music and MP3s created transnational interest groups such as the long-running www.uk-dance.org, and became increasingly resistant to multinational control of both the web and music copyright.[72]

In this respect, record companies tended to censure the increasingly complex and experimental use of sampling, to limit copyright permissions; at the same time much of the most interesting music of this time mixed musical styles, as well as electronic and traditional instruments. The varied adaptations of US hip-hop and rap are a case in point, including groups such as Blak Twang (hip-hop), Fun-Da-Mental (British Asian hip-hop), Goldie, Photek and Roni Size (jungle or drum'n'bass), or Lamb, Massive Attack and Portishead (vocal trip-hop). The success of such artists and groups was in their ability to adapt or incorporate an existing form into local cultural traditions of, for example, West Indian British experience, which was multi-ethnic, technology based and influenced too by the dance music scene.[73] Another tradition of musical fusion was *Mali Music* (2002), a collaboration between African musicians Alef Bocoum, Toumani Diabate and British musician Damon Albarn. Albarn was best known as the lead singer of Blur, but also for his involvement in Gorillaz, a more experimental group with musical influences including rap, dub and Cuban. In the event the combination of Diabate's kora, a 21-string harp, Bocoum's African blues guitar, and Albarn's accordion, with reggae, electronic effects and vocals added, proved surprisingly successful. While 'world music' was firmly established as a marketing category, and while magazines such as *fRoots* promoted an eclectic range of traditional styles from around the world, genuinely equal musical unions remained rare.[74]

Within a varied and dynamic music market, which imported and exported styles and artists, one of the most successful mainstream bands of the period was Coldplay, whose *A Rush of Blood to the Head* (2002) projected a confessional, melodic music around the globe; varieties of dance, rock and psychedelia were mixed for different audiences by, among others, Spritualized (*Let It Come Down*, 2001); while the black British tradition entered the mainstream with great variety and richness, for example on Ms Dynamite's *A Little Deeper* (2002). Additionally, beginning from a narrow musical base, where 'Asian music' meant either ethnic exoticism or the commercial jollity of bhangra and Bollywood, some artists were able to redefine both themselves and their vision of what it meant to belong within a multi-ethnic society, among them Nitin Sawhney.[75] On *Prophesy* (2001), Sawhney redefined 'world music' not as an ethnic marketing label, but as an eclectic, inclusive form drawing on black American, North African, Asian percussive and Australian aboriginal traditions of music and belief. Incorporating a similarly varied selection of sampled voices expanded the album's rich aural textures. Asian Dub Foundation, whose beginnings were in a London community project of the early 1990s, meanwhile developed their own unique blend of socially aware lyrics with 'ragga-jungle propulsion, indo-dub basslines, distorted sitar-like guitars and samples of more "traditional" Asian sounds'.[76] *Community Music* (2000) was defiantly unfashionable, uncommercial even, within an aggressively commercial pop market. Its clear political convictions and innovative 'bhangra punk' rather created a new music by redefining the meaning of 'community'.

British popular music grew up with the generation born around the end of the Second World War, and as that generation grew to maturity their forms of artistic expression entered the mainstream of society. With the rise of film music compilations, of advertisements with pop backing, of pub and supermarket background music, it entered many aspects of everyday life. The status of musicians as privileged, prominent figures allowed the prospect that popular music might also be a medium for political change, as was demonstrated by the Live8 concerts in London and elsewhere during the summer of 2005, echoing the Live Aid event of 1985. The sudden death of BBC music radio presenter John Peel (1939–2004) brought a surprisingly grief-stricken response, emphasizing how popular music had become the collective backing soundtrack to several postwar generations. With a career spanning over thirty years, most of it on BBC radio, Peel's eclectic, open-eared enthusiasm for all kinds of music, from Captain Beefheart to The Fall and the latest hip-hop or thrash noise band, was hugely influential. Recognition of other figures from the wartime and early post-World War Two generation also came to Robert Wyatt (b.1945). Founder member of the sixties psychedelic scene, who continued to produce inimitable, new fusions of jazz, blues, folk and pop, and who was given two lifetime achievement awards in 2004–5. In the search for continuing acts of personal and collective definition Peel's musical discrimination and Wyatt's musical practice – as on *Rock Bottom* (1974) or *Cuckooland* (2003) – described an idiosyncratic, intimate and yet outward-looking vision.

* * *

While popular music was able to thrive by its mix of styles and influences, by its constant efforts to reinvent and reshape the soundtracks of contemporary life,

British film-makers faced a difficult choice between going global or staying local. While industry insiders such as Alan Parker, Chairman of the Film Council in 2002, argued against what they saw as parochial themes director Mike Leigh believed that the local and personal allowed access to the widest possible audience. 'I haven't somehow fallen into some swimming pool in LA and forgotten about what I once cared about as a film-maker . . . I still live in the world and I still care about it. I travel in the Tube every day and it's a feast of possible movies, reflecting life's pageant and tapestry.'[77] Indeed discussing the nomination of his film *Vera Drake* (2004) for three Oscars, Leigh commented: 'A part of me is simply very amused by the irony of what is apparently a tiny film called *Vera Drake*, which actually is an epic, really.'[78] Leigh had established a carefully guarded artistic autonomy; most film-makers were subject to the pressures of high-risk commercial undertakings. Moreover, the spectacular failure of the 'Lottery Franchise' scheme to bring investment returns between 1997 and 2000; the alarming prospect of a major funder, Channel 4's film production arm, closing in 2002; and the 2004 government announcement that tax breaks, which effectively added 15–20 per cent to a film budget, would be scrapped all seemed to offer gloomy prospects. While the real crisis moment for British film had come in the late 1980s with the nearly simultaneous collapse of the UK's two major production companies, Goldcrest and Palace Pictures, film-making remained a hugely expensive and unpredictable business, not least because there was no clear answer as to whether a local or a global route would be more successful.

What funding policy did attempt was a shift of location away from the metropolis and towards other parts of the UK, so that studio facilities were promoted in Scotland and Wales, while a distinctive local culture in, say, Manchester or Liverpool, could become an attractive location for shooting various films, not only dour tales of northern misery. Hence a surprising success was *East is East* (D. O'Donnell, 1999), which is set in Salford in the early 1970s and which, while it deals with the serious theme of race relations at the time of Enoch Powell's greatest influence, nevertheless brings humour into its portrayal of generational differences within a British Pakistani family.[79] Similarly *Going Off Big Time* (J. Doyle, 2000), one of the two dozen-odd British crime films made at the end of the 1990s and early 2000s, was unusual for its Liverpool setting, and for its relatively sympathetic portrait of a workless social world in which criminality and the struggle for survival became difficult to disentangle. These films came in the wake of *Lock, Stock and Two Smoking Barrels* (G. Ritchie, 1998) which, like many of its imitators, combined elements of affectionate gangster movie tribute, comedy and London setting.[80] Such films acknowledged the changed role of men within British society, where physical graft was replaced by casual labour, masculine virtue by an ideal of equality and partnership between the sexes. They did so with reluctance and ambiguity, with a backward glance towards an imagined past of collective, albeit criminal, certainty and solidarity. A more open-ended sense of possibility and complexity, of the jostling mix and competitive confusion in capital life, came through the eyes of a former Bosnian director in *Beautiful People* (J. Dizdar, 1999).

While elements of social observation, comedy, melodrama or tragedy were mixed into these portraits of city living, and while they often had the potential to reach a wider international audience, the concerns of national life and local circumstance were clearly to the fore in these features. Less bound by the constraints of the realist tradition, or by location, were the Anglo-American romantic comedies so popular immediately before and after the Millennium. Set beyond the world of material struggle for survival, beyond ethnicity or class too, films such as *Notting Hill* (R. Michell, 1999) were able to idealize romance and the battle for love by eliminating all other forms of competition.[81] Richard Curtis, writer of *Notting Hill*, *Bridget Jones's Diary* (S. Maguire, 2001) and eventually director on *Love Actually* (2003), established a distinctive style which fitted the late 1990s' moment of New Labour ascent with its flamboyant language, its inclusive portrayal of sexuality and disability, and its consensual, comfortable vision of London as a world city. With its endless gangs of supportive, eccentric pals and its large quotient of available American actresses, 'Curtisworld' occasionally bumped against the harder edged realities of failure or disappointment, though shyness or misunderstanding were more often obstacles to be surmounted in the search for inevitable happiness.[82]

Other directors chose different routes as they attempted to navigate between local and global. Lynne Ramsay's first film *Ratcatcher* (1999), set at the time of the Glasgow refuse workers' strike in the late 1970s, describes the difficult life of a young boy as he faces the brutality of those around him and the rat infestation of his own home, yet one interlude is a hallucinatory visit to the moon by a mouse. Michael Winterbottom's work included a vivid portrait of London (*Wonderworld*, 1999), but his attention to locality took him also to music-obsessed Manchester (*24 Hour Party People*, 2002), to a science fiction Shanghai (*Code 46*, 2003) and to a dangerous journey by two Afghan refugees as they travel through empty landscapes on a journey towards Britain (*In This World*, 2003). Working quickly, with relatively small budgets, and in a variety of styles, Winterbottom's solution was to move as far as possible, imaginatively, formally and geographically, to think with worldwide themes, to intimately attend the specifics of time and place.

Timeline 4: 1998–2005

---1998---

SOCIETY: Scotland Act; Government of Wales Act; White Rose Shopping Centre opens, Leeds. **January:** Monica Lewinski scandal breaks in USA. **March:** UK countryside march joined by 200,000. **April:** Good Friday Agreement in Northern Ireland. **October:** former Spice Girl Geri Halliwell appointed Goodwill Ambassador for the UN Population Fund. **November:** European Union lifts ban on British beef.

ARTS: TV, theatre, film: Shekhar Kapur, *Elizabeth*; John Madden, *Shakespeare in Love*; Guy Ritchie, *Lock, Stock and Two Smoking Barrels*; Anand Tucker, *Hilary and Jackie*. **Visual:** Chris Ofili wins the Turner Prize. **Musical:** Baddiel, Skinner & The Lightning Seeds, *3 Lions '98*'. **Written:** death of Ted Hughes; Iranian fatwa on Salman Rushdie officially lifted; Ian McEwan, *Amsterdam*.

---1999---

SOCIETY: Patten Report on Policing in Northern Ireland; Mitchell Review on weapons decommissioning in Northern Ireland; Immigration and Asylum Act. **January:** launch of the Euro. **February:** publication of the Stephen Lawrence enquiry report. **April:** London gay pub bombing. **May:** Scottish and Welsh Parliamentary election. **October:** Paddington rail crash, London: 31 dead, more than 200 injured. **November:** Northern Ireland power sharing executive set up; Lord Archer withdraws from London Mayoral election.

ARTS: TV, theatre, film: Jasmin Dizdar, *Beautiful People*; Mike Leigh, *Topsy Turvy*; Roger Michell, *Notting Hill*; Lynne Ramsay, *Ratcatcher*. **Visual:** Steve McQueen wins the Turner Prize; Tracey Emin exhibits *My Bed* as part of her Turner Prize exhibition. **Musical:** Geri Halliwell, 'Lift Me Up'. **Written:** suicide of Sarah Kane.

---2000---

SOCIETY: publication of the Parekh Report on Multi-Ethnic Britain. **May:** Ken Livingstone elected Mayor of London. **June:** 58 illegal Chinese immigrants found dead at Dover; hundreds of English hooligans arrested and deported by Belgian and Dutch police during Euro 2000 football championship. **August:** Queen Mother's 100th birthday party. **September:** fuel protests in the UK. **October:** death of Donald Dewar: Scottish First Minister; Hatfield train crash: four killed. **November:** ten-year-old Nigerian boy Damilola Taylor murdered in South London.

ARTS: TV, theatre, film: Gurinder Chadha, *What's Cooking?*; Stephen Daldry, *Billy Elliot*. **Visual:** Wolfgang Tillmans wins the Turner Prize; Tate Modern opens in London. **Musical:** Asian Dub Foundation, *Community Music*; The Beatles, *1*. **Written:** Meera Syal, *Life isn't All Ha Ha Hee Hee*.

---2001---

SOCIETY: February: foot-and-mouth outbreak in the UK; Ellen MacArthur completes round the world yacht race. **April–July:** civil disturbances in Oldham, Burnley and Bradford. **June:** Labour wins UK general election with a majority of 167 seats. **September:** terrorist attacks kill thousands in New York and Washington. **November:** death of George Harrison.

ARTS: TV, theatre, film: Sharon McGuire, *Bridget Jones's Diary*; Richard Eyre, *Iris*. **Visual:** Martin Creed wins the Turner Prize; Grayson Perry, *Claire's Coming Out*. **Musical:** Nitin Sawhney, *Prophesy*; Spiritualized, *Let It Come Down*. **Written:** Peter Carey, *True History of the Kelly Gang*.

-- 2002 --

SOCIETY: Euro becomes legal tender in the Euro-zone. **March:** death of Queen Elizabeth the Queen Mother. **June:** Queen Elizabeth II's Golden Jubilee celebrations. **August:** murder of Holly Wells and Jessica Chapman, two ten-year-old schoolgirls, in Soham, Cambridgeshire. **September:** 400,000 attend Countryside Alliance march in London. **October:** UK suspends Northern Ireland Assembly.

ARTS: TV, theatre, film: Gurinder Chadha, *Bend it Like Beckham*; Stephen Daldry, *The Hours*; Michael Winterbottom, *24-Hour Party People*. **Visual:** Keith Tyson wins the Turner Prize. **Musical:** Ms Dynamite, *A Little Deeper*; Alef Bocoum, Toumani Diabate and Damon Albarn, *Mali Music*; Robbie Williams, *Escapology*. **Written:** Yann Martel, *Life of Pi*; Zadie Smith, *White Teeth*.

-- 2003 --

SOCIETY: January: death of Charlene Ellis and Letisha Shakespeare from gang gunfire on New Year's Eve, Birmingham. **February:** massive worldwide anti-war demonstrations; Tony Blair faces back-bench revolt on Iraq war. **March:** war against Iraq begins.

ARTS: TV, theatre, film: Michael Winterbottom, *In this World*. **Visual:** Grayson Perry wins the Turner prize. **Musical:** Dido, *Life for Rent*; Sugababes, 'Hole in My Head'; Robert Wyatt, *Cuckooland*. **Written:** DBC Pierre, *Vernon God Little*.

-- 2004 --

SOCIETY: November: north-east England rejects regional assembly proposal decisively.

ARTS: TV, theatre, film: Antonia Bird, *Hamburg Cell*; Gurinder Chadha, *Bride and Prejudice*; Mike Leigh, *Vera Drake*; Michael Winterbottom, *9 Songs*. **Visual:** Momart fire destroys work by major postwar artists including Patrick Heron and the Chapman Brothers. **Musical:** death of John Peel. **Written:** Monica Ali, *Brick Lane*; Alan Hollinghurst wins the Man Booker Prize with *The Line of Beauty*.

-- 2005 --

SOCIETY: May: British General Election sees New Labour returned to office with a reduced majority.

ARTS: TV, theatre, film: Mike Newell, *Harry Potter and the Goblet of Fire*. **Visual:** Tracey Emin, 'When I Think About Sex' exhibition; announcement of Trafalgar Square sculpture, Mark Quinn's 'Alison Lapper Pregnant'. **Musical:** Live8 concerts to promote debt relief in Africa; Mojo Prize Lifetime Achievement Award to Robert Wyatt. **Written:** Alexander Masters, *Stuart: A Life Backwards*.

Conclusion

Traditionally studies such as this are expected to reach a conclusion. But reaching a conclusion might in this case mean arriving at one description of identity. Would it be satisfactory to conclude that Britain since 1945 has many faces, many identities? Trivial as it might seem, this would not reduce the variety and complexity presented so far to a few convenient labels. Categorizing and classifying are at odds with selection, however representative, and montage. Identities – loyalties, feelings of belonging, images projected outward – have a density of lived experience when viewed from the individual's perspective. The question of who I am or where I belong may be urgent, troubling; or in may not be consciously admitted. In either case, the answer to it might be found not so much in intellectual debate as in social interaction, in exchanges of viewpoints, jokes, everyday banter and business. Belonging can be deeply embedded in place; it may reside in religious or political belief or simply in loyalty to family and friends. It is through these human connections that pockets of collective opinion and action are formed, that ways of living are extended. As identities and commonalities of interest and action become more public, they also become more self-consciously formed and imagined. The simple, single messages that give impressions but cannot convey the complexities of the everyday are identity's news headlines; individual and local ways of living are its small print (see figure 2).

While this account intentionally devotes space and attention to the individual and the local community as the nexus of varied identity formations, while it investigates the intricate negotiations of a particular time and place which allow a sense of belonging, it also gives consideration to three other connected themes. These are: communal and national identity within the constituent nations of the United Kingdom; the connectedness of social groups within these nations to wider social, economic and political circumstances, to lived experience rather than idealized images; the creative practice of artists as it represents viewpoint or interest by personal or universal themes, as it colours mood and values in the circumstances of the moment.

*　*　*

Compressing the history of postwar nationalism into a brief cinematic sequence, four moments spring to mind. Jack Dorgan, having travelled from the Welsh mining community of Onllwyn to London just after the end of the Second World War, takes part in the Victory Parade. It is a moment of great personal pride for the miner, and of nationwide collective celebration. Dorgan's own achievement is rooted in the traditions and skills of his own neighbourhood, but the powerful

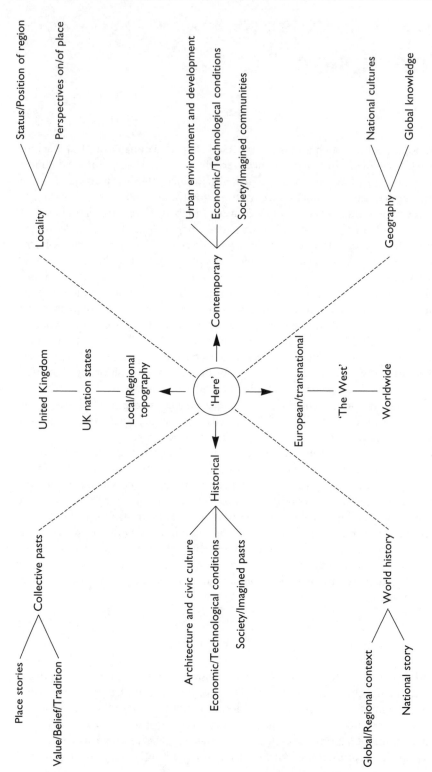

Figure 2 Formation of regional and global identities

emotion of the moment is as much a matter of the common cause, of the collective course of events and common experiences that had helped achieve success. Joy Hendry, a Hackney health visitor in the early 1970s, sits with a glass of 'peculiar lime drink' in the house of a recently arrived Indian woman. The house is in chaos, the two have no common language, Hendry has no idea how she can help. This is a meeting of two cultures which could not have taken place without Britain's colonial heritage, and which marks the connection of two individuals as they begin to share a present and a future. It is a symbolic starting point for the gradual creation of Britain's multi-ethnic society perhaps more than even the arrival of the *Empire Windrush*. Neal Ascherson telephones Tom Nairn from the depressed offices of *The Scotsman* on 2 March 1979 the day after the failed Scottish devolution referendum. The call recognizes the end of the various nationalist campaigns for greater independence, but as Nairn pointed out, it begins a second phase, the result of which is a gradually revised nationalist movement, ratified by the opening of the new Scottish Parliament in 1999. In May 2005 David Trimble loses his majority in the Upper Bann constituency in Northern Ireland as unionists express their frustration at the failure of the Good Friday Agreement to bring lasting peace. After the huge struggle to bring reconciliation and peace, and after providing a new model of multi-ethnic relations for the Britain and Ireland, progress finally seems to halt.

*　*　*

Considering changes in society I myself would pick out five juxtaposed images in this montage of identity's cultural roots. First would be the face of a shrieking woman in a 1950s' sci-fi movie as she runs in terror from a gigantic radioactive ant. This stands for Britain's initial anxiety, or even distrust, towards America over the 'erosion' of national values which subsequently undergoes a metamorphosis, making it more possible to embrace transatlantic novelty and innovation, for worse or better. Second, a vast concrete wasteland where factories once stood, representing Britain's lost nineteenth-century industrial heritage, the ways of life and values that were once so intimately bound up with its routines. Third, an aerial shot of the vast, hedgeless prairie-like farm fields that came to dominate industrialized agriculture and which have raised issues of environment and public health. On the horizon, at the city's edge, there are cranes and skyscrapers as part of the continual attempts to build and renew the urban environments and living conditions. Fourth, a group of women in the early 1960s, the factory hands chatting and laughing in Nell Dunn's *Up the Junction*, who are poised between the traditionalist values of the immediate postwar, and the gradually shifting social scene that is to come. Fifth is Fraggie from the Dongas Tribe wearing her first Stonehenge Festival outfit, who represents both the energy and optimism of youth, but also its statement of defiance.

*　*　*

From the arts three 'still' images fade in, one after another. Eduardo Paolozzi showing slides – a succession of images from advertisements, comic books and horror movies – to a small audience at the Institute of Contemporary Arts in London, 1952. This is a gathering of influential critics, artists and architects who undertake an investigation into popular culture, and who take seriously what they see. The result is a gradually achieved revolution in the visual arts which explores and reflects on the experience of modern living in a mass society. What is remarkable about this investigation is that it takes place so soon after the end of the war and at a time when mass consumerism and popular culture are only beginning to become influential in postwar society. From the films of Derek Jarman, especially *Jubilee* (1977) and *The Last of England* (1987), not so much a single 'still' as a composite image: derelict, rubble-strewn cityscapes, bonfires, punks and guerrilla-uniformed wastrels wandering aimlessly. A representation of all that has gone wrong with Britain through the 1970s and 1980s, Jarman's cinema is often disturbing and politicized. At the same time, with his love for the language and display of sixteenth and seventeenth century literature and society, Jarman is a profoundly English director; an odd mix of radicalism and conservatism that it is hard to imagine anywhere else. Finally Tracey Emin's tent (*Everyone I Have Ever Slept With 1963–1995*, 1995), with its embroidered patchwork of letters, spelling out names from her past; its handwritten messages, framed and stitched to the inside; its odd sensation of trespassing into a private life by looking at the interior. At once profoundly personal and subjective, at the same time opening out to the world, Emin's art recognizes identity as profoundly singular, yet always shared.

Appendices

1 Prime ministers
2 General elections, 1945–2005
3 UK population in millions, 1951–97
4 Industrial change, 1966–91
5 Dwellings and households, 1951–91
6 Scotland – major events
7 Northern Ireland – major events
8 Wales – major events

Appendix 1   Prime Ministers

July	1945:	Clement Attlee
Oct.	1951:	Winston Churchill
April	1955:	Sir Anthony Eden
Jan.	1957:	Harold Macmillan
Oct.	1963:	Sir Alec Douglas-Home
Oct.	1964:	Harold Wilson
June	1970:	Edward Heath
Mar.	1974:	Harold Wilson
Apr.	1976:	James Callaghan
May	1979:	Margaret Thatcher
Nov.	1990:	John Major
May	1997:	Tony Blair

Appendix 2   General Elections, 1945–2005

	Con.	Lab.	Lib.	Plaid Cymru	SNP	Others (GB)	Others (NI)	Total
1945	213	393	12	0	0	18	4	640
1950	299	315	9	0	0	0	2	625
1951	321	295	6	0	0	0	3	625
1955	345	277	6	0	0	0	2	630
1959	365	258	6	0	0	0	1	630
1964	304	318	9	0	0	0	0	630
1966	253	364	12	0	0	0	1	630
1970	330	288	6	1	1	4	6	630
1974 (Feb.)	297	301	14	2	7	2	12	635
1974 (Oct.)	277	319	13	3	11	0	12	635
1979	339	269	11	2	2	0	12	635
1983	397	209	23	2	2	0	17	650
1987	376	229	22	3	3	0	17	650
1992	336	271	20	4	3	0	17	651
1997	165	419	46	4	6	1	18	659
2001	166	413	52	4	5	1	18	659
2005	198	356	62	3	6	3	18	646

Source: Adapted from Electeral Reform Society: www.electoral-reform.org.uk

Appendix 3 United Kingdom population (million), 1951–97

	Scotland	Northern Ireland	Wales	England
1951	5.0	1.3	2.5	41.1
1961	5.1	1.4	2.6	43.5
1971	5.2	1.5	2.7	46.4
1981	5.1	1.5	2.8	46.8
1991	5.1	1.6	2.8	48.2
1997	5.1	1.6	2.9	49.2

Source: Adapted from C. Cook and J. Stevenson, The Longman Companion to Britain since 1945, 2nd edn (Harlow: Longman, 2000) p. 125; J. Hollowell (ed.), Britain since 1945 (Oxford: Blackwell, 2003) p. 242.

Appendix 4 Industrial change, Great Britain, 1966–91 (employment in thousands)

	1966	1971	1981	1991
Agriculture	753	635	515	456
Metal manufacture/Chemicals	1478	1407	941	655
Mechanical engineering	3725	3669	2839	2148
Financial industries	1193	1348	1796	2821
Education	1094	1390	1434	1459
Medical services	900	988	1247	1439
Recreational services	268	260	438	540
All industries	24169	23733	22916	23452
All manufacturing	8460	8125	6194	4828
All services	12039	12362	13699	15784

Source: Adapted from A. H. Halsey, Twentieth-Century British Social Trends (Basingstoke: Macmillan, 2000) p. 284.

Appendix 5 Dwellings and the household/dwelling balance, 1951–91

	Dwelling stock (000s)	Vacant dwellings Number (000s)	Vacant dwellings Proportion (%)	Household/ dwelling balance* (000s)
England and Wales				
1951	12530	138	1.1	−1660
1961	14646	314	2.1	−780
1971	17024	646	3.8	−120
England				
1971	16065	600	3.8	−112
1981	17912	740	4.1	+440
1991	19780	660	3.3	+400

* Minus sign = more potential households than dwellings.
Source: Adapted from A. H. Halsey, Twentieth-Century British Social Trends (Basingstoke: Macmillan, 2000) p. 474.

Appendix 6   Scotland – an outline of events since 1945

1945	Labour General Election victory; Robert McIntyre wins Motherwell by-election for SNP
1946	Development and Industry Council in Scotland formed
1947	Changes in parliamentary procedure and an enquiry into financial relations between England and Scotland proposed in Government White Paper on Scottish Affairs
1948	Scottish Covenant for Home Rule launched
1952	First television broadcast
1954	Recommendation for transfer of responsibilities for electricity, food, roads and bridges to the Scottish Office contained in the Report of the Royal Commission on Scottish Affairs
1955	Scottish Unionist Party (Conservatives) win over 50% of the Scottish vote
1957	Scottish Standing Committee set up to scrutinize Scottish Bills in the House of Commons
1960	Plans announced for a Polaris Missile base at Holy Loch; unemployment in Scotland reaches over 100,000
1961	Establishment of a Scottish Office Development Department recommended in the Toothill Enquiry on the Scottish Economy
1965	Highlands and Islands Development Board established
1967	By-election victory for SNP as Winnie Ewing wins Hamilton
1970	Discovery of North Sea Oil; rise in support for Scottish Nationalists
1971	Scottish Officer sets up a Scottish Economic Planning Department
1974	Rise from seven to eleven SNP MPs over two General Elections
1975	Scottish Development Agency set up
1976	Scottish and Welsh Devolutions Bills fail to get through House of Commons
1979	Failure to reach a required minimum 'Yes' vote (40% of the Scottish electorate) in the devolution referendum; SNP wins two seats in the General Election
1988	By-election victory for SNP as Jim Sillars wins Govan; introduction of the Poll Tax in Scotland; the Campaign for a Scottish Assembly launches its 'Claim of Right for Scotland' campaign
1989	Scottish Enterprise and Highlands and Islands Enterprise set up; widespread opposition to introduction of the poll tax in Scotland
1992	Democracy March at Edinburgh EU Summit; SNP wins three seats in the General Election
1994	Tony Blair promises to establish a Scottish Parliament; Labour changes its name to Scottish Labour Party
1995	SNP win for Roseanna Cunningham in the Perth and Kinross by-election
1996	Labour commitment to Welsh and Scottish devolution if elected
1997	Labour wins a huge majority of 56 seats in Scotland; 'Yes' votes for both Scottish Parliament and tax-raising powers; Scotland Bill published
1999	Election of 129 MPs to the new Scottish Parliament; Donald Dewar becomes First Minister
2001	Jack McConnell appointed First Minister of Scotland
2005	Glasgow launches a bid to host the 2014 Commonwealth Games

Appendix 7   Northern Ireland – an outline of events since 1945

1949	Principal of equal taxation and services for mainland and Northern Ireland established; budgets to be agreed in consultation
1949	Southern Ireland becomes the Irish Republic; high costs of Northern Ireland social services to be met by British Government
1951	Agreement to single National Insurance Fund and transference of funds as required to Northern Ireland
1956–62	Renewed IRA campaign in Northern Ireland
1965	Prime Minister Terence O'Neill exchanges visits with Taoiseach Sean Lemass

1967	Establishment of the Northern Ireland Civil Rights Association
1968	Civil Rights marches and subsequent rioting; investigation by Cameron Commission begins
1969	Belfast to Londonderry march by People's Democracy broken up; British Army arrives in Belfast and Londonderry following civil disturbances; Stormont assumes responsibility for housing allocation
1971	First British soldier killed; IRA bombing campaign intensifies; introduction of internment without trial
1972	Thirteen shot dead by British soldiers during Londonderry civil rights march ('Bloody Sunday'); direct rule from Westminster introduced
1973	Failure of the 'power sharing' agreement; direct rule reintroduced; extended bombing IRA campaign in mainland Britain
1976	Betty Williams and Mairead Corrigan begin the Peace People campaign
1981	Bobby Sands and Francis Hughes die on hunger strike
1984	Five killed in the IRA Grand Hotel, Brighton bombing during the Conservative Party Conference
1985	Garret FitzGerald and Margaret Thatcher's Hillsborough agreement on reconciliation between two parts of Ireland; strong Unionist opposition
1986	Strikes, violence and intimidation in protest at the Anglo-Irish (Hillsborough) agreement
1987	Eleven killed at the Enniskillen Remembrance Day bombing
1991	Anglo-Irish agreement suspended for constitutional talks
1992	Number of dead in the Troubles passes 3000
1994	Ceasefire declared by the IRA; followed by protestant paramilitary ceasefire
1996	IRA ceasefire finished by bombing at London Docklands Canary Wharf
1997	IRA ceasefire resumes; Sinn Fein allowed to peace talks; Downing Street visit by Gerry Adams and Martin McGuinness; ceasefire by protestant Ulster Defence Association and Ulster Volunteer Force
1998	Good Friday agreement concluded; 70 per cent approval in referendum; election of 108 Members to the new Northern Ireland Assembly; David Trimble becomes First Minister; Omagh bombing leaves 28 dead, more than 220 injured
1999	Proposal to form the Northern Ireland Police Force in place of the Royal Ulster Constabulary; arrival of devolved government and power-sharing Executive; six counties claim abandoned by the Irish Republic
2000	Backlash against RUC reforms; crisis over decommissioning of arms; suspension of Executive; agreement that IRA commissioning should put weapons 'completely and verifiably' beyond use
2001	Lack of progress towards peace leads to resignation of First Minister David Trimble; new IRA decommissioning proposals put forward; continued stalemate leads to suspension of devolution by John Reid, Secretary of State, and subsequent restoration 24 hours later; second technical suspension followed by report of 'significant disposal', and returned devolution
2002	Second IRA arsenal tranche dumped; accusations of IRA intelligence gathering at Stormont; danger to assembly if no action taken against Sinn Fein by Government, warns Trimble; return to direct rule
2003	Prime Minister Blair postpones assembly elections until IRA position clarified; DUP and Sinn Fein elected largest unionist and nationalist parties in assembly elections
2004	'Cautious optimism' expressed in Belfast at Good Friday Agreement Review; hopes for breakthrough within weeks as DUP leader Ian Paisley and Irish Prime Minister Bertie Ahern meet; British and Irish governments as well as President G. W. Bush all urge progress on Ian Paisley and Gerry Adams; breakthrough talks fail

Appendix 8   Wales – an outline of events since 1945

1945	General Election: in Wales Labour wins 25 seats, Liberals 7, Conservatives 4
1946	Welsh National Opera established
1947	Nationalization of the mines; Steel Company of Wales; Llangollen International Eisteddfod established
1948	Council for Wales and Monmouthshire
1949	Welsh Joint Education Committee
1951	Minister for Welsh Affairs appointed
1953	First Welsh language television programme
1954	Dylan Thomas's *Under Milk Wood* first broadcast
1955	Welsh capital declared: Cardiff
1956	First bilingual secondary school opens in Flintshire
1957	Cardiff appearance for Bill Haley and the Comets
1958	Commercial television station (TWW) begins
1960	Death of Aneurin Bevan; publication of *Welsh History Review*
1961	Welsh Book Council
1962	*Tynged yr Iaith* ('Fate of the Language') broadcast by Saunders Lewis; Cymdeithas yr Iaith Gymraeg (the Welsh Language Society) founded; Llanwern steelworks opens
1963	Committee on the Status of the Welsh Language set up
1964	BBC Wales established; James Griffiths appointed first Secretary of State for Wales
1966	By-election victory for Plaid Cymru as Gwynfor Evans wins Carmarthen; Aberfan disaster
1967	Welsh Arts Council established; Welsh Language Act comes into force
1969	Prince of Wales Investiture ceremony at Caernarfon Castle
1971	Mudiad Ysgolion Meithrin, the Welsh language nursery movement, established
1972	Sports Council for Wales
1974	Local government system reorganized – eight county councils in the main tier of local government
1976	Welsh Development Agency created
1979	'No' vote in Welsh devolution referendum; Parliamentary Select Committee on Welsh Affairs set up
1982	Launch of Welsh language television station Sianel Pedwar Cymru (S4C)
1986	Welsh Development Agency created
1990	Rhondda Valley's last coal-mine is shut down
1993	Welsh Language Board becomes statutory with the Welsh Language Act
1994	Oscar nomination for Welsh language film *Hedd Wyn*
1997	'Yes' vote to Welsh Assembly
1999	Election of 60 MPs to the new Welsh Assembly; official Royal opening in May; Alun Michael becomes First Minister; Pat Murphy becomes Secretary of State
2000	Rhodri Morgan replaces Alun Michael as First Minister
2001	Corus steel plant job losses. General Election: in Wales Labour win 34 seats, Plaid Cymru 4, Liberal Democrat 2, Conservatives 0
2002	Peter Hain appointed Secretary of State for Wales
2004	Official opening of the Wales Millennium Centre, Cardiff

Notes

Notes to the Introduction

1 For example, L. Colley, *Britons: Forging the Nation, 1707–1837* (London: Vintage, 1996); N. Davies, *The Isles: A History* (London: Papermac, 2000); H. Kearney, *The British Isles: A History of Four Nations* (Cambridge: Cambridge University Press, 1989); R. Weight, *Patriots: National Identity in Britain, 1940–2000* (London: Macmillan, 2002).

2 I am indebted to N. Douglas here for his cogent essay 'Political Structures, Social Interaction and Identity Change in Northern Ireland', in B. Graham (ed.), *In Search of Ireland: A Cultural Geography* (London: Routledge, 1997), pp. 151–73.

3 For an early challenge to this view see M. Hechter, *Internal Colonialism: The Celtic Fringe in British National Development* (London: Routledge, 1975).

4 M. Arnold, 'On the Study of Celtic Literature' (1865–6) in R. H. Super (ed.), *Prose Works*, vol. 3 (Ann Arbor: University of Michigan Press, 1963), pp. 292. See also H.-W. Ludwig, 'Province and Metropolis; Centre and Periphery: Some Critical Terms Re-examined' in H.-W. Ludwig and L. Fietz (eds.), *Poetry in the British Isles: Non-Metropolitan Perspectives* (Cardiff: University of Wales Press, 1995), pp. 47–69. For this reason too the 1960s reply of Welsh nationalists, again echoing a persistent sentiment, 'cenedl heb iaith, cenedl heb galon' (a nation without a language is a nation without a heart).

5 W. Besant, *East London* (London: Chatto and Windus, 1903), p. 200.

6 A. J. P. Taylor, *English History, 1914–45* (Harmondsworth: Penguin, 1982), pp. 235. Characteristically Taylor excludes *Finnegans Wake* on the grounds that 'even the words were gibberish'.

7 For an overview of the subject's development to the mid-1990s see especially R. Samuel, 'Four Nations History', in *Theatres of Memory*, vol. 2: *Island Stories* (London: Verso, 1999), pp. 21–40.

8 Kearney, op. cit., pp. 10–11.

9 The mid-1970s also saw the publication of J. G. A. Pocock's 'British History: A Plea for a New Subject', *Journal of Modern History*, 47 (December 1975).

10 For a recent discussion see B. Graham, 'Ireland and Irishness: Place, Culture and Identity', in B. Graham (ed.), op. cit., pp. 1–15.

11 N. Davies, op. cit., p. xxvi; N. Davies, 'The Decomposing of Britain', *TLS*, 6 October 2000, pp. 15–16; E. J. Hobsbawm, *Nations and Nationalism since 1870*, 2nd edn (Cambridge: Cambridge University Press, 1992).

12 R. Williams, *The Long Revolution* (Harmondsworth: Penguin, 1965); this discussion of 'local feeling' is more directly indebted, though, to I. Taylor, K. Evans and P. Fraser, *A Tale of Two Cities: Global Change, Local Feeling and Everyday Life in the North of England. A Study in Manchester and Sheffield* (London: Routledge, 1996).

13 Taylor, op. cit., p. 33.

14 Ibid., p. 33.

15 On 'space' and 'place' see H. Beynon, R. Hudson and D. Sadler, *A Place Called Teesside: A Locality in a Global Economy* (Edinburgh: Edinburgh University Press for the University of Durham, 1994), pp. 4–7.

16 P. Thane, *Old Age in English History: Past Experiences, Present Issues* (Oxford: Oxford University Press, 2000); F. Mort, *Cultures of Consumption: Masculinities and Social Space in Late Twentieth-Century Britain* (London: Routledge, 1996).

Notes to Chapter I

1 See: 'National Panel Diarist: Blue Clydeside, 1945', in A. Calder and D. Sheridan, *Speak For Yourself: A Mass-Observation Anthology, 1937–49* (London: Jonathan Cape, 1984), pp. 224–6.

2 T. Devine, *The Scottish Nation, 1700–2000* (Harmondsworth: Penguin, 1999), p. 313.

3 Calder and Sheridan, op. cit., p. 225.

4 Ibid., p. 226.

5 Devine, op. cit., pp. 555–6; W. W. Knox, *Industrial Nation: Work, Culture and Society in Scotland, 1800 to the Present* (Edinburgh: Edinburgh University Press, 1999), p. 254.

6 W. P. L. Thomson, *History of Orkney* (Edinburgh: Mercat, 1987), p. 244.

7 Ibid., p. 244; N. Davies, *The Isles: A History* (London: Papermac, 2000), p. 807.

8 Devine, op. cit., p. 558. The Forestry Commission owns 1,600,000 acres according to A. Cramb, *Who Owns Scotland Now? The Use and Abuse of Private Land* (Edinburgh: Mainstream, 1996), quoted in Davies, op. cit., p. 1027.

9 Thomson, op. cit., p. 252.

10 U. Wannop, 'Glasgow/Clydeside: a Century of Metropolitan Evolution', in G. Gordon (ed.), *Regional Cities in the UK* (London: Harper and Row, 1986), pp. 87–8.

11 G. Gordon, 'Edinburgh: Capital and Regional City', in Gordon, op. cit., pp. 160–1.

12 Ibid., p. 164.

13 T. C Smout, 'Patterns of Culture' in W. H. Fraser and R. J. Morris (eds), *People and Society in Scotland*, vol. 2: *1830–1914* (Edinburgh: Edinburgh University Press, 1990), pp. 273–4.

14 G. M. Brown, *Portrait of Orkney* (London: John Murray, 1988), p. 66.

15 See especially J. Littlejohn, *Westrigg: the Sociology of a Cheviot Parish* (London: Routledge and Kegan Paul, 1963).

16 Thomson, op. cit., p. 256.

17 A. Smith, *The Third Statistical Account of Scotland*, vol. 2: *Fife*, p. 83, in Smout, op. cit., p. 269.

18 L. Heron, 'Dear Green Place', in L. Heron (ed.), *Truth, Dare or Promise: Girls Growing Up in the 1950s* (London: Virago, 1985), p. 154.

19 Ibid., p. 163.

20 Ibid., p. 167.

21 B. Devlin, *The Price of My Soul* (London: Pan, 1969), p. 11.

22 Ibid., p. 12.

23 W. R. Rodgers, *The Ulstermen and their Country* (London: British Council/Longmans Green, 1947), p. 1.

24 Ibid., p. 18.

25 W. I. Hunter, 'Agriculture, Forestry and Fishing', in R. H. Buchanan and B. M. Walker (eds), *Belfast and its Region: Province, City and People* (Antrim: Greystone, 1987), pp. 220–1.

26 S. Wichert, *Northern Ireland Since 1945* (London: Longman, 1998), p. 59.

27 Ibid., p. 50; F. Boal and S. Royle, 'Belfast: Boom, Blitz and Bureaucracy', in G. Gordon, op. cit., p. 203.

28 *Industrial Review of Industry* (Belfast: City of Belfast, 1954), p. 23.

29 J. C. Beckett and R. E. Glasscock, *Belfast: the Origins and Growth of an Industrial City* (London: BBC, 1967), pp. 164–6.

30 *Industrial Review*, op. cit., p. 27.

31 For a general account see C. Pooley and J. Turnbull, *Migration and Mobility in Britain Since the Eighteenth Century* (London: UCL, 1998).

32 F. W. Boal, 'Belfast: Boom, Blitz and Bureaucracy', in Buchanan and Walker, op. cit., pp. 125–7.

33 W. Black, 'Industrial Change and the Twentieth Century', in Beckett and Glasscock, op. cit., pp. 157–61.

34 S. Wichert, op. cit., p. 46.

35 B. Devlin, op. cit., p. 25.

36 Ibid., pp. 26–7.

37 F. Boal and S. Royle, op. cit., p. 202.

38 J. Greer and P. Jess, 'Town and Country Planning', in Buchanan and Walker (eds), op. cit., p. 105; Boal and Royle, op. cit., p. 127.

39 W. R. Rodgers, op. cit., p. 17.

40 S. Wichert, op. cit., p. 82.

41 K. O. Morgan, 'Wales Since 1945: Political Society', in T. Herbert and G. Elwyn Jones (eds), *Post-War Wales* (Cardiff: University of Wales Press, 1995), p. 10.

42 K. O. Morgan, *Wales 1880–1980: Rebirth of a Nation* (Oxford: Oxford University Press, 1982), p. 310.

43 Jack Dorgan, Onllwyn miner, June 1946, in H. Francis and D. Smith, *The Fed: A History of South Wales Miners in the Twentieth Century* (Cardiff: University Wales Press, 1998), p. 425.

44 K. O. Morgan, *Wales 1880–1980*, op. cit., p. 318.

45 Museum of Welsh Life MS 3537/27, Mrs Elizabeth Williams Ellis, originally Pencaenewydd, Caerns in S. Minwell Tibbott, *Domestic Life in Wales* (Cardiff: University of Wales Press/National Museums & Galleries of Wales, 2002), p. 127.

46 G. E. Jones, *Modern Wales: a Concise History* (Cambridge: Cambridge University Press, 1999), p. 216.

47 G. A. Williams, *When Was Wales? A History of the Welsh* (Harmondsworth: Penguin, 1991), p. 291; Jones, op. cit., p. 268.

48 N. M. C. Sinclair, *The Tiger Bay Story* (Treforest: Zenith, 1993), p. 8.

49 Ibid., p. 9.

50 J. Davies, *A History of Wales* (Harmondsworth: Penguin, 1994), pp. 635–6.

51 Sinclair, op. cit., p. 89.

52 Morgan, op. cit., pp. 346–7.

52 Ibid., p. 352.

54 F. J. Osborn and A. Whittaker, *New Towns: Their Origins, Achievements and Progress* (London: Leonard Hill, 1977), pp. 370–81.

55 Quoted in Francis and Smith, op. cit., pp. 427–8.

56 C. Logue, *Prince Charming. A Memoir* (London: Faber, 1999), p. 80.

57 M. Abbott, *Family Affairs: A History of the Family in Twentieth Century England* (London: Routledge, 2003), p. 87.

58 See, for example, testimonies by Jamaican immigrants arriving in Britain in 1948 in M. Phillips and T. Phillips, *Windrush: The Irresistible rise of Multi-racial Britain* (London: HarperCollins, 1998), pp. 89–91.

59 Quoted in T. Blackwell and J. Seabrook, *Talking Work: An Oral History* (London: Faber, 1996), p. 61.

60 Ibid.

61 A. Palmer, *The East End: Four Centuries of London Life* (London: John Murray, 2000), pp. 150–1.

62 M. Dintness, *The Decline of Industrial Britain, 1870–1980* (London: Routledge, 1992), p. 5.

63 R. Porter, *London: A Social History* (Harmondsworth: Penguin, 2000), pp. 420–1.

64 J. Richardson, *London and its People: a Social History from Mediaeval Times to the Present Day* (London: Barrie and Jenkins, 1995), pp. 328–9.

65 T. Blackwell and J. Seabrook, op. cit., p. 61.

66 S. Humphries and B. Hopwood, *Green and Pleasant Land: The Untold Story of Country Life in Twentieth Century Britain* (London: Channel 4, 1999), p. 165; M. Abbott, op. cit., p. 97.

67 H. Hopkins, *The New Look: A Social History of the Forties and Fifties in Britain* (Boston, MA: Houghton Mifflin, 1964), p. 48; J. Richardson, op. cit., p. 328.

68 A. Palmer, op. cit., p. 152.

69 Quoted in M. Abbott, op. cit., p. 96.

70 B. Campbell, *Wigan Pier Revisited: Poverty and Politics in the Eighties* (London: Virago, 1984), p. 32.

71 A. Kidd, *Manchester* (Ryburn, Keele: Keele University Press, 1993), p. 220.

Notes to Chapter 2

1   S. Bruley, *Women in Britain Since 1900* (London: Macmillan, 1999), pp. 128–9.

2   P. Parker, 'The Rewards of Hard Labour', in M. Nicholson, *What Did You Do in The War, Mummy? Women in World War Two* (London: Pimlico, 1996), p. 48.

3   Bruley, op. cit., p. 115.

4   J. Lewis, *Women in Britain Since 1945* (Oxford: Blackwell, 1992), p. 16.

5   J. Webb, 'Social Security', in A. H. Halsey and J. Webb (eds), *Twentieth-Century British Social Trends* (Basingstoke: Macmillan, 2000), p. 550.

6   P. Thane, 'Women and Equal Opportunities', in T. Gourvish and A. O'Day (eds), *Britain Since 1945* (Basingstoke: Macmillan, 1991), p. 191.

7   J. Bowlby, *Forty-Four Juvenile Thieves: Their Character and Home-Life* (London: Ballière, Tindall and Cox, 1946), p. 27.

8   S. Rowbotham, *A Century of Women* (Harmondsworth: Penguin, 1999), p. 248.

9   Bruley, op. cit., p. 120; Rowbotham, op. cit., 244.

10 J. C. Spence, *The Purpose of the Family* (Convocation Lecture for the National Children's Home, 1946), p. 51 quoted in J. Lewis, op. cit., p. 19.

11 Quoted in J. Anim-Addo, *Longest Journey: A History of Black Lewisham* (London: Deptford Forum, 1995), p. 91.

12 C. Peach, A. Rogers, J. Chance and P. Daley, 'Immigration and Ethnicity', in A. Halsey and J. Webb, op. cit., p. 137; K. Sword, *Identity in Flux: The Polish Community in Britain* (London: SSEES Occasional Papers No. 36, 1996), p. 35.

13 J. Brown, *The Un-Melting Pot* (London: Macmillan, 1970), p. 61.

14 Peach et al., op. cit., p. 136.

15 B. Maan, *The New Scots: A Study of Asians in Scotland* (Edinburgh: John Donald, 1992), pp. 33–5.

16 R. Ramdin, *Reimaging Britain: 500 Years of Black and Asian History* (London: Pluto, 1999), pp. 127–8.

17 Ibid., 164–5; H. Goulbourne, *Race Relations in Britain Since 1945* (London: Macmillan, 1998), pp. 42–3.

18 M. Rogers, 'Glasgow Jewry', in B. Kay (ed.), *The Complete Odyssey: Voices from Scotland's Recent Past* (Edinburgh: Polygon, 1996), p. 234.

19 A. M. Tomczak, 'Poles in Post-War Britain', in P. Leese (ed.), *Between Two Cultures: Poland and Britain* (Poznan: British Council, 2004) pp. 67–8; B. Maan, op. cit., pp. 34–5.

20 I. R. G. Spencer, *British Immigration Policy Since 1939* (London: Routledge, 1997), pp. 51–2.

21 Tomczak, op. cit., p. 74.

22 E. Ferron, *'Man, You've Mixed': A Jamaican Come to Britain* (London: Whiting and Birch, 1995), p. 33.

23 P. Bailey, 'Jazz at the Spirella: Coming of Age in Coventry in the 1950s', in B. Conekin, F. Mort and C. Waters (eds), *Moments of Modernity: Reconstructing Britain 1945–64* (London; Rivers Oram, 1999), pp. 23–4.

24 Ibid., 25.

25 H. Hopkins, *The New Look: A Social History of the Forties and Fifties in Britain* (Boston, MA: Houghton Mifflin, 1964), p. 143.

26 Ibid., p. 208.

27 DMG, 'Juvenile delinquency', internal Home Office memorandum, CAB 102/790, August 1945, PRO, London, in H. L. Smith (ed.), *Britain in the Second World War: A Social History* (Manchester: Manchester University Press, 1996), p. 17.

28 Hopkins, op. cit., p. 207.

29 Ibid., p. 208.

30 See *The Oxford English Dictionary* (2nd edn) entry, which appears to confirm the horseracing origins of the term, though whether it dates back earlier than the nineteenth century remains unclear. Hence *The Times*, 18 November 2/4 (1947): 'Instead of that brave new Britain all they had left was a land fit for bookies to spiv in.'

31 A. Aldgate and J. Richards, *Best of British: Cinema and Society from 1930 to the Present* (London: I. B. Tauris, 1999), p. 130.

32 BBFC scenario 55a/1949, quoted in J. C. Robertson, 'The Censors and British Gangland, 1913–1990', S. Chibnall and R. Murphy (eds), *British Crime Cinema* (London: Routledge, 1999), p. 21.

33 Quoted in B. Osgerby, *Youth in Britain Since 1945* (Oxford: Blackwell, 1998), p. 11.

34 Bailey, op. cit., p. 25.

35 D. Sylvester, 'End of the Streamline Era', 2 August 1955, *The Times*, reprinted in D. Sylvester, *About Modern Art: Critical Essays, 1948–96* (London: Chatto and Windus, 1996), p. 49.

36 H. Read, 'Threshold of a New Age', in J. R. M. Bramwell (ed.), *This Changing World* (London: Readers Union/George Routledge, 1945), p. 182.

37 See, for example, D. Sylvester, 'Giacometti', op. cit., pp. 52–5.

38 R. Ironside, 'Painting Since 1939', in A. Haskell et al., *Since 1939*, vol. 1, (London: Phoenix House, 1948); D. Masters, 'Going Modern and Being British: Art in Britain 1930–55', in G. Day (ed.), *Literature and Culture in Britain*, vol. 2: *1930–55* (London: Longman, 1997), p. 207.

39 Quoted in F. Spalding, *British Art since 1900* (London: Thames and Hudson, 1992), p. 131.

40 Archbishop of Canterbury's opening speech quoted in B. Conekin, ' "Here is the Modern World Itself": The Festival of Britain's Representation of the Future', in B. Conekin, et al., op. cit., pp. 233–4.

41 *Daily Telegraph*, 28 April 1951, 4, quoted in Masters, op. cit., p. 210.

42 Quoted in M. Whybrow, *St Ives 1883–1983: Portrait of an Art Colony* (Woodbridge, Suffolk: Antique Collectors Club, 1994), p. 125.

43 Quoted in J. A. Walker, *Cultural Offensive: America's Impact on British Art Since 1945* (London: Pluto, 1998), p. 13.

44 John Ormond Thomas, 'Dark Harmony', *Picture Post*, 4 October 1947, in H. Kureishi and J. Savage (eds), *The Faber Book of Pop* (London: Faber, 1995), p. 14.

45 T. Bacon, *London Live* (London: Balafon, 1999) pp. 11–13; I. Chambers, *Urban Rhythms* (London: Macmillan, 1985), pp. 12–13.

46 E. Whitehouse, *This England Book of British Dance Bands from the Twenties to the Fifties* (Cheltenham: This England, 1999), p. 36.

47 C. Brooks, *A Concise History of the Traditional Jazz Revival in Kent* (Chatham, Kent: City, 2000), p. 14.

48 H. Hopkins, op. cit., p. 432; Chambers, op. cit., p. 12; Kureishi and Savage, op. cit., p. 5.

49 Kureishi and Savage, op. cit., p. 17; Bailey, op. cit., 39–40.

50 I. Berg and I. Yeoman, *Trad: An A to Z Who's Who of the British Traditional Jazz Scene* (London: Foulsham, 1962), p. 7.

51 Berg and Yeoman, op. cit., 52–3; Brooks, op. cit., 13–14.

52 Humphrey Lyttelton quoted in Max Jones, 'A New Jazz Age', *Picture Post*, 12 November 1949, in Kureishi and Savage, op. cit., p.16.

53 Ibid., p. 17; Bailey, op. cit., pp. 39–40.

54 See, for example, Richard Attenborough's comments on the Boulting brothers in B. McFarlane, *An Autobiography of British Cinema as Told by the Filmmakers and Actors Who Made It* (London: Methuen, 1997), pp. 34–5, and Michael Balcon's statement in *Kinematograph Weekly*, 11 January 1945, p. 163, quoted in J. Richards, *Film and British National Identity: From Dickens to Dad's Army* (Manchester: Manchester University Press, 1997), p. 134. Also Humphrey Jennings' Festival of Britain film *Family Portrait* (1950).

55 S. Fielding, P. Thompson and N. Tiratsoo, *'England Arise': The Labour Party and Popular Politics in 1940s Britain* (Manchester: Manchester University Press, 1997), pp. 144–5; A. Eyles, 'Exhibition and the Cinemagoing Experience' in R. Murphy (ed.), *The British Cinema Book* (London: BFI, 1997), p. 220.

56 On Anna Neagle see J. Richards, op. cit., pp. 131–2.

57 K. Thompson and D. Bardwell, *Film History: An Introduction* (New York: McGraw-Hill, 1994) pp. 451–2; V. Porter, 'Methodism versus the Market-place: the Rank Organisation and British Cinema', in R. Murphy (ed.), op. cit., p. 123; A. Eyles, op. cit., p. 221.

58 For a fuller account see M. Landy, 'Melodrama and Femininity in World War Two British Cinema', in R. Murphy, (ed.), op. cit., pp. 79–89; and M. Landy, *British Genres* (Princeton, NJ: Princeton University Press, 1991).

59 See especially R. Dyer, *Brief Encounter* (London: BFI, 1993).

60 See especially I. Green, 'Ealing: in the Comedy Frame', in J. Curran and V. Porter (eds), *British Cinema History* (London: Weidenfeld and Nicolson, 1983), pp. 294–311.

61 Linden Travers in McFarlane, op. cit., p. 572.

Notes to Chapter 3

1 Quoted in S. Harris, *Life in Britain in the 1950s* (London: Batsford, 1985), p. 13.

2 Nicolas Tomalin, quoted in J. Hill, *Sex, Class and Realism: British Cinema, 1956–63* (London: BFI, 1986), p. 5.

3 Only in the early 1960s was Bowlby criticized for basing his findings on case studies of children entirely deprived of maternal care by traumatic wartime separation. See S. Yudkin and A. Holmes, *Working Mothers and their Children* (London: Michael Joseph, 1963).

4 Paragraph 47, *Report of the Royal Commission on Marriage and Divorce* (London: HMSO, 1955).

5 A. Myrdal and V. Klein, *Women's Two Roles: Home and Work* (London: Routledge and Kegan Paul, 1956). See also J. Lewis, 'Women's Two Roles: Myrdal, Klein and

Post-war Feminism', in H. L. Smith (ed.), *British Feminism in the Twentieth Century* (Cheltenham: Edward Elgar, 1990), pp. 167–88.

6 E. Chesser, *Is Chastity Outmoded?* (London: Heinemann, 1960), p. 117.

7 J. Lewis, *Women in Britain Since 1945* (Oxford: Blackwell, 1992), pp. 74–5.

8 S. Rowbottom, *A Century of Women* (Harmondsworth: Penguin, 1999), p. 295; M. Abbott, *Family Affairs: A History of the Family in Twentieth-Century England* (London: Routledge, 2003), p. 79, pp. 110–11.

9 Ibid., p. 280.

10 K. Tynan, 'A Taste of Honey', in K. Tynan, *Curtains: Selections from the Drama Criticism and Related Writings* (London: Longmans, 1962), p. 214.

11 C. MacInnes, 'A Short Guide for Jumbles', in *England, Half English* (London: MacGibbon and Kee, 1958), p. 19.

12 Ibid., p. 21.

13 C. Peach, A. Rogers, J. Chance and P. Daley, 'Immigration and Ethnicity', in Halsey and Webb, (eds), *Twentieth-Century British Social Trends* (London: Macmillan, 2000), pp. 131, 137–8.

14 For a brief overview of legislation see I. Curyłło-Klag, 'Migrant Life Stories in the Twentieth Century', in P. Leese, et al. (ed.), *The British Migrant Experience, 1700–2000: An Anthology* (London: Palgrave Macmillan, 2002) pp. 111–13. See also I. G. R. Spencer, *British Immigration Policy since 1939* (London: Routledge, 1997).

15 R. Ramdin, *Reimaging Britain: 500 Years of Black and Asian History* (London: Pluto, 1999), pp. 163–4; K. Sword, *Identity in Flux: The Polish Community in Britain* (London: SSEES Occasional Papers, No. 36, 1996), p. 36.

16 Anim-Addo, op. cit., p. 99.

17 S. Winters, *Nobody Sleeps on the Rooftops Now* (Gravesend: AIM, 1994), pp. 6–7.

18 D. MacAmhlaigh, *An Irish Navvy: The Diary of an Exile* (London: Routledge, 1964), p. 6.

19 A. De la Haye and C. Dingwall, *Surfers Soulies Skinheads and Skaters* (London: Victoria and Albert Museum, 1996), p. 34.

20 For a fuller account see R. Glass, *Newcomers: The West Indians in London* (London: Centre for Urban Studies/George Allen and Unwin, 1960).

21 Ibid., p. 146.

22 Ramdin, op. cit., p. 179.

23 J. Anim-Addo, *Longest Journey: A History of Black Lewisham* (London: Deptford Forum, 1995), p. 99; Glass, op. cit., pp. 203–4.

24 J. Green, *Them* (London: Secker and Warburg, 1990), p. 245.

25 De la Haye and Dingwall, op. cit., p. 34.

26 P. Rock and S. Cohen, 'The Teddy Boy', in V. Bogdanor and R. Skidelsky (eds), *The Age of Affluence, 1951–64* (London: Macmillan, 1970), p. 289.

27 C. Logue, *Prince Charming: A Memoir* (London: Faber, 1999), p. 197.

28 T. Jefferson, 'Cultural Responses of the Teds', in S. Hall and T. Jefferson (eds), *Resistance through Rituals* (London: Routledge, 1996), p. 85.

29 See especially I. Chambers, *Urban Rhythms* (London: Macmillan, 1985), pp. 24–8.

30 K. Tynan, 'Look Back in Anger' (review), op. cit., p. 131.

31 K. Tynan, 'The Angry Young Movement', op. cit., p. 193.

32 See especially H. Richie, *Success Stories* (London: Faber, 1988).

33 J. Nuttall, *Bomb Culture* (London: Paladin, 1968), p. 45.

34 H. Greer, *Mud Pie: The CND Story* (London: Max Parrish, 1964), p. 31.

35 H. Rees, *14:24: British Youth Culture* (London: The Conran Foundation, 1986), p. 18.

36 L. Alloway, 'The Arts and the Mass Media', *Architectural Design*, Feb. 1958, pp. 34–5, in C. Harrison and P. Wood (ed.), *Art in Theory, 1900–90* (Oxford: Blackwell, 1992), p. 701 and p. 703.

37 For a detailed survey see M. Garlake, *New Art New World: British Art in Post-War Society* (New Haven, CT: Yale University Press, 1998).

38 See especially A. Massey, *The Independent Group: Modernism and Mass Culture in Britain, 1945–59* (Manchester: Manchester University Press, 1995), pp. 33–61.

39 E. Paolozzi, 'The Metamorphosis of Everyday Things', in H. B. Chipp (ed.), *Theories of Modern Art: A Source Book by Artists and Critics* (Berkeley and Los Angeles: University of California, 1969), pp. 616–17.

40 Ibid., p. 95.

41 Roger Hilton quoted in F. Spalding, op. cit., p. 172.

42 D. Sylvester, 'Pollock', op. cit., p. 63.

43 See for example J. Berger, 'The difficulty of being an artist', *Permanent Red: Essays on Seeing* (London: Methuen, 1960), pp. 31–57.

44 'A children's uprising' is the phrase used by Harry Hopkins, *The New Look: A Social History of the Forties and Fifties in Britain* (Boston, MA: Houghton Mufflin, 1964), p. 433.

45 F. Cordell, 'Gold Pan Alley', *Ark* 19, Spring 1957, in Kureishi and Savage, (eds), *The Faber Book of Pop* (London: Faber, 1995), pp. 72–7.

46 G. Melly, *Revolt into Style: The Pop Arts in Britain* (Harmondsworth: Penguin, 1972), pp. 25–8. See also F. Newton, *The Jazz Scene* (Harmondsworth: Penguin, 1961).

47 G. Melly, op. cit., p. 32.

48 A. Monro, *The Democratic Muse: Folk Music Revival in Scotland* (Aberdeen: Scottish Cultural Press, 1996), p. 33.

49 Ibid., p. 31.

50 T. Bacon, *London Live* (London: Balafon, 1999), p. 36.

51 See C. McDevitt, *Skiffle: the Definitive Inside Story* (London: Robson, 1997).

52 W. Mankowitz, *Make Me An Offer Expresso Bongo and Other Stories* (London: Hutchinson Educational, 1961), p. 73.

53 See R. Hoggart, *The Uses of Literacy* (London: Chatto and Windus, 1957).

54 L. Anderson, 'Get Out and Push', in T. Maschler (ed.), *Declaration* (London: MacGibbon and Kee, 1957), p. 160; p. 163.

55 S. Harper, 'Bonnie Prince Charlie Revisited: British Costume Drama in the 1950s' in R. Murphy, (ed.), *The British Cinema Book* (London: BFI, 1997), p. 134.

56 F. Manders, *Cinemas of Newcastle* (Newcastle upon Tyne: City Libraries and Arts, 1991), p. 18.

57 See especially P. Hutchins, ' "We're all Martians Now": British SF Invasion Fantasies of the 1950s and 1960s', in I. Q. Hunter (ed.), *British Science Fiction Cinema* (London: Routledge, 1999), pp. 33–8.

58 C. Barr, *Ealing Studios* (Cameron and Tayleur/David and Charles, 1977 (revised edn 1993), pp. 171–2. See also Aldgate and Richards, *Best of British: Cinema and Society from 1930 to the Present* (London: I B. Tauris, 1999), pp. 149–65.

59 *Free Cinema 1 Programme*, 6–8 February 1956; at: www.bfi.org.uk/features/ freecinema; accessed 23 September 2004.

60 E. Hedling, *Lindsay Anderson: Maverick Film-maker* (London: Cassell, 1998), p. 43.

61 G. Lambert, 'Free Cinema', *Sight and Sound*, Spring 1956, pp. 173–7. At www.bfi.org/features/freecinema; accessed 23 September 2004; R. Arnheim, 'Free Cinema II', *Film Culture* 2, February 1958, p. 11. Quoted in E. Hedling, op. cit., p. 43.

62 See, for example, P. Stead, 'I'm All Right Jack', *History Today*, January 1996, pp. 49–54.

63 Val Guest in B. McFarlane, *An Autobiography of British Cinema as Told by the Filmmakers and Actors Who Made it* (London: Methuen, 1997), p. 257.

64 *Films and Filming*, November 1959, p. 5, quoted in A. Spicer, 'Male Stars, Masculinity and British Cinema, 1945–60', R. Murphy, op. cit., p. 151.

Notes to Chapter 4

1 T. Nairn, *The Break-Up of Britain: Crisis and Neo-Nationalism* (London: NLB, 1977), pp. 13–14.

2 On the UK and EEC (Common Market) votes see 'Referendums of 1973 and 1975', Ark Northern Ireland Social and Political Archive, http://www.ark.co.uk/elections/fref70s.htm; accessed 9 November 2004.

3 Quoted in N. Richardson, *Life in Britain in the 1960s* (London: Batsford, 1986), p. 26.

4 B. Abel-Smith and P. Townsend, *The Poor and the Poorest* (London: Occasional Papers on Social Administration no. 17, 1965), p. 65. Townsend's great achievement is *Poverty in the United Kingdom: A Survey of Household Resources and Standards of Living* (Harmondsworth: Penguin, 1979).

5 A. Lynford, *Illustrated London News*, 3 December 1966, quoted in Richardson, op. cit., p. 14.

6 M. Glendenning (ed.) *Rebuilding Scotland: The Postwar Vision, 1945–65* (East Linton: Tuckwell, 1997), pp. 22–3.

7 C. Harvie, *No Gods and Precious Few Heroes: Scotland Since 1914* (Edinburgh: Edinburgh University Press, 1993), pp. 149–50.

8 H. Hazel (ed.) The Orcadian *Book of the Twentieth Century* (Kirkwall: Orcadian, 2000), p. 251.

9 On 7:84 and John McGrath see http://www.784theatre.com; accessed 11 November 2004.

10 Quoted in M. Billington, 'John McGrath', *The Guardian*, 24 January 2002. http://books.guardian.co.uk; accessed 11 November 2004.

11 I am indebted here to T. C. Smout for his provocative essay on 'Patterns of Culture', op. cit., pp. 261–81.

12 See for example, 'Dawn of the Oil Age', in H. Hazel, op. cit., pp. 290–2.

13 W. W. Knox, *Industrial Nation: Work, Culture and Society in Scotland, 1800 to the Present* (Edinburgh: Edinburgh University Press, 1999), pp. 254–6.

14 N. Ascherson, *Stone Voices: TheSearch for Scotland* (London: Granta, 2003), p. 105.

15 Ibid., pp. 105–6.

16 D. Murphy, *A Place Apart* (Harmondsworth: Penguin, 1978), p. 11.

17 Here I mostly follow Murphy's usage, but see below for further comment on place-names.

18 Ibid., p. 71.

19 B. Lacy, *Siege City: The Story of Derry and Londonderry* (Belfast: Blackstaff, 1990), pp. 246–7.

20 Ibid., p. 269.

21 Murphy, op. cit., pp. 75–6.

22 J. C. Beckett, *Annual Register* (1969) in S. Wichert, *Northern Ireland Since 1945* (London: Longman, 1998), p. 107.

23 S. Bruce, *The Edge of the Union: the Ulster Loyalist Political Vision* (Oxford: Oxford University Press, 1994), pp. 19–21.

24 R. G. Crawford, *Loyal to King Billy: A Portrait of the Ulster Protestants* (London: Charles Hurst, 1987), p. 11.

25 Bruce, op. cit., p. 30; N. Douglas, 'Political Structures, Social Intercourse and Identity Change in Northern Ireland', in B. Graham, (ed.), *In Search of Ireland: A Cultural Geography* (London: Routledge, 1997), p. 160.

26 B. Walker, *Dancing to History's Tune* (Belfast: Queen's University, 1996), pp. 82–4.

27 N. Douglas, op. cit., pp. 166–8.

28 For an account of the tensions within Northern Irish society at this time see, for example, J. and J. Harbinson (eds), *A Society Under Stress* (Shepton Mallet: Open Books, 1980), and E. Moxton-Browne, *Nation, Class and Creed in Northern Ireland* (Aldershot: Gower, 1983).

29 'Referendums of 1973 and 1975', op. cit.

30 http://www.geographyinaction.co.uk/Townlands/pnameschange.html; accessed 9 November 2004. I am indebted to this absorbing website for the list of Townland names, and for much of the placenames information presented here.

31 D. Jones, *The Sleeping Lord and Other Fragments* (New York: Chilmark, 1974), p. 96. See also T. Godwin Phelps, 'David Jones's "The Hunt" and "The Sleeping Lord": The Once and Future Wales', *Poetry Wales* 17(4), Spring 1982, pp. 64–71.

32 T. Nairn, op. cit., p. 208.

33 G. A. Williams, *When Was Wales? A History of the Welsh* (Harmondsworth: Penguin, 1991), p. 291.

34 D. Gareth Evans, *A History of Wales, 1906–2000* (Cardiff: University of Wales, 2000), p. 192.

35 J. Davies, *A History of Wales* (Harmondsworth: Penguin, 1994), pp. 529–31.

36 D. Gareth Evans, op. cit., p. 153.

37 H. Francis and D. Smith, op. cit., p. 454 and p. 456.

38 J. Davies, op. cit., p. 631.

39 D. Gareth Evans, op. cit., p. 199; p. 197.

40 D. Beddoe, *Out of the Shadows: A History of Women in Twentieth-Century Wales* (Cardiff: University of Wales, 2000), p. 148; C. Rosser and C. Harris, *The Family and Social Change: A Study of Family and Kinship in a South Wales Town* (London: Routledge and Kegan Paul, 1965).

41 D. Beddoe, op. cit., pp. 147–9.

42 J. Davies, op. cit., p. 671.

43 F. J. Osborn and A. Whittaker, *New Towns: Their Origins, Achievements and Progress* (London: Leonard Hill, 1977), p. 382.

44 Ibid., p. 390.

45 NUM (S. Wales Area) *Annual Conference President's Address* (1976), in H. Francis and D. Smith, op. cit., p. 481.

46 P. Townsend, op. cit., p. 333.

47 G. A. Williams, op. cit., p. 295.

48 A. Palmer, *The East End: Four Centuries of London Life* (London: John Murray, 2000), p. 158.

49 T. Hughes, *Remains of Elmet* (London: Faber, 1979), p. 8. See also M. Strathern, *Kinship at the Core: an Anthropology of Elmdon, a Village in North-East Essex in the Nineteen-sixties* (Cambridge: Cambridge University Press, 1981).

50 R. Fisher, *Poems, 1955–1987* (Oxford: Oxford University Press, 1988), p. 20.

51 A. Sutcliffe, 'The "Midland Metropolis": Birmingham 1890–1980', in G. Gordon (ed.), op. cit., pp. 33–4.

52 J. Brown, *The Un-Melting Pot* (London: Macmillan, 1970), p. 20.

53 'Joy Hendry – Health Visitor', *People's Autobiography of Hackney*, vol. 2 (London: Centreprise, n.d.), p. 72.

54 A. Palmer, op. cit., pp. 157–8.

55 People's Autobiography of Hackney, *The Island: the Life and Death of an East End Community, 1870–1970* (London: Centreprise, n.d.), p. 71.

56 J. Raban, *Soft City* (London: Collins Harville, 1988), p. 190.

57 A. Sutcliffe, op. cit., p. 33.

58 D. Deakin (ed.), *Wythenshawe: The Story of a Garden City*, vol. 2: *1926–84* (Manchester: Northern Civic Society, 1984), pp. 175–205.

59 A. Palmer, op. cit., pp. 158–60.

60 Ibid., p. 161.

61 P. Aughton, *Bristol: A People's History* (Lancaster: Carnegie, 2000), pp. 243–5.

62 D. W. Thoms and T. Donnelly, 'Coventry's Industrial Economy, 1880–1980', in B. Lancaster and T. Mason (eds), *Life and Labour in a Twentieth Century City: The Experience of Coventry* (Coventry: University of Warwick, n.d.) pp. 37–8 and pp. 44–8.

63 R. Hudson and D. Sadler, *A Place Called Teesside: A Locality in a Global Economy* (Edinburgh: Edinburgh University Press for the University of Durham, 1994), pp. 3–4.

64 J. Raban, op. cit., p. 26.

Notes to Chapter 5

1 These figures, and the social situations they describe, appear in but are not confined to two films of the time. Tushingham plays Jo in *A Taste of Honey* (T. Richardson, 1961) and Christie plays Diana in *Darling* (John Schlesinger, 1965).

2 A. Adburgham, 'Mary Quant', *Guardian*, 10 October 1967, in R. Connolly (ed.), *In the Sixties* (London: Pavilion, 1995), pp. 164–9.

3 A. Carter, 'Notes for a Theory of Sixties Style', in Savage and Kureishi, (eds), *The Faber Book of Pop* (London: Faber, 1995), pp. 316–17.

4 Ibid., p. 320.

5 J. Crosby, 'London, the Most Exciting City in the World', *Weekend Telegraph*, 16 April 1965, in R. Connolly, op. cit., p. 78.

6 See H. Gavron, *The Captive Housewife: Conflicts of Housebound Mothers* (London: Routledge and Kegan Paul, 1966), and G. Greer, *The Female Eunuch* (London: MacGibbon and Kee, 1970).

7 *Hansard*, 741 (1966–7), p. 946. Quoted in M. Peplar, *Family Matters* (London: Longmans, 2002), pp. 36–7. See also M. Wynn, *Fatherless Families* (London: Michael Joseph, 1964).

8 D. Coleman, 'Population and Family', in A. H. Halsey and J. Webb (eds.), *Twentieth-Century British Social Trends* (Basingstoke: Macmillan, 2000), p. 63.

9 J. Lewis, *Woman in Britain since 1945* (Oxford: Blackwell, 1992), pp. 44–6.

10 I. Kurtz, 'How do you plead, Mrs John Bull?', *Nova*, February 1968, in R. Connolly, op. cit., p. 154.

11 L. Heron, (ed.), *Truth, Dare or Promise: Girls Growing Up in the 1950s* (London: Virago, 1985), pp. 44–6.

12 N. Dunn, *Up the Junction* (London: Virago, 1988 [1963]), pp. 40–1.

13 C. Holmes, 'Hostile Images of Immigrants and Refugees in Nineteenth- and Twentieth-Century Britain' in J. and L. Lucassen (ed.) *Migration, Migration History, History* (Bern: Peter Lang, 1997), p. 326.

14 A. H. Halsey and J. Webb, op. cit., p. 160; p. 136.

15 B. Emecheta, *Second-Class Citizen* (London: Allison and Busby, 1974).

16 See, for example, P. Marnhan (ed.), *The Private Eye Story* (London: André Deutsch, 1982).

17 R. Perks, ' "You're Different, You're One of us": the Making of a British Asia', *Oral History*, XV (1987), p. 67.

18 M. and T. Phillips, *Windrush: The Irresistible Rise of Multi-Racial Britain* (London: HarperCollins, 1998), pp. 243–4.

19 R. Ramdin, *Reimaging Britain: 500 Years of Black and Asian History* (London: Pluto, 1999), pp. 274–5.

20 J. Anim-Addo, *Longest Journey: A History of Black Lewisham* (London: Deptford Forum, 1995), pp. 115–17.

21 C. Hamblett and J. Deverson, *Generation X* (London: Tandem, 1964), p. 35.

22 A. H. Halsey and J. Webb, op. cit., pp. 221–3.

23 M. Harrison, *Young Meteors: British Photojournalism, 1957–1965* (London: Jonathan Cape, 1998), p. 71.

24 Hamblett and Deverson, op. cit., p. 11.

25 Ibid., pp. 13–14.

26 On Trocchi see A. Campbell and T. Niels (ed.), *A Life in Pieces* (Edinburgh: Rebel Inc., 1997). A. Trocchi, *Cain's Book* (London: Calder and Boyars, 1966); *Young Adam* (London: Heinemann, 1961).

27 R. Neville, *Powerplay* (London: Paladin, 1971), p. 218.

28 Osgerby, *Youth in Britain since 1945* (Oxford: Blackwell, 1998), p. 11.

29 See, for example, J. Clarke, 'The Skinheads and the Magical Recovery of Community', in S. Hall and T. Jefferson (eds), *Resistance through Rituals* (London: Routledge, 1996), pp. 99–102.

30 R. Allen, *Skinhead* (1970) in *The Complete Richard Allen*, vol. 1 (Dunoon: S. T. Publishing, 1992), p. 14.

31 N. Knight, *Skinhead* (London: Omnibus, 1982), p. 11.

32 M. Harrison, op. cit., p. 58.

33 See, for example, 'Pop Art in Britain' in T. Osterwold, *Pop Art* (Koln: Taschen, 1991), pp. 63–81; and on Hamilton, pp. 211–15.

34 See especially N. Stangos (ed.), *David Hockney by David Hockney: My Early Years* (London: Thames and Hudson, 1988).

35 See, for example, A. Caro, *Five Sculptures by Anthony Caro* (London: Arts Council, 1982), pp. 7–10.

36 For Hamilton's account see R. Hamilton, *Collected Works 1953–1982* (London: Thames and Hudson, 1984), pp. 104–6.

37 DIAS, *Press Release* (London, 27 April 1966).

38 Quoted in DIAS, *Preliminary Report* (London: n.d.), p. 2.

39 On Latham see R. Hamilton, *John Latham: Early Works, 1954–72* (London: Lisson Gallery, 1987).

40 Quoted in B. Robertson, 'Introduction and Biographical Note', in B. Riley, *Paintings and Drawings* (London: Hayward Gallery, 1971), p. 7.

41 P. Johnson, 'The Menace of Beatleism', *New Statesman*, 28 February 1964, in H. Kureishi and J. Savage, op. cit., p. 215.

42 M. Figgis, 'Red, White and Blues, Director Interview', http://pbs.org/theblues/aboutfilms/figgisinterview.html; accessed 16 January 2005.

43 See, for example, C. Harper, *Dazzling Stranger: Bert Jansch and the British Folk Blues Revival* (London: Bloomsbury, 2000).

44 M. Watkinson and P. Anderson, *Crazy Diamond: Syd Barrett and the Dawn of Pink Floyd* (London: Omnibus, 1991) in T. Bacon, *London Live* (London: Balafon, 1991), p. 80.

45 J. Green, *Days in the Life: Voices from the English Underground, 1961–71* (London: Pimlico, 1998), p. 221.

46 See Mike Figgis, op. cit.

47 J. Wiener, *Come Together: John Lennon and His Time* (London: Faber, 2000), pp. 280–3.

48 C. S. Murray, *Crosstown Traffic: Jimi Hendrix and the Post-War Rock'n'Roll Revolution* (New York: St Martin's Press, 1990), pp. 40–2.

49 J. Green, op. cit., p. 141.

50 B. McFarlane, *An Autobiography of British Cinema as Told by the Filmmakers and Actors Who Made It* (London: Methuen, 1997), p. 122.

51 On the origins and development of the British 'new wave' see, for example, J. Hill, *Sex, Class and Realism: British Cinema, 1956–63* (London: British Film Institute, 1986) and R. Murphy, *Sixties British Cinema* (London: British Film Institute, 1992).

52 See especially A. Higson, 'Space, Place, Spectacle: Landscape and Townscape in the "Kitchen Sink" Film', in A. Higson (ed.), *Dissolving Views: Key Writings on British Cinema* (London: Cassell, 1996), pp. 133–56.

53 S. Street, *British National Cinema* (London: Routledge, 1997), p. 141.

54 See I. Q. Hunter, 'The Day the Earth Caught Fire', in I. Q. Hunter, (ed.), *British Science Fiction Cinema* (London: Routledge, 1999), pp. 99–112.

55 T. Aldgate, 'Alfie', *History Today*, October 1996, p. 54.

56 C. Geraghty, 'Women and Sixties British Cinema: The Development of "Darling Girl" ', in R. Murphy (ed.), *The British Cinema Book*, pp. 158–9.

57 E. Hedling, *Lindsay Anderson: Maverick Film-maker* (London: Cassell, 1998), pp. 41–61 and 80–112.

58 See especially Aldgate and Richards, *Best of British: Cinema and Society from 1930 to the Present* (London: I. B. Tauris, 1999), pp. 203–18.

59 S. Street, op. cit., p. 141.

Notes to Chapter 6

1 In defence of the 1970s see N. Tiratsoo, ' "You've Never had it so Bad?" Britain in the 1970s', in N. Tiratsoo (ed.), *From Blitz to Blair* (London: Phoenix, 1998), pp. 163–90.

2 A. Carter, *The Passion of New Eve* (London: Virago, 1977); Jonathan Coe, *The Rotters' Club* (Harmondsworth: Penguin, 2001).

3 On Desai and Grunwick see, for example, R. Ramdin, *Reimaging Britain: 500 Years of Black and Asian History* (London: Pluto, 1999), pp. 220–3; on Asian women, work and trade unionism, A. Wilson, *Finding a Voice: Asian Women in Britain* (London: Virago, 1978).

4 Quoted in S. Rowbotham, *The Past Before Us: Feminism in Action since the 1960s* (Harmondsworth: Penguin, 1989), p. 231.

5 S. Bruley, *Women in Britain since 1900* (Basingstoke: Macmillan, 1999), pp. 158–60.

6 A. Oakley, *Housewife* (Harmondsworth: Penguin, 1976), p. 119. See also *The Sociology of Housework* (London: Martin Robertson, 1974) and *Women Confined: Towards a Sociology of Childbirth* (London: Martin Robertson, 1980).

7 A. Wier and E. Wilson quoted in S. Rowbotham, *The Past Before Us*, op. cit., p. 32.

8 J. Lewis, *Women in Britain Since 1945* (Oxford: Blackwell, 1992), pp. 87–8.

9 S. Rowbotham, *Century of Women* (Harmondsworth: Penguin, 1999), p. 431.

10 J. Lewis, op. cit., pp. 104–6.

11 A. Carter, 'Ups and Downs of the Babes in Bondage', *New Society*, 22 December 1977, in Kureishi and Savage, (eds), *The Faber Book of Pop* (London: Faber, 1995), pp. 509–14.

12 J. Anim-Addo, *Longest Journey: A History of Black Lewisham* (London: Deptford Forum, 1995), p. 124.

13 Ibid., p. 125.

14 K. Pryce, *Endless Pressure: A Study of West Indian Life-Styles in Bristol* (Harmondsworth: Penguin, 1979), p. 139.

15 B. Caesar and L. K. Johnson, 'Interview', *Critical Quarterly*, 38: 4, (Winter 1996), p. 96.

16 Ibid., p. 79.

17 Halsey and Webb (eds), *Twentieth-Century British Social Trends* (Basingstoke: Macmillan, 2000), p. 161.

18 Ibid., p. 254; R. Ramdin, op. cit., p. 244.

19 U. Sharma, *Rampal and His Family* (London: Collins, 1971), p. 179.

20 M. and T. Phillips, *Windrush: The Irresistible Rise of Multi-Racial Britain* (London: HarperCollins, 1998), pp. 20–1.

21 D. Widgery, *Beating Time: Riot'n'Race'n'Rock'n'Roll* (London: Chatto and Windus, 1986), p. 26.

22 Pryce, op. cit., p. 107.

23 M. Nissel, 'Families and Social Change since the Second World War', in R. N. Rapport, et al. (ed.) *Families in Britain* (London: Routledge and Kegan Paul, 1982), p. 97.

24 Ibid., p. 100.

25 'Roger Mills' in People's Autobiography of Hackney, *Working Lives*, vol. 2: *1945–77* (London: Centerprise, 1977), p. 222.

26 J. G. Ballard, 'Introduction', *Crash* (London: Vintage, 1995), p. 4.

27 A. De la Haye and C. Dingwall, *Surfers, Soulies, Skinheads and Skaters* (London: Victoria and Albert Museum, 1996), p. 78.

28 J. Savage, *England's Dreaming* (London: Faber, 1991) p. 107.

29 B. Osgerby, *Youth in Britain Since 1945* (Oxford: Blackwell, 1998), pp. 108–9.

30 J. Savage, *England's Dreaming*, p. 112. See also C. Coon, *1988: The New Wave Punk Rock Explosion* (London: Omnibus, 1977).

31 A. Walker, P. Ormerod and L. Whitty, *Abandoning Social Priorities: The Impacts of Cuts in Social Spending on the Living Standards of Poor Families* (London: Child Poverty Action Group, 1979), p. 27.

32 Donald Judd, quoted in M. Raeburn et al., *Vision: Fifty Years of British Creativity* (London: Thames and Hudson, 1999), p. 104. See also L. R. Lippard, *Six Years: The Dematerialization of the Art Object from 1966 to 1972* (Berkeley: University of California Press, 1997).

33 B. Barker, 'An Introductory Note', in *Robert Barry, Victor Burgin, Hamish Fulton, Gilbert and George, Hans Haacke, John Hilliard, Kosuth/Charlesworth, David Tremlett/Lawrence Weiner* (Edinburgh: Scottish Arts Council/Fruit Market Gallery, 1976), p. 3.

34 Ibid., n.p.. See also, for example, V. Burgin, *Some Cities* (London: Reaktion, 1996).

35 M. Gooding, *Bruce McLean* (Oxford: Phaidon, 1990), pp. 63–7.

36 See, for example, B. McLean, *Berlin/London* (London: Whitechapel, 1983).

37 See especially T. Cragg, *Sculpture, 1975–90* (Newport: Harbour Art Museum, 1990).

38 R. Long, 'Five Six Pick Up Sticks', in K. Stiles and P. Selz (eds), *Theories and Documents of Contemporary Art* (California: University of California Press, 1996), p. 565.

39 R. Araeen, 'From Innovation to Deconstruction: My Own Story', at http://www.undo.net/cgi-bin/openframe.pl?x=/Pinto/Eng/eraeen.htm; accessed 17 February 2005. See also R. Araeen, *From Modernism to Postmodernism: A Retrospective, 1959–87* (Birmingham: Ikon Gallery, 1988).

40 M. Kelly, *Post-Partum Document* (London: University of California, 1999).

41 R. Coleman, 'A star is born', *Melody Maker*, 15 July 1972, in T. Thomson and D. Gutman (eds), *The Bowie Companion* (London: Sidgwick and Jackson, 1995), p. 79.

42 See S. Frith, 'Only Dancing: David Bowie Flirts with the Issues', in A. McRobbie, *Zoot Suits and Second-Hand Dresses: An Anthology of Fashion and Music* (Basingstoke: Macmillan, 1989), pp. 132–40.

43 C. Coon, 'Rock Revolution' in H. Kureishi and J. Savage, (eds), *Faber Book of Pop* (London: Faber, 1995), p. 491.

44 D. Laing, 'The Grain of Punk: an Analysis of the Lyrics', in A. McRobbie, op. cit., p. 93.

45 M. E. Smith, *The Fall Lyrics* (Berlin: Lough, 1985), p. 40.

46 See also I. Chambers, *Urban Rhythms* (Basingstoke: Macmillan, 1985), pp. 175–85.

47 On the wider significance of punk see R. Sabin (ed), *Punk Rock: So What? The Cultural Legacy of Punk* (London: Routledge, 1999).

48 See also L. K. Johnson, *Tidings an' Times* (Newcastle upon Tyne: Bloodaxe and LKJ Music, 1991). On the punk–reggae connection, S. Jones, *Black Culture, White Youth: The Reggae Tradition from JA to UK* (Basingstoke: Macmillan, 1988), pp. 78–118.

49 A. Marks, 'Young, Gifted and Black: Afro-American and Afro-Caribbean Music in Britain 1963–88', in P. Oliver (ed.), *Black Music in Britain* (Milton Keynes: Open University, 1990), pp. 110–12.

50 S. Street, *British National Cinema* (London: Routledge, 1997), p. 20; p. 93.

51 Ibid., p. 21.

52 See especially K. Russell, *A British Picture: An Autobiography* (London: Heinemann, 1989).

53 A. Walker, *National Heroes: British Cinema of the Seventies and Eighties* (London: Harrap, 1985), p. 84.

54 B. McFarlane, *An Autobiography of British Cinema as Told by the Filmmakers and Actors Who Made It* (London: Methuen, 1997), p. 505.

55 P. Strick and P. Houston, 'Interview with Stanley Kubrick', *Sight and Sound*, Spring 1972, p. 63. Quoted in J. Chapman, ' "A bit of the old ultra-violence": *A Clockwork Orange*', in I. Q. Hunter (ed.), *British Science Fiction Cinema* (London: Routledge, 1999), pp. 128–37.

56 See 'Mike Hodges discusses *Get Carter* with the NFT audience, 23 September 1997', in S. Chibnall and R. Murphy (eds), *British Crime Cinema* (London: Routledge, 1999), pp. 117–22.

57 D. Sanjek, 'Twilight of the Monsters: the English Horror Film, 1968–75', in W. W. Dixon (ed.), *Re-Viewing British Cinema, 1900–1992: Essays and Interviews* (Albany: SUNY, 1994), pp. 200–3.

58 On Roeg's more general themes see S. Salmolke, *Nicholas Roeg: Film by Film* (London: McFarland, 1993).

59 B. McFarlane, op. cit., p. 490.

60 On Leigh see M. Coveney, *The World According to Mike Leigh* (London: HarperCollins, 1997). On Jarman, S. Dillon, *Derek Jarman and Lyric Film* (Austin: University of Texas, 2004).

Notes to Chapter 7

1 I. Jack, *Before the Oil Ran Out: Britain, 1977–86* (London: Secker and Warburg, 1987), p. 2.

2 C. Tóibín, *The Sign of the Cross: Travels in Catholic Europe* (London: Vintage, 1995), p. 174.

3 W. W. Knox, *Industrial Nation: Work, Culture and Society in Scotland 1800–present* (Edinburgh: Edinburgh University Press, 1999), p. 254; J. Mitchell, *Conservatives and the Union* (Edinburgh: Edinburgh University Press, 1990), pp. 103–4.

4 A. M. Scott, *Modern Dundee: Life in the City Since World War Two* (Derby: Breedon, 2002), pp. 129–30.

5 N. Schoon, *The Chosen City* (London: Spon, 2001), p. 71.

6 A. Marr, *The Battle for Scotland* (Harmondsworth: Penguin, 1995), p. 172.

7 Knox, op. cit., p. 256.

8 Scott, op. cit., p. 130.

9 F. O'Toole, 'Imagining Scotland', *Granta*, 56 (Winter 1996), p. 63.

10 K. Wright, *The People Say Yes: The Making of Scotland's Parliament* (Glendaruel: Argyll, 1997), pp. 140–1. Quoted in Devine, *The Scottish Nation, 1700–2000* (Harmondsworth: Penguin, 1999), pp. 606–7.

11 Marr, op. cit., pp. 178–9.

12 N. Danziger, *Danziger's Britain: A Journey to the Edge* (London: HarperCollins, 1996), pp. 123–4.

13 L. Musgrave, 'High Noon for a High-rise Ideal'; and B. Edwards, 'Great Ocean Liners that Ran Aground', *Independent*, 8 September 1993, p. 13.

14 Devine, op. cit., p. 598.

15 D. G. Thomson, 'Attitudes to Linguistic Change in Gaelic Scotland', in M. M. Parry, W. V. Davies and R. A. M. Temple (eds), *The Changing Voices of Europe* (Cardiff: University Press/MHRA, 1994), p. 128.

16 W. P. L. Thomson, *History of Orkney* (Edinburgh: Mercat, 1987), p. 258.

17 Marr, op. cit., p. 173.

18 J. Kelman, *Some Recent Attacks: Essays Cultural and Political* (Sterling: AK, 1992), p. 81.

19 E. Longley, 'From Cathleen to Anorexia: the Breakdown of Irelands', in *The Living Stream: Literature and Revisionism in Ireland* (Newcastle: Bloodaxe, 1994), p. 194.

20 S. Belfrage, *The Crack: A Belfast Year* (London: André Deutsch, 1987), p. 1.

21 C. Tóibín, *Bad Blood: A Walk Along the Irish Border* (London: Vintage, 1994), p. 83.

22 A. Marwick, *British Society since 1945* (Harmondsworth: Penguin, 2003), p. 258; S. Wichert, *Northern Ireland Since 1945* (London: Longman, 1998), p. 180.

23 'Vision for the Future of Agri-Food Industry: an Economic Note on the Northern Ireland Agri-food Industry' at: www.dardni.gov.uk/file/vision/econ.doc; accessed 15 March 2005.

24 D. Hamilton, 'Peripherality and the Political Economy of Northern Ireland', in P. Shirlow (ed.), *Development Ireland: Contemporary Issues* (London: Pluto, 1995), pp. 27–30.

25 F. W. Boal, *Shaping a City: Belfast in the Late Twentieth Century* (Belfast: Queen's University Press, 1995), p. 50.

26 J. Derby, 'Approaches to Cultural Diversity in Northern Ireland', in M. Crozier and R. Froggatt (eds), *Cultural Tradition in Northern Ireland* (Belfast: Queen's University Press, 1995), p. 50.

27 J. Pitman, 'A Battle to be Cheerful, 25 years after Troops Took to Divided Streets', *The Times*, 13 August 1994, p. 7.

28 D. Childs, *Britain Since 1939* (Basingstoke: Palgrave, 2002), pp. 295–7.

29 T. Paulin, 'Diary', *London Review of Books*, 24 August 1995, p. 24.

30 R. Kearney, *Postnationalist Ireland* (London: Routledge, 1997), p. 101.

31 J. Hewitt, *Regionalism: The Last Chance*, quoted in R. Kearney, op. cit., p. 105. See also T. Clyde (ed.), *Ancestral Voices: The Selected Prose of John Hewitt* (Belfast: Blackstaff, 1987).

32 Longley, op. cit., p. 195.

33 B. Walker, *Dancing to History's Tune* (Belfast: Queen's University Press, 1996), pp. 123–4.

34 B. McIvor, *Hope Deferred: Experiences of an Irish Unionist* (Belfast: Blackstaff, 1998), p. 153.

35 Quoted in Walker, op. cit., p. 125.

36 G. A. Williams, *When was Wales?* (London: Black Raven, 1985), p. 303.

37 J. Davies, *A History of Wales* (Harmondsworth: Penguin, 1994), p. 681.

38 Quoted in K. O. Morgan, 'Wales since 1945: Political Society', in T. Hibbert and G. E. Jones (eds), *Post-War Wales* (Cardiff: University of Wales Press, 1995), p. 12.

39 K. G. Robbins, *Eclipse of a Great Power: Modern Britain, 1870–1992* (London: Longman, 1994), pp. 387–8.

40 Davies, op. cit., p. 681

41 E. Jenkins, *Through the Decades: The History of Swansea and South West Wales as Told by its Own People* (Swansea: People in Print, 1994), p. 53; P. Cope et al., *Chasing the Dragon: Creative Community Responses to the Crisis in the South Wales Coalfield* (n.p: ERGO2, 1997), p. 7.

42 M. O'Neill, 'Family and Social Change in an Urban Street Community', in C. A. Davies and S. Jones (eds), *Welsh Community: New Ethnographic Perspectives* (Cardiff: University Press, 2003), p. 85. See also C. Rosser and C. C. Harris, *The Family and Social Change: A Study of Family and Kinship in a South Wales Town* (London: Routledge and Kegan Paul, 1965).

43 Ibid., pp. 90–2.

44 Ibid., p. 94.

45 G. Day, *Making Sense of Wales: A Sociological Perspective* (Cardiff: University of Wales Press, 2002), pp. 160–1.

46 E. James, 'Research on Your Own Doorstep: Welsh Rural Communities and the Perceived Effects of In-migration', in Davies and Jones, op. cit., p. 50.

47 Ibid., p. 55.

48 Ibid., p. 58–61.

49 B. L. Jones, 'The poetry of speech in a lesser used language', in M. M. Parry, W. V. Davies and R. A. M. Temple (eds), *The Changing Voices of Europe* (Cardiff: University of Wales/MHRA, 1994), p. 264.

50 T. Robin Chapman, *Encounters with Wales* (Llandysul, Dyfed: Gomer, 1995), p. 31.

51 C. Fowler, 'Welsh National Identity and the British Political Process', in C. Caunce et al. (ed.), *Relocating Britishness* (Manchester: Manchester University Press, 2004), p. 210.

52 *Urban Trends in England: Evidence from the 1991 Census* (London: ODPM Urban Research Summary no. 8, 1996), http://odpm.gov.uk; accessed 18 March 2005.

53 P. York and C. Jennings, *Peter York's Eighties* (London: BBC, 1995), p. 111.

54 Danziger, op. cit., pp. 67–8.

55 A. Walker and C. Walker, *Divided Britain* (London: CPGA, 1997), pp. 2–5.

56 R. Weight, *Patriots: National Identity in Britain, 1940–2000* (London: Macmillan, 2002), p. 592; Joseph Rowntree Foundation, 'Housing Conditions in 2000', http://jrf.org.uk; Office of the Deputy Prime Minister, *Your Region, Your Choice* (London: ODPM, 2002) http://odpm.gov.uk; both accessed 18 March 2005.

57 T. Blackwell and J. Seabrook, *Talking Work: An Oral History* (London: Faber, 1996), p. 99.

58 M. Fraser, 'Architecture's Urban Shine and Brutal Reality', in J. Kerr and A. Gibson (eds), *London: From Punk to Blair* (London: Reaktion, 2003), pp. 157–9.

59 I. Sinclair, *Lights Out for the Territory* (London: Granta, 1997), p. 3.

60 H. Beynon, R. Hudson and D. Sadler, *A Place Called Teesside: A Locality in a Global Economy* (Edinburgh: Edinburgh University Press, for the University of Durham, 1994), pp. 1–3.

61 G. L. Dodds, *A History of Sunderland* (Sunderland: Albion, 2001), p. 144.

62 M. Hudson, *Coming Back Brockens: A Year in a Mining Village* (London: Jonathan Cape, 1994), p. 71.

63 P. Driver, *Manchester Pieces* (London: Picador, 1996), p. 18.

64 G. Harvey, *The Killing of the Countryside* (London: Jonathan Cape, 1997); and D.Craig's review, 'Among Flayed Hills', *London Review of Books*, 8 May 1997, pp. 3–4.

65 R. Page, *The Decline of an English Village* (Shedfield: Ashford, 1989), p. 186.

66 Ibid., pp. 182–4.
67 J. Martin, *The Development of Modern Agriculture: British Farming Since 1931* (Basingstoke: Macmillan, 2000), pp. 199–200.
68 P. Addison, *The Road to 1945* (revised edn, London: Pimlico, 1994), p. 280.
69 J. Kerr, 'Blowdown: The Rise and Fall of London's Towerblocks', in Kerr and Gibson, op. cit., p. 190.
70 J. Seabrook, 'An English Exile', *Granta*, 56 (Winter 1996), p. 189.

Notes to Chapter 8

1 C. Churchill, *Top Girls* (London: Methuen, 1982). See also A. H. Kritzer, *The Plays of Caryl Churchill* (London: Macmillan, 1991) pp. 138–47.
2 C. Cook and J. Stevenson, *Britain since 1945*, 2nd edition (Harlow: Pearson, 2000), pp. 142–3.
3 See for example, C. Blackwood, *On the Perimeter* (London: Heinemann, 1984), and J. Keating, *Counting the Cost: a family in the Miners' Strike* (Barnsley: Warncliffe, 1991).
4 S. Bruley, *Women in Britain since 1900* (London: Macmillan, 1999), p. 161.
5 *Women in the Eighties* (Waltham Cross: Tesco, 1982), p. 14.
6 C. Briar, *Working for Women? Gendered Work and Welfare Policies in Twentieth-Century Britain* (London: UCL, 1997), p. 115.
7 S. Westwood, *All Day, Every Day: Factory and Family in the Making of Women's Lives* (London: Pluto, 1984), p. 62.
8 Ibid., pp. 58–60.
9 M. Peplar, *Family Matters: A History of Ideas about the Family since 1945* (London: Longmans, 2002), p. 141; Briar, op. cit., p. 126.
10 Kritzer, op. cit., pp. 162–70.
11 See 'The New Empire within Britain' and 'Outside the Whale', in S. Rushdie, *Imaginary Homelands: Essays and Criticism, 1981–91* (London: Granta, 1991), pp. 129–38, 87–101.
12 R. Ramdin, *Reimaging Britain: 500 years of Black and Asian History* (London: Pluto, 1999), p. 231.
13 B. Bryan, S. Dadzie and S. Scarfe, *The Heart of Race: Black Women's Lives in Britain* (London: Virago, 1985), p. 48.
14 J. Anim-Addo, *Longest Journey: A History of Black Lewisham* (London: Deptford Forum, 1995), pp. 135–9; Phillips and Phillips, op. cit., pp. 324–5.
15 Halsey and Webb (eds), *Twentieth-Century British Social Trends* (Basingstoke, Macmillan, 2000), p. 131.
16 Ibid., p. 137; K. Sword, *Identity in Flux: The Polish Community in Britain* (London: SSEES Occasional Papers No 36, 1996), pp. 50–3.
17 S. Rushdie and The London Consortium, 'Interview about *The Satanic Verses*', *Critical Quarterly*, 38, 2, Summer 1996, p. 65.
18 See especially 'The Rushdie Affair: Dialogue of the Deaf', in D. Hiro, *Black British, White British* (London: Paladin, 1992), pp. 182–93; and L. Appignanesi and S. Maitland, eds, *The Rushdie File* (London: Fourth Estate, 1989).
19 Lord Scarman, *The Brixton Disorders 10–12 April 1981* (London: HMSO, 1981) quoted in J. Beynon (ed.) *Scarman and After* (Oxford: Pergamon, 1984), p. 165.
20 J. Green, *Them: Voices from the Immigrant Community in Contemporary Britain* (London: Secker and Warburg, 1990), pp. 101–2.
21 *i-D*, 1, August 1980. Quoted at http://www.i-dmagazine.com; accessed 26 March 2005.
22 R. Brooks, 'Blitz Culture', *ZG* #1, 1980, in H. Kureishi and J. Savage, *The Faber Book of Pop* (London: Faber, 1995), p 535.

23 D. Rimmer, *Like Punk Never Happened: Culture Club and the New Pop* (London: Faber, 1985), p. 13.

24 M. H. Banks and P. Ullah, *Youth Unemployment in the 1980s: Its Psychological Effects* (Beckenham: Croom Helm, 1988), p. 9; Osgerby, *Youth in Britain since 1945* (Oxford: Blackwell, 1998), p. 156.

25 Banks and Ullah, op. cit., p. 153.

26 See especially G. McKay, *Senseless Acts of Beauty: Cultures of Resistance Since the Sixties* (London: Verso, 1996), and F. Earle *A Time to Travel? An Introduction to Britain's Newer Travellers* (Lyme Regis: Enabler, 1994).

27 C. J. Stone, *Fierce Dancing: Adventures in the Underground* (London: Faber, 1996), p. 160.

28 *Guardian* editorial quoted in F. Earle et al., op. cit., p. 24.

29 H. Rees, *14:24: British Youth Culture* (London: the Conran Foundation, 1984), p. 20; A. De la Haye, *The Cutting Edge: 50 Years of British Fashion* (London: Victoria and Albert Museum, 1997), p. 30.

30 Osgerby, op. cit., pp. 160–2.

31 Quoted in S. Redhead, 'The Politics of Ecstasy', in S. Redhead (ed.), *Rave Off: Politics and Deviance in Contemporary Youth Culture* (Aldershot: Avebury, 1993), p. 11.

32 D. Jarman, *The Last of England* (London: Vintage, 1987), p. 47.

33 See, for example, T. Friedman and A. Goldsworthy, *Hand to Earth: Andy Goldsworthy – Sculpture, 1976–90* (London: Thames and Hudson, 2004); and W. J. T. Mitchell (ed.), *Antony Gormley* (London: Phaidon, 2000).

34 E. Lucie-Smith, *Visual Arts In the Twentieth Century* (London: Laurence King, 1996), p. 43.

35 J. Thompson, *Richard Deacon* (London: Phaidon, 1995); S. Houshiary, *Isthmus* (London: British Council, 1995); G. Celant, *Anish Kapoor* (London: Thames and Hudson, 1996).

36 Lynne Cooke quoted in V. Button, *The Turner Prize: Twenty Years* (London: Tate, 2003), p. 56

37 G. Celant, op. cit., p. 12.

38 For an overview of themes and connections see C. Marshall (ed.), *Breaking the Mould: British Art of the 1980s and 1990s* (London: Lund Humphries, 1997).

39 See M. M. Lisboa, *Paula Rego's Map of Memory: National and Sexual Politics* (Aldershot: Ashgate, 2003).

40 See, for example, H. Chadwick, *Enfleshings* (London: Secker and Warburg, 1989).

41 Quoted in 'Helen Chadwick 1953–1996' at: http://www.portfolio.mvm.edu.ac.uk; accessed 26 March 2005.

42 'Interview with Chris Blackford' at: http://btinternet.com/~rubberneck/chadwick.html; accessed 26 March 2005.

43 S. Rushdie and the London Consortium, op. cit., p. 65.

44 C. J. Stone, op. cit., p. 11.

45 S. Lavers, *Adam and the Ants: 'Kings'* (London: Mirror, 1981), p. 4.

46 J. Savage, 'Androgyny: Confused Chromosomes and Camp Followers', *Time Travel: Pop, Media and Sexuality, 1976–96* (London: Chatto and Windus, 1996), p. 158.

47 D. Hill, *Designer Boys and Material Girls: Manufacturing the '80s Pop Dream* (Poole: Blandford, 1986), p. 8.

48 Ibid., p. 9.

49 See interview with Bragg in M. Roach, *The Right to Imagination: An Essential Collection of Candid Interviews with Top UK Alternative Songwriters* (London: Independent Music, 1994), pp. 55–71.

50 See especially M. Collin and J. Godfrey, *Altered State: the Story of Ecstasy Culture and Acid House* (London: Serpent's Tail, 1998).

51 J. Savage, 'Flaring Up: The Stone Roses at Spike Island', *Time Travel*, p. 265.

52 'Salman Rushdie talks with Terry Gilliam' at http://www.believermag.com/issues/march_2003/rushdie_gilliam.php; accessed 29 March 2005.

53 S. Johnson, 'Charioteers and Ploughmen', in M. Auty and N. Roddick (eds.), *British Cinema Now* (London: BFI, 1985), p. 100.

54 For an opposing view of heritage cinema see A. Higson, 'Re-Presenting the National Past: Nostalgia and Pastiche in the Heritage Film', in L. Friedman (ed.), *British Cinema and Thatcherism* (London: UCL Press, 1993), pp. 109–29.

55 See especially Johnson, op. cit., pp. 105–10.

56 See, however, S. T. Barber, 'Insurmountable Difficulties and Moments of Ecstasy: Crossing Class, Ethnic and Sexual Barriers in the Films of Stephen Frears', in L. Friedman, op. cit., pp. 221–36.

57 On *Scandal* see A. Aldgate and J. Richards, *Best of British: Cinema and Society from 1930 to the Present* (London: I. B. Taurus, 1999), pp. 219–33.

58 See especially L. R. Williams, 'Dream Girls and Mechanic Panic: Dystopia and its Others in *Brazil* and *Nineteen Eighty-Four*', in I. Q. Hunter (ed.), *British Science Fiction Cinema* (London: Routledge, 1999), pp. 153–86.

59 See for example, J. Hill, 'Allegorising the Nation: British Gangster Films of the 1980s', in Chibnall and Murphy (eds), op. cit., pp. 160–71.

60 M. Walsh, 'Allegories of Thatcherism: The Films of Peter Greenaway', in L. Friedman, op. cit., p. 271.

61 Quoted in B. McFarlane, *An Autobiography of British Cinema as Told by the Film-makers and Actors Who Made It* (London: Methuen, 1997), p. 240.

Notes to Chapter 9

1 Quoted in M. Hornblower, 'Wot For? Why Not?' *Time*, 13 December 1993, p. 66.

2 S. Rowbotham, *A Century of Women*, pp. 575–6.

3 K. Figes, *Because of Her Sex: The Myth of Equality for Women in Britain* (London: Pan, 1994), pp. 7–8; p. 18.

4 R. Compton, *Women and Work in Modern Britain* (Oxford: Oxford University Press, 1997) p. 47; C. Briar, *Working for Woman? Gendered Work and Welfare Policies in Twentieth-Century Britain* (London: UCL, 1997), p. 131.

5 Briar, op. cit., p. 130; Bruley, *Women in Britain since 1900* (Basingstoke, Macmillan, 1999), p. 175.

6 S. Innes, *Making It Work: Women, Change and Challenge in the 1990s* (London: Chatto and Windus, 1995), pp. 51–2.

7 Ibid., p. 135; Peplar, *Family Matters A History of Ideas about the Family since 1945* (London: Longmans, 2002), p. 146.

8 Innes, op. cit., p. 265; S. Walby, *Gender Transformations* (London: Routledge, 1997), p. 1.

9 Walby, op. Cit., p. 9.

10 R. McKibbin, 'Mass-Observation at the Mall', in M. Merck (ed.), *After Diana: Irreverent Elegies* (London: Verso, 1998), p. 16.

11 B. Campbell, *Diana, Princess of Wales: How Sexual Politics Shook the Monarchy* (London: Women's Press, 1998), p. 4.

12 R. Norton-Taylor (ed.) *The Colour of Justice: The Stephen Lawrence Inquiry* (London: Oberon, 1999), pp. 5–6; p. 10.

13 See also M. Phillips, 'At Home in England', in O. Wambu (ed.), *Empire Windrush: Fifty Years of Writing about Black Britain* (London: Gollancz, 1998), pp. 426–31.

14 Ramdin, *Reimaging Britain: 500 Years of Black and Asian History* (London, Pluto, 1999), pp. 131–2.

15 Ibid., pp. 308–9.

16 S. B. Mossarib, 'Making My Own Culture', in N. Kassam (ed.), *Telling It Like It Is: Young Asian Women Talk* (London: Livewire/Women's Press, 1997), p. 34.

17 'Alcohol Concern', *Alcohol and the Asian, African and Caribbean Communities: Research and Practice* (London: Alcohol Concern, 1995), p. 4.

18 M. and T. Phillips, *Windrush: The Irresistible Rise of Multi-Racial Britain* (London: HarperCollins, 1998), p. 393; C. Prescod, 'Dealing with Difference Beyond Ethnicity', in O. Wambu, op. cit., p. 410.

19 Ramdin, op. cit., p. 321; H. Mizra, 'The Schooling of Young Black Women', in S. Tomlinson and M. Crafts (eds), *Ethnic Relations and Schooling: Policy and Practice in the 1990s* (London: Athlone, 1995), p. 95.

20 P. Panyani, 'Cosmopolis: London's Ethnic Minorities', in J. Kerr and A. Gibson (eds), *London: From Punk to Blair* (London: Reaktion, 2003), p. 68.

21 B. Temple, 'Telling Tales: Accounts and Selves in the Journeys of British Poles', *Oral History* XVIII (1995), p. 61.

22 J. Green, *Them: Voices from the Immigrant Community in Contemporary Britain* (London: Secker and Warburg), p. 251.

23 Ibid., p. 249.

24 M. Collin, and J. Godfrey, *Altered State: the Story of Ecstasy Culture and Acid House* (London: Serpent's Tail, 1998), pp. 205–10, p. 219.

25 S. Brown, *Understanding Youth and Crime: Listening to Youth?* (Buckingham: Open University, 1998), p. 49.

26 Osgerby, *Youth in Britain since 1945* (Oxford, Blackwell, 1998), pp. 221–2.

27 Brown, op. cit., p. 49.

28 See B. Corby, 'The Mistreatment of Young People' in J. Roche and S. Tucker (eds), *Youth in Society: Contemporary Theory, Policy and Practice* (London: Sage, 1997); and, for example, A. Phoenix, *Young Mothers* (Cambridge: Polity, 1991).

29 See especially A. McRobbie's essay on 'Teenage Mothers: A New Social State', in A. McRobbie, *Feminism and Youth Culture*, 2nd edition (Basingstoke: Macmillan, 2000), pp. 176–8.

30 D. Wiley, 'Out of It', *Granta* 56, Winter 1996, p. 192.

31 B. Bryant et al., *Twyford Down: Roads, Campaigning and Environmental Law* (London: Spon, 1996), p. 192.

32 De la Haye and Dingwall, *Surfers, Soulies, Skinheads and Skaters* (London: Victoria and Albert Museum, 1996), p. 114.

33 'John, of the radical political theory magazine *Aufhaben*' quoted in G. McKay, op. cit., p. 127.

34 M. Collings, *Blimey! From Bohemia to Britpop: The London Art World from Francis Bacon to Damien Hirst* (Cambridge: 21, 1997), p. 15.

35 See especially P. Wollen, 'Thatcher's Artists', *London Review of Books*, 30 October 1997, pp. 7–9.

36 M. Maloney, 'Everyone a Winner! British Art from the Saatchi Collection', in B. Adams (ed.), *Sensation: Young British Artists from the Saatchi Collection* (London: Thames and Hudson, 1997, pp. 26–34.

37 Fiona Rae quoted in S. Kent, *Shark Infested Waters* (London: Zwemmer, 1994), p. 76.

38 On various other of the artists who came to prominence at this time see B. Adams, op. cit.

39 *The Sun* quoted in V. Button, *The Turner Prize: Twenty Years* (London: Tate, 2003), p. 112; Hirst quoted in Kent, op. cit., p. 35.

40 Quoted in P. Wollen, op. cit., p. 8.

41 J. A. Walker, *Cultural Offensive: America's Impact on British Art since 1945* (London: Pluto, 1998), pp. 244–6.

42 A. Dixon-Smith quoted in Button, op. cit., p. 96.

43 Cornelia Parker quoted in L. Buck, *Moving Targets: A User's Guide to British Art Now* (London: Tate, 1997), p. 57.

44 See especially S. Garfield, *The Nation's Favourite: The True Adventures of Radio 1* (London: Faber, 1998).

45 Collin and Godfrey (eds), p. 8.

46 See especially M. Pesch and M. Wiesbeck, *Discstyle: The Graphic Arts of Electronic Music and Club Culture House Techno Electro Triphop Drum'n'Bass Big Beat* (London: Collins and Brown, 1999).

47 Osgerby, op. cit., pp. 198–202.

48 http://regard.ac.uk/research_findings/R000239295/report.pdf; accessed 8 May 2005. See also H. Parker, *Illegal Leisure: The Normalization of Adolescent Recreational Drug Use* (London: Routledge, 1998).

49 John Harris details how heroin and cocaine abuse curtailed the creative musical ambitions of various artists in J. Harris, *The Last Party: Britpop, Blair and the Demise of English Rock* (London: Harper Perennial, 2004).

50 D. Haslam, *Manchester, England: the Story of the Pop Cult City* (London: Fourth Estate, 2000), p. 197.

51 Ibid., p. 186.

52 Harris, op. cit., p. 202.

53 Jon Savage provides some of the most insightful comments on the movement in two articles from 1995; 'Letter from London: Britpop', and 'Oasis: All I Want to Do is Live by the Sea', both in Savage, *Time Travel: Pop, Media and Sexuality, 1976–96* (London: Chatto and Windus, 1996).

54 Collings, op. cit., p. 36.

55 M. Fitzgerald, *Spiced Up! My Mad Year with the Spice Girls* (London: Hodder and Stoughton, 1998), p. 22.

56 See Harris, op. cit., p. 303. On Blur vs. Oasis, A. Richardson, 'The Battle of Britpop', *NME*, 12 August 1995, pp. 28–30.

57 Street, *British National Cinema* (London: Routledge, 1997), p. 26. J. Hallam, 'Film, Class and Identity: Re-imagining Communities in the Age of Devolution', in J. Ashby and A. Higson (eds), *British Cinema, Past and Present* (London: Routledge, 2004), p. 262. I am especially indebted to Hallam's stimulating essay here.

58 J. Hill, *Sport, Leisure and Culture in Twentieth-century Britain* (Macmillan: Palgrave, 2002), p. 71.

59 'Number of UK Feature Films Produced 1912–2003' and 'UK cinema admissions 1933–2003' both at http://www.bfi.org.uk/facts/stats/alltime; accessed 9 May 2005.

60 A. Higson, *English Heritage, English Cinema: Costume Drama Since 1980* (Oxford: Oxford University Press, 2003), p. 17.

61 See J. Hill, 'From the New Wave to "Brit-grit": Continuity and Difference in Working-Class Realism', in Ashby and Higson, op. cit., pp. 249–60.

62 On Leigh see especially R. Carney, *The Films of Mike Leigh: Embracing the World* (Cambridge: Cambridge University Press, 2000). On Loach, A. Hayward, *Which Side Are You On? Ken Loach and His Films* (London: Bloomsbury, 2005).

63 Hallam, op. cit., pp. 262–3.

64 Ibid., p. 268.

65 See S. Laing, 'The fiction is already there: writing and film in Blair's Britain', in S. Bignall (ed.), *Writing and Cinema* (Harlow: Longman, 1999), pp. 139–41.

Notes to Chapter 10

1 A. Aughey, *Nationalism, Devolution and the Challenge to the United Kingdom State* (London: Pluto, 2001), p. 142, and www.scotland.gov.uk, Devolution Factsheet, p. 2; accessed 20 May 2005.

2 On these wider issues see especially the editors' introduction to T. Devine and P. Logue (eds), *Being Scottish: Personal Reflections on Scottish Identity Today* (Edinburgh: Polygon, 2002), pp. x–xi.

3 N. Schoon, *The Chosen City* (London: Spon, 2001), pp. 82–3.

4 *Habitat UK National Report 2001* (London: Department of Transport, Local Government and the Regions, 2001), p. 23; p. 32; www.psi.org.uk/publications/ archivesdfs/ housing; accessed 30 May 2005.

5 M. Hitchins and M. Parkinson, *Competitive Scottish Cities? Placing Scotland's Cities in the UK and European Context* (Edinburgh: Scottish Executive Social Research, 2005), p. 18.

6 J. Allerton, *The Role of Civic Society and the Business Community in Rural Restructuring* (Edinburgh: University of Aberdeen/Scottish Executive Central Research Unit, 2001), pp. 30–1.

7 Devine and Logue, op. cit., p. xiii.

8 Ibid., p. 6.

9 J. Coakley, 'Constitutional innovation and political change in twentieth-century Ireland', in J. Coakley (ed.), *Changing Shades of Orange and Green: Redefining the Union and the Nation in Contemporary Ireland* (Dublin: UCDP, 2002) pp. 1–2; Aughey, op. cit., pp. 129–30.

10 Aughey, op. cit., pp. 134–5.

11 David Trimble and Fionnuala O'Connor respectively, quoted in W. J. V. Neill, *Urban Planning and Cultural Identity* (London: Routledge, 2004), pp. 163–4.

12 E. Longley and D. Kiberd, *Multi-Culturalism: The View from the Two Irelands* (Cork: Cork University Press/Centre for Cross Border Studies, 2001), pp. 39–40; Neill, op. cit., p. 184.

13 Northern Ireland Statistics and Research Agency, *Births and Deaths in Northern Ireland* (2004), www.noi.gov.uk; accessed 25 May 2005.

14 Northern Ireland Executive, *Economic Overview – April 2005*, www.nio.gov.uk; accessed 25 May 2005.

15 Neill, op. cit., p. 211.

16 P. Bew, 'Deal, What Deal?' *The Times*, 8 December 2004, pp. 6–7; A. Christafis, 'Trimble's Unionists Swept Away,' *The Guardian*, 7 May 2005, p. 8.

17 P. Logue (ed.) *Being Irish: Personal Reflections on Irish Identity Today* (Dublin: Oak Tree Press, 2000), p. 288.

18 See especially J. Curtice, 'Is Scotland a Nation and Wales Not?' in B. Taylor and K. Thomson (eds), *Scotland and Wales: Nations Again?* (Cardiff: University of Wales, 1999), pp. 122–3.

19 Aughey, op. cit., p. 150.

20 'Economy', www.walesoffice.gov.uk; accessed 20 May 2005.

21 J. Walsh, 'New Island in the Sun', *Time*, 27 October 1997, p. 29.

22 *Welsh Development Agency Annual Report 2003–4*, www.wda.co.uk.

23 C. Clover, 'Rise of Britain's Homogenised High Street', *Daily Telegraph*, 28 August 2004, p. 12. See also www.thegulbenkianprize.org.uk.

24 See especially V. Robinson, 'Croeso i Gymru – Welcome to Wales? Refugees and Asylum Seekers in Wales', in C. Williams, N. Evans and P. O'Leary (eds), *A Tolerant Nation? Exploring Ethnic Diversity in Wales* (Cardiff: University of Wales, 2003), pp. 181–2.

25 I. Bala, 'On the Island of Gwales: a Postcolonial Parable', in I. Bala, *Here + Now: Essays on Contemporary Art in Wales* (Bridgend: Seren, 2003), pp. 175–6.

26 M. Gooding, 'Foreword', I. Bala, op. cit., p. 7. See also I. Bala, *Process: Explorations of the Work of Tim Davies* (Bridgend: Seren, 2002).

27 Y. Alibhai-Brown, 'Bring England in from the Cold – British Identity', *New Statesman*, 11 July 1997; D. Blunkett, 'A New England: An English Identity within Britain', speech to the Institute for Public Policy Research, 14 March 2005.

28 P. Johnston, 'North-East Delivers Huge Rebuff to Prescott's Regional Assembly', *Daily Telegraph*, 6 November 2004, p. 10.

29 M. Raco, 'Urban Regeneration in a Growing Region: the Renaissance of England's Average Town', in C. Johnson and M. Whitelaw (eds), *New Horizons in British Urban Policy: Perspectives on New Labour's Urban Renaissance* (Aldershot: Ashgate, 2004), p. 41.

30 See especially J. F. Barker, *England in the New Millennium: Are We Prepared to Save our Countryside?* (Sheffield: Gaia Watch, 2000), pp. 99–100.

31 B. Robson, 'Mancunian Ways: the politics of regeneration', in J. Peck and K. Ward (eds), *City in Revolution: Reconstructing Manchester* (Manchester: Manchester University Press, 2002), p. 34. *Habitat UK National Report 2001* (London: DoT, 2001), p. 15.

32 Schoon, *The Chosen City* (London: Spon, 2001), p. 74; Morrison, *English Shops and Shopping: An Architectural History* (London: Yale University Press, 2003), p. 304.

33 Raco, op. cit., pp. 55–6.

34 K. A. Morrison, op. cit., pp. 291–2.

35 For a local view of these events see, for example, 'From Oldham to Bradford: the Violence of the Violated', at www.therevival.co.uk. *The Revival: Voice of the Muslim Youth!*; accessed 29 May 2005.

36 G. Singh, 'Multiculturalism in Contemporary Britain: Reflections on the "Leicester Model" ', *International Journal of Multicultural Studies*, 5 (1) 2003, pp. 50–2.

37 Y. Alibhai-Brown, 'Bring England in from the Cold-British Identity', *New Statesman* 1997 July 11.

38 D. Gritten, 'Why I Put Jane Austen in a Sari', *Daily Telegraph*, 20 September 2004, p. 19.

39 B. Dattani, R. Devadason, S. Kanadola and T. Raj, *Collective Identities, Diverse Lives* (Nottingham: TEDP, 2000) p 9.

40 C. Donnella (ed.), *Gender Roles* (Cambridge: Independence, 2001), p. 37.

41 S. Jenkins, *Gender, Place and the Labour Market* (Aldershot: Ashgate, 2004), pp. 36–7.

42 K. Rowlingson and S. McKay, *Lone Parent Families: Gender, Class and State* (Harlow: Prentice Hall, 2002), p. 43; A. Marwick, *British Society since 1945* (London: Penguin, 2003), p. 462.

43 S. Brisco, *Britain in Numbers* (London: Politico's, 2005), p. 262.

44 Rawlingson and McKay, op. cit., p. 93.

45 J. Carvel, 'Sex education demand after rise in teenage pregancies', *Guardian*, 28 May 2005, p. 10. Jenkins, op. cit., p. 37.

46 N. Barham, *Dis/Connected: Why Our Kids are Turning their Backs on Everything We Thought We Knew* (London: Ebury, 2004) p. 171. See also M. Bunting, 'It isn't Babies that Blight Young Lives', *Guardian*, 28 May 2005, p. 28.

47 B. Zephaniah, 'Me? I Thought, OBE Me? Up Yours, I Thought', *Guardian*, 27 November 2003, at books.guardian.co.uk; accessed 1 December 2003.

48 S. Willman, S. Knafler and S. Pierce, *Support for Asylum Seekers: A Guide to Legal and Welfare Rights* (London: Legal Action Group, 2004), p. vi.

49 'Ethnic Minority Britain in Numbers', *Guardian*, 21 March 2005, p. 4; *Realizing the Vision* (London: Runnymede Trust Briefing Paper, 2004), pp. 5–7.

50 I. H. Malik, *Islam and Modernity: Muslims in Europe and the United States* (Cambridge: Polity, 2004), p. 118. On Muslim and other religious groups see M. Gilbert, *The Routledge Atlas of British History* (London: Routledge, 2003), p. 157.

51 S. R. Ameli, *Globalization, Americanization and British Muslim Identity* (London: ICAS, 2002), p. 278. A. Roy, 'Islamic Reaction too Small to Hurt Blair', *Guardian*, 7 May 2005, p. 6.

52 R. Hyder, *Brimful of Asia: Negotiating Ethnicity in the UK Music Scene* (Aldershot: Ashgate, 2005), p. 20.

53 *Realizing the Vision*, op. cit., p. 8; S. Sandhu, 'Life Lines', *Daily Telegraph Arts*, 28 August 2004, p. 1.

54 Brisco, op. cit., p. 276 and p. 283.

55 Barham, op. cit., p. 306.

56 M. O'Donnell and S. Sharp, *Uncertain Masculinities: Youth, Ethnicity and Class in Contemporary Britain* (London: Routledge, 2000), pp. 28–35.

57 B. Saunders, *Youth Crime and Youth Culture in the Inner City* (London: Routledge, 2005), p. 46.

58 Brisco, op. cit., pp. 262–3.

59 I. Herbert, 'Poverty and Despair of Britain's Lost Generation', *Independent*, 13 December 2004, p. 1.

60 J. Wardhaugh, *Sub City: Young People, Homelessness and Crime* (Aldershot: Ashgate, 2000), pp. 131–2.

61 R. Hollands and P. Chatterton, *Youth Cultures, Identities and the Consumption of Night-life City Spaces* (Newcastle: University of Newcastle, 2002), pp. 12–13. Following quote from Barham, op. cit., pp. 17–18.

62 S. Kent, 'Groundswell', in J. Kerr and A. Gibson (eds), *London: From Punk to Blair* (London: Reaktion, 2003), p. 341 and pp. 351–2.

63 'The Tate Modern is Celebrating its Fifth Birthday', *Daily Telegraph*, 8 May 2005, p. 10.

64 See especially www.graysonperry.co.uk; accessed 18 June 2005.

65 G. Perry, *Guerrilla Tactics*, quoted in A. Wilson, 'Grayson Perry: "General Artist" ' (Amsterdam: Stedelijk Museum, 2004), p. 88. For Perry's earlier comments on beauty and polemic see ibid., p. 24.

66 E. Bearn, 'Torture for the masses', *Daily Telegraph*, 29 October 2002, at www.telegraph.co.uk; accessed 18 June 2005.

67 See also the mock-academic essay included in the catalogue for this exhibition, 'Elements towards a Socio-psychologistical Theory of Faticism by Doctor Suhail Malik', in Jake and Dinos Chapman, *Works from the Chapman Family Collection* (London: White Cube, 2002).

68 Emin quoted in L. Buck, *Moving Targets 2* (London: Tate, 2000), p. 60.

69 See especially C. Townsend and M. Merck, 'Eminent Domain: the Cultural Location of Tracey Emin', in M. Merck and C. Townsend (eds), *The Art of Tracey Emin* (London: Thames and Hudson, 2002), p. 6.

70 'Interview with Tracey Emin', *Modern Painters*, June 2005, at www.lehmann-maupin.com; accessed 18 June 2005.

71 S. Napier-Bell, *Black Vinyl White Powder* (London: Ebury, 2002), pp. 397–8.

72 S. Glaser, 'Bleep: a Journey from Classical to Electronic Music', in P. Lawrence and V. Howard (eds), *Crossfade: A Big Chill Anthology* (London: Serpent's Tail, 2004), pp. 17–18. See also www.greytuesday.org.

73 D. Hesmondhalgh and C. Melville, 'Urban Breakbeat Culture: Repercussions of Hip-Hop in the United Kingdom', in T. Mitchell (ed.), *Global Noise: Rap and Hip-Hop Outside the USA* (Middletown, CT: Wesleyan University Press, 2001), p. 106.

74 M. Hubbard, 'Albarn's Mali Mission', BBC News Online, news.bbc.co.uk; accessed 18 June 2005.

75 See especially A. Bennett, *Cultures of Popular Music* (Buckingham: Open University Press, 2001), pp. 111–15.

76 'Militant Science: Asian Dub Foundation's Approach to Sound and Technology' at www.asiandubfoundation.com; accessed 18 June 2005.

77 A. Smith, 'Small Films, Big Ideas', *The Orange British Academy Awards 2003* (London: Citroen Wolf, 2003), p. 22.

78 L. Benedictus, 'Lynne: People Quote Your Films at Parties. Mike: Those are Lousy Parties', film.guardian.co.uk, 4 February 2005; accessed 21 June 2005.

79 J. Leach, *British Film* (Cambridge: Cambridge University Press, 2004), pp. 228–9.

80 S. Chibnall, 'Travels in Ladland: the British Gangster Film Cycle, 1998–2001', in R. Murphy (ed.), *The British Cinema Book*, 2nd edn (London: BFI, 2003), pp. 281–2.

81 See especially R. Murphy, 'Citylife: Urban Fairy-tales in late '90s Cinema', in R. Murphy (ed.), *The British Cinema Book*, 2nd edn (London: BFI, 2003), pp. 296–8.

82 See, for example, P. French, 'Actually, Love isn't Always Quite Enough', *Guardian* Unlimited Film Reviews, 23 November 2003, at www.film.guardian.co.uk; accessed 15 December 2003.

Selected Bibliography and Further Reading

(1a) Locality and regionalism: general
(1b) Scotland
(1c) Northern Ireland
(1d) Wales
(1e) England
(2a) Social and political accounts: General
(2b) Women
(2c) Ethnicity and immigration
(2d) Youth
(2e) Visual arts
(2f) Popular music
(2g) Cinema
(2h) Website sources

(1a) Locality and regionalism: general

Aughey, A., *Nationalism, Devolution and the Challenge to the United Kingdom State* (London: Pluto, 2001).

Caunce, C. et al. (ed.), *Relocating Britishness* (Manchester: Manchester University Press, 2004).

Danziger, N., *Danziger's Britain: A Journey to the Edge* (London: HarperCollins, 1996).

Davies, N., *The Isles: A History* (Basingstoke: Papermac, 2000).

Gordon, G. (ed.), *Regional Cities in the UK, 1890–1980* (London: Harper and Row, 1986).

Habitat UK National Report 2001 (London: Department of Transport, Local Government and the Regions, 2001).

Harvey, G., *The Killing of the Countryside* (London: Jonathan Cape, 1997).

Hechter, M., *Internal Colonialism: The Celtic Fringe in British National Development* (London: Routledge, 1975).

Humphries, S. and Hopwood, B., *Green and Pleasant Land: The Untold Story of Country Life in Twentieth-Century Britain* (London: Channel 4, 1999).

Jack, I., *Before the Oil Ran Out: Britain, 1977–86* (London: Secker and Warburg, 1987).

Johnson, C. and Whitelaw, M. (ed.), *New Horizons in British Urban Policy: Perspectives on New Labour's Urban Renaissance* (Aldershot: Ashgate, 2004).

Kearney, H., *The British Isles: A History of Four Nations* (Cambridge: Cambridge University Press, 1989).

Ludwig, H.-W. and Fietz, L. (eds), *Poetry in the British Isles: Non-Metropolitan Perspectives* (Cardiff: University of Wales Press, 1995).

Martin, J., *The Development of Modern Agriculture: British Farming since 1931* (Basingstoke: Macmillan, 2000).

Nairn, T., *The Breakup of Britain: Crisis and Neo-Nationalism* (London: New Left Books, 1977).

Neill, W. J. V., *Urban Planning and Cultural Identity* (London: Routledge, 2004).

Osborn, F. J. and Whittaker, A., *New Towns: Their Origins, Achievements and Progress* (London: Leonard Hill, 1977).

Parry, M. M., Davies, W. V. and Temple, R. A. M. (eds), *The Changing Voices of Europe* (Cardiff: University of Wales Press, 1994).

Rushdie, S., *Imaginary Homelands: Essays and Criticism, 1981–91* (London: Granta, 1991).

Samuel, R., *Theatres of Memory*, vol. 2: *Island Stories* (London: Verso, 1999).

Schoon, N., *The Chosen City* (London: Spon, 2001).

Tóibín, C., *The Sign of the Cross: Travels in Catholic Europe* (London: Vintage, 1995).

Walker, A. and Walker, C., *Divided Britain* (London: CPGA, 1997).

Weight, R., *Patriots: National Identity in Britain, 1940–2000* (Basingstoke: Palgrave Macmillan, 2002).

(1b)   Scotland

Allerton, J., *The Role of Civic Society and the Business Community in Rural Restructuring* (Edinburgh: University of Aberdeen/Scottish Executive Central Research Unit, 2001).

Ascherson, N., *Stone Voices: The Search for Scotland* (London: Granta, 2003).

Brown, G. M., *Portrait of Orkney* (London: John Murray, 1988).

Devine, T., *The Scottish Nation, 1700–2000* (Harmondsworth: Penguin, 1999).

Devine, T. and Logue, P. (eds), *Being Scottish: Personal Reflections on Scottish Identity Today* (Edinburgh: Polygon, 2002).

Glendinning, M. (ed.) *Rebuilding Scotland: The Postwar Vision, 1945–65* (East Linton: Tuckwell, 1997).

Harvie, C., *No Gods and Precious Few Heroes: Scotland since 1914* (Edinburgh: Edinburgh University Press, 1993).

Hazel, H. (ed.), *The Orcadian Book of the Twentieth Century* (Kirkwall: Orcadian, 2000).

Hitchins, M. and Parkinson, M., *Competitive Scottish Cities? Placing Scotland's Cities in the UK and European Context* (Edinburgh: Scottish Executive Social Research, 2005).

Kelman, J., *Some Recent Attacks: Essays Cultural and Political* (Stirling: AK, 1992).

Knox, W. W., *Industrial Nation: Work, Culture and Society in Scotland, 1800 to the Present* (Edinburgh: Edinburgh University Press, 1999).

Marr, A., *The Battle for Scotland* (Harmondsworth: Penguin, 1995).

Mitchell, J., *Conservatives and the Union* (Edinburgh: Edinburgh University Press, 1990).

Scott, A. M., *Modern Dundee: Life in the City since World War Two* (Derby: Breedon, 2002).

Thomson, W. P. L., *History of Orkney* (Edinburgh: Mercat, 1987).

Wright, K., *The People Say Yes: The Making of Scotland's Parliament* (Glendaruel: Argyll, 1997).

(1c)   Northern Ireland

Beckett, J. C. and Glasscock, R. E., *Belfast: The Origins and Growth of an Industrial City* (London: BBC, 1967).

Belfrage, S., *The Crack: A Belfast Year* (London: André Deutsch, 1987).

Boal, F. W., *Shaping a City: Belfast in the Late Twentieth Century* (Belfast: Queen's University Press, 1995).

Bruce, S., *The Edge of the Union: The Ulster Loyalist Political Vision* (Oxford: Oxford University Press, 1994).

Buchanan, R. H. and Walker, B. M. (eds), *Belfast and its Region: Province, City and People* (Antrim: Greystone, 1987).

Clyde, T. (ed.), *Ancestral Voices: The Selected Prose of John Hewitt* (Belfast: Blackstaff, 1987).

Coakley, J. (ed.), *Changing Shades of Green and Orange: Redefining the Union and the Nation in Contemporary Ireland* (Dublin: UCDP, 2002).

Crawford, R. G., *Loyal to King Billy: A Portrait of the Ulster Protestants* (London: C. Hurst, 1987).

Crozier, M. and Froggart, R. (eds), *Cultural Tradition in Northern Ireland* (Belfast: Queen's University Press, 1995).

Devlin, B., *The Price of My Soul* (London: Pan, 1969).

Graham, B. (ed.), *In Search of Ireland: A Cultural Geography* (London: Routledge, 1997).

Kearney, R., *Postnationalist Ireland* (London: Routledge, 1997).

Lacy, B., *Siege City: The Story of Derry and Londonderry* (Belfast: Blackstaff, 1990).

Logue, P. (ed.), *Being Irish: Personal Reflections on Irish Identity Today* (Dublin: Oak Tree Press, 2000).

Longley, E., *The Living Stream: Literature and Revisionism in Ireland* (Newcastle: Bloodaxe, 1994).

Longley, E. and Kiberd, D., *Multi-Culturalism: The View from the Two Irelands* (Cork: CUP/Centre for Cross Border Studies, 2001).

McIvor, B., *Hope Deferred: Experiences of an Irish Unionist* (Belfast: Blackstaff, 1998).

Murphy, D., *A Place Apart* (Harmondsworth: Penguin, 2003).

Rodgers, W. R., *The Ulstermen and their Country* (London: British Council/Longmans Green, 1947).

Shirlow, P. (ed.), *Development Ireland: Contemporary Issues* (London: Pluto, 1995).

Tóibín, C., *Bad Blood: A Walk Along the Irish Border* (London: Vintage, 1994).

Wichert, S., *Northern Ireland since 1945* (London: Longman, 1998).

(1d)   Wales

Bala, I., *Here + Now: Essays on Contemporary Art in Wales* (Bridgend: Seren, 2003).

Bala, I., *Process: Explorations of the Work of Tim Davies* (Bridgend: Seren, 2002).

Chapman, T. R., *Encounters with Wales* (Llandysul, Dyfed: Gomer, 1995)

Cope, P. et al., *Chasing the Dragon: Creative Community Responses to the Crisis in the South Wales Coalfield* (n.p: ERGO2, 1997).

Davies, C. A. and Jones, S. (eds), *Welsh Community: New Ethnographic Perspectives* (Cardiff: University of Wales Press, 2003).

Davies, J., *A History of Wales* (Harmondsworth: Penguin, 1994).

Day, G., *Making Sense of Wales: A Sociological Perspective* (Cardiff: University of Wales Press, 2002).

Gareth Evans, D., *A History of Wales, 1906–2000* (Cardiff: University of Wales Press, 2000).

Hibbert, T. and Jones, G. E. (eds), *Postwar Wales* (Cardiff: University of Wales Press, 1995).

Jenkins, E., *Through the Decades: The History of Swansea and South West Wales as Told by its own People* (Swansea: People in Print, 1994).

Jones, G. E., *Modern Wales: A Concise History* (Cambridge: Cambridge University Press, 1999).

Minwell Tibbot, S., *Domestic Life in Wales* (Cardiff: University of Wales Press/National Museums and Galleries of Wales, 2002).

Morgan, K. O., *Wales, 1880–1980: Rebirth of a Nation* (Oxford: Oxford University Press, 1982).

Rosser, C. and Harris, C., *The Family and Social Change: A Study of Family and Kinship in a South Wales Town* (London: Routledge and Kegan Paul, 1965).

Sinclair, N. M. C., *The Tiger Bay Story* (Treforest: Zenith, 1993).

Taylor, B. and Thomson, K. (eds), *Scotland and Wales: Nations Again?* (Cardiff: University of Wales, 1999).

Williams, C., Evans N. and O'Leary, P. (eds), *A Tolerant Nations? Exploring Ethnic Diversity in Wales* (Cardiff: University of Wales, 2003).

Williams, G. A., *When was Wales? A History of the Welsh* (Harmondsworth: Penguin, 1991).

(1e) England

Aughton, P., *Bristol: A People's History* (Lancaster: Carnegie, 2000).

Beynon, H., Hudson, R. and Sadler, D., *A Place Called Teesside: A Locality in a Global Economy* (Edinburgh: Edinburgh University Press for the University of Durham, 1994).

Deakin, D. (ed.), *Wythenshawe: The Story of a Garden City*, vol. 2: *1926–84* (Manchester: Northern Civic Society, 1984).

Dodds, G. L., *A History of Sunderland* (Sunderland: Albion, 2001).

Driver, P., *Manchester Pieces* (London: Picador, 1996).

Haslam, D., *Manchester: The Story of the Pop Cult City* (London: Fourth Estate, 2000).

Hudson, M., *Coming Back Brockens: A Year in a Mining Village* (London: Jonathan Cape, 1994).

Kerr, J. and Gibson, A. (eds), *London: From Punk to Blair* (London: Reaktion, 2003).

Kidd, A., *Manchester* (Ryburn, Keele: Keele University Press, 1993).

Lancaster, B. and Mason, T. (eds), *Life and Labour in a Twentieth Century City: The Experience of Coventry* (Coventry: University of Warwick Press, n.d.).

Morrison, K. A., *English Shops and Shopping: An Architectural History* (London: Yale University Press, 2003).

Page, R., *The Decline of an English Village* (Shedfield: Ashford, 1989).

Palmer, A., *The East End: Four Centuries of London Life* (London: John Murray, 2000).

Peck, J. and Ward, K. (eds), *City in Revolution: Reconstructing Manchester* (Manchester: MUP, 2002).

People's Autobiography of Hackney, *The Island: The Life and Death of an East End Community, 1870–1970* (London: Centreprise, n.d.).

People's Autobiography of Hackney, *People's Autobiography of Hackney*, vol. 2 (London: Centreprise, 1977).

Porter, R., *London: A Social History* (Harmondsworth: Penguin, 2000).

Raban, J., *Soft City* (London: Collins Harvill, 1988).

Sinclair, I., *Lights Out for the Territory* (London: Granta, 1997).

Strathern, M., *Kinship at the Core: An Anthropology of Elmdon, a Village in North-East Essex in the Nineteen-sixties* (Cambridge: Cambridge University Press, 1981).

Taylor, I., Evans, K. and Fraser, P., *A Tale of Two Cities: Global Change, Local Feeling and Everyday Life in the North of England. A Study of Manchester and Sheffield* (London: Routledge, 1996).

York, P. and Jennings, C., *Peter York's Eighties* (London: BBC, 1995).

(2a) Social and political accounts: general

Abbott, M., *Family Affairs: A History of the Family in Twentieth-Century England* (London: Routledge, 2003).

Abel-Smith, B. and Townsend, P., *The Poor and the Poorest* (London: Occasional Papers on Social Administration no. 17, 1965).

Addison P., *Now the War is Over: A Social History of Britain, 1945–51* (London: Jonathan Cape, 1985).

Addison, P., *The Road to 1945: British Politics and the Second World War* (London: Pimlico, 1994).

Appleyard, B. *The Pleasures of Peace: Art and Imagination in Postwar Britain* (London: Faber, 1989).

Bédarida, F., *A Social History of England, 1851–1990* (London: Routledge, 1994).

Black, J., *Britain Since the Seventies: Politics and Society in the Consumer Age* (London: Reaktion, 2004).

Bogdanor, V. and Skidelsky, R. (eds), *The Age of Affluence* (London: Macmillan, 1970).

Booker, C., *The Neophiliacs* (London: Collins, 1969).

Booker, C., *The Seventies: Portrait of a Decade* (Harmondsworth, Penguin, 1980).

Bourke, J., *Working-Class Cultures in Britain, 1890–1960: Gender, Class and Ethnicity,* (London: Routledge, 1994).

Brisco, S., *Britain in Numbers* (London: Politico's, 2005).

Childs, D., *Britain since 1939* (Basingstoke: Palgrave, 2002).

Colls, R., *Identity of England* (Oxford: Oxford University Press, 2002).

Conekin, B. et al. (eds), *Moments of Modernity, 1945–64* (London: Rivers Oram, 1991).

Connolly, R., *In the Sixties* (London: Pavilion, 1995).

Cook, C. and Sked, A., *Postwar Britain: A Political History* (Harmondsworth: Penguin, 1984).

Day, G. (ed.), *Literature and Culture in Modern Britain*, vol. 2: *1930–55* (London: Longman, 1997).

Dutton, D., *British Politics since 1945* (Oxford: Blackwell, 1997).

Gourvish, T. and O'Day, A. (eds), *Britain since 1945* (Basingstoke: Macmillan, 1991).

Harris, S., *Life in Britain in the 1950s* (London: Batsford, 1985).

Hopkins, H., *The New Look: A Social History of the Forties and Fifties in Britain* (Boston, MA: Houghton Mifflin, 1964).

Marwick, A., *British Society since 1945* (Harmondsworth: Penguin, 2003).

Richardson, N., *Life in Britain in the 1960s* (London: Batsford, 1986).

Robbins, K. G., *Eclipse of a Great Power: Modern Britain, 1870–1992* (London: Longman, 1994).

Sinfield, A., *Literature, Politics and Culture in Postwar England* (Oxford: Blackwell, 1989).

Tiratsoo, N. (ed.), *From Blitz to Blair* (London: Phoenix, 1998).

Townsend, P., *Poverty in the United Kingdom: A Survey of Household Resources and Standards of Living* (Harmondsworth: Penguin, 1979).

(2b)   Women

Briar, C., *Work for Women? Gendered Work and Welfare Policies in Twentieth-Century Britain* (London: University College London, 1997).

Bruley, S., *Women in Britain since 1900* (Basingstoke: Macmillan, 1999).

Bryan, B., Dadzie, S. and Scarfe, S., *The Heart of Race: Black Women's Lives in Britain* (London: Virago, 1985).

Campbell, B., *Diana, Princess of Wales: How Sexual Politics Shook the Monarchy* (London: Women's Press, 1998).

Carter, A., *The Passion of the New Eve* (London: Virago, 1977).

Crompton, R., *Women and Work in Modern Britain* (Oxford: Oxford University Press, 1997).

Dattani, B. et al., *Collective Identities, Diverse Lives* (Nottingham: TEDP, 2000).

Donnella, C. (ed.), *Gender Roles* (Cambridge: Independence, 2001).

Dunn, N., *Up the Junction* (London: Virago, 1988).

Figes, K., *Because of Her Sex: The Myth of Equality for Women in Britain* (London: Pan, 1994).

Gavron, H., *The Captive Housewife: Conflicts of Housebound Mothers* (London: Routledge and Kegan Paul, 1966).

Greer, G., *The Female Eunuch* (London: MacGibbon and Kee, 1970).

Innes, S., *Making it Work: Women, Change and Challenge in the 1990s* (London: Chatto and Windus, 1995).

Jenkins, S., *Gender, Place and the Labour Market* (Aldershot: Ashgate, 2004).

Lewis, J., *Women in Britain since 1945* (Oxford: Blackwell, 1992).

Merck, M. (ed.), *After Diana: Irreverent Elegies* (London: Verso 1998).

Myrdal, A. and Klein, V., *Women's Two Roles: Home and Work* (London: Routledge and Kegan Paul, 1956).

Nicholson, M., *What Did You Do in the War, Mummy? Women in World War Two* (London: Pimlico, 1996).

Oakley, A., *Housewife* (London: Harmondsworth, 1976).

Peplar, M., *Family Matters: A History of Ideas about Family since 1945* (London: Longman, 2002).

Rapport, R. N. et al. (eds), *Families in Britain* (London: Routledge and Kegan Paul, 1982).

Rowbotham, S., *A Century of Women* (Harmondsworth: Penguin, 1999).

Rowbotham, S., *The Past is Before Us: Feminism in Action since the 1960s* (Harmondsworth: Penguin, 1989).

Rowlingson, K. and McKay, S., *Lone Parent Families: Gender, Class and State* (Harlow: Prentice Hall, 2002).

Walby, S., *Gender Transformations* (London: Routledge, 1997).

Westwood, S., *All Day, Every Day: Factory and Family in the Making of Women's Lives* (London: Pluto, 1984).

Wilson, A., *Finding a Voice: Asian Women in Britain* (London: Virago, 1978).

(2c) Ethnicity and immigration

Ameli, S. R., *Globalization, Americanization and British Muslim Identity* (London: ICAS, 2002).

Anim-Addo, J., *Longest Journey: A History of Black Lewisham* (London: Deptford Forum, 1995).

Beynon, J. (ed.), *Scarman and After* (Oxford: Pergamon, 1984).

Brown, J., *The Un-Melting Pot* (Basingstoke: Macmillan, 1970).

Emecheta, B., *Second Class Citizen* (London: Alison and Busby, 1974).

Ferron, E., *'Man, You've Mixed': A Jamaican Comes to Britain* (London: Whiting and Birch, 1995).

Fryer, P., *Staying Power: The History of Black People in Britain* (London: Pluto, 1984).

Glass, R., *Newcomers: The West Indians in London* (London: Centre for Urban Studies/George Allen and Unwin, 1960).

Goulbourne, H., *Race Relations in Britain since 1945* (Basingstoke: Macmillan, 1998).

Green, J., *Them: Voices from the Immigrant Community in Contemporary Britain* (London: Secker and Warburg, 1990).

Hiro, D., *Black British, White British* (London: Paladin, 1992).

Kassam, N. (ed.), *Telling It Like It Is: Young Asian Women Talk* (London: Livewire/Women's Press, 1997).

Leese, P. et al. (ed.), *The British Migrant Experience, 1700–2000: An Anthology* (Basingstoke: Macmillan, 2002).

Maan, B., *The New Scots: A Study of Asians in Scotland* (Edinburgh: John Donald, 1992).

Malik, I. H., *Islam and Modernity: Muslims in Europe and the United States* (London: Polity, 2004).

Norton-Taylor, R. (ed.), *The Colour of Justice: The Stephen Lawrence Inquiry* (London: Oberon, 1999).

Phillips, M. and Phillips, C., *Notting Hill in the Sixties* (London: Lawrence and Wishart, 1991).

Phillips, M. and Phillips, T., *Windrush: The Irresistible Rise of Multi-Racial Britain* (London: HarperCollins, 1998).

Pryce, K., *Endless Pressure: A Study of West Indian Life-styles in Bristol* (Harmondsworth: Penguin, 1979).

Ramdin, R., *Reimaging Britain: 500 Years of Black and Asian History* (London: Pluto, 1999).

Smith T. and Winslow, M., *Keeping the Faith: The Polish Community in Britain* (Bradford: Bradford Heritage Recording Unit/University of Sheffield, 2000).

Spencer, I. R. G., *British Immigration Policy since 1939* (London: Routledge, 1997).

Sword, K., *Identity in Flux: The Polish Community in Britain* (London: SSEES Occasional Papers No. 36, 1996).

Tomlinson, S. and Crafts, M. (eds), *Ethnic Relations and Schooling: Policy and Practice in the 1990s* (London: Athlone, 1995)

Wambu, O. (ed.), *Empire Windrush: Fifty Years of Writing about Black Britain* (London: Victor Gollancz, 1998).

Widgery, D., *Beating Time: Riot'n'Race'n'Rock'n'Roll* (London: Chatto and Windus, 1986).

Willman, S., S. Knafler and S. Pierce, *Support for Asylum Seekers: A Guide to Legal and Welfare Rights* (London: Legal Action Group, 2004).

(2d) Youth

Banks, M. H. and Ullah, P., *Youth Unemployment in the 1980s: Its Psychological Effects* (Beckenham: Croom Helm, 1988).

Barham, N., *Dis/Connected: Why our Kids are Turning their Backs on Everything we Thought we Knew* (London: Ebury, 2004).

Barnes, R., *Mods!* (London: Plexus, 1991).

Brown, S., *Understanding Youth and Crime: Listening to Youth?* (Buckingham: Open University, 1998).

Earle, F., *A Time to Travel? An Introduction to Britain's Newer Travellers* (Lyme Regis: Enabler, 1994).

Green, J., *Days in the Life: Voices from the English Underground, 1961–71* (London: Pimlico, 1998).

Hall, S. and Jefferson, T., *Resistance through Rituals* (London: Routledge, 1996).

De la Haye, A., *The Cutting Edge: 50 Years of British Fashion* (London: Victoria and Albert Museum, 1997).

De la Haye A. and Dingwall, C., *Surfers, Soulies, Skinheads and Skaters* (London: Victoria and Albert Museum, 1986).

Hamblett, C. and Deverson, J., *Generation X* (London: Tandem, 1964).

Harrison, M., *Young Meteors: British Photojournalism, 1957–1965* (London: Jonathan Cape, 1998).

Hollands, R. and Chatterton, P., *Youth Cultures, Identities and the Consumption of Night-life City Spaces* (Newcastle: University of Newcastle, 2002).

Knight, N., *Skinhead* (London: Omnibus 1982).

McKay, G., *Senseless Acts of Beauty: Cultures of Resistance since the Sixties* (London: Verso, 1996).

McRobbie, A., *Feminism and Youth Culture*, 2nd edn (Basingstoke: Palgrave Macmillan, 2000).

McRobbie, A. (ed.), *Zoot Suits and Second-Hand Dresses* (Basingstoke: Macmillan, 1989).

Nuttall, J., *Bomb Culture* (London: Paladin, 1968).

Neville, R., *Powerplay* (London: Paladin, 1971).

O'Donnell M. and Sharp, S., *Uncertain Masculinities: Youth, Ethnicity and Class in Contemporary Britain* (London: Routledge, 2000).

Osgerby, B., *Youth in Britain since 1945* (Oxford: Blackwell, 1998).

Parker, H., *Illegal Leisure: The Normalization of Adolescent Recreational Drug Use* (London: Routledge, 1998).

Phoenix, A., *Young Mothers* (Oxford: Polity, 1991).

Redhead, S. (ed.), *Rave Off: Politics and Deviance in Contemporary Youth Culture* (Aldershot: Avebury, 1993).

Roche, J. and Tucker, S. (ed.), *Youth in Society: Contemporary Theory, Policy and Practice* (London: Sage, 1997).

Saunders, B., *Youth Crime and Youth Culture in the Inner City* (London: Routledge, 2005).

Stone, C. J., *Fierce Dancing: Adventures in the Underground* (London: Faber, 1996).

Walker, A., Ormerod, P. and Whitty, L., *Abandoning Social Priorities* (London: Child Poverty Action Group, 1979).

Wardhaugh, J., *Sub City: Young People, Homelessness and Crime* (Aldershot: Ashgate, 2000).

(2e)   Visual Arts

Adams, B. et al., *Sensation* (London: Hodder and Stoughton, 1997).

Araeen, R., *From Modernism to Postmodernism: A Retrospective, 1959–87* (Birmingham: Ikon Gallery, 1988).

Buck, L., *Moving Targets: A User's Guide to British Art Now* (London: Tate, 1997).

Burgin, V., *Some Cities* (London: Reaktion, 1996).

Button, V., *The Turner Prize: Twenty Years* (London: Tate, 2003).

Celant, G., *Anish Kapoor* (London: Thames and Hudson, 1996).

Chapman, J. and D., *Works from the Chapman Family Collection* (London: White Cube, 2002).

Collings, M., *Blimey! From Bohemia to Britpop: The London Art World from Francis Bacon to Damien Hirst* (Cambridge: 21, 1997).

Cragg, T., *Sculpture, 1975–90* (Newport: Harbour Art Museum, 1990).

Farson, D., *The Gilded Gutter Life of Francis Bacon* (London: Vintage, 1994).

Gooding, M., *Bruce McLean* (Oxford: Phaidon, 1990).

Hamilton, R., *Collected Works, 1953–1982* (London: Thames and Hudson, 1984).

Hamilton, R., *John Latham: Early Works, 1954–72* (London: Lisson Gallery, 1987).

Kelly, M., *Post-Partum Document* (London: University of California, 1999).

Kent, S., *Shark Infested Waters* (London: Zwemmer, 1994).

Lippard, L. R. (ed.), *Pop Art* (London: Thames and Hudson, 1996).

Lippard, L. R., *Six Years: The Dematerialization of the Art Object from 1966 to 1972* (Berkeley, CA: UCP, 1997).

Lucie-Smith, E., *Visual Arts in the Twentieth Century* (London: Laurence King, 1996).

Marshall, C. (ed.), *Breaking the Mould: British Art of the 1980s and 1990s* (London: Lund Humphries, 1997).

Massey, A., *The Independent Group: Modernism and Mass Culture in Britain, 1945–59* (Manchester: Manchester University Press, 1995).

Merck, M. and Townsend, C. (ed.), *The Art of Tracey Emin* (London: Thames and Hudson, 2002).

Osterwold, T., *Pop Art* (Köln: Taschen, 1991).

Perry, G., *Guerrilla Tactics* (Amsterdam: Stedelijk Museum, 2004).

Raeburn, M. et al. (ed.), *Vision: Fifty Years of British Creativity* (London: Thames and Hudson, 1999).

Spalding, F., *British Art since 1900* (London: Thames and Hudson, 1992).

Stiles, K. and Selz, P., *Theories and Documents of Contemporary Art* (Berkeley, CA: University California Press, 1996).

Sylvester, D., *About Modern Art: Critical Essays, 1948–96* (London: Chatto and Windus, 1996).

Walker, J. A., *Cultural Offensive: America's Impact on British Art since 1945* (London: Pluto, 1998).

Whiteread, R., *House* (London: Phaidon, 1995).

Whybrow, M., *St Ives, 1883–1993: Portrait of an Art Colony* (Woodbridge, Suffolk: Antique Collectors Club, 1994).

Wollen, R. (ed.), *Derek Jarman: A Portrait* (London: Thames and Hudson, 1996).

(2f) Popular music

Bacon, T., *London Live* (London: Balafon, 1999).

Bennett, A., *Cultures of Popular Music* (Buckingham: Open University Press, 2001).

Berg, I. and Yeomans, I., *Trad: An A to Z Who's Who of the British Traditional Jazz Scene* (London: Foulsham, 1962).

Brooks, C., *A Concise History of the Traditional Jazz Revival in Kent* (Chatham: City Press, 2000).

Chambers, I., *Urban Rhythms* (Basingstoke: Macmillan, 1985).

Collin, M. and Godfrey, J., *Altered State: The Story of Ecstasy Culture and Acid House* (London: Serpent's Tale, 1998).

Coon, C., *1988: The New Wave Punk Rock Explosion* (London: Omnibus, 1977).

Fitzgerald, M., *Spiced Up! My Mad Year with the Spice Girls* (London: Hodder and Stoughton, 1998).

Garfield, S., *The Nation's Favourite: The True Adventures of Radio 1* (London: Faber, 1998).

Harper, C., *Dazzling Stranger: Bert Jansch and the British Folk Blues Revival* (London: Bloomsbury, 2000).

Harris, J., *The Last Party: Britpop, Blair and the Demise of English Rock* (London: Harper Perennial, 2004).

Heckerstall-Smith, D., *The Safest Place in the World: A Personal History of British Rhythm and Blues* (London: Quartet, 1989).

Hill, D., *Designer Boys and Material Girls: Manufacturing the '80s Pop Dream* (Poole: Blandford, 1996).

Hyder, B., *Brimful of Asia: Negotiating Ethnicity in the UK Music Scene* (Aldershot: Ashgate, 2005).

Jones, S., *Black Culture, White Youth: The Reggae Tradition from JA to UK* (Basingstoke: Macmillan, 1988).

Kureishi, H. and Savage, J., *The Faber Book of Pop* (London: Faber, 1995).

Lawrence, P. and Howard, V. (ed.), *Crossfade: A Big Chill Anthology* (London: Serpent's Tail, 2004).

McDevitt, C., *Skiffle: The Definitive Inside Story* (London: Robson, 1997).

Melly, G., *Revolt into Style: The Pop Arts in Britain* (Harmondsworth: Penguin, 1972).

Mitchell, T. (ed.), *Global Noise: Rap and Hip-Hop Outside the USA* (Middletown, CT: Wesleyan University Press, 2001).

Monro, A., *The Democratic Muse: Folk Music Revival in Scotland* (Aberdeen: Scottish Cultural Press, 1996).

Murray, C. S., *Crosstown Traffic* (London: Faber, 1989).

Napier-Bell, S., *Black Vinyl White Powder* (London: Ebury, 2002).

Newton, F., *The Jazz Scene* (Harmondsworth: Penguin, 1961).

Oliver, P. (ed.), *Black Music in Britain* (Milton Keynes: Open University, 1990).

Pesch, M. and Weisbeck, M., *Discstyle: The Graphic Arts of Electronic Music and Club Culture Techno Electro Triphop Drum'n'Bass Big Beat* (London: Collins and Brown, 1999).

Rimmer, D., *Like Punk Never Happened: Culture Club and the New Pop* (London: Faber, 1985).

Roach, M., *The Right to Imagination: An Essential Collection of Candid Interviews with Top UK Alternative Songwriters* (London: Independent Music, 1994).

Sabin, R. (ed.), *Punk Rock: So What? The Cultural Legacy of Punk* (London: Routledge, 1999).

Savage, J., *England's Dreaming: Sex Pistols and Punk Rock* (London: Faber, 1991).

Savage, J., *Time Travel: Pop, Media and Sexuality, 1976–96* (London: Chatto and Windus, 1996).

Smith, M. E., *The Fall Lyrics* (Berlin: Lough, 1985).

Watkinson, M. and Anderson, P., *Crazy Diamond: Syd Barrett and the Dawn of Pink Floyd* (London: Omnibus, 1991).

Whitehouse, E., *This England's Book of British Dance Bands from the Twenties to the Fifties* (Cheltenham: This England, 1999).

Wiener, J., *Come Together: John Lennon and His Time* (London: Faber, 1984).

(2g)   Film

Aldgate, A. and Richards, J., *Best of British: Cinema and Society from 1930 to the Present* (London: I. B. Taurus, 1999).

Ashby, J. and Higson, A. (eds), *British Cinema, Past and Present* (London: Routledge, 2004).

Auty, M. and Roddick, N. (ed.), *British Cinema Now* (London: BFI, 1985).

Barr, C., *Ealing Studios* (London: Studio Vista, 1993).

Bignall, S. (ed.), *Writing and Cinema* (Harlow: Longman, 1999).

Carney, R., *The Films of Mike Leigh: Embracing the World* (Cambridge: Cambridge University Press, 2000).

Chinball, S. and Murphy, R. (eds), *British Crime Cinema* (London: Routledge, 1999).

Coveney, M., *The World According to Mike Leigh* (London: HarperCollins, 1997).

Curran J. and Porter, V. (eds), *British Cinema History* (London: Weidenfeld and Nicolson, 1983).

Dillon, S., *Derek Jarman and Lyric Film* (Austin: University of Texas, 2004).

Dixon, W. W. (ed.), *Re-viewing British Cinema, 1900–1992: Essays and Interviews* (Albany: State University of New York, 1994).

Hayward, A., *Which Side Are You On? Ken Loach and his Films* (London: Bloomsbury, 2005).

Friedman, L. (ed.), *British Cinema and Thatcherism: Fires were Started* (London: University College London, 1993).

Hedling, E., *Lindsay Anderson: Maverick Film-maker* (London: Cassell, 1998).

Higson, A. (ed.), *Dissolving Views: Key Writings in British Cinema* (London: Cassell, 1996).

Higson, A., *English Heritage, English Cinema: Costume Drama since 1980* (Oxford: Oxford University Press, 2003).

Hill, J., *Sex, Class and Realism: British Cinema, 1956–63* (London: BFI, 1986).

Hunter, I. Q. (ed.), *British Science Fiction Cinema* (London: Routledge, 1999).

Jarman, D., *The Last of England* (London: Vintage, 1987).

McFarlane, B., *An Autobiography of British Cinema as told by the Filmmakers and Actors who Made it* (London: Methuen, 1997).

Manders, F., *Cinemas of Newcastle* (Newcastle: City Libraries and Arts, 1991).

Murphy, R., *The British Cinema Book*, 2nd edn (London: BFI, 2003).

Murphy, R., *Sixties British Cinema* (London: BFI, 1992).

Richards, J., *Films and British National Identity: From Dickens to 'Dad's Army'* (Manchester: Manchester University Press, 1997).

Russell, K., *A British Picture: An Autobiography* (London: Heinemann, 1989).

Salmolke, S., *Nicolas Roeg Film by Film* (London: McFarland, 1993).

Street, S., *British National Cinema* (London: Routledge, 1997).

Thompson, K. and Bardwell, D., *Film History: An Introduction* (New York: McGraw-Hill, 1994).

Walker, A., *National Heroes: British Cinema of the Seventies and Eighties* (London: Harrap, 1985).

(2h)   Website sources

The first task of any historian is to consider the validity and accuracy of source material. This remains true for website sources. No data should be taken at face value; double checks and assessment of bias are essential; governmental and major institutional sites have in their favour a degree of credibility and professionalism. With these comments in mind the following sources may be useful starting points.

General: parliament.uk (on contemporary political affairs)
Scotland: scotland.gov.uk and sns.gov.uk (Scotland Neighbourhood statistics)
Northern Ireland: nio.gov.uk and cain.ulst.ac.uk (Conflict Archive on the Internet)
Wales: wales.gov.uk and walesworldnation.com (including history, geography and arts)
England: statistics.gov.uk and environment-agency.gov.uk (contemporary data)

Women: womenandequalityunit.gov.uk (government policy and data)
Immigrants and minorities: movinghere.org.uk (extensive site with interviews and histories)
Youth: dfes.gov.uk (On contemporary affairs)
Visual arts: tate.org.uk (large database of images and biographical information)
Popular music: bl.uk/collections.sound-archive/pop (with links from the British Library to other sources)
Cinema: bfi.org.uk (extensive material on films, themes and individual directors)

Index

Shelton State Libraries
Shelton State Community College

Entries in **bold** indicate major thematic sections.